A Family Approach to Psychiatric Disorders

A Family Approach to Psychiatric Disorders

By

Richard A. Perlmutter, M.D.

**Senior Psychiatrist
Sheppard and Enoch Pratt Hospital
Towson, Maryland**

**Assistant Professor of Psychiatry
The Johns Hopkins University
Baltimore, Maryland**

Washington, DC
London, England

Copyright © 1996 American Psychiatric Press, Inc.
ALL RIGHTS RESERVED
Manufactured in the United States of America on acid-free paper
99 98 97 96   4 3 2 1

American Psychiatric Press, Inc.
1400 K Street, N.W., Washington, DC   20005

Library of Congress Cataloging-in-Publication Data
Perlmutter, Richard A., 1949-
    A family approach to psychiatric disorders / Richard A.
    Perlmutter.
        p.   cm.
    Includes bibliographical references and index.
    ISBN 0-88048-714-3 (cloth)
    1. Family psychotherapy.   2. Mentally ill—Family
    relationships.
    I. Title.
    [DNLM: 1. Mental Disorders—therapy.   2. Family
    Therapy.   WM430.5.F2 P451f   1996]
616.89'156—dc20
DNLM/DLC   96-5703
for Library of Congress   CIP

British Library Cataloguing-in-Publication Data
A CIP record is available from the British Library.

To my family

CONTENTS

FOREWORD

Viewed from a historical perspective, this book by Richard Perlmutter reflects remarkable changes in both psychiatry and family therapy. During much of the last decades, a comprehensive publication on the "family approach to psychiatric disorders" would have been inconceivable. Now, however, the time has come when this volume is urgently needed and wanted.

In the 1950s, during the founding days of the field of family therapy, diagnosing specific disorders was widely disdained by psychiatrists as a distraction from the central task of identifying and treating the psychodynamic conflicts of individual patients. Karl Menninger was representative of many authors and authorities who advocated a unitary theory of mental illness. Not categories of disorders or disease entities, but instead, levels of functioning—conceptualized on sweeping dimensions from health to pathology—were preferred in the conceptualization of psychiatric "diagnosis." Even though the broad concept of a dimensionalized approach remains appealing to this day, there was almost no consensus about the content of the dimensions or methods for their assessment. For the clinician, the unitary theory provided only global, undifferentiated guidelines for treatment planning.

For a number of clinicians and theorists who were seeking to understand and cope with the difficult problems of psychoses, the individualized, psychoanalytic frame of reference that dominated the 1950s seemed inadequate, both conceptually and psychotherapeutically. It was in this context that the field of family therapy arose, not as a protest against unreliable and unsatisfactory psychiatric diagnoses but as an alternative to psychoanalysis.

Meanwhile, in the early 1960s, rumblings of change were heard from two polarities, neither of which was aligned with psychoanalysis or family therapy: psychopharmacology/biological psychiatry and the community mental health movement. From somewhere between psychoanalysis and community mental health, the field of family therapy emerged, staking claim to the most clinically manageable, enduring social context of individual problems, namely, marriage and the family.

During the late 1960s, epidemiological community studies were documenting the gross unreliability of psychiatric diagnosis as then practiced; this lack of reliable diagnoses plagued the evaluation of the new pharmacotherapeutic agents. In retrospect, it is interesting to note that until hypotheses of dopamine receptors came along, there were no theories to guide pharmacotherapy; trial-and-error empirical studies based upon presumptive diagnostic differences were necessary.

The need for more reliable psychiatric diagnoses led to the rapid emergence of operational criteria that would specify the characteristics of populations receiving the new medications. Sometimes, as in the Feighner criteria (the first such diagnostic set that was widely used), social characteristics, such as marital status, were actually identified as differentiating criteria. This practice enhanced diagnostic reliability for research purposes, but remained obviously bereft of a theory for which validity might be claimed. On an atheoretical basis, the concept of operational diagnostic criteria became widely accepted and was adopted for general clinical psychiatric use with the publication of DSM-III (American Psychiatric Association) in 1980.

In sharp contrast, from the 1960s into the 1980s, theories about family therapy flourished with almost no attention to psychiatric diagnosis. These theories energized a wide range of mental health professionals beyond the discipline of psychiatry. Psychiatric diagnoses were generally viewed at best as a distraction from family therapy, and they were often considered to be a stigmatizing, reductionistic deterrent to the therapeutic effort. In this burst of therapeutic enthusiasm, the emphasis was upon theory and clinical demonstrations of treatment techniques for trainees. Unfortunately, the need for buttressing clinical impressions with empirical research was quite belatedly recognized by leaders in the family therapy field. Also, family therapy turned its attention away from schizophrenia and "serious" mental disorders toward problems of marital and parent-child conflict that were unrecognized in the DSM manuals.

Thus, the divergence between "standard" psychiatry and family therapy that had become pronounced during the late 1970s continued during the 1980s as pharmacotherapy became entrenched and community mental health faded.

More recently, the tide has been shifting once again, perhaps beginning with the clear research demonstration that family-oriented approaches contribute significantly to the reduction of relapse rates obtained with medication alone in the treatment of schizophrenia. Even though the DSM approach to psychiatric diagnosis remains controversial among family therapists, there is a belated but growing recognition by family therapists of relatively new points of view.

1. Family therapy can take place with one or more family members individually diagnosed; indeed, if a family member has been so diagnosed, accurately or not, some aspect of this problem is usually the presenting reason for seeking help. Unless there is change in what the patient or family is coming for, treatment cannot be regarded as successful. Thus, the therapist needs to make a detailed appraisal of the difficulties that have been diagnostically labeled and the implications of this diagnosis for the family.

2. Collaborative consultation and treatment with other health care professionals can broaden the range of problems to which family therapists have access.

3. Family therapy and pharmacotherapy can be more effective when integrated than when either approach is used alone.

4. Empirical research on the processes and outcomes of family therapy will not be accepted as meaningful by the wider health care establishment unless information about the presence or absence of diagnosable psychiatric disorders is included as part of the baseline and follow-up assessment. (An entire expanded issue of the *Journal of Marital and Family Therapy,* published in October 1995, describes and critiques outcome research on family approaches to problems classified by DSM criteria.)

5. To enhance communication with other professionals and to improve treatment programs, training in family therapy needs to give more explicit attention to current diagnostic concepts and criteria.

6. Current DSM-IV (American Psychiatric Association 1994) diagnostic concepts can and should be expanded to give much more credence to the relational context of the family. While a two-way street is being paved between individual and relational approaches, consultation and therapy with families of persons diagnosed as having DSM-IV psychiatric disorders are both feasible and fruitful.

At the same time that this pioneering book by Richard Perlmutter will be of enormous relevance to family therapists, it will be of comparable value to individual therapists from psychiatric, psychological, social work, and other mental health disciplines. Not only can individually oriented therapists improve the effectiveness of their work by looking beyond the individual's presenting symptoms, but the families of their patients can also benefit from a more explicit recognition of the impact—often, the burden—of the individual's problems upon the rest of the family. Thus, this timely book by Richard Perlmutter has much to offer both family therapists and those mental health professionals who are being trained in individual approaches. From either starting point, this book opens up new territory: it bridges a gap that has been created by the erroneous belief that psychiatric diagnosis and family therapy are somehow incompatible. It's not so, and Dr. Perlmutter shows how these realms can in fact be joined to improve the effectiveness of both.

Lyman C. Wynne, M.D., Ph.D.
Professor, Department of Psychiatry
University of Rochester School of Medicine and Dentistry
Rochester, New York

ACKNOWLEDGMENTS

The basic idea for this book emerged out of my inspiring conversations with my good friend A. W. R. (Dick) Sipe. Without the support and encouragement of my wife, Barbara (who also helped with the research for several chapters), and the patience and interest of my children, Rebecca and Benjamin, this project would not have made it. Steven Sharfstein, the President of Sheppard–Pratt, was graciously supportive throughout this long venture. My friend and mentor Lyman Wynne was, as always, available and generous with ideas and support.

Chapter 16 needed the input of a child psychiatrist, and so I am very grateful to my friend Peter Kahn for his willingness to collaborate.

Eloise Liberty and her word-processing staff were great about typing and retyping—again and again—the many drafts.

Rudy Lamy, Barbara Jobson, and Anne Dolan of the Kubie Library staff provided an incredible amount of excellent research assistance.

I am most indebted to the many expert readers of the chapters. In alphabetical order, they are Patricia Alfin, David Berenson, John Biggs, Libby Champney, Trish Gaffney, Richard Halpin, Thomas Hobbins, Sushma Jani, Janet Leibowitz, Paul McClelland, Charles McCormack, Israela Meyerstein, Randy Miller, Thomas Monahan, Sheila Murphy, Sandra Phocas, David Roth, Dick Sipe, Dick Smith, Susan Thomas, John Walkup, Neil Weissman, Elizabeth Williams, Donald Wilmus, Sally Winston, and Lyman Wynne.

I was fortunate to have the assistance of one of the world's best editors, Lyn Camire, who not only had 4-wheel drive but also grasped the essence of the book and worked tirelessly to help me make it accessible and clear. I was also fortunate to have the quality support of the staff at APPI, especially Rebecca Richters, Louise Hohensee-Valdov, Pam Harley, Claire Reinburg, Carol Nadelson, and others.

CHAPTER 1

A Treatment Synthesis

A n adolescent's parents announce they are going to divorce just as he is recovering from an overdose of barbiturates and a deep depression.

A man with a mood disorder improves dramatically with medication but then becomes noncompliant and stops taking it, and the therapist discovers that several other members of his family of origin also have mood disorders.

A child patient is pulled out of therapy by his parents at the moment he seemed to be growing less depressed and more assertive.

The Context of Symptoms

My goal in writing this book is to help trainees and practitioners understand the role of the family as a crucial factor in everyday therapeutic phenomena. The substantive knowledge bases of family therapy and psychiatry are selectively synthesized to provide a useful starting point for sitting with and helping psychiatric "patients" and their families.

Families are usually ignored in standard treatment. The natural tendency is for therapists to use tools with which they are already familiar, and these tools are generally those of individual therapy. The language-based, relational methods of family therapy can provide effective tools for use side by side with the traditional individual treatment tools of psychotherapy and pharmacology. Medical differential diagnosis and consideration of biological symptoms can be enhanced by attention to a family's response to a disorder. The biopsychosocial model needs strengthening, and family therapy provides a pragmatic knowledge base for integrating the "social" part of the model.

Clinicians tend to exclude the family to preserve the patient's confidentiality, decrease the therapist's anxiety, and focus on the acute problem. However, avoidance of family sessions may be inefficient and may actually cause more problems in assessment and treatment than it solves. For example, an individual patient's family often clarifies information or corrects misinformation, and the therapist may save time by ascertaining the patient's symptoms and level of function both indirectly during a family interview and directly in response to therapist questions. The families of those with symptoms often have symptoms themselves that require treatment for lasting change to be possible. They also bring high levels of interest, concern, anxiety, or anger that will have a negative effect on the symptomatic family member if left unaddressed.

The family therapy approach in this text focuses on the primary importance of intimate relationships in connection with psychiatric symptoms. Symptoms affect families and families affect symptoms. Social systems outside the family cannot be covered in detail in this manual but must always be kept in mind because they have a bearing in treatment. Therapists who want to consider the effects on and impact of these systems will find that other excellent sources are available (Imber-Black 1988; Wynne et al. 1986).

◼ Positive Objectives

The power of a systemic approach in mitigating the severity of psychiatric and medical disorders is just beginning to be appreciated by health care planners and clinicians. Meta-analysis of two decades of research into the efficacy of marriage and family approaches shows positive effects in the treatment of schizophrenia, depression, health problems, conduct disorders, and marital distress (Pinsof and Wynne 1995).

Family interventions can help reduce the frequency of psychiatric hospitalization and can encourage development of functions once performed only in the hospital. In the family suicide watch, for example, the family resources are mobilized to watch a suicidal member around the clock at home (Landau-Stanton and Stanton 1985). The introduction of family consultation and therapy can help ease the increasing demands on the practitioner's time and health care system resources.

Most important, the clinician learns to routinely explore family resources and consider how they can best be harnessed in support of individual or family treatment. Family support can help prevent prolonged, unnecessarily complicated, or failed treatments. This approach is in keeping with the goals of family therapy, which can be adapted to emphasize brief treatments, enhance the competence of the family, and minimize excessive dependence on the therapist.

One obstacle to incorporating family therapy is the anxiety induced in the clinician by the thought of confronting several agitated people at once in an office or hospital setting. Affect levels can be extremely high in families presenting with a symptomatic member. However, this anxiety can be alleviated by learning helpful interviewer stances and simple pragmatic routines for family consultation as described in later chapters and in many of the references cited.

Families who would refuse family "therapy" may respond well to a request for family consultation. Family members have a chance to offer their own interpretations and feelings about the illness, which can aid the clinician attempting to maintain a treatment plan. Access to previously withheld information can have unexpected and wide-ranging positive results for the family and the individual patient. The benefits of consultation in mitigating social stressors often become apparent to the therapist and the family.

By including a consideration of human grouping and behavior, family psychiatry connects biology and family. This connection is demonstrated in research suggesting that aspects of psychosocial context can "trigger" psychiatric illness. Another example is in mood disorders, where strong research evidence shows that psychosocial stressors function as variables allowing expression of severe mood problems, especially expression of early episodes, in vulnerable individuals (Post 1992). The compelling interdependence between biology and relationships in psychiatric disorders is a model for the treatment synthesis proposed in this manual.

Some mental health policy trends move away from reimbursement for relational problems, but an opportunity may be emerging for family therapy to focus on more serious psychiatric illness embedded within relational problems. This manual should help family therapists orient themselves to psychiatric disorders and see the place for family therapy in anticipation of this expected shift in care.

Clinicians generally must learn to respond more flexibly and more usefully to patient needs within a comprehensive medical and relational model. The days of elegant, single-mode treatments have passed, and specialized treatments can now be combined with other modalities in a more efficacious approach to care.

This manual is intended to bridge the gap between standard individual treatment and family treatment. Chapter 2 focuses on practical guidelines for the first attempts to include a consideration of family as part of standard treatment. In later chapters, therapists can review and select from the case studies, suggested dialogue questions, therapist perspective considerations, concrete assessment categories, and treatment methods provided.

◼ Focus on Disorders

Family therapy and traditional therapies have followed separate though mostly parallel courses, but have diverged on the issue of psychiatric diagnoses. Some family therapists have shunned diagnoses as biased against the individual, preferring to use relational formulations as they looked for the role of the family and its connections to the individual's problem.

This book is organized by the major categories of the *Diagnostic and Statistical Manual of Mental Disorders,* Fourth Edition (DSM-IV; American Psychiatric Association 1994). Those disorders to which family therapy has contributed more highly developed research and clinical data are presented in the early chapters. The family context of disorders such as schizophrenia and mood, eating, and substance abuse disorders is now well established. Ignoring this context in treating an individual patient is not clinically sound.

Thinking and teaching on the basis of DSM-IV disorders offers a bridge to connect family therapists, psychiatric clinicians, and family practitioners. Perhaps in DSM-V this bridge will be fortified by an axis of relational diagnoses, but until then diagnoses will have to do. DSM-IV's reconfigured Axis IV, which includes Psychosocial and Environmental Problems, does require some attention to the context of the illness and the patient's life. In addition, the Global Assessment and Relational Functioning (GARF) Scale, which is included in Appendix B of DSM-IV, rates family functioning in dimensions of problem solving, organization, and emotional climate. The wide acceptance of DSM-IV provides invaluable advantages for communication. Discussion that considers symptoms can also help nonmedical therapists in many clinical situations, and awareness of the disorders can help prepare family therapists as they focus on sicker patients.

A working familiarity with the disorders is assumed. This manual does not attempt to provide an exhaustive review of all existing literature on either psychiatric disorders or family therapy. Numerous suggested dialogue questions and case studies are provided to allow for immediate consideration and use by the busy clinician. The dialogue questions and techniques are offered as a potentially valuable starting point and are not intended to provide a comprehensive or overly didactic guide to the whole field of family therapy.

■ Organization of Chapters 3–17

The sections included in this book are as follows (also see Table 1–1):

Perspective on the Disorders: Provides brief introduction to aspects of the disorder that relate specifically to family considerations.

Connections of the Symptoms to the System (Papp 1983):   Presents clinical family system observations for a particular disorder, with the following subsections:

■ *Effects of the Disorder on the Family:*   Describes the effects of a particular disorder on families. Objectives include enhancing therapist empathy and avoiding blaming of the family.

■ *Family Maintenance of the Symptoms:*   Focuses on ways in which a usually well-meaning family may sustain symptoms. The inadvertent maintenance of symptoms by family members, including those carrying psychiatric diagnoses, is considered without implying that the family *caused* the disorder.

■ *Functions of the Symptoms Within the Family:*   Focuses on hypotheses about symptom functions that enable the clinician to create opportunities for positive change. One dialogue within family therapy and theory focuses on whether symptoms or problems serve a purpose within the family. "Accidentalists" believe that symptoms just happen and that the therapist should focus on the family's reactions to and attempts to solve the problems. "Functionalists" believe in the more traditional family systems view that symptoms themselves serve a purpose within the family and should be considered in that context. Considering functions as hypotheses helps the therapist avoid accepting assumptions as truths or certainties. In this section, I consider the family as a focus for concern, study, opportunity, and evaluation rather than as a focus of blame; function is not equated with cause.

■ *Adverse Consequences of Change:*   Considers family consequences when symptoms are alleviated.

Special Systemic Dimensions: Focuses on special systemic dimensions of family issues as they relate to this disorder. Each chapter includes some or all of the following subsections, as applicable:

■ *Family History and Genetics:*   Comments on selected genetic aspects of the disorder and the environmental influences on the development and progression of a disorder.

Table 1–1.   Sections included in chapters

Perspective on the disorders
Connections of the symptoms to the system
   Effects of the disorder on the family
   Family maintenance of the symptoms
   Functions of the symptoms within the family
   Adverse consequences of change
Special systemic dimensions[*]
   Family history and genetics
   Gender
   Intimacy
   Loyalty
   Map of emotions
   Countertransference
   Posterity
   Ethnicity
Treatment
   Standard individual therapies
   Family modalities
   Psychoeducation
   New stories

---

[*] Subheadings are used only as applicable in each chapter.

Gender: Considers aspects of gender, including traditional gender-role stereotypes, on the course and perceptions of a disorder and the effects on the family.

Intimacy: Considers the particular ways intimacy can be disrupted by a given disorder. Opportunities for renewed trusting relations are explored. Intimacy is defined as mutually trusting self-disclosure (Wynne and Wynne 1986). Martin Buber, the early 20th-century philosopher and theologian, describes intimacy as the moment when the other is treated as a subject ("Thou") rather than an object ("it") being used (Buber 1958).

Loyalty: Focuses on prominent loyalty issues that may be associated with symptoms. Familiarity with loyal and disloyal forces as they are revealed in family responses enhances therapist judgment (Boszormenyi-Nagy 1972). Loyalty is defined as the unwritten laws of kinship that determine what one family member "owes" another (van Heusden and van den Eerenbeemt 1987).

Map of Emotions: Focuses on the strong emotions that may be obscured by moodiness in families presenting with a particular disorder. Because therapy benefits when emotions are recognized and experienced, likely emotional scenarios are suggested to help the therapist elicit more constructive responses from the family (Berenson 1991) (also see Chapter 2).

Countertransference: Considers likely therapist reactions in the family that may cause problems in family treatment of a particular disorder. These issues include overidentifying with either the index person or the family; taking sides; working too hard to rescue the patient and remove symptoms too quickly; showing intolerance of affects during angry, painful exchanges; showing excessive paternalism in insisting on one right way to think or one right course to take; and envying families that move further toward health than the therapist's own family.

Posterity: Considers the impact of a disorder and its treatment on children and future generations.

Ethnicity: Focuses on ethnic and cultural concerns that should be considered when treating a particular disorder.

Treatment: Describes standard individual therapies and practical family approaches to a particular psychiatric disorder. The following subsections are included:

■ *Standard Individual Therapies:* Briefly describes psychotherapies and biological interventions currently in use for treating this disorder.

■ *Family Modalities:* Discusses modalities, including family consultation and conjoint, couple, systemically informed individual, parent-child, and sibling sessions.

■ *Psychoeducation:* Offers ideas about using educational information as part of the therapy plan.

■ *New Stories:* Provides practical relational methods drawn from the narrative constructivist approach (Hoffman 1990; White 1995; White and Epston 1990) to help find new, productive ways to react to, talk about, and think about symptoms (see Glossary for explanation of terms such as *externalization, reauthoring, reconstruction,* and *reframing*).

■ A Few Points on Style

In this book, I emphasize the clinical applications of theory and research. Rather than attempting to provide complete reviews of each topic in this manual, I mention and reference selected relevant research and literature while maintaining the focus on the trainee and clinician wishing for a quick read before going in to face a family with a particular disorder. I discuss the schools of family therapy in terms of their role within a treatment constellation or their contribution to treating a particular disorder.

The terminology used throughout this manual is intended to be quickly and easily understood by a wide range of practitioners in the fields of psychiatry and family therapy. Just a few clarifications may be helpful at the outset:

■ *Family* refers to any cohabiting or formerly cohabiting group of people who rely on each other for nurturance and economic survival. A family may include one or two parents.

■ *Spouse,* though perhaps less flexible than it might be, is used to avoid wordiness in the presentation. A couple may or may not be married.

■ *Index person* refers to the family member who carries the diagnosis. This term identifies the individual for record-keeping purposes and suggests the relation of the patient as part of a larger involved group. *Index person* is preferred over the more familiar *identified patient,* which labels the person or implies that someone else in the family is really the sick one.

The meanings of common family therapy terms, such as *double bind, family system,* and *reframe,* are readily discernible from context. The Glossary provides a full explanation of terminology (*italicized terms* in this chapter are further defined in the Glossary) as it is used in family therapy.

Chapter references provide a guide to further reading in family therapy as desired and feasible. An Additional Reading list is also provided at the end of each chapter.

■ Additional Reading

Gaw A (ed): Culture, Ethnicity, and Mental Illness. Washington, DC, American Psychiatric Press, 1993

Kaslow FW: Relational diagnosis: an idea whose time has come? Fam Process 32:255–259, 1993

McGoldrick M: Ethnicity and the family life cycle, in The Changing Family Life Cycle, 2nd Edition. Edited by Carter B, McGoldrick M. Boston, MA, Allyn & Bacon, 1988, pp 69–90

McGoldrick M, Pearce J, Giordano J (eds): Ethnicity and Family Therapy. New York, Guilford, 1982

Perlmutter RA: Psychopharmacology of attachment: effects of successful agoraphobia treatment on marital relationships. Family Systems Medicine 8:279–284, 1990

Strong T: DSM-IV and describing problems in family therapy. Fam Process 32:249–253, 1993

■ References

American Psychiatric Association: Diagnostic and Statistical Manual of Mental Disorders, 4th Edition. Washington, DC, American Psychiatric Association, 1994

Berenson D: Powerlessness, liberating or enslaving? responding to the feminist critique of the twelve steps, in Feminism and Addiction. Edited by Bepko C. Binghamton, NY, Haworth, 1991, pp 67–84

Boszormenyi-Nagy I: Loyalty implications of the transference model in psychotherapy. Arch Gen Psychiatry 27:374–380, 1972

Buber M: I and Thou. New York, Charles Scribner's Sons, 1958

Hoffman L: Constructing realities: an art of lenses. Fam Process 24:31–47, 1990

Imber-Black E: Families and Larger Systems: A Family Therapist's Guide Through the Labyrinth. New York, Guilford, 1988

Landau-Stanton J, Stanton MD: Treating suicidal adolescents and their families, in Handbook of Adolescents and Family Therapy. Edited by Mirkin MP, Koman SL. New York, Gardner, 1985, pp 309–328

Papp P: The Process of Change. New York, Guilford, 1983

Pinsof WM, Wynne LC: The efficacy of marital and family therapy: an empirical overview, conclusions, and recommendations. Journal of Marital and Family Therapy 21:585–613, 1995

Post RM: Transduction of psychosocial stress into the neurobiology of recurrent affective disorder. Am J Psychiatry 149:999–1010, 1992

van Heusden A, van den Eerenbeemt E: Balance in Motion. New York, Brunner/Mazel, 1987

White M: Re-Authoring Lives: Interviews & Essays. Adelaide, South Australia, Dulwich Centre Publications, 1995

White M, Epston D: Narrative Means to Therapeutic Ends. New York, WW Norton, 1990

Wynne LC, Wynne A: The quest for intimacy. Journal of Marital and Family Therapy 12:383–394, 1986

Wynne LC, McDaniel SH, Weber TT: The road from family therapy to systems consultation, in Systems Consultation: A New Perspective for Family Therapy. Edited by Wynne LC, McDaniel SH, Weber TT. New York, Guilford, 1986, pp 3–15

CHAPTER 2

Getting Started

A third-year psychiatric resident, Dr. R., described a case involving a young woman who presented to the emergency room after a serious drug overdose. Dr. R. performed the traditional assessment for suicide potential and released the patient because she was glad she had been saved and had no further suicidal ideation. The resident said, "She kept telling me to interview her family members, who were in the waiting room, if I wanted to understand the craziness and the issues that drew her to the overdose. I told her that she was my patient and said I didn't want to confuse confidentiality by talking to her family, but now I realize I was afraid both of being outnumbered by them and of being eaten alive. Maybe if I just knew a way to get started, I would have taken the chance."

After a supervision session on how to conduct a first interview, Dr. R. brought the family in, identified the psychosocial precipitants, and agreed on a treatment plan to prevent further suicide attempts.

When a family participates together in therapy, some members are grateful and relieved that a therapist is open and willing to hear their perspective. Other family members assume that their inclusion can only mean that the therapist wants to blame them, expose their role in causing the disorder, and punish them publicly.

The decision to interview the family in addition to the index person opens up a new world of therapeutic possibilities. It can also bring dilemmas and technical challenges. Therapist fears, anxieties, and even cannibalistic fantasies of being "eaten alive" are understandable, given the highly charged emotions of families struggling through long-term problems or an acute crisis.

Different schools and practitioners of family therapy have their own methods of joining and assessing families (Nichols and Schwartz 1991), and much study has been devoted to the first interview (Budman et al. 1992; Satir 1983; Stierlin et al. 1977). The selection of approaches provided here should help therapists successfully begin the first interviews with families presenting with disorders.

The first few minutes of the first interview and some aspects of early consultations are emphasized here. Not all of the following points or suggestions apply to each case, but familiarity with several semistructured ideas will add to therapist confidence and competence during the first fateful meetings.

As Jay Haley (1976) put it, "To end well, therapy must begin well" (p. 9). This point is also true of family consultation if it is to serve the interests of all those involved.

This chapter focuses on these essentials for joining and assessing families:

■ The interviewer's stance
■ Openings
■ Family assessment guidelines

■ The Interviewer's Stance

Some clinical concepts common to all family therapy are particularly useful to ground the therapist theoretically:

1. Participant observation
2. Negotiation
3. Hypothesizing and circular questioning
4. Emphasizing resources, exoneration, and dialogue
5. Thinking and coaching
6. Map of emotions
7. Considering ethnicity and culture
8. The therapist as consultant

Participant Observation

Participant observation is the ability to be both involved and objective at the same time. The therapist conveys empathy for the family's plight and maintains just enough distance to keep from becoming like a member of the family, to maintain the ability to observe, and to remain therapeutically useful (Havens 1976). In consultation, the therapist's effort is to remain sharply interested and yet detached enough from the problem to help determine whether and how family therapy might be most useful.

Negotiation

Negotiation is a process of mutual influence rather than unilateral dictating or prescribing. Patients and families usually present with strong notions of what the problem is and what the solution should be. The therapist comes to his or her own conclusions about the problem and the "required" treatment. For the interview and therapy to be successful, negotiation between the therapist and the family must now take place to establish a common definition of the problem and a shared solution (Lazare 1976; Perlmutter and Jones 1985). Without negotiation, there is little chance that the family will agree to or conform with an action plan.

Negotiation also allows the therapist to elicit additional information that may affect both the strategy and the eventual success of the treatment. The stance of medical paternalism in which the patient lists complaints and the doctor then dictates treatment probably does not work well in medicine, and it definitely does not work well in psychiatry. Negotiation is a useful alternative to paternalism.

A patient might describe feeling hopeless, despondent, suicidal, and sleepless, and the family might describe withdrawal, crying, and personality change. In such a situation, it is difficult for the therapist to resist starting treatment with antidepressants and psychotherapy. This course will work if the therapist's conclusion of a biological depression happens to coincide closely enough with the patient's and family's views. If, however, the family believes that the patient is possessed by the devil and the therapist never elicits this information, real negotiation never takes place. The family may take the prescription politely, throw it away, and disappear from the office forever.

This extreme example suggests not that exorcism should be the prescription, but rather that negotiation is essential. Once the therapist discovers the family's belief in an idea such as possession, for example, he or she can tentatively introduce the idea that depression and possession may be somewhat similar. He or she can discuss medications as treatments for both conditions, or at least as agents to help the exorcism take full effect by first lessening the bad thoughts and enhancing the host's energy. Such stances do not in themselves guarantee compliance, but they may give the therapist a chance to advance toward more useful discussions.

In family consultation, the therapist actually negotiates with the family concerning his or her role and the consultation objectives and methods (Wynne et al. 1986). Here the objective is the negotiated resolution of specific identifiable problems.

■ Hypothesizing and Circular Questioning

In addition to making statements, the therapist interviews by asking questions based on one possible way to synthesize the information. The questions might take this form: "Do you think the drinking has anything to do with the death of your mother?" or "Are you saying that his relapses occur more often at times when there is more or less turmoil in the house?" Ideas are generated from family data, and questioning is used to test the validity of these ideas.

Circular questions (see Glossary) provide one useful way for the interviewer to gather needed systemic (family) information. Circular questions are also designed to allow the family to perceive systemic connections and gain awareness of "feedback loops" that affect their reactions to each other. The therapist asks family members to comment on and classify their actions and the actions of others, to speculate about certain actual or hypothetical events, and to compare people, places, and times in their lives.

Circular questions supply a vehicle for directing family members to consider their own beliefs and attributions about the problems they are facing (Penn 1982; Tomm 1985). This use of language by the therapist helps the family develop their own new stories. Using circular questions replaces the possible presumptions of the therapist with inquisitive interest.

The idea of presenting hypotheses as a way of interviewing is described in general psychiatry (Lazare 1976) and is now a central concept in family theory (Papp 1983; Selvini-Palazzoli et al. 1980), where hypothesizing is used to discuss possible connections of the symptoms to the family system.

> The S. family presented after a drug overdose of the 14-year-old daughter, Jan. The family had a history of affective disorders, and the possibility of biological depression was considered. No symptoms supporting this possibility could be elicited.
>
> Jan had overdosed after a major family battle in which the parents could not agree on a fair set of rules defining limits on her behavior. A hypothesis of a connection between the overdose and parental marital troubles was generated next, but these problems were not confirmed. Surprisingly, marital issues were not the most salient here. The parents seemed to enjoy and respect each other. They were even somewhat entertained by having had a disagreement, because normally they were of predictably similar minds in any decision. All family members believed the parents to be happily married.
>
> When questions then focused on the extended family, a useful connection to the maternal grandparents was found. The grandmother had recently been diagnosed with cancer, and the grandfather had suffered a heart attack. The girl's mother had been distracted, upset, and much more distant in her usually close relationship with her daughter. Jan later said her overdose was an impulse in response to feeling particularly pained by her own powerlessness to help her mother or grandparents.

■ Emphasizing Resources, Exoneration, and Dialogue

Trust-based therapy focuses on the resources of the family (Boszormenyi-Nagy 1987; Boszormenyi-Nagy and Krasner 1986). Blaming is avoided, and communication is emphasized. Family members can address issues of loyalty, fairness, and injustice. Psychiatric disorders are viewed as injustices in themselves, a stance that allows families to relate to the index person in more fair and balanced ways.

Family members address the unjust treatment they may have suffered. They work toward understanding the reasons for the victimizer's actions, a process that may lead to exoneration of the victimizer. Discussing problems in terms of psychiatric disorders may aid in the exoneration process by offering a medical explanation of mood swings, rages, bizarre behaviors, and other symptoms.

> Mr. and Mrs. A., both 42 years old and the parents of two children, presented with marital problems. After four marital sessions, one aspect of the problem was clearly revealed. Mr. A. overreacted to his wife as if she meant him harm, and Mrs. A. felt paralyzed and unable to say anything to him. When his reactions to his wife emerged as related to issues involving his abusive mother, two sessions were held with Mr. A. and his mother. His mother was initially defensive but soon began to cry. She related how she had always wanted what was best for him and could not understand why she couldn't control her temper for weeks at a time.
>
> Later, everyone agreed that Mr. A.'s mother had been suffering from a bipolar illness that was now well treated with lithium and paroxetine. She hoped her son could find a way to understand her plight and avoid letting the unfortunate history destroy his marriage.

In this case, maltreatment was not minimized, but a deeper understanding of the victimizer's life and positive intentions helped free family members from a negative, limiting, and even imprisoning account of the past. This process of exoneration differs from forgiveness in that it does not imply minimizing or excusing but rather offers a deeper understanding that includes intentionality and biological forces. Therapists can develop the ability to sustain multidirectional partiality and to guide dialogue that leads to healing.

■ Thinking and Coaching

Nonemotional, quiet concepts and techniques are essential in work with most families, especially those whose emotionalism is blocking the capacity to consider treatment for a sick family member (Bowen 1994; Kerr and Bowen 1988). For those who present as individuals with family issues, the approach offers a way of conducting systemically oriented individual therapy (Bowen 1994; Carter and McGoldrick Orfandis 1976). This approach draws on the principles of differentiation, which allow for more thinking and less emotional reaction and anxiety. The technique of "coaching" individuals on how to reenter their families is an application of these principles:

"When you enter your family home, begin by doing just what you always do, except turn on your imaginary camera so that you can see clearly and can observe with detachment what each person does when interacting, including yourself. After we discuss this information, we can design some experiments with different responses by you."

This method may allow family members to avoid becoming involved in destructive relational triangles and to resist negative projections. Coaching may also have a role in therapy with children from extremely chaotic homes where the parents are overwhelmed with problems. This approach helps the child deal with day-to-day crises in new planned ways. More examples are found in Chapter 17, Personality Disorders.

Family systems methods have been found to be particularly sensitive to and respectful of variations in perception and attribution. These methods are highly adaptable and thus well suited to meeting the needs of many ethnic minority families (Ho 1993; McGoldrick and Gerson 1985).

■ Map of Emotions

Therapists must develop a way of considering and handling the strong emotions that may emerge in individual or family sessions. Sometimes it is best to discourage expression of affect and encourage thinking. At other times, it is most useful to focus on emotion.

In emotionally focused therapy, underlying emotions are viewed as being obscured by moodiness in family members. An approach developed by David Berenson, the *map of emotions* (see Figure 2–1), can help individuals to experience and accept these emotions so they do not take the usual distracting course into moodiness, which then manifests as anxiety, guilt, or resentment (Berenson 1991).

In this approach, *moods* refer to general discomfort, whereas *emotions* are seen as actual and even physical personal realities. On the map, an imaginary line between emotions and moods would be called *thoughts*—the constant mind chatter that keeps people away from genuine emotions and stuck in disabling moods. The corresponding emotions above the moods are grouped (left to right) from the more external to the more core, vulnerable ones. When family members are helped to stop thought, they begin a journey, first from moods into emotions. If they can face these emotions and let them flow—moving freely one into another—then the possibility is created for arriving at healing *spaces* such as compassion, gratitude, and neutrality. In addition to leading each individual toward more positive personal and relational power, this experience provides an opportunity for family members in the therapy session to achieve a deeper understanding of one another. As a result, they become empowered to consider less defensive and more authentic stances.

The therapist listens for moments when an emotion, such as pain, terror, or powerlessness, is present in the session. At this point, the therapist guides individuals to stop any thought that obstructs real feelings and to allow themselves to experience the dreaded emotion:

> "What are you feeling at this moment? Where do you feel it? Would you be willing to let it stay there for a moment, let it deepen, and see what will happen if your thoughts are not allowed to distract you or help you out of this place? What is happening now?"

Spaces	Love	Compassion	Neutral	Nothingness
	Joy	Beautiful	Witness	Aloneness
	Peace	sadness	Dispassion	Nowhereness
	Gratitude	Amusement	Curiosity	Out of control
Emotions	Anger	Hurt	Fear	Powerlessness
	Rage	Grief	Terror	Loneliness,
	Fury	Loss	Dread	emptiness
	Envy	Sorrow		Despair
				Hopelessness,
				failure
				Shame
Moods	Blame	Self-pity	Anxiety	Confusion
	Guilt	Suffering	Panic	Loneliness
	Resentment	Victim	Worry	Desperation
	Contempt	Martyr	Doubt	Resignation

Figure 2–1.   The map of emotions.
Source.   Copyright © February 1996, David Berenson, M.D. Reprinted with permission.

Families often react to a child's disorder (e.g., schizophrenia) with blaming, guilt, and self-pity. These moods obscure strong emotions that individual family members feel compelled to avoid. Family members can be helped to feel their anger and pain rather than sidestepping these real emotions and continuing to blame their child or each other. Family members who are open and responsive to this technique experience a certain powerlessness as they begin to accept their own emotions, including their powerlessness to change or correct a biological disorder.

By continuing to explore this sense of powerlessness under the therapist's guidance, family members may find that allowing themselves to experience their emotions permits them to discover their own resources of patience and compassion. Emotional "mapping" from mood to emotion can help individual family members move away from blaming and self-pity and toward new ways of relating to each other. With this method, "power over" can become "power to" (Berenson 1991).

In some chapters in this manual, a section under Special Systemic Dimensions discusses emotional concerns for particular disorders. Full use of this method requires some selection and preparation of the family. In the first meetings with a family, therapists need only be alert for hidden emotions and can try to identify which family members, if any, might respond well to an emotional focus later on in the therapy. Potentially receptive members might include those who are particularly moody and blocked from a level of emotional experience and who are able to tolerate such a focus.

■ Considering Ethnicity and Culture

The therapist aims for sensitivity without overfocusing on generalizations about groups, which could lead to stereotypes and prejudice. By attributing conflicts and symptoms exclusively to culture, the therapist may do a disservice to the family. But the therapist also does a disservice by ignoring ethnicity and culture. The desirable stance is an openness to ethnic and cultural influences on the family's understanding of symptoms and the therapist's role. This stance is most attainable for a therapist who is in touch with his or her own ethnic identity and the perceptions and limitations it may imply.

The understanding of families of different ethnic and cultural backgrounds may vary in these areas:

- Meaning of psychiatric symptoms
- Degree of family involvement that will be expected or tolerated
- View of authority, including implied moral authority
- Trust of people of the therapist's ethnic group
- Experience with immigration and trauma in home country
- Attitudes about medications and psychotherapy

An immigrant family that has experienced a harsh government or similar difficulties may be less likely to confront, ask questions, and disagree with the therapist. Families from cultures that stress politeness and respect similarly may not disagree openly, but may quietly not comply with treatment if the therapist misses the issues.

Even though the family's trust of the therapist's ethnic group (or the group to which the family thinks the therapist belongs) is an undeniable factor in therapy, families vary in their responses and distrust should not be assumed.

> One African-American family chose a white therapist, believing they would find high qualifications and interest in their problems.

> Another African-American family asked a white therapist how they could be expected to trust a white therapist and a white hospital that represented to them the institution of slavery.

> A Chinese patient tried to stay with a Japanese therapist, but finally gave up. She could not develop trust because of thoughts of the Second World War.

Families that include nontraditional relationships, such as single parents and mixed-race or single-sex couples, may be especially sensitive to a perceived moral judgment implicit in the authority of the therapist. Other more traditional families may have so much natural acceptance for authority that the therapist will need to encourage their active participation in treatment.

Also relevant is the expected and desired role of the family in dealing with the psychiatric illness. Cultural variations often reflect the difficult balancing of family loyalty and autonomy.

One white Protestant family was perplexed by the therapist's request for their involvement in their 20-year-old daughter's treatment for an eating disorder because they felt she was autonomous and deserved privacy.

The next hour, sitting in the same chairs, the members of an Italian-American family were relieved at the therapist's willingness to meet with them and their 22-year-old son over his depression and impulsiveness. Though ashamed of what they considered their Old-World ideas, they were willing to join in the therapy out of distress over the son's plans to move out of their home.

Those who value family ties above all else may be indignant and resist treatment if the therapist refuses to allow participation of other family members. Those who value individual privacy and autonomy may desire more distance from the therapy and may be indignant if the therapist suggests participation of other family members.

The therapist's cultural and ethnic sensitivity will help him or her adjust treatment to create an environment that offers the greatest possibility for trust and compliance.

▪ The Therapist as Consultant

Family anxiety about psychiatric intervention can be greatly reduced by introducing the idea of consultation rather than therapy. Family consultation is presented as a model that focuses on the family's objectives and current state and is not a search for people to blame or "fix."

The potential benefits of this stance include greater accuracy in assessing symptoms and an increased likelihood that the family will support a future treatment plan, if all agree that therapy is desirable and indicated. Family consultation also respects the struggles of the family and may help relieve some pressures of living with psychiatric illness. A variety of family modalities can be considered for a particular family.

With serious psychiatric illness, the therapist-consultant makes no assumptions about the family's expectations from consultation (Wynne 1991a) but instead attempts to discover what their priorities are. Every effort is made to avoid increasing the blame that many families already feel by the time they present for family consultation. Most families with a seriously ill family member have had many frustrating experiences with the mental health system and will be most grateful for the opportunity to get clear information (Wynne 1994). Considering the family's goals first can help increase the satisfaction of all involved and improve the prospects for a positive outcome.

Especially in the consultation model, psychoeducation focuses on explicit educational information within a comprehensive therapeutic context (Wynne 1991b). Psychoeducational efforts focus on providing information that will help families make their own decisions. A strong effort is also made to provide information on care alternatives, possibly outside the family home, and to build support networks with other families who are experiencing similar difficulties and are working to find similar solutions (Wynne 1991b).

■ Openings

Social greetings, introductions, comments about finding the office, and inquiries about parking are necessary moments of joining that also generate much information about the family, including its openness to meeting with a stranger.

The family also assesses the therapist during these first minutes. Although everyone knows the assessment is mutual, the therapist may elect to state this fact to help the family feel more of a sense of power and control. Though the family will be making all decisions about whether there will be future meetings with the therapist, family members may lose sight of their control and instead feel overwhelmed by a feeling of powerlessness that comes from dealing with family problems and emotional disorders. Opening questions can help restore a healthy sense of control.

If the family is acting tentative and seems afraid of the therapist, this beginning can be effective:

> "Part of the point of this meeting is for you to assess me and what this process offers, to see if you feel you can work with me, and to judge whether these consultations could be useful in helping you solve some problems or see things in new ways."

It may be helpful to mention explicitly that this is a nonjudging, information-gathering consultation and not a meeting focused only on problems or based on the assumption that the family will be sent for help. If confidentiality concerns interfere with joining, they should be discussed openly. In general, confidentiality for the index person or any other family member applies only if the clinician has made an explicit or implicit contract with an individual, in which case there will be limitations on family discussion. Problems with confidentiality can be reduced if all individuals understand and agree on the rules from the beginning.

After greetings are exchanged, the therapist may continue with one of these semistructured openings to the first interview. The suggestions should help the therapist become more comfortable with family interviews. After a while, each therapist develops his or her own special style based on personality, training, and experience.

These openings are described in the following sections:

1. The dream question
2. History of the idea of therapy
3. History of the referral
4. Focus on beliefs and attributions
5. Focus on the symptom
6. Focus on psychiatric treatment of index person
7. Solution history
8. Genogram (multigenerational history)

■ The Dream Question

The dream question approach is a competence-based, future-oriented way of enlarging the limited focus on pathology to include hopes and wishes (Satir 1983). For many emotional family situations, this approach is a way to open the session without immediately focusing on central problems.

Before the usual family interactions, complaints, and attacks take over, the therapist gives each person a chance to present his or her idea of the therapy goals:

> "I will leave time to talk about the pain, problems, and struggles you have been going through. First I wanted to ask each of you to share with me your dream or fantasy of what might come out of this hour if you could rule the universe and your wishes could come true in any way. In this dream, what would life be like in the family when we were done with our work?"

■ History of the Idea of Therapy

This approach is an indirect way of entering the family system by finding out who comes to the first session as allies of the therapy idea, who is being coerced, and who is actively opposed. The responses will help shape the therapist's early strategies:

> "Whose idea was it to come here today? Who liked the idea, and who did not? I would like to hear from each of you what it is like for you to be here now."

■ History of the Referral

This approach focuses on the person who referred the family and the reactions of each family member to the referral:

> "Who recommended that you make the appointment to come here today? Did you agree with this idea, or did you disagree? I am wondering how each of you felt when this person suggested you come here."

The family's answers may introduce larger context concerns that could be factors in treatment. For example, the therapist may want to contact the school principal, primary physician, caseworker, and others involved in the referral to be sure the agenda is clear.

■ Focus on Beliefs and Attributions

The traditional opening of the medical interview ("What's the problem here?") can be adapted to a constructivist psychotherapeutic mode by eliciting each family member's beliefs about the problem:

> "I would like to begin by asking each of you to share a bit about what you *see* as the problems in the family that need attention and what you *believe* is behind these problems."

The attributions of the family are elicited. How does the family understand its crisis? What meanings are attributed to the symptoms? Each family responds to a symptom or event in unique, symbolic, and dynamic ways. Families respond differently to specific events, such as the departure of children for college. Families vary in many other ways, including their reactions to unusual events. In the case of a drug overdose, for example, some families react with support and a wish to understand, and others react with rage at the individual for ruining their week or trying to make them feel guilty. They may even be angry that the individual wasn't able to overdose "correctly."

■ Focus on the Symptom

Sometimes the simplest and most traditional approach is best. Continuing to focus on the index person may initially prevent the family from discovering new ways of problem solving, but in the first minutes of the first interview this focus may be a respectful way of meeting the family where they are.

Even if scapegoating is one dimension of the family's problems, the "scapegoat" has been in that role for some time and can handle it for a while longer. In fact, moving quickly to broaden the focus to a family problem may meet with more than just family resistance, and the scapegoat may become the most agitated. This reaction may reflect an expectation of being the focus, or it may show loyalty to family members, who this person fears will fall apart if other issues are addressed. The agitation may show guilt that the psychiatric problem is such a burden to the family. Many other factors may have an effect.

The therapist asks a series of questions:

> "I understand from the phone call that you are consulting me about some of the problems that John is having and how to be most helpful to him. Okay, then. Let's begin there. Could each of you tell me a bit about John's problems? When did they begin? How have they evolved? How do they affect you? What do you think he goes through? Which of his treatments thus far has seemed most helpful and least helpful?"

■ Focus on Psychiatric Treatment of Index Person

Many cases are referred for family consultation by therapists who are well established in the individual treatment of the index person. The family therapist attempts to discover any thoughts the family may have about previous treatment and the referring therapist. Each person can begin by describing his or her understanding of the individual therapy. The therapist asks family members to discuss their knowledge or impressions of the referring therapist, their judgment of the individual therapy's effectiveness, and their ideas about which points or issues are not being addressed:

> "Let me understand who sent you here. What is your sense of what Dr. X does and what my role should be? Have you ever met Dr. X? What was your impression? How much does he (or she) know about the family?"

As part of this modified medical approach, the therapist can include a history of past psychiatric treatments, medications, and consultations. It may also be prudent to inquire about the family members' attitudes toward medications.

■ Solution History

The solution-oriented family therapy schools offer a methodology for assessing the family's attempted solutions to the problem. Strategically, the solutions are viewed as part of the problem. Any new interventions will be aimed at blocking the family's attempts to help in the old ways so that more useful solutions can emerge.

Such solution-oriented interviewing can be used either as an effective opening or as a conceptualization that will guide an ongoing solution-oriented therapy. The family's responses can help the therapist empathize with their many futile attempts to deal with the problems before seeking help.

The responses may also help the therapist avoid "more of the same." Solutions may have included visits to different authority figures who lectured a wayward adolescent. Based on this response, the therapist knows that the family is likely to try to get him or her to lecture the adolescent again. The therapist also knows that this approach will not work and can avoid being pulled into the trap.

The therapist may open the session this way:

> "It sounds like this problem has been faced by all of you for some time. What have you done to try to help? What has worked, and what has not?"

◼ Genogram

Because the multigenerational family therapist will eventually need family history information to become oriented for family intervention, one possibility is to open the session with matter-of-fact data gathering before going on to the family complaints and requests:

> "I think better if I can make a picture of the family as a whole. As a way of my getting to know you and getting oriented about your family, could you each tell me a little about your families of origin? Who is around now? How do they get along? How are they affected by or responding to the troubles you are having?"

The genogram can be recorded on a pad or board and shown to the family. Most families have never seen their history represented in this way and will find the information interesting. Conventions for recording genograms are readily available (McGoldrick and Gerson 1985). Usually the picture uses squares to represent men, circles to indicate women, horizontal lines for marriages, and vertical lines to indicate children.

Talking about the extended family can also lower the family's anxiety by focusing on relatively manageable issues. This approach must be balanced over time with the family's need to address other issues. Telling the extended family history serves to launch the therapy.

◼ Family Assessment Guidelines

◼ Traditional Psychiatric Assessment

Early in the consultation, the therapist gives attention to the basic psychiatric evaluation. Assessment emphasizes attention to medical differential diagnoses, especially for toxic states and for medical conditions affecting mental function. This evaluation includes assessment for suicide/homicide potential, the ability of the patient to care for him- or herself, and major disorders manifesting in other family members.

◼ Systemic Assessment

When getting started in the first interview and early consultations, it is helpful to have a sense of the eventual goal. General assessment criteria are considered even at this early stage, with the objective of attaining the fullest possible picture of the family after a few meetings.

Many existing schemata and matrices suggest ways to categorize and classify families. In discussing families and psychiatric disorders, the most useful assessment dimensions focus on the family's capacity to deal with adversity and crisis. The therapist does not try to answer assessment questions in every category. A few key components should be kept in mind and developed early in the consultation.

The following assessment dimensions are drawn from a number of systemic models and are among the most useful for the therapist's purposes:

- Flexibility–rigidity
- Closeness–distance
- Autonomy–dependence
- Loyalty–antisystem perception
- Openness–restriction
- Anxiety–capacity to think
- Maturity–immaturity

Flexibility–rigidity.   How does the family respond to a change in circumstances? The ability of the family to adapt to crises, stressors, and developmental events is assessed by considering the family's flexibility and openness to change. The more flexible families look forward to and celebrate developmental events such as a grown child's marriage. They readily rise to the challenge of problem solving through a crisis such as a job loss. The more rigid families enjoy sameness and are more fearful and frozen when a situation demands adaptation and problem solving.

Closeness–distance.   How closely are the family members connected to each other? In an overly close family, the pain of one member is felt by all as if it were their own personal pain. In an overly distant family, the pain of one member is not noticed and never elicits an empathic response. A balance is seen in families who share each other's pain and offer support to the person in crisis through separate though connected selves.

Autonomy–dependence.   How does the family respond to the strivings for independence by its members? The family that emphasizes dependence insists on keeping family members together. A child's leaving home for college can devastate this family. Because everything must be subjugated to the family of origin, leaving home is seen as an angry, disloyal act and possibly a sign of parental failure: "What did we do wrong that our children feel so little for their family?" In a family that places a high value on autonomy, the same act may be seen as partly painful but mainly as a cause for pride and celebration. The attribution is of parental success: "We must have done a good job to raise children who can stand on their own."

Loyalty–antisystem perception. How does the family perceive the particular symptoms in terms of their congruence with or threat to the family? In a family that forbids expression of emotion, depression and anxiety are perceived as disloyal and stoicism is perceived as loyal. In a family more open to emotions, the family may react supportively to the same depressed or anxious presentation without questioning the sufferer's loyalty to them. This family might feel shut out if a family member were strongly stoic. "Disloyal" symptoms will lead to attempts for solutions or requests for outside help more often than "loyal" symptoms might. Where the perception of disloyalty is strong, an effort may be needed to guide the family toward more positive interpretations of the disorder and other problems.

Therapists trying to assess and heal family relationships may feel progress is being made as the family takes part in angry, confrontational sessions or, in individual therapy, as the person reveals the story of unjust treatment by parents. However, any progress represented by these turbulent sessions will dissipate rapidly unless loyalty forces are considered. The therapist must take into account these hidden but powerful family allegiances and must recognize that a strong sense of betrayal of family may follow such outpourings. The "contractual intimacy" of therapy and transference must be compared with loyalty to family and considered in context. As the saying goes, "Blood is thicker than therapy."

Openness–restriction. How thick is the barrier to outsiders? In a closed family, the most threatening aspect of the crisis may be not the crisis itself, but the involvement of outsiders in family affairs. The involvement of agencies and the request for psychiatric help will be seen as especially invasive. In a more open family, the request for help and therapy is supported and seen as a mature attempt to adjust.

Either stance can be adaptive or maladaptive. The closed family turns away from possible help. The open family may be too reliant on helpers from outside, at the expense of developing their own resources within the family.

Anxiety–capacity to think.   What is the anxiety level of the family in relation to its critical reasoning point? Individuals and families can think and problem-solve up to a certain anxiety level. After that level is exceeded, the family cannot think calmly through a crisis.

The level of anxiety rises in any family or individual undergoing a traumatic event. The therapist attempts to assess the family's baseline and crisis anxiety levels. Is the family at or above its critical anxiety level? A high-functioning family may fall apart during a crisis because anxiety goes over a critical point. Another family with the same baseline anxiety level may tolerate increased anxiety in crisis more readily.

Maturity–immaturity.   What is the maturity level of the family's functioning? Maturity of function is related to the anxiety level. At times of crisis, anxiety moves a family's maturity of function toward the immature end of the spectrum.

A family presents in crisis because the parents have announced an impending divorce. In a more maturely functioning family, those who receive the announcement react by acknowledging emotions, requesting clarification, and offering support. In a less maturely functioning family, the two families of origin react by intensifying gossip and triangulation, which creates rage and vengefulness and exacerbates the crisis.

The marital couple in an immaturely functioning family deals with their anxiety and stress by projecting their disappointment and rage onto the children or by pulling the children toward one parent at the expense of the other. In the more maturely functioning family, the couple makes an effort to do whatever they can to repair the marriage. If this is not possible, they separate in a way that preserves the children's stability and loyalty to both parents.

■ Summary

These suggestions for interviewing and assessing can help the therapist evaluate the current concerns and needs of the family, gather information, and often form a valuable alliance. Even if the decision is not to undertake family therapy at this time, at least an environment open to family involvement has been established. Therapists may find that individual treatment will proceed more smoothly when the family feels involved as a result of these consultations.

One final point: Families and the problems they present are sometimes so complex that they cannot be adequately addressed with any set of techniques. No matter how skilled or well trained the therapist may be, sometimes nothing seems to work. The essence of getting started may be in having the courage and willingness to sit with families, in approaching families with respect and flexibility, and in attempting to interview and intervene to the best of the therapist's ability.

■ Additional Reading

Breunlin DC, Schwartz RC: Sequences: toward a common denominator of family therapy. Fam Process 25:67–87, 1986

Gaw A (ed): Culture, Ethnicity, and Mental Illness. Washington, DC, American Psychiatric Press, 1993

Resnikoff RO: Teaching family therapy: ten key questions for understanding the family as patient. Journal of Marital and Family Therapy 7:135–142, 1981

Weber T, McKeever JE, McDaniel SH: A beginner's guide to the problem-oriented first family interview. Fam Process 24:357–364, 1985

■ References

Berenson D: Powerlessness, liberating or enslaving? responding to the feminist critique of the twelve steps, in Feminism and Addiction. Edited by Bepko C. Binghamton, NY, Haworth, 1991, pp 67–84

Boszormenyi-Nagy I: Foundations of Contextual Therapy: Collected Papers of Ivan Boszormenyi-Nagy. New York, Brunner/Mazel, 1987

Boszormenyi-Nagy I, Krasner BR: Between Give and Take: A Clinical Guide to Contextual Therapy. New York, Brunner/Mazel, 1986

Bowen M: Family Therapy in Clinical Practice, 9th Edition. Northvale, NJ, Jason Aronson, 1994

Budman S, Hoyt MF, Friedman S: The First Session in Brief Therapy. New York, Guilford, 1992

Carter EA, McGoldrick Orfandis M: Family therapy with one person and the therapist's own family, in Family Therapy: Theory and Practice. Edited by Guerin PJ. New York, Gardner, 1976, pp 193–219

Haley J: Problem Solving Therapy. San Francisco, CA, Jossey-Bass, 1976

Havens L: Participant Observation. New York, Jason Aronson, 1976

Ho MK: Family Therapy and Ethnic Minorities. Washington, DC, American Psychiatric Association, 1993

Kerr ME, Bowen M: Family Evaluation. New York, WW Norton, 1988

Lazare A: The psychiatric examination in the walk-in clinic: hypothesis generation and hypothesis testing. Arch Gen Psychiatry 33:96–102, 1976

McGoldrick M, Gerson R: Genograms in family assessment. New York, WW Norton, 1985

Nichols MP, Schwartz RC: Family Therapy Concepts and Methods. Needham Heights, MA, Allyn & Bacon, 1991

Papp P: The Process of Change. New York, Guilford, 1983

Penn P: Circular questioning. Fam Process 21:267–280, 1982

Perlmutter RA, Jones JE: Assessment of families in psychiatric emergencies. Am J Orthopsychiatry 55:130–139, 1985

Satir V: Conjoint Family Therapy. Palo Alto, CA, Science & Behavior Books, 1983

Selvini-Palazzoli M, Boscolo L, Cecchin G, et al: Hypothesizing–circularity–neutrality: three guidelines for the conductor of the session. Fam Process 19:3–12, 1980

Stierlin H, Rucker-Embden I, Wetzel N, et al: The First Interview With the Family. New York, Brunner/Mazel, 1977

Tomm K: Circular interviewing: a multifaceted tool, in Applications of Systemic Family Therapy: The Milan Approach. Edited by Campbell D, Draper R. Orlando, FL, Grune & Stratton, 1985, pp 33–45

Wynne LC: Family consultation for major psychiatric disorders. Psychoterapia 2:5–13, 1991a

Wynne LC: Systems consultation for psychosis: a biopsychosocial integration of systemic and psychoeducational approaches, in Schizophrenia and Youth: Etiology and Therapeutic Consequences. Edited by Eggers C. Berlin, Springer-Verlag, 1991b, pp 159–168

Wynne LC: The rationale for consultation with the families of schizophrenic patients. Acta Psychiatr Scand 90 (suppl 384):125–132, 1994

Wynne LC, McDaniel SH, Weber TT: The road from family therapy to systems consultation, in Systems Consultation: A New Perspective for Family Therapy. Edited by Wynne LC, McDaniel SH, Weber TT. New York, Guilford, 1986, pp 3–15

CHAPTER 3

Adjustment Disorders

Margaret M.

Margaret M. presented with depression after the overdose of her 15-year-old daughter, Carolyn. Carolyn claimed that she was distressed in part because of her difficulty dealing with her mother's depression. She felt sorry for her mother and wanted to save her, but she was also angry that she could not rely on her mother.

Margaret thought her own depression was related to her daughter's depression. After the overdose, Margaret's mood worsened because she felt incompetent as a mother. Other members of the family were considered in the treatment plan to keep Carolyn's overdose from pulling Margaret even further from the family into her depressive world.

Edward O.

A 50-year-old man, Edward O., married and the father of two children, presented with anxiety and depression following the loss of a job he had held for 25 years. Edward was seen individually, seemed cooperative in sessions, and was agreeable to a trial of medications as part of the plan. Interestingly, he never took the medications.

Edward's "noncompliance" became understandable after a family meeting, in which it was clear that the family idolized him. The children had only a vague sense that his job was in trouble and had no idea that it had been lost 2 months earlier. The treatment team recognized the need for Edward to remain the strong head of the family and became more tolerant of his resistance to taking antidepressants or to doing anything else that might indicate weakness or sickness if discovered by the family. The family was very effective in conveying their support and convincing Edward that getting help was viewed as a strength. Soon after this, he benefited from medications and found another job.

■ Perspective on the Disorders

Adjustment disorders are usually characterized by mood, conduct, or behavioral symptoms judged to be related to stressors rather than to some other psychiatric disorder. An adjustment disorder might present as a moderate depression in a person with no prior mood problems and in the context of a recent divorce. If the symptoms are in reaction to a stressor and meet the criteria for a major depression, major depression is diagnosed and an Axis IV rating is used to describe the concomitant life stressor.

Only one or two people in a family may show psychiatric symptoms, but the stressful situation affects all family members and is best resolved for everyone if the whole family is involved. Adjustment disorder symptoms signify that the family needs assistance as they grieve over a death or cope with difficulty or change.

An adjustment disorder can be a symptomatic response to crisis, which is defined here as a stressor of sufficient magnitude or symbolic meaning to throw an individual or family into a painful, threatening state of disequilibrium that demands resolution. A crisis often results from *a significant loss:*

■ Diminishment in status
■ Joblessness
■ Loss of relationships through separation, divorce, or death

A crisis may result from *developmental changes:*

■ The birth of a child
■ A move
■ A remarriage
■ Decisions about care of elderly family members

Interpersonal conflicts that may lead to a crisis include disagreements, disappointments, and struggles for control between adolescents and their parents. *Disasters* (earthquakes, fires) and *accidents* (falls, car accidents) can also precipitate a family crisis.

The time pressure involved in crisis presentations requires a methodology for rapid assessment along these dimensions: the family's degree of openness to outsiders, flexibility, closeness, maturity, ability to solve problems, and perception of loyalty or disloyalty in the presenting symptoms (also see Chapter 2).

Table 3–1 summarizes some aspects of the family context of these disorders, which are described in more detail in the next section.

■ Connections of the Symptoms to the System

■ Effects of the Disorder on the Family

A consultation-liaison psychiatrist was called to the bedside of a man recently diagnosed with terminal cancer. The diagnosis itself was the

---

Table 3–1.   Adjustment disorders in context

Effects of the disorder on the family

- Panic and anger in reaction to stressor
- Increased closeness and resourcefulness among family members
- Shame over idea of defect in family member

Family maintenance of the symptoms

- Deficient problem-solving ability in family
- Organization of family around symptoms
- Dysfunctional behaviors and conflicts within family
- Poor coping mechanisms within family

Functions of the symptoms within the family

- Sending of interpersonal message
- Signal of underlying depression
- Expression of entire family's depression or hopelessness
- Solution of hidden family dilemmas
- Distraction from parents' problems
- Plea for nurturance

Adverse consequences of change

- Need for others in family to face own issues
- Going against family's newly vigilant and suspicious stance
- Loss of family closeness found in crisis

---

crisis. The psychiatrist held a family meeting in the hospital room, and the rest of the family showed by comments and physical closeness that they were sadder and more supportive than the man had thought. He saw that his family was not disappointed with him, angry, or rejecting in reaction to his illness. Only this reassurance could defuse his initial rage and allow the family to move on to the next tasks.

The ability to handle crisis varies widely among different families. A catastrophic event can destroy trust in the world and devastate family union. With a job loss or a diagnosis of illness, the index person and the whole family panic and develop symptoms. If serious illness affects one family member, a perfectionist family may feel panic and shame over this person's "defect."

In another family, the same catastrophic event can bring family members closer to each other as they become more sympathetic but remain able to solve problems and offer help. A diagnosis of illness is seen as an extremely disturbing but normal part of life and can be accommodated. The family is grateful if the disease is not terminal.

All crises resolve one way or the other within a relatively short time. The question is not *whether* the crisis will pass, but *how* it will pass and how much growth or damage will take place as the crisis is resolved.

■ Family Maintenance of the Symptoms

After the crisis passes, a family's inability to adapt may maintain a residual problem. Another family may feel sadder but wiser after dealing with a crisis together and adapting to its effects. This family is now ready to move on to sending children to college, looking forward to a marriage, or supporting a parent's career change.

Some family crises concern issues within the family, such as separation, divorce, disclosure of secrets, or a grown child's leaving home. In these cases, symptoms may be maintained by dysfunctions within the family, such as an inability to make decisions or resolve conflicts. Family intervention must address these dysfunctions to resolve the family crisis.

When crisis results from events outside the family, such as a car accident, weak coping mechanisms within the family may maintain the symptoms. Family therapy focuses on strengthening coping abilities and on normalizing the family's response: "Any family would be in crisis now if they were dealing with the difficulties you are facing."

■ Functions of the Symptoms Within the Family

A family may see an adolescent's drug overdose as an attempt to get more attention. The therapist is alert for signs of an underlying depression that connects to the suicidal impulse and also notes the interpersonal message of the overdose. The overdose may be an attempt to reconnect to or get closer to family members from whom the adolescent has been unable to elicit a response.

Depression in one family member could be the expression of the entire family's depression or hopelessness. Anxiety of one family member may represent fear and uncertainty in facing a crisis. One member of the family may be unconsciously "picked" to carry all the symptoms of depression and grieving, which allows other family members a respite from their pain as they focus on the depressed person.

> One 19-year-old young man was brought in for therapy by his parents because of depression and personality change. It emerged that the young man's brother had been killed 10 months earlier. The onset of symptoms correlated with this event. The parents clung to their focus on the 19-year-old, and only gradually did they face their own grief over the son who had died. All three family members were then seen as depressed and struggling.

Adolescent presentations, such as delinquency, overdoses, running away, truancy, academic failure, and substance abuse, may form the overt crisis, but these behaviors may also be covert attempts to solve hidden family dilemmas. The symptoms can distract from problems in the parents' marriage or from depression or panic disorder in one of the parents. The adolescent's symptoms may be an affective expression related to the actual or impending loss of a grandparent or other person when emotional expression has been suppressed by the family.

The adolescent may be trying to obtain nurturance from parents who are busy, ill, or distracted. An adolescent female may say after an overdose that the role of women in her family is so dismal that she wanted to escape her plight. The symptoms may be a reaction to violence or financial stressors in the family.

In crisis intervention with adolescents, symptoms often have meanings that extend beyond the immediate family members. Even in the middle of the night in an emergency room, the therapist should ask about multigenerational issues with almost every family seen in crisis and should draw a genogram that includes past and present central players. Often the present crisis can be connected to the major illness or death of a grandparent or a worsening of the relationship between the child's parents and the grandparents.

The symptoms of one member may be conducive to healing. As one family dealt with their child's drug overdose, both parents realized how distracted they had been by work and by financial and health problems. They recognized that they had distanced themselves from their children and treated them unfairly, and at the bedside they resolved to change.

■ Adverse Consequences of Change

Problems may result when the index person improves and others in the family must face their own issues. The family member who is over-whelmed with grief after a death in the family is being loyal and helps distract others in the family from their own grief. If the person begins to recover from the symptoms, the rest of the family may accuse him or her of forgetting about the person who died.

When an accident, robbery, or assault has shattered a sense of trust, anxiety fits the family's newly vigilant and suspicious stance. If the index person becomes less anxious, other family members may fear exposure to further loss.

If the crisis response has pulled together a previously disconnected family, the former distance and withdrawal could return when the crisis is resolved.

■ Special Systemic Dimensions

■ Family History and Genetics

Biological and psychological factors contribute to family styles of handling crises. A biological influence on family coping mechanisms can be inferred from the influence of such variables as concomitant mental illness, levels of anxiety, problem-solving abilities, intelligence, and vulnerability to physical illnesses.

Psychological factors have more to do with the learned patterns of crisis response through the generations, the "legacy of coping." Some families tell of ancestors who were unable to cope after the death of a spouse or who attempted suicide after a job loss. The family history of other families reveals hardy types who suffered severe hardships with an unbelievable capacity to cope with trauma. These stories alert the therapist to the family's current expectations regarding how they should deal with crisis.

■ Gender

A man may be violent or threaten violence after a woman has threatened to end a relationship. If a woman presents with an adjustment disorder and in a terrified state, the therapist must first consider possible danger to the woman and not jump to an impulsive, angry decision that could further jeopardize the woman's safety.

In a typical emergency presentation, an emotionally dependent man presents in abject despair, hopelessness, terror, and desperation after his wife has told him she plans to leave. The man plans and may possibly carry out a violent act against her or himself to prevent the breaking of this bond.

> One 45-year-old alcoholic and impulsive man said that he would shoot himself if his wife followed through on her threat to leave him. The wife did not want to be blackmailed into staying and knew that her husband's behavior would again become intolerable, but his intensity convinced her that he was very likely to harm himself. She could not allow herself to be responsible for the death of the father of her children, so she decided to stay a little longer.

Women are the ones who express feelings in many cultures. Men don't cry and are instead taught to deny and dissociate from painful affects. When a family presents in acute grief, a man is likely to request help for his wife, daughter, or mother: "Doc, can you give her something to calm her down?" Often, the man is in a kind of frozen denial and may present later with an even more disabling difficulty in dealing with the loss. Therefore, therapists cannot afford to ignore the needs of men to be reached and helped with their coping styles.

■ Intimacy

A crisis may avert abandonment. The person being left becomes depressed and anxious, which leads the person leaving to feel too guilty to carry out this act.

One 33-year-old woman told her husband she would cut her wrists if he left. She had disclosed a recent affair, and he felt too angry to stay. Even under these circumstances, however, her mutilation threat made him wonder whether she might really love him and whether he should take the drastic step of breaking up the family.

■ Loyalty

If a wife feels more loyalty to her family of origin than to her new family, she may blame her husband for a job layoff even if the layoff was beyond his control. Her immature response is an expression of loyalty to her family of origin that interferes with an empathic response toward her husband. In a different family, the same stressor might evoke strong, positive expressions of loyalty toward the newly unemployed person. The spouse in this family expresses confidence that the family will pull together and survive. He or she may offer to get a second job and generally works to soothe the anxiety of the unemployed member.

The diagnosis of medical illness, such as cancer, may bring desperate attempts by family members to demonstrate affiliation and affection for the sick person. Family members must determine what they owe and do not owe to the parent as they consider whether to place a parent in a nursing home.

In separation and divorce, children are especially affected as they try to find ways to remain loyal to two parents, each of whom may perceive closeness to the other parent as disloyal.

An adult child who finds out that his parent is afflicted with depression may feel a pull toward depression. After the death of a loved one, the survivors may feel disloyal if they get over the "depression" too early or too easily.

The departure of an adult child for college or for married life can bring painful loyalty conflicts. The person who is leaving feels simultaneous pulls to stay with the family and to move on to new opportunities in a college or work career or the new life of a marriage.

■ Map of Emotions

Crises may evoke rage or self-blame that denies underlying powerlessness and fear—"I am to blame for the layoff, so at least I am in control." Blaming and numbness are ways of avoiding deep sadness. Couples who present in intense anger, anxiety, and depression after the overdose of their child may be avoiding a sense of shame or a feeling of inadequacy as parents. After divorce or separation, a couple may be unable to face mutual responsibility related to their situation.

A husband may feel ashamed to hear his wife, who presumably knows him best, express negative opinions about him and say she wants him out of her life. Psychiatric symptoms that express demandingness, blaming, rage, and anxiety help avoid the shame, hurt, loss, grief, sadness, and fear that lurk beneath the surface. The therapist's ability to read hidden emotional levels allows for incisive, helpful statements about impediments to progress.

Countertransference

The therapist may feel pulled toward the family's level of anxiety and toward their reduced level of functioning. Therapists working with adjustment disorders and crises must constantly monitor their own level of anxiety and fear.

Crises can blur identities and boundaries between the therapist and the family, especially when the crisis involves a universal human event such as birth, death, or severe conflict. The therapist must consider boundary issues in his or her own current family and family of origin. This awareness can help the therapist remain capable of preserving boundaries, first between the therapist and family and then among family members.

Treatment

Standard Individual Therapies

Brief individual psychotherapy focuses on resolving the symptoms and on decreasing perturbation from the event. Individual crisis intervention therapies include analyzing the individual's coping mechanisms and modifying his or her maladaptive coping styles through psychotherapy. In posttraumatic stress disorder (PTSD), psychotherapy also focuses on the symbolic meaning of the catastrophic event and the expected psychophysiological coping reactions of the mind (Horowitz 1986; van der Kolk 1987) (also see Chapter 7).

Medications may be used to soothe or control acute symptoms. After sudden catastrophic events, benzodiazepines are commonly prescribed on a brief, emergency basis, though they must be used carefully because of addictive potential.

Standard treatment for depression is warranted for clinical biological depression. For example, a depressive grief reaction may appear several years after the death of a parent. Anhedonia, guilt, sense of worthlessness, and morbid preoccupation with the deceased are assessed psychiatrically to see if a true mood disorder can be diagnosed and treated. If a mood disorder is diagnosed, treatment is likely to include antidepressants and psychotherapy.

■ Family Modalities

Dealing with family crisis.   In one study of families presenting in an emergency room, psychiatric emergency patients were accompanied by family members in more than half the visits. Among these cases, about 80% of the problems were related to family issues (Perlmutter 1983).

A traditional individual psychiatric interview may be preferable to a conjoint interview, especially where violence is a concern. In most cases, the conjoint interview offers great advantages for assessing paranoia, psychosis, and potential for suicide. The most seriously suicidal patients may reassure the interviewer that they are not suicidal. The family may then supply crucial information about a personality change, strange morbid notes, or the recent purchase at the gun shop. A paranoid patient is often guarded and can hide delusional symptoms from the therapist, but family members may describe the suspiciousness and irritability and the negative effects at home and work.

Certain variables, such as age, affect the choice of individual or family meetings. The younger the person, the more essential the family's involvement. A suicidal adolescent may need individual sessions if the parents are ill or otherwise unavailable as a present resource and the survival of the adolescent depends on finding inner resources. When the family is available and willing, the therapist judges the family's ability to serve as a resource in problem solving.

In the most severe posttraumatic situations, such as the murder of a child, individual and family work is urgently needed. Individuals may resist family meetings out of fear that they will hurt others even more by sharing their pain, but therapists should encourage these sessions.

One argument for conjoint sessions in these severe situations is the high percentage of marriages that break up after the death of a child. One reason for this phenomenon is the unbearable pain felt by both spouses as they face each other daily and assume each is blamed by the other for the traumatic death. Shame, depression, and self-blame lead to isolation of each spouse, and negative projections onto other family members lead to the belief that others really are blaming. Soon one spouse determines that he or she must flee to survive. These family patterns are more amenable to reality testing, soothing, and healing if the whole family is seen together.

When the crisis involves suicidality and the person or family are refusing hospitalization, the therapist can offer the last-resort alternative of the "family suicide watch" (Landau-Stanton and Stanton 1985). The family is assigned the job of 24-hour care of the suicidal person. A family member must be at the person's side at all times. If necessary, members of the extended family are recruited to accomplish this task until the person emerges from the suicidal state.

Phases of therapy.   Crisis intervention is brief and immediate and often requires the use of crisis teams to intervene quickly and on-site in family domestic crises. The length and spacing of sessions must be flexible. In this work, it is common to see a family daily for 1 week and to have several of the sessions last 2 hours or more. The following week, the family may be seen two or three times. By the third week, the family may be wondering what all the fuss was about.

After emergency interventions, a follow-up visit is scheduled to take place in 1 or 2 months with the idea of stopping therapy at that time if the family is ready. Compliance is usually partial, even with very brief therapy. Once the anxiety of the initial crisis is reduced, most families lose motivation and disappear from therapy. Compliance can be enhanced by continuity, as when the therapist who sees the family in the emergency room does the follow-ups, and by keeping the goals limited and focused, with only the minimum required sessions being scheduled.

A somewhat more comprehensive goal of crisis intervention in treating adjustment disorders is to strengthen the problem-solving abilities of the family so that future crises can be handled more effectively. If this is the plan for a given family, a second phase of therapy can be negotiated to focus on the development of coping abilities.

If the crisis involves the overdose of an adolescent, the first phase might include only enough sessions to ensure the safety of the child, assess for depression, and begin a preliminary inquiry into the family story and the possible significance of the overdose. In a second phase, the family might focus on underlying marital difficulties and possible severe problems in another family member. Some families may wish to continue into a third and longer-term phase that allows them to work on relational conflicts.

■ Psychoeducation

Education and normalization are the most important first interventions with families or individuals after massive catastrophic stress. The therapist explains that intrusive thoughts, nightmares, and emotional flooding that alternate with denial or numbing are normal reactions, the attempts of the mind to deal with overwhelmingly traumatic events. Many victims of violence, accidents, and other catastrophic events feel great relief when they understand that at least they are not losing their minds.

> One father presented with his three small children and said all three children were having nightmares, crying spells, and intrusive images of the death of their mother, which they had witnessed 3 weeks earlier. Reluctantly, the father admitted that he too was having unwanted thoughts and was convinced he was losing his mind. They were reassured that their reactions were normal and universal, and should be seen as a kind of healing. Therapy continued periodically over the next 2 years to help with vast life adjustment.

■ New Stories

What has worked?   Solution-oriented approaches may be useful:

> "In what ways have you and your family coped well, or even exceedingly well, with the tragedy you just described? How will you know when you have resolved and mastered this difficulty as well as it can be mastered?"

Nonblaming dialogue with other family members may be a useful way to facilitate joining and reduce anxiety. A positive perspective is essential. The interviewer can comment on the family's connectedness, caring, and willingness to serve as a resource rather than focus on their difficulties. The family can be praised for their openness to seeking help at this time. The interviewer then takes a careful history of all efforts the family has made up to now to solve the problem.

Counterprojection. Counterprojective techniques are essential at times of maximum stress and crisis. If a mother is very sensitive to being blamed, the therapist asks if she is one of those people who thinks mothers are always to blame for everything and whether she is thinking or feeling that now. Many families are going through "if only" phases after a devastating event: "If only I had worked harder," "If only I had visited him before he died," "If only I had given her more money or time." These responses can be framed as understandable but futile attempts to feel in control of events over which they are sadly but realistically powerless.

New opportunities. A crisis may open up a family to new possibilities that challenge old values, beliefs, perceptions, and coping styles. In these cases, a relatively small intervention can facilitate much therapeutic change. The family may then be able to solve other old problems with their newly discovered solutions.

> The T. family presented in crisis after the myocardial infarction of the father, Anthony. Anthony T., an immigrant from Italy like his wife, had been consulted on every family question and made all decisions. The family presented in a state of paralysis, and the internist referred them for family therapy to help restore them to function. The brief, crisis-oriented therapy addressed the past and present styles of problem solving and considered what had and had not worked.
>
> The family was in consensus that the rigidly father-oriented stance was no longer possible. The panic created by the crisis was sufficient to open the family to new ways of relating, and a more egalitarian structure emerged. The seemingly meek and helpless wife took over decisions that involved not only her husband's care but also broad family concerns, including the family business. Two of the children reported a positive shift in their own marriages as they felt less need to control every detail of family life.

Circular questions. Problems can be phrased in terms that reflect attachment and interpersonal themes:

"What can you do to send clear messages of what you need?"
"How can you keep her from leaving?"
"Is there anything he or you could do to turn this around?"
"Who do you think will be the first family member to heal from this crisis?"

Unhappiness right now is normal.   Another possible approach focuses on the idea that anxiety and unhappiness at times of stress do not necessarily imply ill health. Negative affects are part of the temporary and healthy attempts to cope with change in times of mourning or during life transitions (pregnancy, birth, marriage, change of jobs, new school, new home, medical illness).

Development and breaking away.   Crises resulting from adolescent running away, delinquency, and conduct problems may be revealed as the child's effort to communicate in a way that cannot be ignored or as an earnest, if misguided, attempt to force the family into therapy to address dysfunctional patterns. Families usually view their children's behaviors as mean and delinquent or crazy and out of control, rather than as actions with positive intent.

The problem can be discussed as a developmental issue in that the child is functioning at a more immature level than the family had realized. The job of the parents is seen as not quite done.

> In a discussion with a family and their 15-year-old daughter, who had just overdosed, the interviewer commented that the adolescent seemed to be committing outrageous acts in the hope of distracting the mother from her own depression (i.e., as a way to offer the mother what the daughter thought she needed). The interviewer later asked the family to consider how they might take this pressure off the adolescent: "How can you convince your daughter that she does not need to hurt herself to protect you, because you can take care of yourself?"

■ Additional Reading

Adam KS, Bouckoms A, Scarr G: Attempted suicide in Christchurch: a controlled study. Aust N Z J Psychiatry 14:305–314, 1980
Bowen M: Family Therapy in Clinical Practice, 9th Edition. Northvale, NJ, Jason Aronson, 1994

Everstein DS, Everstein L: People in Crisis. New York, Brunner/Mazel, 1983

Imber Coppersmith E: "Developmental" reframing: he's not bad, he's not mad, he's just young. Journal of Strategic and Systemic Therapies 1:1–8, 1981

Langsley DG, Kaplan DM: The Treatment of Families in Crisis. New York, Grune & Stratton, 1968

Perlmutter RA, Jones JE: Assessment of families in psychiatric emergencies. Am J Orthopsychiatry 55:130–139, 1985

Perlmutter RA, Jones JE: On not recommending family therapy to families in psychiatric emergencies. Family Systems Medicine 5:333–343, 1987

Pittman FS: Managing acute psychiatric emergencies: defining the family crisis, in Techniques of Family Psychotherapy: A Primer. Edited by Bloch D. New York, Grune & Stratton, 1973, pp 99–107

Puryear DA: Helping People in Crisis. San Francisco, CA, Jossey-Bass, 1979

Richman J: Symbiosis, empathy, suicidal behavior, and the family. Suicide Life Threat Behav 8:139–148, 1978

Richman J: The family therapy of attempted suicide. Fam Process 18:131–142, 1979

Rubinstein D: Rehospitalization versus family crisis intervention. Am J Psychiatry 129:715–720, 1972

Walsh F, McGoldrick M (eds): Living Beyond Loss: Death in the Family. New York, WW Norton, 1991

■ References

Horowitz M: Stress Response Syndromes, 2nd Edition. Northvale, NJ, Jason Aronson, 1986

Landau-Stanton J, Stanton MD: Treating suicidal adolescents and their families, in Handbook of Adolescents and Family Therapy. Edited by Mirkin MP, Koman SL. New York, Gardner, 1985, pp 309–328

Perlmutter RA: Family involvement in psychiatric emergencies. Hosp Community Psychiatry 34:255–257, 1983

van der Kolk BA (ed): Psychological Trauma. Washington, DC, American Psychiatric Press, 1987

CHAPTER 4

Mood Disorders

William E.

A 72-year-old man, William E., had suffered from recurrent unipolar depression for years, especially since his retirement. The problem had become unbearable for him and his devoted wife. After multiple treatment failures with psychotherapy and medications, his psychiatrist found an effective antidepressant. When William subsequently stopped taking the medication, the therapist, in frustration, referred him for family consultation.

The consultants assessed the marriage as loving and functional and turned to family-of-origin issues. William said his father had been severely depressed, very irritable, and frequently physically abusive and left the family when William was 8 years old. The consultants pointed out the differences between William and his father. As bad as William's depression was, he had worked to keep it in check. No matter how unhappy or irritable he felt, he had always provided for his family. Clearly, he had already surpassed his father in terms of family satisfaction. The consultants suggested that he might now feel a reluctance to be happier or to have a better life than his father.

The consultants hypothesized that William was holding on to the negative mood style of his father as an indirect way of staying loyal to his father and that his conscious feelings of rage for the beatings and abandonment had obscured this longing for his father and his wish to be loyal. At this point, William started to cry and said, "Wouldn't it be something if that's it?" He returned to his psychiatrist and was compliant with medications, to which he responded well. His wife was impressed and touched that the therapists had reached such a hidden side of her husband in one family session.

Paula B.

Paula B., 17 years old, presented with a severe suicidal depression and an eating disorder with obesity. She was seen by a psychiatrist in individual sessions monthly and responded dramatically to fluoxetine and psychotherapy. Three years later, a trial of lower-dose maintenance medications was discussed. She refused to change medications because of the risk of relapse.

Paula discussed this refusal in a family-oriented individual session. She revealed that she was living at home because of economic conditions, and she saw her severely depressed father every day. He had been depressed for many years and refused help, even after seeing his daughter's recovery. Paula could not risk feeling or being like her father, even for a few hours. She could not stand the thought of burdening her mother further, after seeing what the father's illness had done to the family. Paula also said she would never marry and risk passing on this illness to her children.

James and Ellen D.

A family-oriented therapist asked James D., a 30-year-old man, to join the therapy sessions of his 28-year-old wife Ellen, who was being treated for a unipolar depression. Even though Ellen responded to medication, the therapist thought something was holding her back from a more complete recovery.

During the family session, the couple described their behavioral pattern. When Ellen got mildly depressed, James became agitated, panicky, and withdrawn and eventually started drinking. Ellen then became desperate in response to his emotional withdrawal and, even in her depressed state, tried to reassure him that her depression would be brief and had nothing to do with him. When this effort was ineffective, she became more deeply depressed and felt like a burden to her family. As her depression deepened, her husband's withdrawal intensified and she became more depressed.

This destructive cycle was broken after several weeks of work. James revealed that, as a small boy, he had watched his usually stalwart father enter melancholic depressions that lasted for months and for which he would refuse help. The last depression ended in the father's suicide when James was 16 years old. In one emotional session, James had the painful realization that he was confusing these traumatic scenes with his wife's much less severe mood disorder.

The key to ending the cycle came when James saw clearly the differences between the two stories, especially Ellen's responsible openness about treatment and rigorous compliance, her responsiveness to medications, her lack of suicidality, and the vastly better marital relationship they enjoyed compared to that of his parents.

The M. Family

In another case, Alan M., a highly successful 40-year-old accountant, and his wife, Miriam, an equally accomplished 38-year-old philosophy professor, presented because of marital problems, ostensibly over disagreements about money, but other issues were prominent: the couple's 15-year-old daughter Natalie, who caused them pain and constant dilemmas; depressive disorders in both spouses, which needed urgent attention because they were cyclical and often severe; alcohol abuse in both spouses, especially in the husband, which had been a taboo subject in the family; Miriam's obsessional disorder, which was under her control much of the time but took over the household when it was not; and related marital problems.

After careful discussion, the family requested that one family-oriented psychiatrist address as many of the treatment needs as possible. Conjoint meetings were the modality for about three-quarters of the visits, with occasional individual sessions with each spouse. The therapist successfully prescribed antidepressants for both spouses and focused on the drinking problems until both spouses were dry. The therapist and couple implemented strategies for consistent communication with the distressed and defiant daughter.

The middle phase of therapy was characterized by family battles, but the couple's relationship improved. The therapy ended by mutual agreement after 1 year. Five years later, Alan called the same therapist to see his daughter. She was now in college and had been doing well until a crisis had occurred. The therapist met with Natalie and found her in urgent need of treatment for depression and panic disorder. She responded dramatically to treatment. The attempt to address the underlying discord between Natalie and her

parents led to some very painful family sessions, and a partial rec-
onciliation was achieved.

■ Perspective on the Disorders

Research suggests that psychosocial stressors are crucial variables affecting the expression of severe mood problems in prone individuals
(Post 1992). The therapist should consider the individual's symptoms,
biology, intrapsychic processes, and relationships when treating mood
disorders.

Addressing family issues in treatment of depression adds significantly to treatment outcomes, and combined research findings make
one of the strongest cases for a treatment approach that emphasizes
the family (Glick et al. 1985; Haas et al. 1988; Keitner and Miller 1990).
This research provides the psychiatric clinician with the new possibility
of a psychotherapy that treats individual and family factors and can
also be combined with modern pharmacotherapy.

Table 4–1 summarizes some aspects of the family context of these
disorders, which is described in more detail in the next section.

■ Connections of the Symptoms to the System

■ Effects of the Disorder on the Family

A severely depressed family member can depress an entire family. The
spouse often feels anger, guilt, and deprivation, and may also fear that
the depressed person will leave or will no longer be alive at the end of
the day. The spouse must function for two people, and he or she may
see the depressed person's withdrawal as a deliberate, aggressive act.
The therapist must consider the attributions of the spouse.

> One woman reacted to her husband's depression with anger and
> pain because she assumed it was proof of her inadequacy and of his
> lack of love for her. In discussions with the therapist, the woman
> revealed that her mother had suffered from depression. The wom-
> an was responding to her husband as she had responded to her
> mother as a child.

The effects on a child raised by a chronically depressed parent can be as devastating as the effects of any other disorder in a parent, including psychosis (Beardslee et al. 1983; Downey and Coyne 1990). The child thinks, "I must be a bad (or unimportant) child if my mother doesn't care whether she lives or not or whether she can take care of me, so I must care for *her.*" The parentified child is at increased risk of

Table 4–1. Mood disorders in context

Effects of the disorder on the family

- *Depression*
    - Depression of whole family
    - Marital stress in response to depression in spouse
    - Devastation for children as associated with parent's apathy, irritability, and other symptoms; eventual expression of depression or other disorders in children
- *Bipolar disorder*
    - Confusion and vigilance in response to mania
    - Assumption of executive tasks by children

Family maintenance of the symptoms

- Malfunctioning relationships correlate with increased frequency and severity of disease episodes and increased likelihood of relapse
- Likelihood of need for marital therapy if relationship dysfunctional

Functions of the symptoms within the family

- *Depression*
    - Distraction from even more serious depression in another family member
    - Creation of better power balance
    - Elicitation of nurturance
- *Bipolar disorder*
    - Introduction of vitality into everyday life by behavior of person with bipolar disorder
    - Needed attention to children

Adverse consequences of change

- Consequences especially strong if detouring has been primary function of disorder
- Previously overresponsible person vulnerable to resuming overfunctioning role
- Withdrawal of nurturance after symptoms clear
- Resumption of abuse
- Need for new balance of power without mood swings

developing eating disorders and psychosomatic problems or of experiencing dissatisfaction with interpersonal relationships.

The study of "children of depression" is expanding, and it drama-
tizes the effects of depression in the general population (Beardslee and
Podorefsky 1988; Downey and Coyne 1990). Research findings indicate
psychiatric disturbance in about half of those children with one depressed parent (Coyne 1987). More complex studies demonstrate that
negative effects on children are related not simply to a parent's depression, but also to marital discord and general family stress (Downey and
Coyne 1990). Interpersonal research approaches have reported that
certain capacities in children of depressed parents, such as self-understanding and strong commitments to relationships, may indicate resil-
ience to adjustment problems and psychiatric disorders (Beardslee and
Podorefsky 1988). Postpartum depression requires particularly close
study because of the high incidence rate and the resulting health implications for children.

In bipolar disorder, the mood of the family swings. Family members
may eventually become confused by features of mania that appear positive, such as high energy, creativity, and capacity for enjoying life. Confusion enters as the family tries to decide when these features are
healthy expressions and when they are signs of a disordered, dangerous
process (Moltz 1993). Vigilance for relapses and dangerous behaviors
is the usual state. All actions of the person with bipolar disorder are
viewed from an illness perspective: "Is he or she buying that as part of
the next spending spree even before we're out of debt from the last
one? Does that sleepless night last night mean that the next siege is
coming?"

One complaint voiced by children is uncertainty about when the
parent with bipolar disorder is to be treated as a parent in charge and
when that parent is to be considered ill and the roles must shift. During
relapses, children are often recruited to help with family tasks and to
pick up some executive functioning. This shift often means parenting
the parent.

Withdrawal is a particularly common adaptation in a child of a
bipolar parent as a way to get off the emotional roller coaster. This
withdrawal can be healthy if the child can express family loyalties while
also finding friends and families who become alternative models of
interpersonal interaction. Withdrawal can easily become maladaptive
if avoidance transforms into delinquency, excessive risk taking, truancy,
or running away.

■ Family Maintenance of the Symptoms

Malfunctioning relationships in the family correlate with increased frequency and severity of depression episodes and an increased likelihood of relapse after successful treatment (Beach et al. 1990; Brown and Harris 1978; Clarkin et al. 1988). The frequency of critical comments directed toward the symptomatic individual correlates with relapse rate. These critical comments are typical:

> "Why can't you be more friendly (or more fun)?"
> "After all we've done for you, why are you so ungrateful?"
> "Why do you always have to dress so carelessly?"
> "You're a bad father."

Also relevant is the association of positive family functioning, especially the index person's subjective view of his or her family as a healthily functioning one, with achieving and maintaining a recovery from a major depressive episode (Keitner et al. 1995).

Although marriage seems to convey some decreased risk of depression, being married and unable to talk to the spouse correlates remarkably strongly in research studies with the risk of depression (Coyne and Downey 1991). If a relationship is troubled, marital therapy or at least addressing marital issues is essential to recovery (Coyne 1987; Keitner et al. 1993).

■ Functions of the Symptoms Within the Family

Depression in one person may distract from a more serious depression in another family member. The presentation with the index person brings other members into contact with potentially helpful treatment settings.

> One woman presented with a severe recurrent depression. She and her family related her pattern of overfunctioning, especially in parenting and family decisions. During her depressed episodes, her passive, underfunctioning husband was forced to exert parental authority and take over as the head of the family. This established a new balance of power and demonstrated a healthier model of intimate relationships for the children.

If a woman finds herself increasingly fearful of a husband who is becoming increasingly dominant and abusive, especially when she expresses her own opinion, she may become clinically depressed and helpless, submissive, anergic, and emotionally nonreactive. Her husband may express concern or fear, and his physical threats may stop temporarily.

Although the cost is extremely high, bipolar disorder introduces life and vitality into certain families with extremely low affect levels. Some observers describe mania as a couple's way of regulating intimacy. The mania increases interpersonal distance and replaces intimacy with control. The spouse is forced to control the manic spouse until the episode is over.

In some families with bipolar disorder, expressions of nurturance and caring are severely suppressed except when one member becomes ill. A child's attempt to get attention and nurturant parenting falls on the deaf ears of two parents who are absorbed with their own suffering or personal stress. The parents' self-absorption may modify only when the child attempts suicide or becomes so nonfunctional that school authorities recommend hospitalization for depression. These events wake up the parents to the needs of their child, and a corrective effect may generalize to other children and may last beyond symptom remission.

◼ Adverse Consequences of Change

> In one family, the 21-year-old son presented with a moderate depression that was successfully treated with antidepressants and family sessions. The mother began to face her own issues and became depressed and suicidal and requested treatment, during which she revealed intrusive memories of sexual abuse by her father 50 years earlier. The memories had been continuous since childhood but devoid of affect.
>
> The woman went through a phase of being enraged at her son for reminding her of her own intolerable affects. She admitted to feeling envious that he could recover from his mood disorder when she doubted such a good outcome for herself, but she was also grateful that his depression and therapy had brought the possibility for her to get help for herself.

With the "cure" of the depression, the previously overresponsible index person may be pulled back into the overfunctioning role. If the family has improved the distribution of responsibilities, the index person may be sad to lose a familiar place in the family, even if it was impossible to maintain that role. Where abuse is an issue, therapy may mean the wife has lost her protection and could be abused again.

The spouse of a person with bipolar disorder may fear the unknown, which is a relationship free from extreme affective swings. This fear is especially common if the healthy spouse has adapted to assuming control of family functions during manias and severe depressions, and the person with bipolar disorder is the executive during euthymic periods. If mood stabilizers and psychotherapy are effective, the couple must establish a new way of relating.

■ Special Systemic Dimensions

■ Family History and Genetics

A patient with a mood problem is routinely assessed for a family history of mood disorders. Bipolar disorder has an especially strong genetic transmission rate, showing about a 70% concordance rate for monozygotic twins and about a 20% rate for dizygotic twins (Mendlewicz 1985). Unipolar depression research also indicates a genetic contribution, but is complicated by the commonness of "depression" in reports about family members. These reports may or may not represent bona fide mood disorders. Affected offspring have a good chance of responding to an agent similar to one that worked for the parent.

Twin studies hint at genetically related aspects of personality and temperament that determine how a person gets along with others, suggesting that some people have a genetic load for mood disorders *and* poor interpersonal skills. If these people get sick, the protective influence of relationships is not available (Kessler et al. 1992). Intervention should emphasize and build upon family supports or should focus on shyness, social phobia, or paranoid processes between episodes.

■ Gender

A research field now points to strong correlations of depression in women with interpersonal distress, especially marital unhappiness (Beach et al. 1990; Clarkin et al. 1988). The severity of women's depression correlates with the amount of inequality in the decision-making process in the marriage and also increases where the couple reports dissatisfaction with the sharing of household tasks (Whisman and Jacobson 1989). Research data implicate a bad marriage as the single most potent predictor of major unipolar depression in women and strongly indicate that depression did not "cause" the deterioration of the marriage. Problems in the marriage precede the onset of depression (Beach et al. 1990; Weissman 1979).

These findings are probably related to the often-described connection between identity and relationship in the socialization of women. The clinician must be alert to depressed women who function with impossible traditional role expectations, as when a woman is socialized into a homemaker role that is then devalued by society, husband, and self.

Although research studies have focused more on women, men also react to distressed or interrupted relationships with alteration in mood. Work stress or layoffs are somewhat more likely to trigger mood problems in men than in women.

■ Intimacy

The quality of relationships has repeatedly been shown to correlate with response to treatment of depression and proneness to relapse. The lack of a close primary relationship is itself a risk factor for depression (Brown and Harris 1978; Coyne and Downey 1991). A positive intimate primary relationship seems to offer protection against the expression of mood disorders. For example, the likelihood of a woman's recovery from a severe depression has been found to be predicted by her rating of her husband's support of her (Goering et al. 1992; Keitner et al. 1993).

A healthier balance of power and enhanced demonstration of an empathic connection are examples of the positive effects of mood disorders on intimacy.

> A 42-year-old man recovering from a major depression related that his wife was critical of everything he said or did and subjected him to vituperative attacks. The only exception was in the early days of an impending depressive episode, when she would become caring and accepting and would tell him what a good man and husband he was.

The projection of negative feelings about self threatens intimacy. Depressed people assume another person looks at them with the same disdain and shame that they feel toward themselves, and eventually others *do* become frustrated and disgusted with confronting irritable, unreasonable stances. Negative projections cause others to doubt their empathic connection with the depressed person. Interpersonal distance is ensured, and other people are pushed away as enemies.

■ Loyalty

Some people express loyalty invisibly (Boszormenyi-Nagy and Krasner 1986) by not succeeding too far beyond the success of their family, by covertly remaining bound to the family, or by adopting similarly negative ways of thinking. A mood disorder may balance success and happiness in adult life. Clinically, this condition can be observed in overachieving adults who secretly feel they don't deserve so much good in their lives. These adults are pained to see the ongoing suffering in their families of origin and develop intense mood problems.

Negative thoughts are projected onto children: "You shouldn't be happier than we are, and we are sure miserable." These powerful projections can bring a negative outcome for the child. The child who goes against such projections risks family anger, abandonment, and attacks.

■ Map of Emotions

Moods represent the avoidance of emotions. Though the experience of sadness offers the potential for movement and change, it can be more intensely painful than depression. Sadness means facing the limits of what a person can do to alter any unhappy or even tragic realities that may loom.

The concentration of a depressed person is often impaired by repetitive, obsessive thoughts of guilty responsibility for events and painful realities. The exaggerated sense of self-blame and worthlessness conveys a grandiosity that opposes the sense of powerlessness.

Mania may be an emotional detour from depressive suffering. In biologically vulnerable individuals, mania alternates with severe depressions characterized by a particularly deep level of despair and anergy. In bipolar disorder, one reality being avoided is the sense of powerlessness over having the disorder at all, a problem that can be lifelong, extremely disruptive, and costly.

Depression could be seen as a temporary victory of shame, which saps the person's energy and sense of self and forces withdrawal from other people to avoid more shame. Mania is the avoidance of shame via externalization. All inadequacies are denied and all problems projected in a blaming irritable frenzy.

■ Countertransference

> A therapist finds himself feeling inadequate and without enough energy to correct the depressive way several members of a family are distorting his comments and those of other family members.

It is critical for the therapist to be aware when negative moods and thoughts are projections of a family's depression. He or she must refuse to absorb this depression.

Manic families are more likely to elicit in the therapist a desire to dominate and control or to withdraw anxiously.

■ Ethnicity

Some minority families may distrust professional and medical institutions because of perceived or actual discrimination, language barriers, and general misunderstanding of their culture. Families that distrust institutions have probably tried for years to deal with problems themselves before even considering treatment. Mood disorders are often severe and well advanced by the time these families present for help. Asking for treatment is a last desperate act.

Affective disorders are generally alike among the various ethnic groups, although a few differences are worth noting. Depression in African Americans may be more directly related to loss, as dramatically substantiated by the frequency with which these families have been touched by violence (B. Dorsey, personal communication, June 1993). One elderly man said, "You call this depression in black folk a *disorder?* When you've been suppressed, repressed, and oppressed for so long, what else do you expect us to act like but depressed?" (Freda Hall Lewis, "Affective Disorders in African Americans" lecture, September 1993).

Families who have come to this country as refugees often suffer a severe sense of loss and develop frequent clinical depressions. The issue for therapy is to determine how to judge when the situation is extreme and requires intervention.

■ Treatment

■ Standard Individual Therapies

Psychotherapies. Cognitive therapy focuses on understanding and modifying the array of negative thoughts that are habitual for the depressed person. Interpersonal therapy studies and works with the individual to examine the family and social stressors, with an emphasis on modifying the interpersonal world so that the index person has more supports. Group therapy of mood disorders addresses the relationship of interpersonal patterns to the demoralization and isolation that can be expressed as depression.

Psychoanalytically informed therapies address underlying drives, conflicts, and character problems that exert a downward pull on mood. Even though psychoanalytic therapy may require supplementation by other therapies, it continues to play a role in treatment. Intrapsychic conflicts exert a dysphoric pull on mood, and character pathology can contribute to treatment failures even with promising pluralistic therapies. For character disturbances that do not respond to other treatments, psychoanalytic psychotherapy may offer the ability to deal with the deeper levels of personality development.

Biological treatments. Biological psychiatry has focused much of its effort on treatment methods for mood disorders. These methods include electroconvulsive therapy, medications, and therapy with high-intensity fluorescent lights.

While some professionals might still advocate psychotherapy alone for depressive disorders, fewer would advocate this course for bipolar disorder. Bipolar patients spend much time in states that cannot be reached through words and relationships. While seemingly opposite, mania and bipolar depression both involve the person's preoccupation with mood and the inability to fully process new cognitive information. Lithium's demonstrated effectiveness in bipolar disorder obligates professionals to consider biological intervention when bipolar mood disorder is suspected.

Despite the undisputed effectiveness of lithium and the antidepressants, large patient subgroups do not benefit. The new mood-stabilizing applications of carbamazepine and valproic acid have helped, as have newer antidepressants, new combinations, and augmentations. However, limitations of response to medications are notable for both those with unipolar disorder and those with bipolar disorder (Sachs et al. 1994; Shea et al. 1992). This sobering observation should keep all clinicians open to both new biological interventions and psychotherapies.

■ Family Modalities

The psychiatrist who is both prescribing medications and providing family consultation should be aware of potential opportunities and also obstacles to success. Does the person taking medication feel as if the therapy has shifted to focus on him or her as the source of the problem? Does the prescribing of medication allow the spouse to escape from shared responsibility for problems and to assume the role of caregiver for the "sick one"? If these potential drawbacks are considered, one psychiatrist can effectively treat an individual with medications and also work with the family. The strong advantage is that relational, intrapsychic, and biological forces can then be efficiently addressed and integrated.

It is sometimes possible to treat more than one family member for a mood disorder, including the use of psychotropic agents as part of family treatment. Added perspectives may then be accessible, especially the relationship of moods to marital and parent-child issues. New possibilities for dialogue are worth some of the complexities of therapeutic boundaries and confidentiality when treating several members of the same family. Where competition, distrust, and the need for especially clear boundaries are prominent, referral to other therapists may be necessary.

Sibling sessions are underutilized as a modality and can contribute to strengthening the potentially curative sibling bond, especially where children in the family are suffering from the effects of one person's depression.

■ Psychoeducation

A body of literature now exists that focuses on psychoeducational methods and effectiveness in the treatment of depression (Anderson et al.

1986; Berkowitz 1988), as well as a new application for families with bipolar members (Miklowitz and Goldstein 1990). Other research literature focuses on the role of expressed emotion and critical comments in depressed patients, similar to the findings in schizophrenia (Florin et al. 1992; Goldstein 1992). Research into the social origins of schizophrenia has been extended to depression and bipolar disorder (Brown and Harris 1978; Goldstein and Miklowitz 1994; Miklowitz et al. 1988).

Psychoeducational methods have great power, but they should be used with care. Education should not support the belief that the *only* problem is a disease in one member of a family—a belief that can increase blame, negative projections, and isolation of the index person (factors already likely to be contributing to the depression).

Medically modeled psychoeducation can help reduce blame and guilt. The mood disorder is framed as a physical disease for which no one is any more at fault than with diabetes. Motivation to work on relationship issues is increased. The therapist explains improvements in relations and biochemistry work synergistically. Individuals recovering from mood disorders often gratefully report the benefit they have received from their family's continued expression of warmth and support, even when the individual was unable to respond in kind.

Individuals in the family can be helped to maintain a focus on themselves, to pay attention to their own health, needs, feelings, and reactions as they live with the symptomatic person, as in this comment to the wife of the index person:

> "You're saying that when you're tired and he's depressed, you become hurt and angry more easily. Then the children have to deal with *two* distressed parents."

Discussion can also focus on how the family can influence the affected one to get help, even if he or she resists.

Through education, the family can acquire a useful understanding of mood disorders, including an awareness of how to avoid "catching" negative thoughts. With this increased understanding of the disorder and the likely shift away from blaming, the family may be open to the possibility of identifying treatable psychiatric disorders in other family members.

Psychosocial factors, such as criticizing comments, can be examined in connection with their role in obstructing recovery or encouraging relapse:

> "Over the next week, pay attention to how many critical exchanges take place every day, and we'll discuss them in our next meeting."

The therapist can encourage the continued expression of support by family members, even when the index person seems unreceptive.

The therapist can help the index person and the family identify *prodromes* of depressive or manic episodes so that early intervention is possible. What are the symptoms, and in what order do they develop, as reported by both the internal experience and the observations of the family? Sometimes the index person will be able to detail the sequence completely: "First I can't sleep, then I get these thoughts, then I lose energy." Sometimes the index person has difficulty recognizing the prodrome but the family has long been silently aware of the pattern: "First we'll notice the irritability, then the withdrawal, then the slowness of speech and motion, then the strange comments."

Perhaps most important, a psychoeducational approach can call attention to the special needs of children to ensure that they receive maximum care and nurturance and minimum shame. This focus can exert pressure on the adults to push toward their own recovery.

Grown children are concerned about inheritability, and these concerns must be addressed directly. Information on inheritability can be used indirectly to increase motivation for mature behaviors or to provide incentive for family consultation. The role of family and social life on transmission of the disorder can be emphasized:

> "We agree that your children are genetically at somewhat higher risk to develop mood disorders, and yet you have control over only the aspects of transmission that are affected by environment and home life. Let's see what can be done to maximize effective, positive family communication."

■ New Stories

Mania. Families expect therapists to see manic behaviors as purely negative, destructive, immature, and impulsive. Therapists may find it useful to inquire about other less obvious meanings and beliefs. In a particular family, the hypothesis may be that mania is helping the family bring excitement into relationships that otherwise seem mundane and predictable. The therapist might ask, "Are you saying that you sometimes enjoy the manic state because of the high level of creativity and energy?" Children might find their mother's manic states positive because, painful as they are, they draw out a normally shy or passive father into a stronger role in the family.

Depression.   For a family that is angry at the index person and hurt by his or her withdrawal, depression can be reframed as a form of conservation of energy in response to biological illness or as protection from intrapersonal stresses (i.e., reactions that may be part of the mind's attempt to adapt and survive), such as rejection.

The positive effects of a depressive episode can be emphasized to support family members who feel guilty because they believe they are responsible for the illness. For example, the therapist can comment on the rallying of support and nurturance expressed in the face of the depressive crisis.

The family members can be freed from the burden of direct efforts to reassure or cheer up the depressed person. This common-sense approach can be tried a few times and abandoned if it is unsuccessful. Such a well-meaning effort can backfire if the person cannot be cheered up and feels only a compounded sense of failure when he or she is unable to laugh at family jokes. The index person ends up more depressed, and the family feels angry and rejected by the ungrateful one.

Belief systems.   Depression can be described as an unwanted form of suffering and as a sign of such intense self-criticism that no family member could possibly put a more negative cast on the problem than the sufferer already does.

On the other extreme, the beliefs of some families do not allow the depressed member to carry *any* responsibility for the effects on others of the depressive withdrawal, and the family is solicitous to the point of infantilizing the patient. It may be prudent to suggest that the disorder is at least in part an indulgence and to see if the family is willing to increase tasks and responsibility:

> "Are you saying that your husband has it pretty good when in the depressed state, and that even though you know the depression is an illness, there is a concern that he holds back (maybe understandably) from getting effective treatment?"

Externalizing the disorder as an unwanted enemy of the whole family, especially the sufferer, can be helpful:

> "So what I hear is that the family is being attacked by this force
> called depression, which no one wants and which you are all pulling
> together to defeat."

This approach can offer the beginning of a new story to replace the old
one in which the index person had been unproductively labeled as
irresponsible, hostile, lazy, and self-pitying.

Circular questions.   If detouring is identified during the assessment
as a primary function of the depression, the therapist can ask, "What
might be some other issues the family would face if the depressive
symptoms were cured?"

The function of the depression may be identified as evoking nurturance. In this case, the focus can be on ways the family might express
positive regard for the index person at times when the disorder is
quiescent.

If the function of the mood disorder is identified as regulating
intimacy, the therapist inquires into ways members of the couple or
family can signal when they need more closeness and when they need
more space and freedom.

The roles adopted by each family member in the bipolar cycle can
be assessed through circular questions:

> "Who stands for fun and spontaneity, and who stands for harmony
> and control? Who is the head of the family during depressive times,
> and who is the boss during manic times?"

Psychopharmacology of attachment.   The therapist must consider
the family's views about medication, especially in treating mood disorders, where medication is likely to be a substantial part of treatment.
Family attitudes will have a significant influence on compliance.

Family attitudes about antidepressants and mood stabilizers can
vary widely.

> In one case, the therapist, a biologically and individually oriented
> psychiatrist, believed that his patient Robert, a young man of 17,
> had a severe mood disorder and needed antidepressants, but felt
> sabotaged and defeated by Robert's family. Although the youth's
> parents had presented a superficially compliant stance in the of-
> fice, at home they disparaged the doctors and the medication, re-
> fused to get the prescription filled, and repeatedly told their son
> that his depression was a moral weakness, not a biological disease.
> Robert sank deeper into melancholia. During his subsequent hos-

pitalization, the family revealed the deep fear and shame they had felt when antidepressants were prescribed for Robert, because to them medication symbolized a very serious and possibly hopeless disorder.

Conversely, some families vigorously pursue a purely biological etiology and intervention to forestall any discussion of family secrets or conflicts. When a family's insistence on biological treatment is motivated by a wish to avoid discussion of painful interpersonal issues, the therapist must try to address both medical and relational dimensions.

Family-oriented therapists begin by finding components of the family's theory with which they can agree and by finding demands to which they can accede. If the family is strongly opposed to biological treatments, the therapist can first comment on how some families oversimplify such issues and believe every problem is a matter of chemistry. Later the therapist can gently introduce the idea that medications may help, but treatment must also include changing attitudes.

If the family holds a definite biological view of the disorder and demands medications, the therapist's agreement with this assessment helps build an alliance with the index person and the family. Indirect questioning about family functioning and conflict can be introduced gradually. Sometimes the therapist asks the family to look for correlations between family or social stressors and the severity of the negative moods. This method can help decrease family members' resistance to exploring interpersonal issues.

◼ Additional Reading

Costell RM, Reiss D: The family meets the hospital: clinical presentation of a laboratory-based typology. Arch Gen Psychiatry 39:433–438, 1982

DiNicola VF: The child's predicament in families with a mood disorder: research findings and family interventions. Psychiatr Clin North Am 12:933–949, 1989

Framo JL: Symptoms from a family transactional viewpoint, in Explorations in Marital and Family Therapy. Edited by Framo JL. New York, Springer-Verlag, 1970, pp 11–57

Goering PN, Lancee WJ, Freeman SJJ: Marital support and recovery from depression. Br J Psychiatry 160:76–82, 1992

Heim SC, Snyder DK: Predicting depression from marital distress and attributional processes. Journal of Marital and Family Therapy 17:67–72, 1991

Kaslow NJ, Carter AS: Gender-sensitive object-relational family therapy with depressed women. Journal of Family Psychology 5:116–135, 1991

Keegan DL: General management issues in depressive illness—family interventions. Psychiatric Journal of the University of Ottawa 14:421–425, 1989

Sher TG, Baucom DH, Larus JM: Communication patterns and response to treatment among depressed and nondepressed maritally distressed couples. Journal of Family Psychology 4:63–79, 1990

Sloman L, Gardner R, Price J: Biology of family systems and mood disorders. Fam Process 28:387–398, 1989

Snyder DK, Heim SC: Marriage, depression and cognition: unraveling the Gordian knot—reply to Ettinger et al. Journal of Marital and Family Therapy 18:303–307, 1992

Weber G, Simon FB, Stierlin H, et al: Therapy for families manifesting manic-depressive behavior. Fam Process 27:33–49, 1988

■ References

Anderson CM, Griffin S, Ross A, et al: A comparative study of the impact of education vs. process groups for families of patients with affective disorders. Fam Process 25:185–205, 1986

Beach SRH, Sandeen EE, O'Leary KD: Depression in Marriage: A Model for Etiology and Treatment. New York, Guilford, 1990

Beardslee WR, Podorefsky D: Resilient adolescents whose parents have serious affective and other psychiatric disorders: importance of self-understanding and relationships. Am J Psychiatry 145:63–69, 1988

Beardslee WR, Bemporad J, Keller MB, et al: Children of parents with a major affective disorder: a review. Am J Psychiatry 140:825–832, 1983

Berkowitz R: Family therapy and adult mental illness: schizophrenia and depression. Journal of Family Therapy 10:339–356, 1988

Boszormenyi-Nagy I, Krasner BR: Between Give and Take: A Clinical Guide to Contextual Therapy. New York, Brunner/Mazel, 1986

Brown GW, Harris TO: Social Origins of Depression: A Study of Psychiatric Disorder in Women. New York, Free Press, 1978

Clarkin JF, Haas GL, Glick ID (eds): Affective Disorders and the Family: Assessment and Treatment. New York, Guilford, 1988

Coyne JC: Depression, biology, marriage and marital therapy. Journal of Marital and Family Therapy 13:393–407, 1987

Coyne JC, Downey G: Social factors and psychopathology: stress, social support, and coping processes. Annu Rev Psychol 42:401–425, 1991

Downey G, Coyne JC: Children of depressed parents: an integrative review. Psychol Bull 108:50–76, 1990

Florin I, Nostadt A, Reck C, et al: Expressed emotion in depressed patients and their partners. Fam Process 31:163–172, 1992

Glick ID, Clarkin JF, Spencer JH, et al: A controlled evaluation of inpatient family intervention, I: preliminary results of the six-month follow-up. Arch Gen Psychiatry 42:882–886, 1985

Goering PN, Lancee WJ, Freeman SJJ: Marital support and recovery from depression. Br J Psychiatry 160:76–82, 1992

Goldstein MJ: Commentary on "Expressed Emotion in Depressed Patients and Their Partners." Fam Process 31:172–174, 1992

Goldstein MJ, Miklowitz DJ: Family intervention for persons with bipolar disorder, in Family Interventions in Mental Illness. Edited by Hatfield AB. San Francisco, CA, Jossey-Bass, 1994, pp 23–35

Haas GL, Glick ID, Clarkin JF, et al: Inpatient family intervention: a randomized clinical trial. Arch Gen Psychiatry 45:217–224, 1988

Keitner GI, Miller IW: Family functioning and major depression: an overview. Am J Psychiatry 147:1128–1137, 1990

Keitner GI, Miller IW, Ryan CE: The role of the family in major depressive illness. Psychiatric Annals 23:500–507, 1993

Keitner GI, Ryan CE, Miller IW: Role of the family in recovery and major depression. Am J Psychiatry 152:1002–1008, 1995

Kessler RC, Kendler KS, Heath A, et al: Social support, depressed mood, and adjustment to stress: a genetic epidemiologic investigation. J Pers Soc Psychol 62:257–272, 1992

Mendlewicz J: Genetic research in depressive disorders, in Handbook of Depression. Edited by Beckham EE, Leber WR. Homewood, IL, Dorsey Press, 1985, pp 795–815

Miklowitz DJ, Goldstein MJ, Nuechterlein KH, et al: Family factors and the course of bipolar affective disorders. Arch Gen Psychiatry 45:225–231, 1988

Miklowitz DJ, Goldstein MJ: Behavioral family treatment for patients with bipolar affective disorder. Behav Modif 14:457–489, 1990

Moltz DA: Bipolar disorder and the family: an integrative model. Fam Process 32:409–423, 1993

Post RM: Transduction of psychosocial stress into the neurobiology of recurrent affective disorder. Am J Psychiatry 149:999–1010, 1992

Sachs GS, Lafer B, Truman CJ, et al: Lithium monotherapy: miracle, myth and misunderstanding. Psychiatric Annals 24:299–306, 1994

Shea MT, Elkin I, Imber SD, et al: Course of depressive symptoms over follow-up: findings from the National Institute of Mental Health treatment of depression collaborative research program. Arch Gen Psychiatry 49:782–787, 1992

Weissman MM: The psychological treatment of depression. Arch Gen Psychiatry 36:1261–1269, 1979

Whisman MA, Jacobson NS: Depression, marital satisfaction, and marital and personality measures of sex roles. Journal of Marital and Family Therapy 15:177–186, 1989

CHAPTER 5

Schizophrenia and Other Psychotic Disorders

Philip M.

The M. family presented to the emergency room with their blatantly psychotic 19-year-old son, Philip. During the interview, they revealed that Philip had been psychotic for more than a year and emerged from his bedroom only to harass the family. He read the Bible constantly, talked to himself, and was convinced that he was Jesus. He lost weight, rarely washed or brushed his hair, and had terrified the family and held them hostage. Even so, they sought no help until Philip began shouting at their cherished 7-year-old daughter and threatening to hit her. The trip to the emergency room was followed by hospitalization, medications, and therapy, to which Philip responded well. It is unclear how far the family would have let him deteriorate had his symptoms not taken on this anti-family dimension.

Matthew H.

Matthew H., a 17-year-old diagnosed with schizoaffective schizophrenia, was quite difficult to treat because his relapses were frequent, severe, and long-lasting. His delusional state and occasional self-mutilation were only partially responsive to antipsychotic and mood-stabilizing medications. A family assessment revealed a complex wealthy family with problems in most family members. Matthew's relapses were found to correlate with the disappearance from the family of the mysterious father, who left the family periodically on extramarital "flings" that lasted up to 4 months at a time. During these absences, Matthew and three other siblings were left trying to comfort the distressed mother.

The family work consisted of two sets of sessions, one that included the mother and all the children and another set that included Matthew and his father, who would participate in sessions with this child only and refused to meet with the rest of the family. During the months of separate sessions, Matthew remained highly symptomatic and psychotic. When the sessions were able to bring about harmony and cooperation between the two groups, especially when the father recommitted himself to the family, Matthew responded beautifully to his treatment regimen and was at relative peace.

◼ Perspective on the Disorders

Family therapy began with the "hopeless cases." Much of the early research and clinical experimentation by the founders of the family field (including N. Ackerman, G. Bateson, I. Boszormenyi-Nagy, M. Bowen, D. D. Jackson, T. Lidz, V. Satir, M. T. Singer, J. H. Weakland, C. A. Whitaker, and L. C. Wynne) worked with families with a chronically psychotic member, and the impact of this influence persists. Schizophrenia is one of the areas where family therapy has had the greatest impact in the treatment of individuals and their families. Early theoretical models of family therapy reflected the focus on chronic psychosis. Several family-oriented research groups (Anderson et al. 1986; Falloon et al. 1982, 1985; Goldstein et al. 1978) continue to focus productively on the impressive effects of family treatments on the course of chronic schizophrenia and on the potential for families to be helpful as therapeutic allies (Goldstein and Miklowitz 1995). One of the greatest challenges is the application of these family research findings to clinical work with people with chronic psychotic illness.

A discussion of families and schizophrenia must include the increasingly complex body of research on family interaction communication styles. This research began with early descriptions of such relational aberrations as "pseudomutuality" and "rubber fences" (Wynne et al. 1958). These ideas evolved into the concept of communication deviance, communication patterns that confuse and distract the listener and prevent a shared focus of attention (Singer and Wynne 1965; Singer et al. 1978). Later, the concept of "expressed emotion" (Vaughn and Leff 1976, 1981) became useful in measuring family attitudes about the symptomatic person. Many of these studies demonstrated the connection between psychotic relapse and the frequency of negative, critical, intrusive (emotionally overinvolved) comments made about the person to an observer. The quality of the family's face-to-face comments to the person is considered as part of the family's affective style. Family affective style can be benign, negative, or mixed. In each area, critical comments and intrusiveness are the crucial variables correlating with poor outcome.

By exerting an effect at a series of intermediate steps, a psychosocial intervention can help prevent a serious biological condition, such as tardive dyskinesia. In one often-reported finding, greatly decreased frequency of relapse has been linked with family interventions that decrease critical comments and emotional overinvolvement (Hogarty et al. 1988, 1991). Family interventions directly reduce the dosages of neuroleptics required to maintain remission and thus reduce exposure to tardive dyskinesia risk.

As in Alzheimer's disease, chronic schizophrenia affects observers as strongly as it affects the symptomatic person. The severe disruption of thoughts, feelings, and behavior that defines this disorder is associated with an intensity of suffering and devastation that is felt by everyone in the family.

Table 5–1 summarizes some aspects of the family context of these disorders, which is described in more detail in the next section.

■ Connections of the Symptoms to the System

■ Effects of the Disorder on the Family

Effects vary in relation to phase and diagnosis. A family is affected differently by a first-break schizophreniform episode than by the seventh hospitalization for a chronic problem. In the first case, the family may be confused and concerned; in the second case, the family may be completely fed up with the individual's problems.

Table 5–1.   Schizophrenia in context

Effects of the disorder on the family
- Differences in effects based on illness phase and diagnosis
- Shame
- Financial struggles
- Focus of family life on disorder
- Confusing or distracting communication (communication deviance; expressed emotion)
- Marital stress
- Sibling guilt and envy
- Development of positive caregiving roles

Family maintenance of the symptoms
- General caveat against blaming the family
- Role of unclear communications
- Tendency of chaotic or unpredictable family life to overwhelm defenses of symptomatic person
- "Loyal" symptoms may be tolerated

Functions of the symptoms within the family
- Symptomatic person reinterprets stimuli to protect self
- Symptoms provide person for caregiver to tend
- Dealing with illness may hold family together

Adverse consequences of change
- Risk of tardive dyskinesia
- Need for new, less rigid family structure
- Dependence on mental health system
- Deinstitutionalization and resulting care dilemmas

Shame and blame are inevitable dimensions of chronic psychosis because of the public nature of the person's dysfunction. Each person in the family is prompted by a sense of social ostracism to look at self and others to see who is to blame.

The disorder brings serious and sometimes devastating financial struggles. The loss of income is secondary to the loss of earning potential and the burden of health care costs that may have to be borne for the life of the individual.

Psychotic disorders affect every area of family life, and it is not surprising that families organize around the index person's symptom. Murray Bowen, a pioneer in the family therapy field, was working with schizophrenia when he described a family in his lectures as "an autocracy ruled by its sickest member."

Family communication patterns are usually discussed as contributing to symptom maintenance, but these patterns may also reflect the effects of the disorder. For example, having a child with schizophrenia may lead to rage or disappointment, and this effect results in critical comments directed at the child. Similarly, parents understandably respond with excessive emotional involvement to the demands of caring for a symptomatic grown child who still requires protection. Inferences about causation must be made cautiously, if at all. A negative affective style may be an *effect* of despair over the child's future rather than a *cause* of the disorder. Parental statements that disconfirm (Holte et al. 1987) the symptomatic offspring can be viewed as the desire to avoid validating the child's psychotic reality.

Schizophrenic behaviors exert stress and pressure on marital relationships. Sometimes spouses tend to blame each other for the child's disease or are critical of each other's ideas about the symptoms. One spouse may end up in the lenient role to avoid crushing the child; the other spouse may assume the role of the strict parent who tolerates very little deviant behavior.

Effects are related to the quality of relationships before the onset of schizophrenia. Marriages that are already stressed will be even more strained by the onset of illness. Ambivalence among siblings will be associated with intense survivor guilt in the healthy siblings and mutual envy between the sick and healthy siblings.

Although these negative effects cannot be denied or minimized, some families find deep meaning in devoting their attention to the chronically psychotic member. This effect can lead to other positive results, such as participating in the National Alliance for the Mentally Ill and potentially having an impact on social policy.

■ Family Maintenance of the Symptoms

Family maintenance of symptoms is discussed here with caution because families living with schizophrenia are often blamed by society in general and by mental health professionals in particular, even if the blaming is inadvertent or unconscious. Even sophisticated new concepts of expressed emotion and emotional overinvolvement have been interpreted as only slightly more sophisticated versions of such misleading early concepts as "the schizophrenogenic mother," or "disordered family communication." Each practitioner must think carefully about the subtle ways families can be blamed for having a psychotic member.

It is possible to examine the influence of family relational sequences on the disorder without implying causation and blame. Many clinical and research findings can be described as associations in search of explanations, such as findings that link high rates of critical comments in face-to-face contacts with psychotic relapse (Hogarty et al. 1988), associate communication deviance with development of schizophrenic-spectrum disorders in high-risk offspring (Asarnow et al. 1987; Singer et al. 1978), and suggest an increased relapse rate in families with a high level of communication deviance. The patient may simply not be able to figure out what is being said, and he or she is under constant stress that is inadvertently imposed by the family.

Families with a symptomatic member also show an unusually high rate of disconfirming feedback to the person with schizophrenia when the conversation involves conflict. Families in conflict but without a psychotic member may convey disagreement with the speaker but treat the speaker's comments as valid and real. Families with a psychotic member often fail to communicate that the receiving person understood the comments of the psychotic person or saw them as valid (Holte et al. 1987).

People with schizophrenia tend to be extremely sensitive to change. Chaotic and unpredictable family life may be associated with worsening symptoms. Violence and frightening affects may also overwhelm schizophrenic defenses. The therapist should always search for these family events when assessing schizophrenic relapses.

For a family to be open to face the risk and expend the time, money, and energy needed to obtain psychiatric help, the index person's symptoms must be sufficiently noxious and antifamily to motivate family members toward change. Psychotic behavior may be tolerated until the symptomatic individual begins to hurt or annoy a favorite child in the family. Until this point, family members may not perceive the seriousness of the symptoms and may delay seeking help (as was done by the family of Philip M. in the case study at the beginning of this chapter).

■ Functions of the Symptoms Within the Family

A discussion of hypothetical functions that schizophrenia may serve at the family level does not imply that the family caused the syndrome or that the syndrome exists because it has a function. Nevertheless, therapists must not miss themes and forces out of fear of being "blamed for blaming," because awareness of these functions may form the building blocks for helpful interventions in selected cases.

The filter theory of schizophrenia describes a neural circuitry unable to adequately screen out and select from constant sensory input. At an individual level, the symptoms may be an adaptive attempt to block out or reinterpret stimuli in a way that protects the mind from being overwhelmed. Within the family, the person must stay somewhat removed from day-to-day family life to avoid being overwhelmed by stimuli and to protect others in the family. Many family members see this distance as a blessing because it reduces painful contact with the psychotic person.

Sometimes dealing with the extremes of psychotic behavior requires such intense problem solving and teamwork that these efforts become the "cement" that holds the family together. One couple described their marriage as "a mess"—they had separated 11 times. They said they reunited only to join forces to care for their daughter, who has schizophrenia.

■ Adverse Consequences of Change

Compliance with neuroleptic treatment may mean a lifetime with reduced symptoms but also an increased risk of tardive dyskinesia.

Symptom reduction can threaten existing behavioral patterns in the family and may require the creation of a new, more flexible family structure. Families often adopt relatively rigid behavioral patterns when someone in the family has schizophrenia, and relationships among other family members may have become close partly in response to the difficulties and even tragedy of dealing with the symptomatic member. The coalitions that develop may exclude the person with schizophrenia. When the person improves and presses to be included in these coalitions, the comfortable structures and alliances are jeopardized.

With successful treatment, the family may become dependent on the mental health system. They might find themselves emotionally vulnerable to a therapist, a powerful new figure who has entered within the family boundary. The therapist and other helpers may be sources of support and knowledge, but they may also be expensive, blaming, destructive, and ineffective.

Deinstitutionalization may be an additional adversity associated with symptom improvement. As long as a patient stays severely ill enough to justify being in a state hospital, families usually feel chronic sadness but also relative safety. The person with schizophrenia who gains some symptom relief may be released to a community mental health center, some of which are less than optimal for care of this type. Now the patient is at increased risk of noncompliance, inadequate self-care, poor judgment, and subsequent homelessness. Medicare, disability, and veterans benefits may be lost if the individual is considered well enough to leave the hospital.

Alternatively, the state may exert pressure on the family to take the patient home. Although sometimes this situation may lead to a meaningful reunion that the family has prayed for, more often it is associated with a severe disruption of family life and rage that the family must once again accommodate the sick member. If the family has closed ranks, it may be extremely difficult to readmit a family member who has essentially been mourned as if gone forever.

The mental health field has added to family dilemmas by encouraging families to live up to their "obligation" to care for the very ill family member at home. Often no professional or practical support is offered with these expectations, which greatly increases the burden on families (Wynne 1994).

■ Special Systemic Dimensions

■ Family History and Genetics

The genetic aspects of schizophrenia have probably been studied more extensively than those of any other psychiatric disorder. Early twin studies of schizophrenia showed monozygotic concordance rates between 25% and 86%, far short of the rate expected if schizophrenia were a completely genetic disease. These findings launched an entire field investigating the genetic component of psychiatric disorders. Other studies have shown 48% concordance for monozygotic twins and 3.6% for dizygotic twins (Kendler 1983; Tienari 1991). An often replicated finding suggests that the risk that a first-degree relative of a schizophrenic individual will also develop schizophrenia is about 10 times the rate in the general population.

Social and biological (prenatal and postnatal) environmental factors may affect expression of the disease. The diathesis-stressor model is the most promising model to emerge from numerous studies of these issues. A person is born with a certain potential vulnerability *(diathesis)* to schizophrenia that is genetically determined. Whether this genotype is expressed depends largely on family environmental factors. These data support a nonblaming stance toward the family. It may be that dysfunctional families do not cause schizophrenia (although they can increase the chance of its expression), and a healthy family may in fact offer protection from the expression of the disease (Tienari et al. 1987).

Family members often want genetic counseling and request information about the probability that their children will have schizophrenia. Many want to know whether they "should" have children. These questions are often left unasked, probably because of the shame associated with the disorder; they should be raised by the alert interviewer when heritability is likely to be a concern.

■ Gender

The psychoses exert their devastating effects without respect to gender. Schizophrenia in particular affects both genders similarly, and differences are not as prominent as they can be with other disorders. Some findings indicate a more prominent affective component in women with schizophrenia as compared with men. Also, women are more likely to want to be in relationships, whereas men are more likely to be isolated (Apfel and Handel 1993). This observation reflects trends found in the healthy population.

Men with schizophrenia suffer from the societal view of work accomplishments as "the measure of a man," though this behavior no longer follows strict gender lines. Work-related limitations associated with schizophrenia take a major toll on self-esteem and may contribute in part to the high rate of suicidal behaviors. Some men can be motivated to comply with medications only when they realize that a job will be lost if they go unmedicated.

Women with schizophrenia must face their diminished capacity for mothering. Schizophrenic women are more likely to want children than are schizophrenic men. Concern about the ability to care for small children is therefore a common consideration for women patients during treatment and crisis evaluations. Often the difficulties of these women are related to the sense of loss. Schizophrenia has a negative effect on the social and interpersonal abilities needed to form a family. Because psychosis is characterized by self-involvement and a diminished ability to empathize with others, many symptomatic women who do become parents experience a similar loss of the capacity to take pleasure in children.

The issue of pregnancy in young women with schizophrenia raises the risk-benefit dilemma of prescribing neuroleptics during pregnancy. Another concern is the crisis in the extended family and in society when a woman who is functionally close to being a child becomes a mother.

> Susan P., a severely psychotic 18-year-old, was seen with her family in crisis after she became pregnant. Her parents said that their worst fear had now been realized. The mother reluctantly volunteered to care for the baby, and the extended family reorganized around the new task of ensuring the best possible outcome for their daughter. Susan's psychosis and self-destructive behaviors continued throughout the pregnancy and postpartum period, and she was uninterested in mothering and unable to offer much to her child. Her mother's offer to raise the child became a reality.

■ Intimacy

Chronic psychotic thought processes severely damage the capacity for intimacy. No other problem can compare with paranoia in its power to negate the trust and capacity for empathy that are required for intimate relatedness. The specific interference factors are the self-referential dimensions of the disease, the poor reception of external stimuli caused by preoccupation with internal signals, a tendency toward the defensive mechanisms of projection and externalization, and the bizarre aspect of the behaviors.

The negative symptoms exert a strong pull away from situations that involve social scenes and meeting new people. An additional impediment is the negative self-image that results from the sense of being disabled and "crazy." These factors contribute to a severe loss of social skills that precludes even asking for a date, which suggests a lack of possibility for any intimate relationships.

■ Loyalty

Loyalty dimensions can be described in terms of four family categories: parent-child, spousal, sibling, and child-parent. Loyalty issues also surface in multiple pulls from larger systems outside the family.

Parent-child loyalty.   Parental loyalty is an innate biopsychosocial devotion that is focused on taking care of a relatively defenseless child. In many cases of schizophrenia, development toward autonomy and maturity has been impaired so severely that the index person functions at the level of a child.

Spousal loyalty.   Examples of spousal loyalty dimensions can be found in marriages that continue despite massive disruption by psychosis, bizarre behaviors, and frequent hospitalizations. An informal study of family loyalties and bonding could be made on Sunday afternoons in the remaining chronic inpatient units of state hospitals anywhere in the country, where a noble minority of spouses will be found visiting.

In several ways, the person with schizophrenia can also show loyalty toward the spouse. One symptomatic woman always seemed able to keep her behavioral symptoms under control at crucial times during the marriage or when her husband's career was at a delicate point. In another example, a male patient tended to become symptomatic in such a way that hospitalizations were necessary. A pattern in these events was noted, and it was found that they occurred as soon as his wife began to give messages that she needed a break from the uncertainty and chaos of the schizophrenic process.

Sibling loyalty.   Sibling loyalties are complex. It is common to observe detachment of siblings from the child with schizophrenia and sometimes from the whole family. Sometimes this response is necessary as a person tries to survive and not be overwhelmed by fears of his or her own craziness. Just as commonly, however, siblings may demonstrate a lack of shame and an openness to helping the sibling with schizophrenia and including him or her in their family life.

The success of the effort to include the symptomatic person varies with the nature of that person's symptoms and with the ability of the healthy siblings to tolerate the particular illness behaviors exhibited. Some siblings may be able to tolerate a range of bizarre delusional ideas, fantasy worlds, paranoia, and disordered thought processes that occur in conversation. The same siblings may be completely intolerant of particular gestures, sounds, or mannerisms.

The loyalty of parents to one child or another illustrates another level of complexity. Parents may ally with their ill child against the healthy siblings, who may feel anger and envy toward the sick one for receiving all the attention. Other parents might feel loyalty toward the healthy siblings, who in turn may feel guilty about their good health and consequently ally themselves against the sick sibling for reminding them of this guilt.

Survivor guilt can also become a prominent issue in terms of how guilt is incorporated into the siblings' defenses. Survivor guilt may contribute to the siblings' devotion to the child with schizophrenia, no matter how difficult the person is. The guilt may just as commonly result from the rejection of the symptomatic person that can occur as siblings avoid facing or experiencing the unpleasant effects of the caregiving burden.

Child-parent loyalty.   Some patients may be able to express their regret over the burden they were to their families when they were actively psychotic. In families where the index person does not have such moments of clarity and insight, loyalty may be expressed more indirectly. A previously suspicious child may become compliant with treatment. Such an effort represents significant homage to the parents, because the child may perceive no benefit from taking drugs that make his or her nerves feel as if they are on fire.

In many cases, even the suicidal act seems to be more than the patient's attempt to end the suffering of delusions, hallucinations, and intrapsychic symptoms. This act may be an attempt to remove a huge burden from the family. Although it is difficult to prove such intentions, the therapist should be open to perceiving the disguised modes in which family loyalties can be expressed.

Outside systems.   The involvement of so many treaters, agencies, case managers, house managers, hospitals, and third-party payers creates many possible loyalty conflicts for the family and index person. If the family feels blamed by any person or group involved in treatment, they may reject advice from that quarter and leave the index person in the difficult position of choosing between family and professionals. If there are any treatment disagreements among case managers, therapists, peers, roommates, insurance companies, and family, the loyalty conflict can completely obstruct effective treatment. Caught in a web of conflicting advice, the index person may find it more difficult to maintain remission.

■ Map of Emotions

Nonpsychotic emotional maps contain complexity and surprises, and psychotic maps can be particularly dramatic and intense. The issue of loss is central. The pervasiveness of the losses and the sense of tragedy for the patient and family are so intense that all involved may deny the degree of pain, sadness, and rage. Therapists and family may handle this pain by distancing and seeing the person as only an illness rather than a person.

As the index person attempts to avoid intolerable affects, the sense of loss may become anger and then despair. Chronic helplessness may give way to shame and guilt. Fear or anxiety may become paranoia or panic. The experiencing of sadness may detour via hallucinations and delusions. One patient said he was so overwhelmed with feelings of sadness for the world that it was intolerable, and he preferred his psychotic world and hallucinations. Anger may be externalized as paranoia. The individual who is enraged at the world and wishes to destroy it projects these feelings onto the world, which then becomes full of frightening people who are angry at him and want to destroy him.

Denial connects to noncompliance with therapies and medicines. The response of denial is understandable. The person who emerges from denial confronts certain awareness of powerlessness over a disorder that makes the person very different from other people.

■ Countertransference

Therapists who need to see results to be reassured of their worth and ability will find it difficult to work with chronically ill patients. Treatment progress may be difficult to measure, relapses are part of the work, and the condition of some patients deteriorates no matter how expert and caring the treatment may be. Especially in front of the family, the therapist may feel inadequate if the care offered is insufficient to eliminate suffering.

Several other factors may encourage an avoidance of very sick patients. The strangeness of language and behavior may create a wish to keep a wide distance. The fear of one's own craziness or irrationality may be triggered by close work with psychotic people and their families.

Family work with schizophrenia also involves translating scientific information into clear language that is free of jargon. Not every therapist has this skill.

■ Posterity

Concern for children becomes prominent when one or both parents are chronically psychotic. The family-oriented therapist can practice preventive psychiatry by considering the impact of the illness on the child.

The therapist can intervene on behalf of the children when a symptomatic parent is hospitalized. Children experience intense emotions when a parent is removed from the home for extended periods, and these emotions should be considered as attempts are made to help correct misunderstandings and maximize the chances for healthy adaptation. Explaining hospitalization to small children can serve as a useful focus of discussion. Younger children often blame themselves for the hospitalization of a parent. The understanding and awareness of this universal point can help healthy family members become better listeners and mitigate damage to the children's self-image. The therapist must also respect the effect of hospitalization on the parent-child bond. On the one hand, hospitalization can provide a needed respite to repair the damage in a relationship that is being disturbed by continuous bizarre behaviors and damaging actions. On the other hand, a prolonged separation can damage the parent-child bond.

Children, grandchildren, nieces, and nephews describe living in the shadow of their ancestors with schizophrenia. Although this awareness may not impair functioning or even be a preoccupation, relatives of the next generation carry this awareness and are therefore more sensitive to their own mental state (their fear of going crazy) and the mental state of others.

◼ Treatment

◼ Standard Individual Therapies

The field has now evolved into a complex interweaving of therapies. The effectiveness of neuroleptics and significant evidence of a biological component to the disorder have led to a view of biological treatments as the mainstay of therapy for chronic schizophrenia.

The effectiveness of neuroleptics in decreasing relapse rates is one of the success stories of psychopharmacology. Most treatment centers emphasize some form of medication regimen as a key aspect of treatment. In these programs, the appearance of symptoms or early indications of relapse are monitored, medication dosages are adjusted, and side effects of the medication are managed. The injectable depot forms of haloperidol and fluphenazine are commonly used and have had a major effect in resolving complex problems of patient compliance with medications.

The new generation of neuroleptic drugs, such as clozapine and possibly risperidone, is associated with a lower rate of movement disorders and is becoming a standard treatment option. These agents are the first to have a notable therapeutic effect on the so-called "negative" symptoms that include apathy, withdrawal, and lack of motivation. These agents are likely to encourage a revolutionary shift in our ways of thinking about and treating positive and negative symptoms. As more patients experience a decrease in negative symptoms, they may be amenable to and may even demand psychotherapy to help them adjust to improvements in outlook, motivation, mood, and function and to mourn the "lost years."

The standard treatment of schizophrenia differs from that of other psychiatric disorders because it customarily includes some attention to family context. Most programs and practitioners routinely incorporate some form of family psychoeducation and family involvement.

■ Family Modalities

One distinctive feature of therapy for families who have a member with schizophrenia is that the patient and family may have different therapists. The family may not know or attend meetings with the patient's primary therapist, and the patient may not attend meetings with the family's therapist, especially if the therapy is oriented toward psychoeducation.

The two modalities complement each other best when the individual therapist knows that the family is working in the adjunctive psychoeducational model. The therapist then knows that the family will be trained to be vigilant about prodromal symptoms of relapse and will notify the therapy team. The individual therapist also perceives the family's interest in the therapy and in their role in the patient's day-to-day life. This knowledge can enhance the usefulness of both the individual therapy and the family's psychoeducational consultation.

Individual and family therapies must have enough of a shared agenda to avoid raising loyalty conflicts and fears about what is going on in the other therapy. These conflicts can interfere with problem solving by the individual and family.

The main convergence of the two therapies occurs as the individual and family are prepared separately for the worsening or improving of symptoms. If the illness gets worse, the family can be trained in how to obtain help. If the illness gets better, the family can be prepared for autonomous functioning and the adjustments that will be required.

Another modality that promises high effectiveness is the structured psychoeducational family group. Families of hospitalized acutely psychotic patients meet at regular intervals, and the therapist asks each family to report on recent events, dilemmas, and problem-solving efforts. The other families then contribute their ideas and relate how they have handled similar problems and traumas. A structured psychoeducational program is included in these groups (see below).

One large research study of this modality has shown a highly significant decrease in 2-year relapse rates as compared with single-family psychoeducation (McFarlane et al. 1995). It is possible that much of the demonstrated efficacy of psychoeducational programs may be related to the support and ideas of other families who face similar struggles.

■ Psychoeducation

Educational programs have become powerful tools in work with families, especially if the therapist adopts a consultation model. A highly developed array of techniques, clinical experiences, and research into the use and effectiveness of these interventions has been established (Anderson et al. 1986; Falloon et al. 1982; Goldstein 1981; Goldstein and Miklowitz 1995; Hogarty et al. 1988, 1991). Excellent self-help literature is also available to help families feel less alone in their plight (Bernheim et al. 1982; Sheehan 1982; Torrey 1988; Vine 1982; Wasow 1982).

In addition to self-help books, self-help groups, such as the National Alliance for the Mentally Ill, are an essential component of therapy. This referral helps the therapist avoid unhelpful struggles and furthers the therapeutic alliance by serving as a "counterprojection" that refutes the family's assumption that a therapist is blaming and defensive. The therapist might even encourage families toward political action, including advocacy and other efforts to ensure health care and even to oppose a therapy style that blames families.

A number of family psychoeducational models exist, and the elements of the complete package include the following:

1. **Allies.** "How can we help you help the patient?" The educational package may work as much by helping to build an alliance with the family as it works by offering specific content.

2. **Education.** Focus on phenomenology and treatment of psychotic illnesses.

3. **Training in specific skills.** Patient and family pick a problem to work on together and are taught the skills needed to bring problems to a solution.

4. **Getting along better.** The consultant works for interactional change. "Let's work together to achieve the environment that is best for the patient to come home to and that is also fair to the family."

5. **Environmental engineering.** "Let's be sure you, the parents, are in charge and also have a chance for respite."

6. **Contact with other families.** "I never knew others were going through what we go through." As described previously, multifamily education is one of the most promising modalities for effective prevention. New social contacts with those who understand the difficulties of living with a family member with schizophrenia can help rebuild family life.

Most modules share the vulnerability-stress model for the expression of schizophrenia, largely because this model addresses specific stressors over which the family does have some control. All implications of blame and family causation are avoided, although the idea is introduced that better coping styles, reduced stress, clearer communication, more reasonable expectations, and more knowledge can reduce the risk of relapse. The models also share a view of the disorder as a biological disease that may require biological treatment.

The format of the educational component is largely didactic, utilizing lectures, readings, videotapes, tests, and role play. Delivery is clear and focused; for example, "Schizophrenia is one of the types of psychotic illness that affects the way a person thinks, feels, organizes, and behaves. Patients may experience what are referred to as positive symptoms, such as hallucinations and delusions. They may also demonstrate what are referred to as negative symptoms, such as apathy, lack of motivation, boredom, and withdrawal." The therapist then defines these terms.

In other sessions, the therapist attempts to describe the experience of schizophrenia. A psychiatrist may speak about new biological treatments and about side effects of commonly used medications. A lawyer may provide information on estate planning and guardianship laws. The psychiatric rehabilitation model, which builds on skills and aims at realistic achievements, adds a way to ally with the index person and the family against the limitations of illness.

Families learn to tolerate certain behaviors, such as idiosyncratic use of words and some strange mannerisms, but to be less tolerant of other behaviors, such as violence or medication noncompliance.

One important theme of an educational or case management approach is identifying and studying each patient's *prodrome*, the sequence of symptoms that predicts and leads to a psychotic episode. The focus on relapse prevention requires this study by the family, the individual, and the therapy team, who become experts in the prodrome. They become co-observers with a shared mission of "catching" the next relapse early.

Families can also be educated about the need to contact the therapist in connection with the occurrence of certain life events. An educational discussion held early in the therapy focuses on which events are known to be particular stressors (e.g., changes in routine, vacations, moving, weddings). Later sessions can be scheduled before these upcoming events to help head off symptom development (L. C. Wynne, personal communication, May 1994).

■ Communication Training

Communication training has been developed so that families can be taught specific ways to express positive and negative feelings: "It is known that schizophrenia is predominantly a brain disease that is unlikely to be caused by life events or family life. It is likely that patients do better if they live with families with clear communication, active listening, and fewer critical exchanges. Let's discuss these observations in more detail and get specific about some of the skills needed to achieve those goals."

The therapist helps the family develop communication skills by responding to negative comments with constructive requests: "Try giving that feedback again, beginning with 'I feel' instead of 'You did.' " The training includes practice making specific requests, and reviewing problem-solving techniques for both day-to-day and larger issues. The family is seen as an ally of the treatment team, and the approach is competence based rather than pathology based.

Partly to emphasize the fact that the family is not the patient, the index person usually does not attend the early meetings. During these first meetings, the family attends a series of educational workshops, multifamily group meetings, and meetings with the therapist to work at decreasing guilt and stress. Part of the goal is to give the family some cognitive distance. This distance helps them become less emotionally reactive at home and allows them to provide quieter, more stable surroundings for the index person in recovery.

■ New Stories

The main themes of new stories are supporting family strengths, building upon existing resources, and enhancing motivation for therapeutic change.

Externalization.   The family who feels ashamed and blamed may respond well to the idea that a chronic psychotic disorder affects the whole family, not just the index person. Parental guilt can be diverted toward acceptance of the fact that schizophrenia is mostly a disease of the brain.

However, relief from guilt is not the same as relief from responsibility for either the patient or the family. Therapeutic consultation and psychoeducation can focus on defining reasonable responsibility to provide an atmosphere that is less critical and intrusive and more conducive to symptom stabilization or improvement.

Just like asthma.   Chronic psychosis can be described as a chronic illness that is affected by stress, similar to asthma, diabetes, angina, and high blood pressure. In this way, the quest for a cure can be replaced by efforts to cope with the illness and to minimize traumatic, stressful events. The family is the expert in the index person's emotional makeup and is the main resource for helping to develop strategies that improve coping and create a less stressful environment.

Acceptance of the disorder.   This stance can help families reduce the rage and blame directed at the psychotic member. This view is appropriate for use with families who attribute negative intentions to the person with schizophrenia and negative meanings to the person's behavior.

The family may accept biological illness as a partial explanation of the problem. Their guilt is reduced, but they can then be helped to face the thought that a person with schizophrenia cannot change through willpower. The family's request for symptom improvement may contain a hidden request that the therapy change the person into someone who does not have schizophrenia. When symptoms appear, the family believes that the index person is "acting like a schizophrenic" just to hurt them. Therapy will be most successful if the family stops focusing on changing the person and instead emphasizes aspects that can be controlled.

Causation versus maintenance.   The difference between causing and maintaining symptoms can be highlighted. Sometimes the first family interview discloses a family that is already self-blaming, feels "dysfunctional," and believes this dysfunction caused the psychosis. Simple reassurances are unlikely to be effective.

The therapist can concede that the family may be partially correct in that research evidence does support the idea that unclear or critical family communications may increase frequency of relapse or prevent the fullest possible recovery. The therapist emphasizes, however, that this idea in no way implies that they could cause the illness. They are not powerful enough to create this disease through their own actions.

Enmeshment and separateness.   Patients who are discharged and return home to critical and overinvolved families will be more likely to relapse or to require higher doses of neuroleptics to stay well. Some therapists tend to use such data to justify the therapeutic goal of removal of a person with schizophrenia from his or her parents.

Such "parentectomy" represents an oversimplified reading of research findings. Perhaps this interpretation results from a linear misapplication of the observation that in many cases families of severely disturbed psychotic patients are chaotic, poorly functioning, and confusing, and thus constitute a harmful influence from which the patient should be removed. However, a therapeutic team that moves to separate a person with schizophrenia from his or her family too quickly and without attention to context can threaten family bonds and integrity. The family may feel pressed to regroup and close out the therapist instead of the index person.

Instead of forming quick assumptions, the therapist should consider differences among families. One family may appear hopelessly enmeshed as the parents show overprotection and overresponsibility for all their children. Their belief system equates encouragement of autonomy with parental irresponsibility. A gradual introduction of conversations about the responsibility of parents to foster growth and independence must occur before this family can even consider ideas about having the index person live outside the home or acquire independent activities.

By contrast, other families have inordinately high expectations of all members and cannot modify these views even for a child with chronic psychosis. The family prematurely pushes the regressed individual into colleges or demanding business positions. The family appears intolerant of the patient's low level of functioning and denies the extent of the deficit. The therapist examines where the family's seemingly outrageous stance may have some merit, perhaps in attempting to maximize function, decrease infantilization, and create an aura of hope. As the conversation progresses, the family may be able to consider that the achievement of avoidance of hospitalizations or arrests for 2 years may be as good in its own way as a corporate presidency. The family's inordinate expectations are treated respectfully and compassionately as understandable wishes to adapt gradually to the full impact of the disorder.

The medical-model frame of schizophrenia as a disease that affects maturation and level of function can be useful. It can help the family objectify their dilemmas and find compassion for both the patient and other family members. This approach respects the family's need to be helpful and combines it with a realistic awareness of the individual's limitations. If the therapist judges that the family ideas are not readily modifiable, conversations can emphasize parental responsibility for an adult child who cannot be released into the adult world without some family involvement.

Therapist to consultant.   The role of the professional is often usefully recast from that of a therapist treating illnesses to that of a consultant sitting with patients and families to see what they may identify as needs and how best to help them cope with the psychotic processes that have invaded their lives.

"Schizophrenic" to person.   The family's way of thinking about the index person can be modified by changing from a view that labels the person a "schizophrenic" to one that separates the person from his or her symptoms of schizophrenia. Such a stance may allow the family and the treatment team to identify and build upon the index person's strengths, positive traits, and competencies.

Psychopharmacology of attachment.   Family forces strongly affect compliance in the treatment of schizophrenia, where taking or not taking neuroleptics becomes a family affair. Any unresolved control issues in the family will manifest as noncompliance. The index person may oppose medications, which may cause the parents and siblings to become more controlling and intrusive. The index person then grows more obstinate and distant. These cycles may end in relapse of the index person or in burnout and withdrawal of the family.

If the patient develops tardive dyskinesia, the family that must witness this condition can often be as distressed as the person experiencing it. The family may respond to this distress by allowing the patient to stop taking medication, which brings the threat of imminent relapse. These difficult choices confronted by families show why medication compliance is another essential area requiring alliance between the family therapist and the individual therapist.

An interpersonal approach to medications could frame the possible benefits as more than the possible reduction of symptoms and pathology. The therapist can emphasize the potential return of the index person to the family. If hallucinations are quieted, for example, the person's ability to respond to what others are saying would have a direct effect on family function. As the person's negative symptoms remit, the family regains a motivated useful member to help reach goals and ensure economic survival. The reestablishment of mutual relationships is one goal of using medications.

■ Additional Reading

Bateson G, Jackson DD, Haley J, et al: Toward a theory of schizophrenia. Behav Sci 1:251–264, 1956

Boszormenyi-Nagy I: The concept of schizophrenia from the point of view of family treatment. Fam Process 1:103–113, 1962

Bowen M: A family concept of schizophrenia, in The Etiology of Schizophrenia. Edited by Jackson DD. New York, Basic Books, 1960, pp 346–372

Bowen M: Family psychotherapy with schizophrenia in the hospital and in private practice, in Intensive Family Therapy: Theoretical and Practical Aspects. Edited by Boszormenyi-Nagy I, Framo JL. New York, Harper & Row, 1965, pp 213–243

Falloon IRH, Boyd JL, McGill CW: Family Care of Schizophrenia. New York, Guilford, 1984

Goldberg SC, Schooler NR, Hogarty GE, et al: Prediction of relapse in schizophrenic outpatients treated by drug and sociotherapy. Arch Gen Psychiatry 34:171–184, 1977

Goldstein MJ, Rodnick EH, Evans JR, et al: Drug and family therapy in the aftercare of acute schizophrenics. Arch Gen Psychiatry 35:1169–1177, 1978

Hatfield A: What families want of family therapists, in Family Therapy in Schizophrenia. Edited by McFarlane WR. New York, Guilford, 1983, pp 41–68

Hooley JM: The nature and origins of expressed emotion, in Understanding Major Mental Disorder: The Contribution of Family Interaction Research. Edited by Hahlweg K, Goldstein MJ. New York, Family Process Press, 1987, pp 176–194

Jackson DD, Weakland JH: Schizophrenic symptoms and family interaction. Arch Gen Psychiatry 1:618–621, 1959

Koenigsberg HW, Handley R: Expressed emotion: from predictive index to clinical construct. Am J Psychiatry 143:1361–1373, 1986

Leff JP: Schizophrenia and sensitivity to the family environment. Schizophr Bull 2:566–574, 1976

Lidz T, Fleck S: Schizophrenia, human integration, and the role of the family, in The Etiology of Schizophrenia. Edited by Jackson DD. New York, Basic Books, 1960, pp 323–345

Matthews SM, Roper MT, Mosher LR, et al: A non-neuroleptic treatment for schizophrenia: analysis of the 2-year postdischarge risk of relapse. Schizophr Bull 5:322–333, 1979

McGill CW, Falloon IRH, Boyd JL, et al: Family educational intervention in the treatment of schizophrenia. Hosp Community Psychiatry 34:934–938, 1983

Parker G, Johnston P, Hayward L: Parental "expressed emotion" as a predictor of schizophrenic relapse. Arch Gen Psychiatry 45:806–813, 1988

Schnur DB, Friedman S, Dorman M, et al: Assessing the family environment of schizophrenic patients with multiple hospital admissions. Hosp Community Psychiatry 37:249–256, 1986

Strauss J, Carpenter WT: Schizophrenia. New York, Plenum, 1981

Whitaker CA, Malone TP: The Roots of Psychotherapy. New York, Blakiston, 1953

Wynne LC: Knotted relationships, communication deviances, and meta-binding, in Beyond the Double Bind: Communication and Family Systems, Theories, and Techniques With Schizophrenics. Edited by Berger MM. New York, Brunner/Mazel, 1978, pp 177–188

Wynne LC: Current concepts about schizophrenics and family relationships. J Nerv Ment Dis 169:82–89, 1981

Yee WK: Psychiatric aspects of psychoeducational family therapy. Psychiatric Annals 19:27–34, 1989

■ References

Anderson CM, Reiss DJ, Hogarty GE: Schizophrenia and the Family. New York, Guilford, 1986

Apfel RJ, Handel MH: Madness and Loss of Motherhood: Sexuality, Reproduction, and Long-Term Mental Illness. Washington, DC, American Psychiatric Press, 1993

Asarnow JR, Ben-Meir SL, Goldstein MJ: Family factors in childhood depressive and schizophrenic-spectrum disorders: a preliminary report, in Understanding Major Mental Disorder: The Contribution of Family Interaction Research. Edited by Hahlweg K, Goldstein MJ. New York, Family Process Press, 1987, pp 123–138

Bernheim K, Lewine R, Beale C: The Caring Family: Living With Mental Illness. New York, Random House, 1982

Falloon IRH, Boyd JL, McGill CW, et al: Family management in the prevention of exacerbations of schizophrenia. N Engl J Med 306:1437–1440, 1982

Falloon IRH, Boyd JL, McGill CW, et al: Family management in the prevention of morbidity of schizophrenia. Arch Gen Psychiatry 42:887–896, 1985

Goldstein MJ (ed): New Developments in Interventions With Families of Schizophrenics. San Francisco, CA, Jossey-Bass, 1981

Goldstein MJ, Miklowitz DJ: The effectiveness of psychoeducational family therapy in the treatment of schizophrenic disorders. Journal of Marital and Family Therapy 21:361–376, 1995

Goldstein MJ, Rodnick EH, Evans JR, et al: Drug and family therapy in the aftercare of acute schizophrenics. Arch Gen Psychiatry 35:1169–1177, 1978

Hogarty GE, McEvoy JP, Munetz M, et al: Dose of fluphenazine, familial expressed emotion, and outcome in schizophrenia: results of a 2-year study. Arch Gen Psychiatry 45:797–805, 1988

Hogarty GE, Anderson CM, Reiss DJ, et al: Family psychoeducation, social skills training, and maintenance chemotherapy in the aftercare treatment of schizophrenia, II: two-year effects of a controlled study of relapse and adjustment. Arch Gen Psychiatry 48:340–347, 1991

Holte A, Wichstrom L, Erno KO, et al: Confirmatory feedback in families of schizophrenics: theory, methods, and preliminary results, in Understanding Major Mental Disorder: The Contribution of Family Interaction Research. Edited by Hahlweg K, Goldstein MJ. New York, Family Process Press, 1987, pp 139–155

Kendler KS: Overview: a current perspective on twin studies of schizophrenia. Am J Psychiatry 140:1413–1425, 1983

McFarlane WR, Lukens E, Link B, et al: Multiple-family groups and psychoeducation in the treatment of schizophrenia. Arch Gen Psychiatry 52:679–687, 1995

Sheehan S: Is There No Place on Earth for Me? Boston, MA, Houghton Mifflin, 1982

Singer MT, Wynne LC: Thought disorder and family relations of schizophrenics, IV: results and implications. Arch Gen Psychiatry 12:201–212, 1965

Singer MT, Wynne LC, Toohey ML: Communication disorders and the families of schizophrenics, in The Nature of Schizophrenia. Edited by Wynne LC, Cromwell RL, Matthysse S. New York, Wiley, 1978, pp 499–511

Tienari P: Interaction between genetic vulnerability and family environment: the Finnish adoption family study of schizophrenia. Acta Psychiatr Scand 84:460–465, 1991

Tienari P, Lahti I, Sorri A, et al: The Finnish adoptive family study of schizophrenia. J Psychiatr Res 21:437–445, 1987

Torrey EF: Surviving Schizophrenia: A Family Manual. New York, Harper & Row, 1988

Vaughn CE, Leff JP: The influence of family and social factors on the course of psychiatric illness: a comparison of schizophrenic and depressed neurotic patients. Br J Psychiatry 129:125–137, 1976

Vaughn CE, Leff JP: Patterns of emotional response in the relatives of schizophrenic patients. Schizophr Bull 7:43–44, 1981

Vine P: Families in Pain. New York, Pantheon, 1982

Wasow M: Coping With Schizophrenia. Palo Alto, CA, Science & Behavior Books, 1982

Wynne LC: The rationale for consultation with the families of schizophrenic patients. Acta Psychiatr Scand 90 (suppl 384):125–132, 1994

Wynne LC, Ryckoff I, Day J, et al: Pseudomutuality in the family relations of schizophrenics. Psychiatry 21:205–220, 1958

CHAPTER 6

Substance-Related Disorders

Elizabeth A.

Elizabeth A., 40-year-old homemaker with a 2-year-old daughter, a Ph.D. in economics, and a prominent lawyer husband, presented to a family-oriented psychiatrist with complaints of depression, marital problems, and family-of-origin problems. The depression had never been treated, but on this presentation it was diagnosed as a bipolar disorder, with a clear family history of major affective disorders and an even clearer history in retrospect of cyclical suicidal depressions alternating with weeks of high energy, elevated grandiose mood periods during which she required almost no sleep.

Elizabeth adamantly denied alcoholism to family and doctors, even after a hospitalization for pancreatitis. Two weeks after her second hospitalization for pancreatitis of unknown etiology, she hit bottom and realized she was an alcoholic. This experience came as a kind of strange revelation, as if she were discovering a fact about someone she knew. She told the complete story of her many years of heavy alcohol intake during the day while she was alone at home. She felt that the self-medication of the affective disorder was only part of the story and that the main issue was denial of family problems. Avoidance of the deadness of her marriage had paralyzed her. The hopelessness of her role in her family of origin had depressed her.

After detoxification and an earnest connection to the fellowship of Alcoholics Anonymous, Elizabeth's behavior changed and the lies ended. The couple attempted to work on their problems in therapy until she decided clearly and unilaterally that she wanted a divorce. Five years later, she was remarried, sober, recovering, and back in her career, and she would not hear of changing her lithium and sertraline regimen.

Donald T.

Donald T., a 47-year-old impoverished and often homeless man with alcoholism and chronic schizophrenia, presented to the emergency room in the most recent of many visits. The staff knew Donald well and referred to him affectionately as the "nose-picking drunk." As usual, he demanded hospitalization, which could not be justified based on symptoms and presentation. Donald's elderly parents were contacted and asked to come to the hospital so that they could be interviewed with the patient.

Donald was embarrassed that his frail parents had been brought into the situation, and yet their involvement seemed to motivate him to more action and participation in the disposition than he had ever shown in previous visits. As it turned out, the upset had been a misunderstanding between Donald and his community mental health therapist, which he had interpreted as rejection. The therapist was contacted, and this problem was straightened out.

The parents had been so completely uninvolved for so long that it seemed a reasonable request for them to provide a few nights of housing for their son while he worked on finding a new place to live. Donald's knowledge of all the treatment and housing options in the region was emphasized with the parents, who were instructed not to get drawn into helping with placement. Donald was labeled as the expert who in fact knew more about available resources than did the parents, the staff, or the therapist. Donald laughed at this description of his competence and expertise and yet acknowledged that it was true. He withdrew his demand for admission and went home with his mother and father. Within 1 week, he arranged a 30-day rehabilitation program and a halfway house residence.

◼ Perspective on the Disorders

The rich interrelationships among substance abuse, psychiatric disorders, and family issues are clinically evident. The interface of substance abuse and family dynamics has become a field of study in its own right, and yet the fields of chemical dependency, psychiatry, and family therapy leave room for much more work in expanding a treatment synthesis. Most practicing clinicians choose and focus on a single approach, which is needlessly limiting. Without a broad treatment approach, the painful symptoms of these disorders pose an extreme threat to sobriety.

The chemical dependency field brings a deep understanding of the experience and defenses of addicted persons. The insights of Alcoholics Anonymous (AA), Narcotics Anonymous (NA), Nar-Anon, and Al-Anon and the power of the fellowship offer a definitive approach to addiction and a method for transformation to a healthier state. Psychiatry allows for recognition and treatment of comorbid states such as depression and panic.

The clinical and research insights of family therapy bring a deeper understanding of intimacy, secrecy, loyalty issues, and unhelpful transactions. Family therapy offers families in advanced recovery a way to accomplish some of the interpersonal goals of the 12 steps, as in orchestrating conversations that move the family toward change, healing, and repair. The goal of fairness in relationships is accomplished in part by the process of making amends.

Table 6–1 summarizes key aspects of the family context of substance abuse disorders, which is described in more detail in the next section.

■ Connections of the Symptoms to the System

■ Effects of the Disorder on the Family

The effects of substance use, abuse, and addiction on those around the addicted person have generated a vast amount of popular and clinical research literature and several popular family educational and support groups, including Adult Children of Alcoholics, Adult Children of Dysfunctional Families, Al-Anon, Nar-Anon, and many others.

The presence of an addiction in a family affects every family member. A parent who sees a teenager engaging in heavy substance use may become completely preoccupied with the question of addiction. The spouse of an addicted individual may learn to organize his or her life around the substance and to prevent the consequences of substance use. In the modal case of a nondrinking wife with an alcoholic husband,

---

Table 6–1.   Substance-related disorders in context

Effects of the disorder on the family

- Family preoccupied with addiction
- Conflict between letting go and wishing to help
- Distinction between family that includes person with alcoholic behavior and "alcoholic family"
- Connections between violence and alcohol
- Dependence of addicted individual on family
- Overachievement of child without addiction

Family maintenance of the symptoms

- Behavior that maintains symptoms makes it easier for addict to use
- Complementary relationship between addicts and enablers
- Incorporation of addiction into family routines
- Fear of change

Functions of the symptoms within the family

- Adaptive consequences of substance use: anxiety reduction, problem solving
- Regulation of maturity of function
- "Solution" for boredom, lack of intimacy, and other problems
- Attempt to get nurturance

Adverse consequences of change

- Need to face damage already done
- Loss of sense of superiority to person with addiction
- Need to establish new relationships within family

---

the wife deals with issues of survival, keeps the alcoholic functioning at work, and protects herself and the children from behavioral excesses during intoxication phases.

In opioid use, the parents of the addicted person may struggle for years in conflict between letting go to avoid enabling their son or daughter and wishing to help the desperate individual, who has constant life-threatening and legal troubles. The successful 12-step programs specify that "you have to love an addict differently." Implementing this difficult change is one of the tasks of family therapy.

One of the most useful models to emerge is the Family Life History Model (Steinglass et al. 1987). The pervasiveness of the effects of drinking on the family is assessed by how much the family is organized around the alcoholism, and the penetration of the substance usage into day-to-day rituals, such as the dinner hour or holiday celebrations, is the major dimension. If the alcoholism has taken over the regulatory mechanisms of the family in such a way that day-to-day problem solving requires a few drinks first, the family is considered an "alcoholic family." If the nonalcoholic spouse refuses to allow drinking to disrupt certain family rituals and functions, then the family may be closer to being a "family with an alcoholic member."

The effects of the substance use are different in these two types of families, especially in terms of the effects on the next generation. Many children raised in the alcoholic family enter adult life with their thinking organized around unpredictability, distrust, survival, vigilance, hyperresponsibility, and isolation of affect. Some will develop a separate identity and will have compassion for the alcoholic while also understanding the need to set firm limits on behaviors. If the substance abuse is contained in location and duration and if at least one adult is present who acknowledges and labels problems accurately, then the child might enter adult life with a relatively preserved sense of trust and with wisdom about human nature.

Research suggests that the modal alcoholic family is quiet and nonabusive, although there is some potential for violence in substance-related disorders (Steinglass et al. 1987). Wives and children bear the brunt of family victimization. Suicide and self-destructive acts are highly associated with drugs and alcohol. Substances and violence are associated through direct disinhibition by the drug, desperate acts committed in attaining the substances, and the abusive childhoods of so many individuals with addictions (Kaufman 1985).

At one time it was thought that drug-addicted persons had little to do with their families (Alexander and Dibb 1975). However, subsequent clinical and research observations regarding boundaries and launching have repeatedly found that young adults with addictions are quite dependent, very often living with and tied to their families of origin (Pattison and Kaufman 1981; Stanton 1980; Todd and Seleckeman 1990; Vaillant 1966).

This connection is easy to miss because a rebellious, counterdependent bravado often hides the dependent relationship with the family (Bernal et al. 1990; Stanton and Todd 1979). Such relationships are often complex and are deciphered only over time.

> Melissa B., a 17-year-old addicted to cocaine and alcohol, had been living with dealers and sometimes on the streets. Whenever she presented for detoxification or help, her only concern was that she wanted to return to her parents and be accepted. Her parents and

siblings were burned out and enraged and wanted nothing to do with her. Their stance seemed to be a sensible attempt to be strong and responsible in facing a situation where direct attempts to help the daughter were inevitably followed by relapse and outrageously hostile and provocative behaviors.

On closer examination, it emerged that the parents' rejection and negative projection onto their daughter predated her current addiction behavior and began when she was a small child. The father confused feelings toward her with his feelings toward his drug-addicted, irresponsible brother. The mother saw a rival for the sexual attention of father and the other men in the family. From early on, this child had been seen as the source of all the family problems. This emphasis hid the family secret that she had been abused as a child by an older brother, a fact that the family knew but denied and never addressed. They acted as if the family were ideal except for the young adult daughter, which was striking because her brother was also substance addicted.

The child who is not addicted often has a story that is not told. This child may overachieve and be especially good as a way to survive. If a sibling is addicted, the child without addiction tries to make up for the pain caused to the parents by being strong and competent. The success of this overachieving sibling may obscure the silent suffering that can continue throughout life because he or she still does not want to burden anyone (Coleman 1979). This individual will show a persistent pattern of absorbing the pain of others and of sacrificing him- or herself to alleviate this pain.

■ Family Maintenance of the Symptoms

It is often difficult to distinguish the effects of substance-abuse disorder on the family from the effects of family behavior on the disorder. "Enabling" or sometimes "coalcoholism" or "coaddiction" is often implicated in the addiction. The addicted individual continually uses more and denies more intensely. At the same time, the enabler rescues, supports the addict's rationalizations, makes excuses, becomes hyperresponsible, and gives more pep talks. Then the phase of punishing and nagging takes over.

Sometimes the enabler gives mixed messages about the use of substances and the effects on the family. In one extreme example, a wife threw a cocktail party to celebrate her alcoholic husband's return from a 30-day rehabilitation program.

A more subtle maintenance of symptoms in family life occurs when the substance is allowed to become part of the structure of rituals and daily functioning of the family. The family may also take responsibility for the substance use and become self-blaming and depressed. Then they may avoid the person with the addiction or begin to use substances in the same pattern.

Once the use of substances has become an intimate part of family life, the maintenance of the symptoms by the family can be partially explained by the fear of the unknown and the wish for stability. The family hesitates when confronting change, even positive change, especially if it would bring a completely different way of life.

■ Functions of the Symptoms Within the Family

In 1971, Gregory Bateson's seminal article, "Cybernetics of Self: Toward a Theory of Alcoholism," proposed the idea that substance use was an attempt to reach a higher state of mind. It is helpful to consider the expansive and adaptive effects sought by the individual who uses mood-altering substances.

Substances such as alcohol and marijuana may be among the best-known antianxiety drugs and at least initially reduce anticipatory anxiety. By helping the person avoid painful feelings such as anxiety, the substance use helps the family in many ways. In some families, a parent may be able to solve problems or be in control of the family only when alcohol reduces anxiety, takes away inhibitions associated with shyness and withdrawal, and allows the person to feel empowered.

> Mr. B., a businessman, was socially phobic. He credited his moderate success in his career to a liberal use of alcohol at important lunch and dinner functions. The alcohol helped him to be gregarious, assertive, and humorous.

> Steinglass et al. (1987) tell the story of an alcoholic mother who felt that her drinking had saved her child's life. One night the child was ill with a fever, and she was concerned. The child was more lethargic than she had ever seemed before. The mother didn't want to bother her pediatrician, but she finally called him. He advised

her to administer aspirin and to bring the child in the next day if necessary. The child's symptoms persisted, and the woman began to drink. By midnight the child was still sick, and the mother, made bold by the alcohol, called the doctor again—this time she was intoxicated, furious, aggressive, and demanding. The doctor told her to go to an emergency room, where the child was found to have a ruptured appendix requiring emergency surgery.

Another positive effect sought by the user and the family is the regulation of maturity of function. By using the substance, some people are able to stay young and immature and to avoid the responsibility and drudgery of adult life. This avoidance may extend to other family members, who then have permission to be childlike and play while others become hyperresponsible to pick up the slack. The intoxicated state may represent the closest the addicted person and his or her family can get to enjoyment and playfulness.

The substance use may function as a "solution" to other problems, such as boredom, lack of assertiveness, and lack of intimacy. Addiction can also function partly as an attempt to get nurturance that was not given earlier in life. The addiction may help address the sense of "destructive entitlement," or "holding the world accountable for what was not received from family" (Controneo and Krasner 1976).

■ Adverse Consequences of Change

The person who stops using mood-altering substances must face the damage that has already been done to body, soul, and family and may have to tolerate the rage of family members who could not express their anger earlier out of fear of the addict's retaliation. With sobriety comes a new fear of relapse.

The family may have developed a sense of self-worth from feeling morally superior to the addicted member. The focus on that person may have relieved or distracted the other family members from confronting their own pain or defenses. If the substance-addicted individual goes straight, others in the family may have to face their own issues.

The change from addiction to sobriety is drastic and can mean that each family member now has to relate differently with the recovering person. The family may react almost with grief and may relate with the now sober individual as they would with a stranger. It can be very uncomfortable for a family, especially children and adolescents, to find themselves starting a new relationship with someone they have lived with most of their lives.

The family therapy of substance-related disorders involves helping the family become "ready" for sobriety and able to handle the positive and negative consequences of this desirable yet traumatic change.

■ Special Systemic Dimensions

■ Family History and Genetics

The study of family history factors in addiction is an immense and active field. Alcoholism has been most thoroughly investigated, and many studies now point to the greatly increased chance that children of alcoholic parents will develop alcoholism themselves as they become adults.

Genetic studies show that alcoholism of one or both parents is found with approximately 20% to 45% of alcoholics. The few twin studies on chronic alcoholism offer estimates of 71% concordance for monozygotic twins and 32% for dizygotic twins. The genetic component of chronic alcoholism appears strong (Cotton 1979; Goodwin 1971; Kaij 1960).

One prominent study produced the fascinating finding that two factors could offer a protective force against the transmission of the alcoholic family culture from parent to child: 1) family rejection of intoxication, and 2) preservation of holiday and family rituals from the effects of the drinking (Steinglass et al. 1987). These research findings point toward the importance of family consultation and intervention in attempts to mitigate transmission of substance-related disorders.

■ Gender

Gender issues, such as power, control, and responsibility, are central to understanding addictive relationships. A man who feels inadequate in comparison with his dominant wife can experience the pleasure of power and control while in the intoxicated state. The wife is then "put in her place," possibly through abuse. After the husband falls asleep, his wife regains power and control of the family. Often, family members have no models that show a balance of power in partnerships, and these major oscillations of control and dominance are seen as the only ways to relate.

Women's potential hyperresponsibility for others can play out in many ways. The most common example is the enabling wife of the male alcoholic. A less obvious example is the heroin addict's mother who says she understands what Nar-Anon is saying but sees no way to refuse her son's or daughter's request for money and shelter when he or she is high or desolate.

Addictions to all substances are found in both men and women, but men may tend to use substances more than women do at least partly to avoid intolerable affects such as shame and a sense of inadequacy. In general, women have more options for the expression of affect. Where a woman might be in a therapist's office complaining of depression and insomnia, her husband might be drinking, denying problems, and refusing outside help.

Women are injured more often by their alcoholic husbands than husbands are by alcoholic wives. The disinhibiting effects of many substances thus become an instrument of dominance and suppression.

■ Intimacy

Substances function as regulators of distance and intimacy, and relationships can form around the attainment and use of substances. Drinking, getting high, and using the substance together become an essential activity that is soon associated with closeness and bonding. In relationships that are already formed, the development of substance abuse and addiction is so powerful that soon the relationship is completely organized around the addiction. Other facets of the relationship present when the addiction becomes so severe that the relationship itself must drop in priority.

A "wet-dry" cycle begins as the substance-abusing couple starts complaining one evening about each other and their lack of closeness. The next morning the user wakes up in a bad mood and begins to use, the spouse begins to nag, and the user uses more until evening. By this point, the intoxicated user is yelling and abusing, may cause injury or property damage, and then falls into a deep sleep. When he wakes up and sees the damage done, he is contrite and remorseful. He promises, "I'll never do it again, honey. Will you forgive me?" His wife gives in, and the couple experiences a moment of intimacy that is in itself so intensely rewarding that it could also be seen as addictive. Soon, however, both people realize that even that moment of extreme intimacy does not fill all the voids. They each continue to feel bad, the user begins to use, and the spouse begins to nag. By evening, the user is intoxicated and the cycle continues.

■ Loyalty

When a child of an alcoholic grows up, marries, and forms a new family, a decision must be made regarding the role of alcohol or other substance use. If the family of origin is still actively drinking, a loyalty force is exerted on the adult child. The individual may feel so guilty for moving away and leaving the alcoholic parent or parents alone with each other, for not taking care of them, and for having his or her own life, that he or she feels homage must be paid to the parent or parents in other ways.

One way to express loyalty to the family of origin is to be a drinker. Drinking is a way for the parents and grown child to be together, and it also reduces the child's pain in letting go of the relationship with the parents. Another expression of loyalty is to shape the new family like the old one. Loyalty toward the family of origin may contribute to marital or other problems in the new family. If the grown child makes a decision to change the relationship with alcohol, he or she must deal with the disloyalty implicit in this choice.

These examples show vertical loyalties across generations, but horizontal loyalty forces are also pertinent (Bernal et al. 1990). The sober spouse may need to maintain the role of caretaker and the person in control, and the substance user's dependence may show loyalty to the spouse.

This complementary functioning replicates the role of each spouse in their families of origin. Often the substance abuser was considered incompetent, irresponsible, and dependent. The same attributions that kept the individual tied to his or her family of origin now tie the individual to his or her spouse. The only time the individual is not constrained by these patterns is when he or she is drinking. The sober spouse was likely to have been a parentified, overresponsible child in the family of origin and was able to subjugate his or her own needs to the needs of others. He or she is well suited to the role of spouse of an addicted person.

If the adult child is not addictive, the pull may be to prevent the new marriage from developing into a relationship that is closer and more trusting than the parental marriage. The adult child is then doomed to repeat history through a distant and untrusting (though perhaps sober) marriage relationship.

Some alcoholic couples manage to make it possible or grant "permission" for their children to marry well. However, it is excruciatingly difficult to give this gift if the family is absorbed in active addiction.

■ Map of Emotions

The concept of emotional mapping evolved during work with alcoholics and their families. Active alcoholism is rooted in the alcoholic individual's "dis-ease," or inability to sufficiently deny the dark sides of the soul that contribute to the irresistible urge to use substances (Berenson 1987). Substances serve as a way of circumventing the pain not only of shame but also of inadequacy, sadness, and fear. By not passing through these emotions, the person avoids the sense of emptiness, powerlessness, and hopelessness that he or she expects will be so intolerable.

The person with a substance-related illness alternates between moods of self-pity, suffering, resignation, and disgust. When moods threaten to give way to true emotions, a state of numbing ensues. If the individual gets close to feeling shame or despair, he or she quickly reaches for the bottle, pills, or syringe. Helping the person navigate the shame and despair, pass on through emptiness, powerlessness, and hopelessness, and finally arrive at compassion, neutrality, and truth is the task of therapy.

■ Countertransference

Prejudice and powerlessness are the key countertransference issues. Some mental health professionals cannot feel empathic toward an alcohol- or drug-addicted individual. Several factors play a role in this inability to treat substance-related disorders. Substance use is common in families. It is likely that the therapist has experienced substance abuse in his or her own family and cannot tolerate being reminded of this experience. The therapist may see alcoholic and addicted people as evil, nasty sociopaths whose dishonesty will prevent them from gaining anything from psychotherapy. Therapists may not believe that the person who abuses substances can learn a new cognitive processing style or delay of gratification.

The first of the 12 steps is an honest facing of that over which the person has no control, and therapists also face their own powerlessness. If therapists are driven by an urge to pursue and fix, they will get caught in some of the same enabling traps that family members are caught in. One signal might be therapist anger at a person who is still actively drinking after 2 months of therapy. Another sign of enabling might be therapist denial that the drunk-driving charge and the complaints of family members about alcohol mean there is a problem. Complete detachment on the part of the therapist is also not an ideal stance for bringing change. Treatment can proceed only if the therapist can convey that the people matter and also that he or she is comfortable with powerlessness. To treat addictions, the therapist models comfort and familiarity with limits of power over someone else's life.

■ Treatment

■ Standard Individual Therapies

One well-known text on substance abuse medicine is more than 1,000 pages long (Lowinson et al. 1992). It would be impossible to convey the vast body of knowledge and treatment options available. The tools for dealing with addictions include detoxification; individual and group psychotherapy (with the emphasis on group psychotherapy throughout the denial phases); pharmacotherapy of comorbid conditions, such as depression; and pharmacotherapy to reduce cravings and likelihood of relapse with agents such as alcohol deterrents (e.g., disulfiram [Antabuse]), narcotics antagonists (e.g., naltrexone [Trexan]), selective serotonin reuptake inhibitors, and tricyclic antidepressants.

Several variables determine the mix of clinical interventions chosen for treatment, and comorbidity is one important variable. Where there are two diagnoses, the addiction is usually attended to first to ensure that the patient is drug free before an assessment of underlying problems is made. Even psychopharmacological interventions may need a "clean" host. Mood-altering substances tend to adhere to the same receptors as antidepressants and other agents and hence block therapeutic effects.

Another variable is peer involvement in maintaining the addiction of young adults or adolescents. More of the individual's problems will be related to struggles with parents than is true for older adult patients.

Individuals with substance-related disorders vary in their acceptance of 12-step programs. Alcoholics Anonymous and Narcotics Anonymous have demonstrated vast success and must be considered resources for all patients working toward sobriety. The treatment approach described here assumes that the therapist is working in conjunction with a 12-step program. Therapists who refer successfully to AA or NA usually attend open meetings and familiarize themselves with the basic literature of the program.

Some individuals will discontinue treatment if the therapist insists on participation in the program. Although they are a minority, some people do find sobriety without the fellowship of a 12-step program. The therapist must respect the beliefs of the individual, especially in the opening phases of therapy. The patient who resists AA, for example, can be challenged to see whether sobriety can be obtained without the fellowship.

Finally, individuals with addictions vary in their expectations from the treatment. Therapy must assess the patient's agenda, both overt and covert. If addiction is not acknowledged at first (the usual situation), attention must be paid to the presenting complaint before the addiction is addressed. A gradual easing of resistance is required because a forceful confrontation of the problem will only raise more defenses.

■ Family Modalities

For an addicted individual with a significant other, marital and couples therapy can be the main treatment modality. Children, siblings, and members of the family of origin can increase the sense of despair, break through denial, and supportively confront the individual in ways that can help the person with addiction hit bottom.

Multifamily groups for addictions have also been a popular adjunct in some centers and may provide the support needed to implement the most difficult changes in the family, such as "closing the back door," that is, refusing to take youngsters with substance problems back into the home and thus forcing them to accept the rigors of treatment (Kaufman and Kaufman 1977).

Family therapy is now used most often as an adjunct modality with individual and group therapies and AA or NA. A strictly individual approach may be appropriate in situations where the family is seriously disengaged, absent, or violent. In most cases, however, it is limiting to work with the individual in isolation.

"Network Therapy" is a relatively new approach in addiction psychiatry (Galanter 1993; Rueveni 1979; Speck and Attneave 1973).

The person is treated both individually and in conjunction with a support network consisting of family and close friends. This group is sensitized to cues connected to relapse. These cues appear as the conditioned associations of substance use with certain places, people, moods, thoughts, and sensations. The cohesiveness of the group then becomes a therapeutic force against the cues. The cohesive networks are strengthened by a mix of family therapy, AA, couples groups, and multifamily groups. The network pays attention to the cues during the early months of sobriety, and they report and confront early relapse, threats to sobriety, and reemergence of denial.

Therapy with addictive problems can be divided into three phases:

1. Addressing denial and stopping active addiction.
2. Adjusting to dry state and preventing relapse.
3. Addressing marital or other relational issues.

A three-phase family treatment plan for addiction combines knowledge of chemical dependency with family systems therapy (Berenson 1986, 1994). With married alcohol-addicted individuals, the treatment begins with a couples approach to stopping the substance abuse and then focuses on gradual movement toward relational meaning and intimacy.

Phase 1: Addressing denial and stopping active addiction. The central goals of this "wet phase" are to maintain engagement, to gradually help the person become aware of the high cost to self and others of continued use, and to bring an end to drinking.

The therapist's language must be respectful. Extreme denial in a substance-addicted individual may increase the importance of family or co-worker involvement in the assessment. The person comes to see that drug use in fact *causes* rather than *relieves* pain and problems. Gradually, the therapist introduces a confrontation with the individual and uses information given by others to motivate the person to care about his or her own well-being.

In couples with alcoholism, the initial focus is often best directed toward the nondrinking spouse, who must realize the hopelessness of his or her position and hit bottom. The spouse can then focus on him-

or herself and find enough energy and emotion to stop enabling, to detach, and to allow the alcoholic to experience despair and hit bottom. The therapist diagnoses a "drinking problem," explains the disease concept, and labels enabling and codependence. The 12-step programs are introduced, and the issue of powerlessness is addressed.

Phase 2: Adjusting to dry state and preventing relapse.　　Once the individual has stopped drinking, the couple must adjust to the dry state. The therapist can attempt to introduce some gradual improvement in family functioning, including balancing parental functions and addressing family-of-origin issues. Continued participation in AA and Al-Anon is encouraged. Discussions of hurt are allowed, but the therapist maintains calmness as the family adjusts to sobriety.

Phase 3: Addressing marital or other relational issues.　　In Phase 3, when the family has been in sobriety for at least 2 years, the treatment can begin to address marital intimacy and deemphasize labels such as alcoholism and codependency. Marital therapy begins to replace AA and Al-Anon. If the person is still attending daily AA meetings at this stage and is withdrawn or defensive about being available to the family, this may now be labeled an avoidance of intimacy. Examining resources in the relationship, dealing with past injustices and grudges, and rebuilding trust now become the focus of therapy.

■ Psychoeducation

Many individual therapies for addictions involve psychoeducation. Treatment programs usually include lectures about addictive substances, denial, and defense mechanisms. This teaching should be straightforward and nonjudgmental. The spiritual foundations of the 12 steps are introduced as a new framework for thinking. This method introduces a new view of life as the addicted person and his or her family members hear their own experiences reflected in stories that reveal the denial, rage, hopelessness, fear, and enabling of living with addictions. The hardest step is getting the person with the addiction and the family to the lecture.

In family therapy, psychoeducation aims to decrease denial and shame; increase motivation, joining, and hope; and prepare the family for the tough road ahead. The experiences of other families are introduced. The therapist explains the "map of emotions" (see Figure 2–1) to introduce the idea that substances help avoid emotional pain (Berenson 1991). Network Therapy focuses on social and environmental cues.

Education may also be used to offer information about normal family life. The individual may have never seen a balanced parent-child relationship, a balanced spousal relationship, or normal use of substances such as alcohol. The family may respond enthusiastically to learning about basic concepts of boundaries, self, intimacy, giving and receiving, and commitment.

■ New Stories

Thank God I am an alcoholic. The therapist listens for hints of the person's awareness of the special opportunities possible in recovery from an addition. This awareness is used to reflect a strange kind of gratitude to the addiction for allowing for a greater possibility for transformation. Unlike other diseases, such as cancer, addiction can be "cured" by abstaining from certain behaviors. The journey toward hitting bottom and then coming back again creates a new chance for an honest, sober experiencing of life for the first time.

A higher state of mind. A focus on the individual's desire for a higher state of mind helps detoxify the family's notion that the addicted member is merely weak, dishonest, and opportunistic. Discussion focuses on the ways in which the substance may have helped the person become stronger, more assertive, closer to others, and happier with him- or herself.

If substances were used to attain a feeling of self-worth, an attempt is made to discover other ways to attain this positive state. If substances were the means for social relation, perhaps the individual can learn to sneak out to an AA or NA meeting the way he or she used to sneak out to a bar (Berenson 1987).

Adolescent launching attempt. Substance use by an adolescent often relates at least in part to efforts toward autonomy, maturation, and self-differentiation, though the method is dangerous. The family and adolescent can be asked to find other ways for the child to move from dependence to self-sufficiency. Conversely, substance use can also indicate a reluctance to give up dependence for maturity. Can a common ground be found where child and parents discover they share the same goals? The parents may be able to help the adolescent accomplish his or her objectives without having the child suffer or even die from substance abuse.

Experimentation versus addiction.   The adolescent substance abuser is often brought to therapy by parents concerned about a life-threatening addiction. The therapist can help the family determine whether the behaviors represent peer-related experimentation or dependence and addiction.

The therapist can explain the high risk that substance use will lead to substance dependence for certain at-risk adolescents. The adolescent and family can then confront the different possible meanings of the behaviors.

> One adolescent was initially gratified when the therapist asked her parents whether addiction was the only possible explanation for what they were observing, because she felt the therapist would reassure the parents that she was not addicted.
>
> Later she became frightened by the secrets shared in the session, in which substance abuse, addiction, and subsequent tragedies were revealed in the parents' families of origin. The young woman suddenly realized that she *was* at risk for addiction. Subsequently her attitude toward drugs changed dramatically.

Hopelessness and despair are desirable.   Therapy is likely to fail unless the individual hits bottom and transforms. The family is helped to see the importance of feeling worse before being able to climb back up. As 12-step programs often say, "You can't solve a problem you don't have."

The issue of surrender may meet with resistance because willfulness is a primary dynamic of the person and family. Surrender can be described as a step the person has already taken in choosing to surrender to the substance. Now this question can be asked: "Can you choose to surrender in a different way, as in admitting powerlessness?"

Detaching with love.   The many interpersonal dimensions of addictions can be emphasized in new interpretations. The role of the substance as a regulator of intimacy was described earlier, and another possible focus is the idea of detaching with love. This concept may be an especially helpful reconstruction for those who have trouble showing closeness and affection in any way other than rescuing and hyperresponsibility. It can be suggested that a closer, more mature relationship is actually the goal of such detachment. Learning to not enable, not rescue, and not punish or nag can be described as a new way of showing affection.

"Power over" to "power to."   The concept of powerlessness can help reveal reality in a new way. Many people resist the idea of powerlessness because it connotes helplessness, passivity, and resignation. The therapist can help the family accept their lack of "power over" others and may show the family those areas in which the individual and family *do* have power. Recovery attempts to teach "the wisdom to know the difference."

When the person and family realize that one person has no true control over another, the energy that was directed toward changing others is liberated. This energy can now be used to develop and to relate in ways other than dominance or submission. "Power over" can become "power to," and this can bring a fundamental shift for family members (Berenson 1991).

Options can be discussed with the spouse trying to decide about staying in a relationship: 1) stay as is, 2) leave, or 3) stay with powerlessness. The last choice opens up a new possibility of staying in the relationship with a focus on self, without a mission to change the other, and with clear communication of needs and expectations. This choice is not resignation or masochism, but is experienced as lightness, lifting of a burden, and new freedom.

Welcoming relapse.   Most people who abuse substances, especially alcohol, begin by claiming they could control their drinking if they thought it were really a problem. In therapy, they might be asked to carry out a contract in which they control their drinking as an experiment, with results to be evaluated in 2 months. The specific assignment is for the individual to have two drinks per day, no more and no less, every day for 2 months. A failure of this contract has helped alcoholics discover their powerlessness to control (Treadway 1987).

Relapses can also be seen as welcome in that they increase the individual's awareness of the depth of his or her own powerlessness over life and addiction. This awareness is an essential part of recovery. A relapse prevention plan, in which specific high-risk thoughts and events are labeled and alternatives to drinking are found, may result.

Courage to recover.   The addicted person can be praised for having the courage to consider the idea of sobriety and to face the painful emotions of recovery and of life without the substance. Family members may be confused initially by this view because they are so used to thinking of the substance as evil. They can be helped to see the individual's decision to stop using substances as a willingness to face shame, anxiety, sadness, and even boredom.

Enabling as common sense.   The enabling and pursuing spouse may be able to see how his or her efforts have not worked and may actually be helping to maintain the situation as it is. Nevertheless, such efforts deserve a balanced view that considers them at least partly as well-intended attempts to protect the stability of the family. Even nagging and overprotection can be discussed positively as natural and sensible reactions designed to make the person stop using substances. The only problem is that these efforts do not work.

Adaptiveness of intoxication.   The adaptive aspects of drinking and the adverse consequences of change are themselves new views that may be shocking to the family. The adaptive aspects of using substances include a decrease in shyness, fear, anxiety, and depressive paralysis, and an enhanced capacity for relatedness, assertiveness, and problem solving. David Treadway said, "It took me a long time to fully appreciate how traumatic it is for a family to have an alcoholic member go sober" (Treadway 1987, p. 22).

■ Additional Reading

Berenson D: Alcohol in the family system, in Family Therapy Theory and Practice. Edited by Guerin P. New York, Gardner, 1976, pp 284–297

Berenson D: The therapist's relationship with couples with an alcoholic member, in Family Therapy of Drug and Alcohol Abuse, 2nd Edition. Edited by Kaufman E, Kaufman P. New York, Gardner, 1992, pp 224–235

Berenson D: A systemic view of spirituality: God and twelve-step programs as resources in family therapy. Journal of Strategic and Systemic Therapies 9:59–70, 1990

Crowley P: Family therapy approach to addiction. Bull Narc 40:57–61, 1988

Fossum MA, Mason MJ: Facing Shame: Families in Recovery. New York, WW Norton, 1986

Gibson DR, Sorenson JL, Wermuth L, et al: Families are helped by drug treatment. Int J Addict 27:961–978, 1992

Kaufman E: A workable system of family therapy for drug dependence. J Psychoactive Drugs 18:43–50, 1986

O'Farrell TJ: Marital and family therapy in alcoholism treatment. J Subst Abuse Treat 6:23–29, 1989

Steinglass P, Davis D, Berenson D: Observations of conjointly hospitalized "alcoholic couples" during sobriety and intoxication: implications for theory and therapy. Fam Process 16:1–16, 1977

■ References

Alexander BK, Dibb GS: Opiate addicts and their parents. Fam Process 14:499–514, 1975

Bateson G: Cybernetics of "self ": toward a theory of alcoholism. Psychiatry 34:1–18, 1971

Berenson D: The family treatment of alcoholism. Family Therapy Today 1:3–7, 1986

Berenson D: Alcoholics Anonymous: from surrender to transformation. Family Therapy Networker 11:24–31, 1987

Berenson D: Powerlessness, liberating or enslaving? responding to the feminist critique of the twelve steps, in Feminism and Addiction. Edited by Bepko C. Binghamton, NY, Haworth, 1991, pp 67–84

Berenson D, Schrier EW: Current family treatment approaches, in Principles of Addiction Medicine. Edited by Miller NS. Chevy Chase, MD, American Society of Addiction Medicine, 1994, pp 1–11

Bernal G, Rodriguez C, Diamond G: Contextual therapy: brief treatment of an addict and spouse. Fam Process 29:59–71, 1990

Coleman SB: Siblings in session, in Family Therapy of Drug and Alcohol Abuse. Edited by Kaufman E, Kaufman P. New York, Gardner, 1979, pp 131–143

Controneo M, Krasner B: Addiction, alienation, and parenting. Nurs Clin North Am 11:517–525, 1976

Cotton NS: The familial incidence of alcoholism: a review. J Stud Alcohol 40:89–116, 1979

Galanter M: Network therapy for addiction: a model for office practice. Am J Psychiatry 150:28–36, 1993

Goodwin DW: Is alcoholism hereditary? a review and critique. Arch Gen Psychiatry 10:209–214, 1971

Kaij L: Alcoholism in Twins. Stockholm, Sweden, Almquist & Wiksell, 1960

Kaufman E: The role of alcohol and drugs in family violence, in Substance Abuse and Family Therapy. Edited by Kaufman E. Orlando, FL, Grune & Stratton, 1985, pp 75–83

Kaufman E, Kaufman P: Multiple family therapy: a new direction in the treatment of drug abusers. Am J Drug Alcohol Abuse 4:467–478, 1977

Lowinson JH, Ruiz P, Millman RB (eds): Substance Abuse: A Comprehensive Textbook. Baltimore, MD, Williams & Wilkins, 1992

Pattison EM, Kaufman E: Family therapy in the treatment of alcoholism, in Family Therapy and Major Psychopathology. Edited by Lansky MR. New York, Grune & Stratton, 1981, pp 203–229

Rueveni U: Networking Families in Crisis. New York, Human Sciences Press, 1979

Speck RV, Attneave C: Family Networks. New York, Vintage Books, 1973

Stanton MD: A critique of Kaufman's "myth and reality in the family patterns and treatment of substance abusers." Am J Drug Alcohol Abuse 7:281–289, 1980

Stanton MD, Todd TC: Structural family therapy with drug addicts, in Family Therapy of Drug and Alcohol Abuse. Edited by Kaufman E, Kaufman P. New York, Gardner, 1979, pp 55–69

Steinglass P, Bennett LA, Wolin SJ, et al: The Alcoholic Family. New York, Basic Books, 1987

Todd TC, Seleckeman M (eds): Family Therapy Approaches With Adolescent Drug Abusers. Needham Heights, MA, Allyn & Bacon, 1990

Treadway D: The ties that bind. Family Therapy Networker 11:16–23, 1987

Vaillant G: A 12-year follow-up of New York narcotic addicts. Arch Gen Psychiatry 15:599–609, 1966

CHAPTER 7

Anxiety Disorders

Hannah W.

A 55-year-old woman, Hannah W., was severely impaired by obsessive-compulsive rituals in which she attempted to prevent contamination. A shower could take 3 hours, and a trip to the bathroom could take 1½ hours. Her pre-bedtime handwashing and checking rituals would begin at 11 P.M. and often lasted until 5 A.M. She was referred for family therapy after years of treatment failures. The family treatment consisted of behavioral therapy (supportive exposure and response prevention), pharmacotherapy trials of many combinations, and meetings every 4 weeks over many years.

Hannah's husband was included in the therapy and medication sessions. He was very resistant to psychological "stuff," but he was willing to work on what bothered him—his anger and impatience with Hannah's rituals. He wanted to find ways to be more patient. Although his wife's disorder proved particularly resistant to intervention, the couple expressed improvement over time. Improvement was attributed to medications (a combination of clomipramine [Anafranil] and paroxetine [Paxil]), the interest of the therapist, and the couple's new understanding of the disorder.

The therapist explored with Hannah's husband alternative ways to deal with her requests that he wash compulsively, share her scrupulosity, and participate in her rituals. Simultaneously, the couple introduced other family problems: "While we're here, we just thought we'd ask about alcohol treatment services for our daughter," or "By the way, I'm concerned about my husband's health and his drinking." These problems were then dealt with effectively.

Jim P.

Jim P., a 30-year-old man with agoraphobia and a terror of traveling alone, was responding extremely well to treatment. As his anxiety, panic, and avoidance were remitting, however, he became extremely depressed. He finally realized that when he no longer needed his wife solely as a safe companion, his recovery would mean facing a marriage that he experienced as empty and taking the dreaded steps toward separation.

Judy N.

As Judy N., a very bright 40-year-old woman, improved with treatment and began to express her readiness to return to work, her husband, whom she had seen as perfectly strong and mentally tough, confessed that he had been plagued by his own panic attacks for many years and that this problem was leading to serious inefficiency at work. His disclosure of this secret helped explain certain aspects of their marriage, such as his long hours at work. He was adapting to reduced efficiency because of his own panic, and his absence was exacerbating Judy's agoraphobic fear of being alone.

■ Perspective on the Disorders

Anxiety disorders encompass a range of common and often disabling syndromes, and an interpersonal dimension is prominent. The panic disorders, especially agoraphobia, are strongly related to interpersonal attachment. Several research groups (Chambless and Goldstein 1982; Marks and Herst 1970) focus on agoraphobia as predominantly related to interpersonal conflict, most notably to the feeling of being trapped in a relationship.

In this chapter, I focus on the interpersonal dimensions of panic disorders, with some attention to obsessive-compulsive disorder, generalized anxiety disorder, and posttraumatic stress disorder (PTSD).

Table 7–1 summarizes some aspects of the family context of anxiety disorders, which is described in more detail in the next section.

Table 7–1.   Anxiety disorders in context

Effects of the disorder on the family

- Anxiety as "world's most contagious disease"
- Family organizes around symptom and allows clinging dependence (phobic companions)
- Vicarious traumatization through witnessing of the other's distress and feeling helpless and angry

Family maintenance of the symptoms

- Family avoidance of whatever triggers the anxiety
- Association of agoraphobia with person's sense of being trapped in relationship; variations in response of spouse to first signs of treatment success
- Importance of considering spouse in complete treatment package

Functions of the symptoms within the family

- Protection of other family members
- Restraining of change, which may occur just before separation or child's or spouse's major move toward independence
- Panic distracts couple or family from other conflict

Adverse consequences of change

- Too-fast improvement may bring setbacks
- Paranoia of spouse as he or she becomes capable of functioning well socially
- Likelihood of marital problems at midphase in therapy

◼ Connections of the Symptoms to the System

◼ Effects of the Disorder on the Family

The interpersonal dimension of anxiety has led to its reputation as "the world's most contagious disease." Anxiety in one family member makes others in the family more anxious, sometimes to the point where the entire family—instead of just one person—is anxious. This transformation is similar to that seen in alcoholic families. Anxiety becomes the crucial component of most family decisions, activities, and rituals.

In panic disorder, the terror of experiencing a panic attack pushes the desperate person to do anything to relieve this extremely unpleasant feeling. Faced with an inability to comfort him- or herself, the person seeks the comfort or distraction of being with others. In couples, the spouse allows the anxious person to move naturally toward a clinging dependence. It is not long before the spouse, child, or parent becomes known affectionately as "the phobic companion."

Agoraphobia, characterized by phobic avoidances of places where panic is feared, also becomes a family phenomenon. The spouse and children begin planning their lives around the task of ensuring that the agoraphobic member is not left alone or exposed to fearful situations, and anxious attachments quickly develop. The family commonly avoids vacations and air travel and may take circuitous routes to avoid beltways or bridges. They avoid theaters unless the phobic person can sit on an aisle seat near an exit. Families will climb hundreds of stairs to avoid an elevator. The Statue of Liberty can be visited only in one highly aerobic way, or not at all. Shopping can be done only when lines or closed-in spaces can be avoided.

In posttraumatic and acute stress disorders, the family is not prepared for the intensity of the symptoms and the suddenness of change in one family member. Sometimes these families undergo a kind of vicarious traumatization as they witness the traumatized person's ordeal and feel helpless and angry as the story of the traumatic event is told and retold.

Pam C.

After she was raped, Pam C., a 22-year-old college student, was obsessed with the rapist's face and was extremely fearful of people. She had to take a leave of absence and return to her parents' home because she could not concentrate on schoolwork. Her parents were enraged at the offender, the police, and the criminal justice system. They felt helpless and did not know if they should talk about the incident. They found themselves pretending that the rape did not happen, thinking that would spare their daughter any further pain.

Stephanie N.

Stephanie N., a 20-year-old college student, had been raped near her apartment 2 months before her visit to an emergency room in her hometown. She presented with nightmares, depression, and agitation and was brought in by her parents, but she asked to be interviewed alone. In the individual interview, she tearfully revealed that her parents knew nothing about the rape. She feared that her father would not be able to handle the news and would die of a heart attack. The daughter had been suffering silently and secretly, but she could no longer contain her distress. In a family meeting in the emergency room, she was able to share her story. The parents were very emotional but rallied to provide empathic support.

■ Family Maintenance of the Symptoms

One way to understand maintenance of anxiety symptoms is by considering family avoidance. The wish to prevent discomfort in the loved one results in family avoidance of whatever triggers the anxiety. The agoraphobic individual receives support from the family to avoid facing his or her fear. Inadvertently, the well-meaning family is pulled into excessive reassurances, overdependence, and overprotection. These responses work against recovery.

Maintenance of a symptom also occurs in couples. Most agoraphobia develops within marriages (Rohrbaugh and Shean 1988; Vandereycken 1983) and reflects the feeling of being trapped in a relationship (Chambless and Goldstein 1982). Clinical and research groups often observe that improvement in agoraphobic symptoms may be accompanied by marital troubles or symptoms in the spouse (Goodstein and Swift 1977; Hafner 1977; Hand and Lamontagne 1976; Perlmutter 1990), though this result is not inevitable. The nonphobic spouse may be thankful that the agoraphobic spouse has finally obtained symptom relief and can be left alone. He or she is grateful for being able to travel and for no longer having to do all the shopping. This spouse is highly supportive of treatment.

Conversely, the nonsymptomatic spouse may seem ungrateful and angry in proportion to how well the agoraphobic spouse is responding to treatment. He or she may begin to subtly sabotage the treatment—problems with payment, complaints about the fee, or disparaging comments that provoke anxiety about psychiatry or medications: "How do you know *for sure* these pills won't harm you? Did you see the article about psychiatrists as pill-pushers? I heard that people taking drugs shouldn't drive or take care of children."

The index person's spouse must be considered in treatment of anxiety disorders to mitigate the chances of noncompliance and relapse.

■ Functions of the Symptoms
Within the Family

Anxiety symptoms may serve to protect another member of the family. A husband is allowed to feel even stronger compared with his fearful wife, and she "agrees" to the weak and fearful role to protect him from the exposure of his underlying weakness and self-doubt.

The symptoms may also function to restrain change. This result is observed most clearly just before a separation or before a child's or spouse's major move toward independence. Anxiety becomes a kind of a change meter, increasing if the rate of change is too rapid or if the type of change is too threatening, and decreasing when all agree to maintain the status quo.

An unresolved interpersonal conflict often leads to panic levels of anxiety. The panic can then function to distract the couple or family from the initial conflict and thus confine them even more within that conflict. Alternatively, the pain of the anxiety can force the eventual resolution of the main problem.

> One woman felt strongly that her marriage should end, but each time she considered leaving she panicked. For weeks she could focus on nothing but the fear of another panic attack. During these weeks, she would be grateful even to her immature husband for at least being a safe, predictable phobic companion.

> Another woman with agoraphobia had previously complained bitterly about her husband. She reported that a genuine transformation in her relationship with him had occurred during a prolonged, distressing housebound period when she and her husband had felt mutually close and interdependent. She then began to see the marriage as one of her main satisfactions in life.

From the anxious person's standpoint, symptoms function to delay or block new, challenging, and threatening experiences. The anxious person may later admit that being a housebound agoraphobic protected him or her from the complexities of life in the outside world with its stressors, temptations, and dilemmas. One woman said that agoraphobia gave her a way to avoid growing up until she absolutely had to.

■ Adverse Consequences of Change

If treatment progresses too rapidly, the clinician will observe setbacks as the person becomes resensitized and is unable to approach certain places or activities. One dimension of this setback is relational. A number of studies show family symptoms emerging in the context of rapid improvement (Goodstein and Swift 1977; Hafner 1984).

Now that the person is free and able to get out of the house, the husband or wife may then imagine that the spouse is having affairs or becoming outrageously successful. These fears may not be totally unfounded. The person may be an extremely attractive, underfunctioning person who has been housebound by the disorder and can now be appreciated by others for his or her strengths and talents.

Many treatment programs have spousal groups or other ways to address marital issues because marital problems occur so often at midphase in therapy. Although marital problems may have been denied in early phases, couples in this midphase are often in bad shape. Not all marriages survive this phase.

■ Special Systemic Dimensions

■ Family History and Genetics

Children not only learn anxiety behavior from their parents but also inherit it genetically. A phobic parent can easily raise a phobic child because the child is constantly exposed to worries, expectations of catastrophes, and anxious "what if " thinking. The child begins to think of the world as a fearful place where bad things are always about to happen.

The study of the genetic contribution to anxiety disorders is a complex and active research field that is moving toward the observation that anxiety is highly familial. For example, family studies show that 15% to 20% of the first-degree relatives of subjects with panic disorder also have diagnosable anxiety disorders, compared with 1% to 2% of the general population (M. Weissman, "Genetics of Anxiety Disorders" grand rounds, Baltimore, MD, May 1992).

Work on phobias indicates a continuum of inheritability. Panic disorder tends to be the most inheritable, social phobia is moderately inheritable, and the simple phobias are probably the least inheritable (Kendler et al. 1992).

■ Gender

The seeming predominance of anxiety disorders in women probably has as much to do with the sociocultural permission to express anxiety and fears as it does with the actual prevalence of anxiety. Men may be more likely to present with sociopathy or alcoholism, and only later is an underlying anxiety disorder uncovered. Older demographic data reported the modal agoraphobic individual as a married woman, with 75% to 95% of persons with agoraphobia found to be women (Agras et al. 1969). Newer observations show that panic is a disorder of both men and women (S. Winston and P. Alfin, personal communication, October 1993).

The notion of agoraphobia as "housewife's disease" shows gender bias in suggesting that anxiety restores a woman to a traditional place in the home. Perhaps the anxiety-prone nervous system helps solve a woman's dilemma of whether to enter the working world. For some, the solution works; for others, it backfires. Agoraphobia leaves the woman home with a feeling of being trapped, terrified, and miserable. The agoraphobic couple may resemble a caricature of the traditional marriage, with the wife adopting a stance of the helpless, unassertive woman and the husband appearing to be the strong, silent protector.

Male agoraphobia more often involves work issues than does female agoraphobia: "Unless I can fly without panicking, I can't take any of the promotions that are being offered to me and that I deserve," or "I should be much more successful in the company, but my fear of talking in front of a group cramps my presenting style and turns my times to shine into agonies of anxiety."

■ Intimacy

High anxiety levels occur with the fear of losing intimate relationships. Anxiety may also occur with the thought that there is not enough true closeness in a relationship, and this thought may lead to panic. Conversely, anxiety is often described when relationships get too close. The mind reacts with panic at the fear of being consumed, engulfed, and lost.

Because each person uses the other, the relationship of a person with phobia and his or her phobic companion is not truly intimate. The symptomatic person uses the spouse as company to help shut out unwanted feelings, and the spouse uses the symptomatic person as an object of possession. The discomfort of high anxiety may lead to true relatedness if, for example, it forces the family into a therapy or experience where these relationships are examined and deeper resources and affection are revealed.

■ Loyalty

The therapist assesses loyalty forces in establishing why the patient and family have presented for help at this time. Does the symptom show loyalty toward the family, as with the housebound wife whose symptoms reassure her jealous husband? The "disloyal" symptom is more likely to be a motive for change, as with a woman with an obsessive-compulsive syndrome whose family likes outdoor camping or with a woman who becomes housebound in a family that values achievement, leadership, and gregariousness. Which will be more loyal to the family: agoraphobic avoidances or an unrestricted active life? The therapist who assesses these dimensions will be better able to help family members adjust to and even enjoy the changes and challenges of recovery.

A child with overanxious disorder and school phobia is behaving in a way that keeps him or her around a mother who hates being alone. By assuming the role of phobic companion, the child has expressed a form of filial devotion. The mother's guilty appreciation of her child's offer of relief from the terror of aloneness and panic may coexist with the stronger wish for the child to be well.

Agoraphobic adults commonly have at least one agoraphobic parent, and sharing this experience implies an expression of loyalty: "Only my mother can really understand what I go through in panic, because she's been through this." Giving up the symptoms often leaves the parent behind, and the recovering patient may feel guilty for causing the parent's increased loneliness and anxiety.

■ Map of Emotions

Behind panic there may be fear, terror, dread of being alone, powerlessness, and sadness. Panic preoccupies the patient and helps him or her avoid these intense emotions. In relationships, anxiety that seems free-floating may contain specific fears, such as fear of losing a spouse. As the moment just before panic occurs in the therapy session, subtle thoughts about aloneness, abandonment, or death emerge in rapid succession.

Anxiety is not invariably based on fear. One patient was shocked to discover that her underlying emotion before panicking was rage at her husband for his unrelenting selfishness. A link between anger and anxiety is neuroanatomically consistent. Anxiety, fear, and anger follow very similar pathways in the limbic system. Sometimes the panic is derived from unresolved grief and loss.

> Joanne V., a 50-year-old married librarian, presented with severe anxiety attacks and major depressive episodes, which had led to at least one hospitalization. In tracing the affects to their origin, she was moved to find that the feelings were the same she had experienced 40 years earlier when she was a child and her mother had died suddenly. She was sent away and placed in the care of aunts. Joanne recalled one horrible moment at the funeral when she was confronted by her aunts, who told her she was to blame for her mother's death. At that moment, she experienced the feelings of dread, despair, and panic that were to become so familiar in later life.

In PTSD, the core symptoms are related to the uncontrolled nature of affects. The map of emotions helps elucidate which affects are repeated to excess and which are intolerable and lead to numbing. On the interpersonal level, it may help to map out why certain feelings, fears, suspicions, or flashbacks are triggered by certain individuals and actions.

In obsessive-compulsive disorder, a particular thought gets stuck in an individual's mind. Some patients obsess on whether they will hurt a child, and others fear blasphemy, contamination, or violence. The symptom is often the behavior that is most offensive and creates the most negative affects of fear, shame, panic, and dread. The rituals represent driven, compulsive attempts to distract the patient from these dreaded affects.

■ Countertransference

Anxiety is contagious. Picking up the patient's urge to be instantly relieved of anxiety, the therapist may give in to the urge to fix the problem right away, even before it is understood. The clinician must be able to control his or her own anxiety before being able to help the patient accept dreaded feelings.

■ Treatment

■ Standard Individual Therapies

Psychotherapy. There is some consensus that attention to the presenting symptom and some relief from the crippling level of anxiety may be necessary before focusing on conflicts, childhood antecedents, or character structure. Well-developed protocols of cognitive and behavioral therapies, hypnosis, and a form of behavioral therapy called *supportive in vivo exposure* have emerged to directly teach how to cope with anxiety symptoms.

In supportive in vivo exposure, patients are trained to accept the panicky feelings. The therapist attempts to correct fearful misattributions concerning the danger of the symptoms themselves, to stimulate sensory refocusing of attention, and to explore a counterintuitive approach toward anxiety-producing stimuli, such as welcoming rather than fighting the panic attacks or bad feelings.

The integration of psychotherapy modes includes a careful, persistent elucidation of the exact thoughts and emotions experienced in the moments before the onset of panic, high anxiety, or an impulse to perform a ritual. This effort may unearth a wealth of dynamic, cognitive, and learned issues.

Pharmacotherapy. Anxiety and panic overlap not only in phenomenology but also in medication response. The medications for generalized anxiety disorders include benzodiazepines, tricyclic antidepressants, and selective serotonin reuptake inhibitors, as well as the nonbenzodiazepine anxiolytic buspirone and the pharmacologically distinct antidepressants trazodone and nefazodone. Panic attacks can be helped with tricyclics, monoamine oxidase inhibitors, and selective serotonin reuptake inhibitors. Treatment is complicated by sensitivity to side effects and a tendency for some individuals to react with greater anxiety to the idea of ingesting foreign agents into their bodies. Low doses must be used in the beginning.

For initial treatment of those with newly diagnosed disorders, selective serotonin reuptake inhibitors may eclipse the benzodiazepines, which are effective and work almost immediately but can be addictive and sedating.

In social phobia, phenelzine is supported as being highly effective. Beta-blockers such as atenolol can be used 1 hour before an event if anxiety is performance related (Liebowitz et al. 1992).

In obsessive-compulsive disorder, the serotonin reuptake inhibitors clomipramine, fluvoxamine, and fluoxetine show well-documented effectiveness (Rasmussen et al. 1993). However, symptom improvement with any of these agents is almost always partial, with improvement of 20% to 35% being seen as a positive response. A sizable subgroup of patients, approximately 40% to 60%, are considered nonresponders (Goodman et al. 1992, 1993).

The evolving pharmacotherapy of PTSD is one of the most exciting areas in the field. Tricyclics, monoamine oxidase inhibitors, and especially selective serotonin reuptake inhibitors (van der Kolk et al. 1994) all show promise in treating the hyperarousal and intrusive reexperiencing of traumatic events. Benzodiazepines, especially clonazepam, have been useful in this dampening or soothing, but caution about addiction and disinhibition is essential. The importance of intervening early in PTSD is reinforced by preliminary work on changes in brain structure associated with severe chronic trauma (van der Kolk 1987).

Combinations of psychotherapy and pharmacology have not been adequately studied with research protocols. Clinically, these combinations show great promise, and they are likely to become the centerpieces of standard individual therapy for the anxiety disorders.

▓ Family Modalities

The therapist thinks about family members who could be brought in as part of the assessment. Even if the treatment then continues as individual therapy, family members have at least been introduced to the therapist(s) and have had a chance to share their perspectives.

Many families respond well to the chance to participate in the treatment. In some couples, the spouse is open to discussing family maintenance of anxiety and to experimenting with new behaviors. Spouses of those with obsessive-compulsive disorder are particularly desperate for guidance. Their lives have become so tied up with the rituals that even their attempts to help through reassurance have become rituals in themselves. Children appreciate the chance to describe the effect of anxious parenting, even if they are also afraid of being disloyal and hurtful to the parent.

> One couple, Mr. and Mrs. G., has been seen jointly once a month for 6 years to treat Mrs. G.'s severe agoraphobic condition, which she had had for more than 20 years, many of them housebound. Mrs. G. has been in agoraphobic recovery for 3 years. She shows no avoidances, and although she continues to have occasional panic attacks, she has confidence in her ability to cope with them.
>
> Over the years, Mr. G.'s trust has increased gradually. He is now willing to share his own anxieties and to look at the role of family problems in the agoraphobia. The marriage has improved greatly, resolving Mrs. G.'s initially hidden and later openly revealed sense of being trapped in an unhappy relationship. Although the physiological tendency toward adrenalin surges and panic remains, the psychological and interpersonal fuel that feeds the panic is now controlled by Mrs. G. and continues to be addressed in therapy.

■ Psychoeducation

Often, the most prudent way of dealing with marital problems involved in anxiety is not to declare the marital problems an issue, but to conduct the therapy in a way that involves the spouse. Psychoeducation can achieve this objective early in the therapy. Family members can be taught directly about the syndromes of anxiety.

The whole family can be encouraged to attend lectures, if available, and learn as much as they can. This knowledge may lead the family to consider the problem with compassion instead of seeing it as part of a manipulative power game: "I see now that she's not trying to control us. She's trying to survive, and she's terrified."

This strong, particularized compassion may allow other family members to attempt some very difficult and seemingly counterintuitive efforts. Family members may be asked to encourage the symptomatic person to face the terror, one small step at a time. They can then gradually withdraw responses that, although well intentioned, may add to the depth of the agoraphobic avoidances. The therapist can teach the family members how to handle demands for reassurance and may give them permission not to reassure. The family is taught that although agoraphobia is a real physiological disorder, they need not panic whenever the person with agoraphobia does.

The phobic companion and other family members can also be taught not to keep confronting the anxious person with questions such as, "How are you today? What are you going to do next? Aren't you sick of living this way?" Instead, family members—especially spouses—can be given suggestions about how to make their response constructive: "It's okay to be anxious, and I will help you with this. It's not the place, it's the thought. You can do it no matter what you feel. I admire your courage to face into the fear. How can I help you now?" (Anxiety and Stress Disorders Institute of Maryland 1992).

In obsessive-compulsive disorder, where a biological component is most convincing, patient and family may benefit from a description of the obsessive thoughts as emanating in part from an area of the brain that is misfiring. This idea has helped patients resist impulses to act on obsessive thoughts, sometimes even by visualizing their use of the cortex to override the caudate. It has also helped spouses find another way to understand why the symptoms are so persistent and difficult to change.

■ New Stories

Much of the distress of persons with anxiety disorders comes from misattributions about the panic attack or an action: "This panic attack will kill me," "I'll never be free of this problem," "Touching doorknobs and not washing will make me sick," and so on. Much of the family's distress is also related to misattributions in the form of "stories" about the disorder.

It's just your nerves.   One focus is the idea that the panic attack is caused by nerves. A panic attack usually lasts from 10 to 20 minutes. The wish to have no panic attacks at all or to be rid of them instantly fuels the "second fear" and creates a functional handicap characterized by avoidance of everything associated with panic. This handicap results in the limitations and avoidances that lead to the destruction of a lifestyle. Supportive exposure that includes the family can allow panic to be interpreted not as a power that must be fought or eliminated but rather as an event that is expected, accepted, and allowed to wash over the person.

The panic attack itself is framed by the therapist as actually benign even though still terrifying to the patient—as just an adrenalin surge pumped out by a hyperaroused nervous system that has been stimulated by an anxious thought, a feeling, or a physical stimulant. This reframe counters the patient's conviction that he or she is going to die, go crazy, or carry out some humiliating act.

Helping as not helping.   The degree to which family members change their day-to-day lives and routines as part of their response to the index person's anxiety symptoms is called "family accommodation." This phenomenon has been studied in obsessive-compulsive disorder, where accommodation to the affected person's rituals has been associated with family dysfunction and stress (Calvocoressi et al. 1995). Hence, the idea emerges that family member's seemingly helpful behaviors may not be so helpful and may in fact increase the symptomatic person's "stuckness" in an anxiety trap. This effect of excessive accommodation has implications for treatment, because it provides a rationale for encouraging the family to minimize their involvement in rituals, reassurances, or avoidances while remaining compassionate about the disorder.

He'd (she'd) do anything for you.   Family treatment emphasizes the positive intentions of family members. The special bond that forms between persons with anxiety and their phobic companions can be built upon rather than destroyed, even if the person with anxiety no longer needs a phobic companion. The therapist can note and discuss elements of intimacy and adult mature dependence in the relationship. Reconstructions based on loyalty dimensions can be enlightening and can help the couple deal with painful issues:

> "Now that you are no longer so fearful, you don't need to have your husband treat you so carefully and protectively. How can you let him know that you want to try to be more on your own and also thank him for the years of sacrifice and devotion as he moves toward retirement from this job as protector?"

Free your children.   An agoraphobic mother reported that her children were refusing to leave her. In one interview, the children hinted at some level of concern about their mother's loneliness, and they did not note her strengths and capabilities. In a joint session with her and her school-phobic children, the focus was kept off the mother's troubles at first, and this question was asked:

> "Your children seem to think you need them at home. How can you convince them that you are strong and that you don't need to have them give up their lives and their schooling to be with you?"

Build a nonanxious bond.   A period of recovery requires consideration of how to adjust. Some treatment conversations focus on how the parent-child or husband-wife relationship can still be close and intimate even if the anxious lifestyle is no longer the bond. Family members can discover new ways to express nurturance other than joining in anxiety or being a phobic companion.

The anger that spouses of persons with agoraphobia direct at the anxious person for limiting their lifestyle can be shown to have dimensions of gratitude for how the person has either helped them avoid their own symptoms or helped them feel needed and worthwhile, even when they were complaining.

Let's try another response.   Solution-oriented interventions can be useful in breaking behavior sequences in response to the symptom. A panic-disordered or obsessive-compulsive patient draws the sometimes-willing spouse into anxiety rituals. The spouse can be asked if he or she is willing to experiment with not reassuring or with not ritualizing his or her response to anxious requests. The therapist can then teach alternatives, such as showing the phobic companion how to negotiate steps forward rather than pushing, ridiculing, or reassuring.

In obsessive-compulsive disorder, the index person's spouse often must be included in the actual exposure and response-prevention sessions. Homework is assigned to both partners, and the therapist gives clear instructions about what they must do.

> In one case, after several weeks of preparation, an obsessive-compulsive wife was told to touch the dreaded toilet and cleaning liquid three times a day and then to not wash. Her spouse was instructed to help distract her when she reported panic from thoughts of contamination. He was also told to experiment with not reassuring her when she asked if the table was clean enough. At first, the only task assigned the spouse was to carefully observe and record the effects of his own changed participation.

Co-recovery.   Co-recovery can bring an important revision of the family stories.

> One husband who had been described as a "rock" by his wife had to be hospitalized with a major depression 2 months after his wife began to recover from an agoraphobic disorder.

> Another husband reacted to his wife's dramatic progress by panicking that she would leave him. In a tantrum one night, he threw himself on the floor and fractured his neck.

The emergence of these underlying problems can be predicted when the anxiety patient has his or her first major treatment success. Sometimes it can be explained that in a family that is close and caring, other members of the family must take a parallel or complementary course, such as co-recovery, when one person begins to recover. The therapist helps the spouse see complex problems and take responsibility for him- or herself.

As the anxious person progresses, the other spouse may be given permission to focus more on his or her own anxieties, insecurities, and fears. Spouses may be helped to discover that they do indeed have resources—perhaps surprising ones—and that these resources will make them feel strong enough to deal with a newly competent, stronger partner. Developing the capacity for deeper, more mature interactions can save some relationships.

Flashbacks and numbness as healing.   In PTSD, patients are afraid of losing their minds. Families share the worry. The therapist can provide much solace and clarification by explaining that flashbacks are part of the mind's way of dealing with overwhelming trauma. *Any* person would be perturbed and sleepless after experiencing such an event.

The numbing forgetfulness and confused times are described as the mind's way of healing by shutting down when the memories are too much to take at that time. Such oscillation between numbing and reexperienced terror becomes understandable to both patient and family, who can then be more tolerant of both the intrusive nightmare phases and the confused, absent, and forgetful phases.

Circular questioning.   One use of circular questioning is to address the effects of the index person's anxiety on others and the possible adverse consequences of rapid change:

"When you have a panic attack, who gets most involved, who is most sympathetic, who gets most annoyed? Who offers the most reassurance, and who offers the least? How will each family member react to your improvement? Who will be most pleased? Some people in your family have been especially helpful. How will they fill their time when they no longer have to deal with the agoraphobia? What will you do when someone tells you to wash the counter or your hands?"

These questions can be rephrased and asked of other family members, not just the index person.

Psychopharmacology of attachment.   Treatment with medication may be more effective if the spouse can be involved, either directly or indirectly. The spouse can be asked for an opinion about this form of treatment. The clinician observes whether the spouse will be an ally and treatment resource or a saboteur after the prescription is given.

The therapist considers the different meanings the medications have for the individual, spouse, and family. Families respond in widely varying ways when medications are suggested as part of the treatment. On a given day, one family might say that this is great news. A biological intervention is what they thought would be useful, and they are very pleased. Later that same day, a different family might receive the suggestion anxiously: "Why would you just give her drugs? Does this mean she's crazy? Can she still take care of the children? Can she drive? If she takes medicines, will she become addicted? I've read that pills are not the way to go."

If the therapist does not address these issues, the anxious person will be exposed to the spouse's anxiety at home. He or she will be caught between spouse and therapist. One unsatisfactory solution to the triangle is more panic and the addition of the treatment setting to her list of agoraphobic avoidances.

Occasionally, patients benefit from the suggestion to keep some of their progress a secret for a short time. In this way, patients can keep both their own and their family's expectations from rising too high too fast, and creating more anxiety for everyone. The family also may avoid investing too much confidence in the medications as an easy cure. They will be more free to recognize and credit the changes in self-confidence and identity that emerge from therapy.

The therapist focuses on the anxious person's relational goals:

"The medications are aimed at the panic attacks and the anxiety so that you can be calmer throughout all the other family tasks and problems."

◼ Additional Reading

Alfin PL: Agoraphobia: A Study of Family of Origin Characteristics and Relational Patterns. Northampton, MA, Smith College Studies in Social Work, March 1987, pp 134–154

Arnow BA, Taylor CB, Agras WS, et al: Enhancing agoraphobia treatment outcome by changing couple communication patterns. Behavior Therapy 16:452–467, 1985

Benum I: A composite formulation of agoraphobia. Am J Psychother 40:177–188, 1986

Hafner RJ: Agoraphobic women married to abnormally jealous men. Br J Med Psychol 52:99–104, 1979

Kendler KS, Neale MC, Kessler RC, et al: Generalized anxiety disorder in women: a population-based twin study. Arch Gen Psychiatry 49:267–272, 1992

Milton F, Hafner RJ: The outcome of behavior therapy for agoraphobia in relation to marital adjustment. Arch Gen Psychiatry 36:807–811, 1979

National Institutes of Health: Consensus statement. Bethesda, MD, NIH Consensus Development Conference on Panic, September 25–27, 1991

Oppenheimer K, Frey J: Family transitions and developmental processes in panic-disordered patients. Fam Process 32:341–352, 1993

◼ References

Agras WS, Sylvester D, Oliveau D: The epidemiology of common fears and phobias. Compr Psychiatry 10:151–156, 1969

Anxiety and Stress Disorders Institute of Maryland: Panic Disorders: Guidelines for Loved Ones. Baltimore, MD, Anxiety and Stress Disorders Institute of Maryland, 1992

Calvocoressi L, Lewis B, Harris M, et al: Family accommodation in obsessive-compulsive disorder. Am J Psychiatry 152:441–443, 1995

Chambless DL, Goldstein AJ (eds): Agoraphobia: Multiple Perspectives on Theory and Treatment. New York, Wiley, 1982

Goodman WK, McDougle CJ, Price LH: Pharmacotherapy of obsessive compulsive disorder. J Clin Psychiatry 53 (suppl 4):29–37, 1992

Goodman WK, McDougle CJ, Barr LC, et al: Biological approaches to treatment-resistant obsessive compulsive disorder. J Clin Psychiatry 54 (suppl 6):16–26, 1993

Goodstein R, Swift K: Psychotherapy with phobia patients: the marriage relationship as the source of symptoms and the focus of treatment. Am J Psychother 31:285–292, 1977

Hafner RJ: The husbands of agoraphobic women and their influence on treatment outcome. Br J Psychiatry 131:289–294, 1977

Hafner RJ: The marital repercussion of behavior therapy for agoraphobia psychotherapy. Psychotherapy 4:530–542, 1984

Hand I, Lamontagne Y: The exacerbation of inter-personal problems after rapid phobia removal. Psychotherapy: Theory, Research, and Practice 13:405–411, 1976

Kendler KS, Neale MC, Kessler RC, et al: The genetic epidemiology of phobias in women: the interrelationship of agoraphobia, social phobia, situational phobia, and simple phobia. Arch Gen Psychiatry 49:273–281, 1992

Liebowitz MR, Schneier MD, Campeas R, et al: Phenelzine vs. atenolol in social phobia: a placebo-controlled comparison. Arch Gen Psychiatry 49:290–300, 1992

Marks IM, Herst ER: A survey of 1,200 agoraphobics in Britain. Soc Psychiatry 5:16–24, 1970

Perlmutter RA: Psychopharmacology of attachment: effects of successful agoraphobia treatment on marital relationships. Family Systems Medicine 8:279–284, 1990

Rasmussen SA, Eisen JL, Pato MT: Current issues in the pharmacologic management of obsessive compulsive disorder. J Clin Psychiatry 54 (suppl 6):4–9, 1993

Rohrbaugh M, Shean GD: Anxiety disorders: an interactional view of agoraphobia, in Chronic Disorders and the Family. Edited by Walsh F, Anderson C. New York, Haworth, 1988, pp 65–85

Vandereycken W: Agoraphobia and marital relationship: theory, treatment and research. Clinical Psychology Review 3:317–336, 1983

van der Kolk BA (ed): Psychological Trauma. Washington, DC, American Psychiatric Press, 1987

van der Kolk BA, Dreyfuss D, Michaels M, et al: Fluoxetine in posttraumatic stress disorder. J Clin Psychiatry 55:517–522, 1994

CHAPTER 8

Eating Disorders

Louise T.

Louise T., a 21-year-old woman, presented with bulimia nervosa and was accompanied by both of her divorced parents and three siblings. At first, it was difficult for the family to discuss anything but the eating symptoms. Only gradually did the story begin to emerge that Louise was not the only troubled person in the family. The mother suffered from depression, and one sister had overdosed repeatedly. After 3 months, the father's severe alcoholism was mentioned in discussions for the first time. Once this family secret was in the open, the daughter with the eating disorder became compliant with treatment and responded well.

Katherine F.

A severely ill 16-year-old with anorexia nervosa, Katherine F., presented for individual therapy and refused the offer of family meetings. Family dysfunctions were so blatant that it was hard to imagine recovery without some family awareness and change. The anorexia had developed after Katherine's mother died after a long battle with cancer. One sister also had an eating disorder and depression. One brother was diagnosed with schizophrenia with a tumultuous course that seemed to have correlated with Katherine's course. He was often hospitalized for psychotic breaks at roughly the same times Katherine was dangerously underweight and also hospitalized.

Katherine's father, David, was barely surviving this tragic situation and was overridden with anxiety and obsessive-compulsive symptoms. He was still in charge of the family, and all were dependent on him. He was desperate for advice on how to handle his children, especially for advice on how to react to the terrible dilemma of his daughter with anorexia, who communicated that she wanted to be left completely alone but who would starve if he did as she asked.

Meetings with David were held to help him work on his own issues and anxiety first. Then approaches to each of the children's problems were developed that helped him feel empowered in some aspects and accepting of those behaviors about which he could do nothing. He understood the futility of attempting to cajole his very defiant daughter into eating, but he could adopt a series of expectations about her living in the home.

David became the spokesman for reasonable expectations about Katherine's behavior and for the idea that she might have a chronic illness. She would be given care, attention, and treatment but would not be allowed to rule the family. She was to begin to help out around the house, she was not to keep the family awake with her obsessive kitchen roamings, and she would be sent to the hospital if her weight went below 80 pounds.

■ Perspective on the Disorders

The eating disorders are characterized by the seeming loss of control over the regulation of food intake. Though they appear primarily in adolescent girls and young women, the age of symptom onset may extend to include both younger and older women. Men may also show bulimia nervosa symptoms.

The larger context is a culture that is obsessed with food, provides food in abundance, and also prescribes that women can never be too thin. Within the family, developmental processes leading to maturation are somehow impaired, contributing to and often inadvertently maintaining the disorder. Some observers point to a possible correlation between eating disorders and abuse (Rorty et al. 1994).

The family therapy of eating disorders is a well-described application of family systems thinking to a psychiatric disorder. Early systems thinkers studied families with daughters who were severely anorexic and usually required inpatient treatment (Minuchin et al. 1978). One school developed early theories of circularity, paradox, and systemic interventions through work with severely ill patients with anorexia and their families (Palazzoli 1978). Later, eating disorders were studied as examples of symptoms connected to system or context (Papp 1983). More recently, a family therapy model for eating disorders that emphasizes a constructive and positive approach toward the family has emerged (Vandereycken 1987). Family dysfunction or family causes need not be assumed because one member has an eating disorder.

Family therapy has also focused on families with eating disorder because of the intensity of the presentation. A family appears with a young daughter who is either starving (in anorexia nervosa) or engaging in deviant and mysterious behaviors such as bingeing and vomiting (in bulimia nervosa). Because both disorders can be life threatening and both affect young adults and adolescents, family involvement in assessment and treatment is inevitable.

Table 8 1 summarizes some aspects of the family context of eating disorders, which is described in more detail in the next section.

■ Connections of the Symptoms to the System

Families of individuals with anorexia have traditionally been described as showing the following five family interaction characteristics:

1. **Enmeshment.** Family members are highly sensitive to each other and tend to "feel" each other's movements.
2. **Overprotectiveness.** The parents' nurturance and watchfulness become overprotectiveness and exert a strong negative force against the forces of development and change in launching the child into adulthood.
3. **Rigidity.** Sequences and behaviors are characterized by rigidity and tend to be expressed the same way no matter what the outside situation or the need for modification may be.
4. **Lack of conflict resolution.** Arguments are never finished, problems are never resolved, and a chronic state of tension and disagreement reigns.
5. **Involvement of a vulnerable symptomatic child.** Unresolved conflict between the parents leads to involvement of a vulnerable symptomatic child (Minuchin et al. 1978).

Three additional qualities characterize families of individuals with bulimia: the *isolation* of the index person, a hyperconsciousness about *appearances,* and the attachment of *special meaning to food* and eating (Schwartz et al. 1984). Although this prototype has some clinical utility, it cannot be seen as descriptive of a particular family with an eating disorder (Grigg et al. 1989).

Table 8–1.   Eating disorders in context

Effects of the disorder on the family
- Terror of losing child
- Sense that preoccupation with eating and health has turned against family
- Overprotectiveness and enmeshment
- Concern over obvious starvation effects of anorexia nervosa
- The "fall" of the perfect daughter
- Discovery of bulimia leads to disbelief over secret life
- Organizing of family around eating

Family maintenance of the symptoms
- Increased anxiety leading to anxious preoccupation with disorder
- Escalation of attempts to control
- Family and child's preoccupation with image of perfection; fear of emergence of family imperfections and conflicts
- Individual's continued search for mastery and perfection

Functions of the symptoms within the family
- Detour and distraction from covert marital discord
- Resolution of impossible parent-child dilemma
- Balancing of conflict between autonomy and dependence
- Effort to maintain perfectionism or to break cycle of performance expectations
- Drawing of boundary between child and parents
- Expression of anger without disloyalty
- Forcing treatment and opening up of a closed family

Adverse consequences of change
- Burden of assuming adult responsibilities and decisions
- Need to cope with child's new and potentially intimate relationships with people outside the family
- Loss of specialness for individual
- Need to face other family problems; possibility of focus on other family member
- Accepting end of perfection myth

■ Effects of the Disorder on the Family

Because symptoms develop in families that focus strongly on health and eating, an eating disorder can become fairly severe before treatment is sought. The family presents in crisis only after they recognize that the young, previously "perfect" daughter is starving herself to death or compulsively engaged in a binge-purge cycle.

Overprotectiveness and enmeshment are just as likely to be effects as they are to be causes of the disorder. The family may be reacting in a nurturant way to the troubled and often frail offspring. The onset of bulimia within peer groups of young women can lead some families to move to protect the young adult child from what they fear to be the evils of dormitory life.

Anorexia nervosa is apparent to other family members and is likely to draw their attention. The family commonly presents with extreme concern about the problem. Bulimia nervosa is characterized by secrecy. The family expresses much concern about the symptoms, but the primary issue may be shock and disbelief. They may express concern that their "perfect" daughter has betrayed the family by carrying out her actions without their knowledge or involvement. The family is surprised and disappointed that they now must face problems with the very family member about whom they least expected to worry. They may also be disturbed to discover that the symptomatic daughter has serious concerns about the family.

The entire family organizes around the symptom of eating as they accommodate to pressure from the symptomatic daughter to focus on the symptom. The perfectionist family members see their efforts as supportive of the symptomatic daughter and are often unaware of the degree to which family life has become constricted and limited to concerns about food.

Growing up with a parent with an eating disorder can have a dramatic effect on children. For example, adult children of a parent with bulimia nervosa may describe their childhood impressions of a strange, special secret their mother or father had that was connected to that parent's disappearance to the bathroom after meals.

■ Family Maintenance of the Symptoms

Once anorexia nervosa is identified as a problem, other family members reflexively focus even more on the affected child (usually a daughter). Mealtimes draw more interest and attention as the family monitors the eating behavior of the child. As the preoccupation with the symptomatic child increases, both the child and the family become more fearful of losing control. The family moves toward increasing control and away from healthy boundaries and autonomy. The child's perception of increased parental control can begin to escalate the symptoms as a defiant statement of the child's control over her own body and food intake.

Some families that include a person with bulimia (again, usually a daughter) are happy and functional. In those that are not, the problems can be hidden by the family's distinctive concern for the appearance of happiness. Underlying family conflict may escalate the daughter's bingeing and purging, and she then feels extreme discomfort over her shameful secret. She attempts to look perfect to fit the family's image of her, which increases her shame over her secret and will most likely contribute to more bingeing. The daughter's search for mastery and perfection through the perfect body works to some degree, but family tension and problems continue. The realization that there is nothing that she can do about the family problems is an overwhelmingly sad thought that she tries to soothe with food. Even the guilt after the binge is "preferred" to facing the sad state of family affairs and disturbing the image of happiness.

■ Functions of the Symptoms Within the Family

As covert disagreements and distancing between the parents become overt, the child develops dramatic symptoms that force the attention of the whole family onto the need to save the child's life (Minuchin et al. 1978). This function is important, but the detouring idea should not be overplayed as the only systemic meaning of the symptoms.

For some families, the symptoms are an attempt to resolve an impossible parent-child dilemma. The child's maturation and striving for autonomy are perceived by the family as so threatening and disloyal that the effects become painful and even intolerable. A symptom that keeps the patient small and dependent emerges to balance this covert conflict between autonomy and dependence. Eating disorder symptoms can isolate the symptom bearer from others while increasing her dependence on the family, thus regulating autonomy.

Unattainable perfectionism in families with eating disorders can come from the parents *or* the child. Eating symptoms themselves derive from perfectionism but can also serve to break the family cycle of increasingly demanding expectations of performance. Anorexia can be seen as a declaration of imperfection, an attempt to break the pattern. Similarly, bulimia allows the child to look perfect but secretly to be in a kind of rebellion against the parents, who would hate the binge-purge cycle if they knew about it.

Bulimia can serve to draw a boundary between the child and parents. The after-dinner behaviors are private, behind closed doors. The expression of the symptom differs from the family's normal modes of expression. The symptom is seen as originating outside the family—"something picked up at school"—and no amount of overprotection will be enough to stop it. Bulimia has been called "the perfect rebellion" (Root et al. 1986).

One other function concerns the expression of anger. Many families with children with eating disorders do not tolerate direct expressions of anger, especially from women. In these families, anger seems to be associated with the destruction of relationship. The eating disorder may serve as a sanctioned way for a young woman to express anger without seeming disloyal or threatening to the family.

The dramatic nature of the symptoms can also function to force families to get treatment, which can help open them up to new ways of looking at their methods of adapting to their world.

◼ Adverse Consequences of Change

Recovery of the child from anorexia presents the child with the burden of becoming an adult. Responsibilities and decisions loom ahead. The acceptance of maturation may mean recognizing and accepting physical and sexual development and relating independently with men.

This change "threatens" the individual with the prospect of developing serious intimate relationships outside the family, and it threatens the family of origin with the "loss" of their child. Recovery also means the patient must face the loss of the specialness that the symptoms conveyed. If the major source of self-esteem has been the ability to limit food intake and be thinner than anyone else, the loss of this source is painful and must be balanced in some way. Therapy attempts to compensate for this loss by enhancing a sense of uniqueness and value in areas other than eating and weight.

If the symptom has functioned to distract family members from their own despair, recovery pushes family members to either face their problems directly or find a new vulnerable member on whom to focus.

In families with bulimia, successful treatment means the end of the myth of perfection and also grief over the lost image. For the young adult, discovery of the secret by the family means enduring a period of shame and sense of failure. She may experience increased guilt for burdening family members with her problem and being unable to protect them from it any longer.

■ Special Systemic Dimensions

■ Family History and Genetics

There is evidence of familial transmission for both anorexia nervosa and bulimia nervosa, though this research continues to evolve. Anorexia nervosa is found significantly more often in first-degree relatives of a person with anorexia. Studies of sisters of individuals with anorexia show a prevalence of anorexia of between 3% and 10%, and a family history of anorexia nervosa is found in approximately 29% of research subjects with anorexia. By comparison, the lifetime incidence of anorexia nervosa is about 1%; that of bulimia nervosa is about 2%. Twin studies show concordance for anorexia nervosa significantly more often in monozygotic twins. A related observation is that bulimia is commonly found in the first-degree relatives of patients with anorexia nervosa (Strober and Humphrey 1987).

■ Gender

Eating disorders are connected with our culture's views and expectations of women. The disorders reflect the perception of the relative powerlessness of women as compared with men. A young woman tries to exercise power in a "feminine" way by pursuing thinness, but instead loses control and becomes "boylike," as in anorexia. In bulimia, she may become powerful in other ways that reflect a connection to her father. In one family, a daughter with bulimia completely avoided men but became a professional in the same field as the father, with whom she was often identified because of their similar personalities. The symptom helped balance the connection to both parents.

The societal obsession with thinness and health is disproportionately carried by women. Self-esteem in women is tied to body image, and the perception of body image is inversely proportional to weight. These ideas push women toward a relentless pursuit of thinness. The societal connection of thinness to goodness and specialness is evident in advertisements, magazines, and movies. It is not surprising that this phenomenon could lead vulnerable women to a morbid and uncontrolled pursuit of thinness. The evolution of the body image concept in girls relates to eating disorders for several reasons, including the general cultural concern with weight and thinness and the clinical observation that girls are becoming preoccupied with this issue at younger ages. Normal-weight or underweight 6-year-old girls may be heard discussing how fat they are.

In bulimia, gender themes express the relentless search for the perfect body and for the most acceptable ways of expressing anger and other feelings. The themes also reflect the fear of rejection and provide the ideal way of protecting others from their own problems by perpetuating the image of perfection (Goodsitt 1984; Orbach 1984; Surrey 1991). As societal forces shift, men are likely to develop similar concerns with body, perfection, and food.

■ Intimacy

Obsessive preoccupation with food, eating, and weight interferes with the capacity for genuine, open relatedness. Other people are viewed in terms of their weight, their eating habits, and how much concern they express about the patient's eating disorders. For the person with anorexia, the pursuit of thinness is not so much a craving for closeness as an obsession with how one is seen by others and a concern for being special. The capacity for mutuality, empathy, and openness to another person's ideas or feelings is compromised. The relentless pursuit of thinness and self-starvation brings with it a rigidity of thinking and a view of others as objects.

The capacity to relate to others in the complex ways needed for intimacy may be preserved to a greater degree in bulimia than it is in anorexia. Individuals with bulimia tend to be ruled by the fear of rejection, whereas individuals with anorexia are ruled by the fear of being consumed or merged with the other.

■ Loyalty

By drawing the focus away from marital concerns, the symptomatic person unconsciously attempts to give her parents the gift of either distraction or respite from facing these problems. The illness may reflect an attempt to find a solution by forcing the parents to work together to save the life of their little girl. If the family legacy includes grandparents who were anorexic, obese, or otherwise focused on food, the child carries on the legacy in a way that may disturb her parents but is also familiar to them (Roberto 1986). The conflict may be identical to the parents' own adolescent struggles.

The choice of food as the symptom can be loyal. If the family includes one or more members who are obese and preoccupied with being overweight, the child's thinness might please the parent who is obsessed with not passing on the "sin" of being fat. If other family members are preoccupied with weight, thinness, diet, and health, the child's choice of symptom is loyal to the family values and norms. The person with bulimia also exhibits loyalty by the long and valiant attempt at secrecy in the hopes of sparing the rest of the family.

■ Map of Emotions

In eating disorders, shame is measured by weight and fat. A determined attempt to decrease shame is made by eliminating extra fat and skin folds. The map of emotions also includes a terror of aloneness. Anorexia keeps the patient dependent, young, and distracted from awareness of the separateness inherent in maturing and becoming further differentiated within the family. The patient's sense of powerlessness over her life, her body, and her family's happiness can lead to an intense fear of further loss of control.

In anorexia, the fear of facing powerlessness becomes so intense that the individual attempts to compensate by controlling one of the few controllable elements available—her caloric intake. Ironically, the attempt to fight against powerlessness leads to an uncontrollable obsession. Bulimia is also an attempt to master impulses and body size. By giving in to powerlessness (through bingeing and purging), the person with bulimia makes a strong statement of power ("I will achieve whatever I want, no matter what the cost").

■ Treatment

■ Standard Individual Therapies

The psychotherapies are the treatment mainstay for the eating disorders, although adjunctive medications are now common. As with most disorders, the early psychotherapy experience was psychoanalytic. The particular ego deficits of the eating disorders have been described, and suggested technique modifications have been offered (Bruch 1973). The early drive-conflict models emphasized self-starvation as a defense against sexual fantasies and oral impregnation. Starvation was seen as a neurotic symptom deriving from oral sadistic drives.

These ideas were later altered by object relations theorists, who viewed anorexia as the result of conflicting introjects. These introjects could become hostile and destructive when the individual's life moved toward separation from parents (Goodsitt 1984).

The eating disorders are easily viewed as prototype disorders of self. The hatred of one's own body has been interpreted as part of the failure to develop an empathic "selfobject." This failure is seen as related to the failure of the parent to mirror and confirm the child's value (Goodsitt 1984).

During the last decade, some observations culled from psychoanalytic research on eating disorders have highlighted a series of specific cognitive defects and distortions. This work evolved into what is now the most common psychotherapeutic approach to the disorders, the cognitive-behavioral therapies (Garner and Bemis 1984). These treatments emphasize the modification of intense misperceptions of body and self. The cognitive distortions usually relate to body size, food, eating, weight, personal worth, and interpersonal relationships.

The eating disorders field has also established a strong role for group therapy for patients with both anorexia and bulimia. The two disorders share aspects such as the common drive for thinness, but there are also major differences. The week-to-week crises of dedicated self-starvers revolve around food and survival, while those with bulimia tend to struggle with intimacy and differentiation issues.

The role of pharmacotherapy is expanding, as are the number of papers on the use of medications in eating disorders. Medications are now used often to treat the coexisting symptoms of anxiety, depression, and obsessionalism. There is no consensus that any medication is specifically able to counteract the cognitions or behaviors involved in the binge-purge cycle, but most antidepressants have been found to be useful. The serotonin reuptake inhibitors tend to suppress impulsivity and are often useful in counteracting the binge-purge cycle.

Families often inquire about the role of medications in treating eating disorders, especially when the disorder is life threatening. The therapist must be conversant with the benefits and limitations of medications or have access to consultation. Inquiries about conflicting media reports regarding agents such as fluoxetine should be anticipated.

■ Family Modalities

The need for whole family or parent-child consultations increases with the relative youth of the index person and the severity of the disorder. Systemically oriented individual therapy will be the treatment of choice for many older patients whose adolescence is a memory but whose development in young adult life is constrained by disordered eating symptoms. Parents are not a daily factor in their lives, and the index person will be too assaulted at first by the idea of conjoint meetings. Such meetings may still be fruitful after a few sessions of preparation, where the goals of family sessions can be clarified. The goals of blaming and confronting, for example, may be replaced by clarifying, sharing, and building on new understandings.

Errors will result if generalities are taken as rules.

> Individual therapy with a 22-year-old woman with bulimia was stuck until her family was brought in. To the surprise of the therapist, both the woman and her family members were eager to deal with multigenerational and parent-child conflicts.

In comparison, some families with anorexia are unable to tolerate the anxieties and affects of conjoint meetings until later in the treatment. Before convening family sessions, the therapist must assess the family's willingness to be seen, the predominance of parent-child or sibling dilemmas, the proximity of the family, and the level of function and maturity of the family.

Couples therapy.   Eating disorders are being expressed later in life and may be the chief complaint in the request for marital therapy. Either spouse may be symptomatic.

> One couple presented for marital therapy over the issues involved in the husband's increasingly out-of-control bulimic symptoms. Investigation of the pattern revealed that he binged when angry at his wife. Alternative ways of handling his affects had been vetoed because of an underlying conviction that more direct expressions would lead to rejection and abandonment. He began to change only after his wife reassured him that she much preferred anger to his vomiting after meals. Situations like these have led to the development of couples therapy as a new field (Woodside et al. 1993).

If the couple believes that marital issues and the eating behaviors may be related, the therapy can focus directly on communicational and relational problems. Bingeing and purging can be framed as partly an interpersonal message. If the symptoms are severe and the focus is on the index person, the initial therapeutic focus moves toward medical evaluation and enlistment of the spouse to help break the cycle. Both members of the couple may be asked to study their families of origin for useful information, such as signs of relationships organized around food and eating symptoms. If a conflict around excessive closeness is involved, the couple can initially discuss other ways to maintain a safe distance. If power and control issues predominate, the therapy can include having the index person experiment with asserting him- or herself in ways other than food behaviors while the spouse examines the cost of overcontrolling.

The disclosure of the symptoms may initially be received by the spouse as hurtful and rejecting. This disclosure can be reframed as an expression of trust and vulnerability about a shameful topic and as a sign of a move toward intimacy.

■ Psychoeducation

A positive, nonblaming approach is essential in working with families with eating disorders. Many have already been blamed for years, both implicitly and explicitly, by helping professionals, such as pediatricians and therapists, and by the extended family, friends, and the media. Eventually the parents may blame the symptomatic person for publicly humiliating them and making them feel so bad about themselves as parents. The recalcitrance of the symptoms can lead to anger, rage, and rejection as the child clings "stubbornly" to starving or bingeing and purging. If the therapist also blames the family, the sequence worsens quickly.

A didactic, nonblaming, and medically oriented approach helps the family understand and accept the prevalence and phenomenology of the eating disorders. The therapist suggests the hypothesis that the family is struggling with a medical disorder of unknown etiology and, at the present time, with good but not curative treatment. The goal is not to seek and cure the family pathology but to help all family members survive the disorder, limit morbidity in other family members, and help the family stay calm enough to solve problems.

For "stuck" families where lack of motivation is an issue, statistics on morbidity (including changes in stomach and esophagus, changes in teeth and hair, and electrolyte abnormalities) and mortality (greater than 10% in hospitalized patients with anorexia nervosa [American Psychiatric Association 1994] and 3% to 20% in longer-term follow-up studies [Halmi 1992]) can dramatize the stakes and help open the family to new possibilities, motivate them toward change, and mandate their involvement. Later discussions might focus on the importance of clear boundaries in family life, the goals of differentiation, or the painful but essential process of launching of children into adulthood.

■ New Stories

The common enemy.   One way to reduce anxiety and defensiveness in the early phase of therapy is to discuss the eating disorder as a disease that comes from outside and against which all family members struggle. Rather than attributing evil intent in either direction (that the person is using the eating behaviors to torture the family or that the parents are torturing the child with their protectiveness), the therapist sees the person and the family as waging a valiant struggle against a common enemy (White and Epston 1990). This enemy most commonly manifests as a disorder of perceptions and thoughts about food and one's body.

The better-than-average family.   With certain families it is possible to present eating disorders as a behavioral norm, in recognition of the very high prevalence of eating disorders among young women, the common (though strange) societal ideas about food and weight, and the high regard families with eating disorders often have for appearances. If the family somehow manages to help their child develop a balanced sense of health and body image, they will cure the illness and also exceed the accomplishments of other "normal" families.

"The greatest" or "good enough."   Anorexia symptoms can be described as the person's attempt to achieve specialness, especially to be the best by being the thinnest. Such a person could be admired for his or her many strengths, including willpower and persistence.

In bulimia, the attempt may be to maintain the most perfect possible image by keeping the illness behavior a secret at all times. In this case, the challenge is to learn how to be "good enough" instead of "the greatest" and best.

Gender themes.   Sometimes a family is open to gender themes, and the idea is offered that the female patient is a victim of her culture and deserves understanding rather than rejection for her symptoms. The family can discuss the culture in terms of how it suppresses women by forcing them into thinness and into a way of thinking that links goodness and value to self-starvation.

More-powerful adults.   If the child unknowingly is using the eating symptoms to control and organize the family, the family can consider how unhelpful it is both for a child to control an entire family and for competent adults to be dominated by a child. The power that the child has over the family is challenged. The parents learn that they must somehow regain executive control as a way to help the child, rather than as a way to suppress the child's actions or thoughts.

Loyal detouring.   The therapist suggests the hypothesis that the eating problems have a loyalty dimension:

> "Could there be any way that the eating symptoms are also part of your daughter's overall attempts to be a good girl? I even wonder if she thinks you are depressed or interprets your fights as meaning that you are having troubles in your marriage and so finds herself distracting, protecting, and indirectly helping you by drawing so much concern."

Where a child's seeming martyrdom is an issue, words must be chosen carefully when considering such themes as the child's willingness to sacrifice herself and even die for the family. This idea should be discussed as a perception rather than a reality. In cases of anorexia, an effort is made to critically examine the child's perception that the family will be destroyed if it changes too rapidly or has to deal with the individuation or autonomy of its adolescent members.

The family can discuss whether the family unit is really so fragile that it cannot accommodate the changing needs and lives of adolescents and other family members. They can be challenged to convince the child with anorexia that they can indeed tolerate family members' growing, moving on to different households, leaving for college, developing new interests, and expressing new allegiances and loyalties. Parents may then assure the child of their underestimated strength and resiliency, allowing him or her to give up the exaggerated sense of obligation to protect them.

"Just a predictable child."   Sometimes the early assessment phase provides multigenerational hypotheses of patterns and legacies that the child is acting out in hidden, unconscious ways. The index person may perceive his or her symptoms as particularly innovative, unique, self-determined statements, and will be surprised to discover that he or she is actually carrying out established family patterns. The awareness of past determinants for present behavior will be detested by a defiant adolescent and may then become a motivator for change.

Too much responsibility.   Discussion may focus on responsibility and hyperresponsibility. For example, the symptom can be discussed as the child's "wishing" to dramatically call attention to the issue of eating and health, perhaps in relation to a parent who is either obese or self-starving. The therapist can then ask the parent if there is some way to release the child from this sense of responsibility. The parents can be challenged to convince the child that parents are responsible for their own bodies and that the child need not take on this job. In fact, parents may be helped to convey their desire to be unburdened of the guilt they feel when they see the child being held back because of his or her concern for them.

More mature relationships.   The importance of family closeness can be emphasized as the discussion focuses on the development of more mature relationships between the adolescent child and others in the family. The therapist must avoid suggesting that the therapy will cut off or distance the child from her parents. The new relationships can be held out as a rewarding goal, even if the change must be accompanied by the sadness of having lost the different kind of closeness that exists between a parent and a small child.

Psychopharmacology of attachment. The role of medications can be framed largely as attempts to treat concomitant problems such as depression, obsessive-compulsive symptoms, and anxiety and impulse disorders. Although medications may help with the eating symptoms, the therapist must emphasize that the issue is not simply weight gain. Focusing only on the issue of weight will lead to counterproductive power struggles among the family, patient, and therapist.

Special systemic issues are involved when considering the use of psychopharmacological agents to treat eating disorders. The person's attitude toward medication may reflect familial issues such as control, fear of dependence, worries about bodily damage, and concern about expense. Conversations in therapy can help the family reassure the index person that he or she can be compliant without being disloyal.

The deceptions, misattributions, and lies about food intake suggest that determining the family's true attitude toward medication is likely to be challenging. Assessment of efficacy and compliance will be extremely complex and difficult. If the patient takes a medication early in the therapy and achieves symptomatic improvement, the therapist must consider whether the family and the patient can tolerate such rapid change. Some families are grateful for the patient's improvement and supportive of further efforts to help remove symptoms; in these families, the medications can work synergistically with family therapy themes. In other families, noncompliance represents a form of loyal self-reliance as the patient and family rebel against the medications. Questions about drug side effects and effectiveness and comments about the expense, the weight gain, and possible damage to their child may be heard just at the time when improvement is first evident. The family's attitude toward medications must be determined in every case, early in the medication trials.

Closing frames. During the last phase of therapy, each family member acknowledges the joy and sadness they feel about what they have accomplished. The family may want to stage a ritual to demonstrate their celebration of the child's launching into adulthood relatively free from symptoms that were keeping him or her a small child. The conversation can then focus on reasonable rules and on the degree to which the family should be involved in handling symptoms, participating in future therapy, and being part of the child's everyday life. The child's involvement in the parents' life also becomes an issue for discussion. If the young adult has been living at home, this phase may involve a move to an apartment. The emphasis may shift from family therapy to the person's individual therapy.

The parents may express some of their dilemmas and problems with each other as a test to see whether the child can possibly express concern for them but also maintain a boundary and stay out of the middle of the relationship. Can he or she allow the parents to function as adults who can handle their own problems?

Essential closing conversations should focus on the ongoing difficulties of change, on what to do in case of relapse, and on who will be the first to contact the appropriate therapist if necessary in the future.

■ Additional Reading

Fairburn CG: Cognitive-behavioral treatment for bulimia, in Handbook of Psychotherapy for Anorexia and Bulimia. Edited by Garner DM, Garfinkel PE. New York, Guilford, 1984, pp 160–192

Sargent J, Liebman R: Family therapy for eating disorders, in The Eating Disorders: Medical and Psychological Bases of Diagnosis and Treatment. Edited by Blinder BJ, Chaitlin BF, Goldstein RS. New York, PMA Publishing, 1988, pp 447–455

Sargent J, Liebman R, Silver M: Family therapy for anorexia nervosa, in Handbook of Psychotherapy for Anorexia and Bulimia. Edited by Garner DM, Garfinkel PE. New York, Guilford, 1984, pp 257–279

Vandereycken W, Kog E, Vanderlinden J: The Family Approach to Eating Disorders. New York, PMA Publishing, 1989

White M: Anorexia nervosa: a transgenerational system perspective. Fam Process 22:255–273, 1983

■ References

American Psychiatric Association: Diagnostic and Statistical Manual of Mental Disorders, 4th Edition. Washington, DC, American Psychiatric Association, 1994

Bruch H: Eating Disorders: Obesity, Anorexia Nervosa, and the Person Within. New York, Basic Books, 1973

Garner DM, Bemis KM: Cognitive therapy for anorexia nervosa, in Handbook of Psychotherapy for Anorexia and Bulimia. Edited by Garner DM, Garfinkel PE. New York, Guilford, 1984, pp 107–146

Goodsitt A: Self-psychology and the treatment of anorexia nervosa, in Handbook of Psychotherapy for Anorexia and Bulimia. Edited by Garner DM, Garfinkel PE. New York, Guilford, 1984, pp 55–82

Grigg DN, Friesen JD, Sheppy MI: Family patterns associated with anorexia nervosa. Journal of Marital and Family Therapy 15:29–42, 1989

Halmi KA: Psychobiology and Treatment of Anorexia Nervosa and Bulimia Nervosa. Washington, DC, American Psychiatric Press, 1992

Minuchin S, Rosman B, Baker L: Psychosomatic Families: Anorexia Nervosa in Context. Cambridge, MA, Harvard University Press, 1978

Orbach S: Accepting the symptom: a feminist psychoanalytic treatment of anorexia nervosa, in Handbook of Psychotherapy for Anorexia and Bulimia. Edited by Garner DM, Garfinkel PE. New York, Guilford, 1984, pp 83–104

Palazzoli MS: Self-Starvation: From Individual to Family Therapy in the Treatment of Anorexia Nervosa. New York, Jason Aronson, 1978

Papp P: The Process of Change. New York, Guilford, 1983

Roberto LG: Bulimia: the transgenerational view. Journal of Marital and Family Therapy 12:231–240, 1986

Root M, Fallon P, Friedrich W: Bulimia: A Systems Approach to Treatment. New York, WW Norton, 1986

Rorty M, Yager J, Rossotto E: Childhood sexual, physical, and psychological abuse in bulimia nervosa. Am J Psychiatry 151:1122–1126, 1994

Schwartz RC, Barrett MJ, Saba G: Family therapy for bulimia, in Handbook of Psychotherapy for Anorexia and Bulimia. Edited by Garner DM, Garfinkel PE. New York, Guilford, 1984, pp 280–307

Strober M, Humphrey LL: Familial contributions to the etiology and course of anorexia nervosa and bulimia. J Consult Clin Psychol 55:654–659, 1987

Surrey JL: Eating patterns as a reflection of women's development, in Women's Growth in Connection: Writings From the Stone Center. Edited by Jordan JV, Kaplan AG, Baker-Miller J, et al. New York, Guilford, 1991, pp 237–249

Vandereycken W: The constructive family approach to eating disorders: critical remarks in the use of family therapy in anorexia nervosa and bulimia. Int J Eat Disord 6:455–467, 1987

White M, Epston D: Narrative Means to Therapeutic Ends. New York, WW Norton, 1990

Woodside DB, Shekter-Wolfson L, Brandes JS, et al: Eating Disorders and Marriage: The Couple in Focus. New York, Brunner/Mazel, 1993

CHAPTER 9

Somatoform Disorders

Sandra M.

Sandra M., a 48-year-old woman and the mother of a grown daughter, presented with massive muscle tension and spasms throughout her body but especially around the shoulders, upper back, and neck. She had had hundreds of procedures for these problems: injections, massage, exercises, acupuncture, and medications. Nothing helped, and psychotherapy sessions were an endless reciting of bodily complaints relayed in a friendly, matter-of-fact way. It was impossible to interpret the complaints in terms of physical illness. Three therapists had given up.

Sandra's husband was asked to attend a couples session. He was asked what he believed were the reasons for the somatic problems. Without hesitation, he said he had thought about this point for a long time and was convinced the reasons were his wife's perfectionism and overgiving at work and her cold parents, who responded nurturantly only to physical complaints. He also mentioned casually that he was partially crippled from a car accident and that his rage about this disability had spilled over into several years of mostly verbal abuse of his wife, a difficult time from which they were both recovering. Sandra's symptoms had worsened during the abusive period. In the session, her husband expressed his guilt over his outbursts and his "other theory" that he was really the culprit to blame for her somatization.

Joni R.

Joni R., a 40-year-old mother of two, was seen for a psychiatric consultation in a general medical hospital because of muscle weakness, "floppiness," and also "blindness." No neurological dysfunction could be found, and conversion was considered. In a psychiatric interview, Joni and her family revealed that her ex-husband was dying of progressive multiple sclerosis in a nursing home. He was blind and had lost his muscle tone, which made him "floppy." He was the father of her two children.

Even though Joni was remarried, she often visited her ex-husband with the children. The last visit had been too much. She left flooded with guilt for leaving him 5 years earlier, for not taking care of him, and for somehow causing his disease. The emotional pain was unbearable until 3 days later, when she woke up "unable to see" and with "floppy," weak muscles. She was in a good mood except for her concern about these symptoms.

The jealousy of Joni's current husband had developed into a serious problem, and he had become increasingly tyrannical and oppressive. During an assessment interview, she stated that her options were poor and that she "couldn't stand to see" how trapped she was. Her husband needed reassurance that her feelings about her ex-husband did not imply she did not love her current husband. He also needed and responded to clear limits and clear messages that continued oppression would cost him his marriage.

In this case, the conversion led to such extreme symptoms that hospitalization in a medical hospital was essential. A psychiatric consultation forced the attention of the family to Joni's distress and need for help. The symptoms became less of a focus after a few sessions in the hospital, followed by meetings with an outpatient psychiatrist. Once other guilt and life issues were discussed, the physical symptoms were barely mentioned. Soon the floppiness disappeared and function returned in full. It was more difficult to help effect change with the husband, but he did begin to reduce his oppressiveness and learn alternative, more mature expressions.

Rachel F.

A 70-year-old Jewish woman, Rachel F., presented to our Somatic Symptoms Clinic with desperate complaints about her skin, bowels, urinary tract, and eyes. She had workups with physician experts in four different states and had been hospitalized repeatedly at a cost of nearly $1 million. Her pattern with physicians was initial idealization and hope, followed by disillusion, disappointment, noncompliance, and the search for the next doctor.

As part of our routine workup, family members are brought in for an interview. Initially Rachel could not think of any family to involve and almost reluctantly mentioned a son and a daughter living in town. She was certain they would want nothing to do with her and said her "real" family was her paid companion. The children were grateful to be contacted and were brought in. They had struggled for many years to find ways of maintaining contact with their mother, but they had given up because she never spoke of anything but pain and disease and workups. The patient had never even seen two of her grandchildren.

The family meetings were used to describe the family history, the relationships, the resources, the beliefs about Rachel's complaints and somatoform lifestyle, and the family transactions about physical complaints. During the interviews, the children found some ways they could give to their mother, which Rachel desperately wanted, and she found some ways she could receive and give back. Rachel was not allowed to complain about her body except at agreed-upon times, and then only to certain people. In a follow-up visit 2 months later, she said to her therapist, "Those doctors still can't find what's wrong and help me, but at least you've given me back my family."

■ Perspective on the Disorders

During the past four decades, much innovative research has pointed toward a comprehensive view of somatization and medical illness. With origins in the early thinking of family theory, the new and exciting field of "family somatics" is growing. Gregory Bateson, an early theorist, had a strong interest in the connections between psyche, somatics, and relationship and made a plea for a thinking shift that eliminated the distinctions between *psych* and *soma*.

In the 1960s and 1970s, others began focusing almost exclusively on what they referred to as "psychosomatic families" (Coyne and Anderson 1989) and on the connections of medical illness with family anxiety and other illness. The field of medical family therapy emerged, appropriately signaled by the first appearance of the *Journal of Family Systems Medicine*.

The theory of medical family therapy (McDaniel et al. 1992) is comprehensive in considering both physical and relational systems. This theory addresses both somatoform disorders and medical illness because all pain or illness has physical and relational components. The person's physical systems, other individuals, and the family as a whole represent interconnected systems that are considered together. Relational issues are prominent in a person's response to physical pain of any kind, such as when a child who suffers minor injury responds differently depending on whether he or she is alone or if parents are nearby.

A body of literature has developed on interpersonal dimensions of pain, and the new field of medical family therapy will contribute to an understanding of the connections among somatization, physiological illnesses, and relationships. It is useful to think in terms of a family *ecology* of medical illness, with physicians and therapists as "ecological detectives" (Auerswald 1971). There is a need for a new form of healer who is equally proficient at treating medical illness, psychiatric disorders, and relationships (Friedman 1985).

Table 9–1 summarizes key aspects of the relational context of the somatoform disorders, which is discussed in more detail in the next section.

■ Connections of the Symptoms to the System

■ Effects of the Disorder on the Family

In general, the effect of a somatoform disorder or medical illness on the family is that the family organizes around the affected organ systems (except in somatization disorder, where the involved organ systems are multiple and shifting). The particulars of the effects differ according to whether the illness is acute medical, chronic medical, or somatoform.

A serious, acute medical illness is the biggest test of a family's coping abilities as a unit. The family has no time to prepare for this sudden, catastrophic stress. The family must confront immediate threats, such as the possible death of their family member and critical decisions concerning emergency triage, vigils, loss of function (e.g., income and nurturance), residual disability, rehabilitation, and the expense of cata-

Table 9–1.   Somatoform disorders in context

Effects of the disorder on the family

- Family organizes around the affected organ systems
- In medical illness, family must accommodate sudden, unexpected, catastrophic stress—both emotional and financial
- In somatoform disorders, families may react with anger, guilt, rage, disengagement; alternatively, may react with excessive concern
- Neglect of children as result of parents' emotional exhaustion
- Development of somatization or other disorder in other family members

Family maintenance of the symptoms

- Relational phenomena connected with illness viewed as mutual effects of individuals on each other
- Certain critical, negative ways of treating person can increase severity of psychosomatic symptoms
- Influence of family's teaching of responses to pain

Functions of the symptoms within the family

- Transfer of anxiety from one family member to another; "agreement" out of loyalty or other basic emotional ties
- Metaphor of immune system to illustrate hazards of family in which members largely undifferentiated
- Communication of emotional pain
- Plea for rescue
- Pain behaviors may be associated with marital satisfaction
- Face-saving justification for the family's inability to achieve and succeed

Adverse consequences of change

- Loss of power of sick role, including nurturance and support
- Indecisiveness and other difficulties if illness served to help resolve conflicts
- Remission may leave other family members confused and "unemployed"

strophic illness. The family may need to find and liquidate assets to fund medical care, and they must try to understand a complex health care system.

In chronic medical illness, families are more slowly drained of their emotional and financial resources. The family itself may undergo change as children become the caregivers or assume the former functions of the sick member. A child may become the family organizer or the legs of the paralyzed mother. Family members suffer together when one person confronts the pain of a medical illness. Watching a loved one suffer is itself one of the most painful human experiences.

In somatoform disorders, family reactions are complex in a different way. If the patient is recognized as having a tendency to somatize feelings and to complain in general, families may react with anger, guilt, rage, and disengagement. The family may also show an excessive concern that adds to the patient's anxiety, often by questioning whether physicians have been thorough enough in their tests. This reaction is especially strong when dramatic symptoms develop rapidly, as in conversion.

In a family preoccupied with hypochondriacal illness, the persistent symptoms of somatization disorder, or the dramatic symptoms of a conversion disorder, little energy is available for other tasks such as nurturing children, playing sports, or attending school activities. Often another family member develops a somatization disorder, a psychophysiological disorder such as ulcers, or a psychiatric disorder such as depression. Family members may become enraged and rejecting.

■ Family Maintenance of the Symptoms

The classic characteristics of the psychosomatic family (overprotection, enmeshment, triangulation, rigidity, and poor conflict resolution [Minuchin et al. 1978]) may be more productively considered in terms of symptom *maintenance* rather than *cause*. The therapist should not oversimplify the situation by assuming that a particular family type can cause medical illness or somatization. The relational phenomena connected with illness are more profitably viewed as the mutual effects on each other of individuals with different vulnerabilities and psychological makeups.

Certain disease types are more likely than others to increase the severity of psychosomatic family patterns. Unhelpful family behavior toward the prone individual has psychological effects, and these effects may be transmitted to the body and expressed as somatic or medical illness.

> The members of the J. family began to criticize the 14-year-old daughter, Nancy, one of three children, accusing her of being lazy and irresponsible. Nancy had a lifelong tendency to somatize when stressed. She denied her emotional pain with adolescent bravado ("I really don't care what they say") but developed severe headaches and stomach cramps. The family then responded compassionately to the illness and brought Nancy to the pediatrician, who noticed the strained family relationships and referred the family for therapy.

During therapy, it was discovered that Nancy's parents had compassion only for physical illness and pain. Gradually, the resources in the family were expressed, and the girl's parents saw Nancy's pain and wanted to find ways of giving to her. Her father saw how he had confused his daughter with his own depriving, uninterested mother. Nancy's mother realized that her resentment of her daughter was related to residual hurt from a painful rivalry with her own sister. The sister had always been treated as "all good," while this woman was treated as "all bad," except when she was ill. Nancy's somatic symptoms faded as these discussions continued.

Families also influence the course of illness by teaching specific responses to pain. Behavioral theories of operant pain conditioning observe that expressions of pain tend to evoke automatic caregiving responses from others. For both children and adults, the ease with which pain complaints and illness behaviors can be reinforced by family members has major treatment and evaluation implications (Kremer et al. 1985; Turk et al. 1985). Family anxiety may inadvertently encourage unnecessary procedures and surgeries. Evaluation of a chronic pain complaint must include an assessment of the family's reactions to pain.

■ Functions of the Symptoms Within the Family

The symptoms may serve as an anxiety transfer from one member to another. If family members tend to be less anxious or to get along better when serving in the caregiver role, the person who becomes symptomatic allows the caregivers to be less anxious and "agrees" out of loyalty to express the anxiety for them. This is not to say that one member "wants" another member to be sick or dysfunctional; instead, an elemental and communal emotional bond allows family members to cooperate in such a way that one becomes ill, thereby providing the caregiver with someone to care for (Friedman 1985). One member may express another person's stress by becoming ill.

Differentiation within the family is often an issue, and the idea of a relational immune system can serve as a helpful metaphor. As long as family members are undifferentiated and others are seen as "self," the entire system is vulnerable to the illness or anxiety of any member. This situation threatens the survival not only of the individual but also of the system itself. When family members are differentiated, the system recognizes illness in one member as something "other." The family system can ensure its own survival for all members by "rejecting" the illness as part of the system while also responding to it. More differentiation of individuals within the family correlates with less emotional reactivity and more helpful response among family members.

Physical complaints may serve as a communication of emotional pain. The expression of pain may be a request for nurturance, especially in those families where it is in short supply. Physical complaints may also communicate a need to attend to growing loneliness, despair, or even abuse within the family that is not being addressed.

The symptom may communicate a plea for rescue. The dramatic presentation of somatization disorders forces attention to the family from outsiders, such as doctors and mental health professionals, to help investigate and relieve underlying relational dysfunctions. Hence, pain and illness could serve a positive, corrective role.

Strangely enough, the organization of the relationship around one spouse's expressing pain and the other spouse's perpetuating of pain behaviors seems to be associated with marital satisfaction (Kremer et al. 1985). In these and other situations, pain communications may serve as a substitute method for resolving conflict that cannot be discussed or managed in any other way. The expression of pain may communicate a loyalty to the family's culture or ethnicity if that background values the role of suffering.

For a family that is functioning at a low level, the index person's symptoms allow for a face-saving justification for the family's inability to achieve and succeed.

■ Adverse Consequences of Change

The person who loses the power of the sick role also loses the nurturance and support that may have been elicited from family and medical caregivers. If the symptom served to absorb or reduce the anxiety of others in the family, those members may become symptomatic and resist the recovery of the index person.

If the symptoms served to help resolve conflict, the recovery of the index person can throw the family into the chaos of indecisiveness. If the symptoms served to communicate other relational problems in the family, such as unbalanced power or abuse, remission must be accompanied by alternative ways of relating; otherwise, the symptoms may easily return. Somatization and illness alter the roles of family members so intensively that remission may throw the other members into confusion and "unemployment." The former caregiver begins a search to find new meanings, functions, and ways of contributing to the family other than through caregiving.

■ Special Systemic Dimensions

■ Family History and Genetics

With most inherited diseases, penetrance is partial. It appears that a person inherits a vulnerability or increased tendency toward a disease rather than the guaranteed expression of the disease. This partial role of heredity has been established for a number of pain syndromes, most notably for migraine.

The family environment and its connection to somatization has received some research attention. First-degree relatives of patients with pain disorder have more injuries and illnesses than the general population (American Psychiatric Association 1984). Growing up with a hypochondriacal parent has a dramatic effect on development. The connection between nurturance and the expression of pain and illness symptoms in childhood contributes to a learned pattern that is difficult to break. When relatives of chronic pain patients are studied, more than three-quarters (78%) also report chronic pain (Violon and Giurgea 1984). A family obsessed with health and bodily sensations creates a force toward somatization disorders in adulthood. Experiences of family deprivation and abuse are found in a high percentage of pain patients in adulthood (Violon 1985).

■ Gender

Women typically assume the caregiver role within the family. A family crisis results when the caregiver becomes overwhelmed and rebels against the intensity of a caregiving role that has subjugated her. If the caregiver becomes ill, she may be uncomfortable with the focus on her own illness and needs and may persist in overfunctioning for the family, even from the sickbed. Some families are relieved by the denial of the disability or illness in this overplaying of the role. Others are frustrated by their inability to help the chronic caregiver at a time when she most needs assistance.

The "counterdependent" man may also become sick, which exposes the fear of vulnerability behind his characteristically excessive strength. The family must face the crisis of his disability and must attempt to deal with a dependency that is now impossible to avoid.

Medical illness and somatization offer opportunities for couples to demonstrate more flexible gender roles to their children. A woman locked into a caregiver position can demonstrate a broader role if she also accepts the temporary sick role and is comfortable with acknowledging her needs and receiving help from others. A counterdependent man who suffers the loss of physical health can find new forms of strength and new expressions of appreciation for caregiving, a new model of "maleness" for the next generation.

■ Intimacy

Pain and illness can shock family members into an awareness of their love and need for each other and can bring a genuineness in communication that the family may never before have experienced. The medical family therapist aims at healing relationships and considers illness an opportunity to maximize dialogue, closeness, and expressions of vulnerability among family members.

The same events can have a negative effect on intimacy and can push people apart, as when somatoform complaints become intolerable to other family members. The anger and disgust shown by some families when they bring in their chronically complaining hypochondriacal or somatizing members can be just as remarkable as the healing, intimate moments seen in other families.

■ Loyalty

Medical symptoms and pain complaints can demonstrate loyalty to the degree that they work toward correcting family dysfunctions. One family engaged in a course of therapy around the issue of migraine headaches, which were found to be in good control. Abuse and alcoholism then emerged as the issues in need of therapeutic attention.

In their most chronic and unrelenting forms, somatoform disorders may in part represent an indirect and more acceptable way to express outrage at the family of origin. The expression of pain and worries in somatoform disorders may be a direct emulation of family styles and behaviors observed throughout the child's life. Expressions of pain in dealing with difficult transitions and emotions are understood by family members.

In medical illness, loyalty forces exert a pull for the index person to express concerns and exhibit illness behaviors learned in childhood. The family anxiety level is raised by illness. This anxiety in turn contributes toward returning to the less mature but familiar attitudes and responses learned in the family of origin.

Not all loyalty expression is indirect. Illness and response to pain also create opportunities for healing and giving among family members and for enhanced direct expressions of family loyalties.

■ Map of Emotions

Somatization can be viewed as a complex form of moods. Underlying emotions are converted into somatic concerns through the mediation of distracting thought processes. The body and mind cooperate to express discomfort through pain and physical symptoms rather than through direct experience of rage, hurt, grief, and shame.

Underlying emotions may be expressed somatically in many different ways. Fear and terror may become concern over headaches and abdominal pain. A deep intolerable sadness over past losses may be expressed as obsession over bodily symptoms and a lifelong dedication to a search for a cancerous growth. Despair may be avoided by focusing on the health care system, which has failed by not finding the organic disease the index person believes is there.

In medical illness, the map of emotions relates to the complex emotional reactions of each family member to one member's illness. The therapist helps other members recognize, understand, and face the underlying emotions in a way that makes it easier to heal relationships. Each family member has a dramatic need to move through loss, pain, grief, fear, and despair. If these journeys are detoured, relationships in the family deteriorate as family members avoid and withdraw from the symptomatic person. The attempts of family members to minimize their own painful affects may magnify the negative impact of the illness on future generations.

◼ Countertransference

The therapist treating families with serious medical illness must be aware of his or her own "illness map." This map includes the history of medical illness and loss in one's own family; one's own fear of illness, aging, and death; and knowledge of one's own reactions and behaviors when ill. Without this awareness, the therapist will inadvertently impose his or her attributions on families.

If the therapist sees illness as self-induced or as a sign of weakness, he or she will reject or subtly blame the families. A therapist who is fearful of death must be aware of this dynamic before he or she can help families face the implications of terminal illnesses. The therapist who also has a chronic illness must work to use this knowledge empathically, without projecting his or her own scenario onto families.

In treating somatoform disorders, professional helpers often feel anger when faced with complaining patients. This response results from confusion and helplessness over not being able to elicit physical findings or offer sound medical treatment. The therapist working with such patients benefits from a stance of curiosity, interest, and true systemic understanding. This stance enables the therapist to see through the superficial complaining to other levels of meaning and communication. From a systemic vantage point, the symptom is seen as a meaningful signal that warrants respectful investigation—just like any other symptom.

◼ Posterity

Medical illnesses and somatoform disorders are ideally suited to draw children into roles as overfunctioners. Out of loyalty, they smoothly and sometimes unconsciously pick up the functions that the parents abdicate. In somatization disorder and hypochondriasis, the children are easily drawn in to minister to the parents' complaints. Children often give willingly for years, not only out of loyalty but also out of fear that the parent will die, get sicker, or abandon them.

The injustice of this situation for the child emanates not from the child's being asked to contribute, but from the lack of credit given for the child's efforts. Injustice results if the sick person acts as if he or she is entitled to the child's services and criticizes the child instead of expressing appreciation. Further injustice occurs when the child's needs are subjugated to the needs of the parents and the child's feelings are routinely discounted. After many years of bringing the parent tea and medicine rather than playing with peers, the child realizes that no medical problem has ever been found. Children then feel that the parent has taken away their childhood and that they themselves may have "enabled" the sick role. Adult children seen at this stage may be overtly cut off and uninterested in discussing the now elderly parent's complaints and dilemmas.

■ Ethnicity

Few behaviors better illustrate cultural and ethnic differences than the experience and communication of pain. The main point is to stay open to each family's specific messages about pain, illness, and requests for help. Some generalizations suggested by research indicate that Jews and Italians complain about pain, while white Anglo-Saxon Protestants (so-called WASPs) and the Irish say little. People in these four groups have different ideas about the expected objectives of treatment: 1) Italian patients tend to look for an immediate remedy; 2) Jewish patients disdain medications or the quick fix, preferring to understand the symptom thoroughly and to treat underlying problems; 3) Irish patients expect very little from helpers because they feel responsible for their symptoms; and 4) WASP patients tend to have confidence in medical science and feel that the doctor's advice plus their self-help measures will lead to a cure (Zborowski 1969).

Asian Americans, Hispanics, Italians, and Jews tend to somatize emotional pain. This generalization can be complicated by issues such as the trauma of recent immigration, where a language barrier, fear, and lack of support make discussion difficult. The attitude toward expressing emotional pain and pain complaints in general can vary greatly in different generations of a given culture. Cultural or racial generalizations can be useful, but they should not be considered absolute truths for a particular family.

Americans combine a belief in the mind-body connection with an overvaluation of their own willpower and fortitude, and they may see a deficiency of mental power and strength as a cause of medical illness (i.e., a recurrence of cancer is attributed to a lapse in personal drive). Americans may search for a mind-over-matter cure in response to a diagnosis of serious medical illness. Their confidence in the belief that a cure is available through sheer willpower and a strong wish to live can then be taken to extremes.

The will to fight shifts subtly to shame and self-blame, and patients may then feel ashamed of having a serious disease. When this emotion is mapped, the individual reveals the belief that power of mind can control anything. Illness is seen as a punishment for which the person him- or herself is responsible. As one commentator has put it, "Americans are the only people on Earth who believe that death is optional" (P. Boss, remark made during American Family Therapy Academy Meetings, San Diego, CA, June 1991).

■ Treatment

■ Standard Individual Therapies

Commonly, a medical physician refers patients to mental health professionals because of problems in compliance or because the physician suspects a coexisting psychiatric disorder or believes the patients' complaints are disproportionate to the disease.

Patients with somatoform disorders are treated predominantly by nonpsychiatric physicians who usually feel frustrated and helpless because of their inability to offer definitive help. Some attempts to refer to mental health professionals are received well and are successful, but these referrals are more commonly rejected by the patient, who feels hurt and also angry at the physician for saying that "it's all in my head." The patient may continue to see medical physicians until he or she finds one who will do further medical procedures or surgeries.

Some medical physicians skilled in handling these patients may break the cycle of "dependent" patient and "resentful" physician by actually scheduling visits. During these brief, supportive visits, the physician inquires about aspects of the patient's life other than illness. Discussion focuses on how the patient can learn to live with the symptoms rather than try to eliminate them. The physician searches for treatable psychiatric disorders and finds a way to present a need for psychiatric-psychological referral that allows the patient to save face (Bass 1990; R. Shochett, personal communication, October 1992):

> "At this point, I'm not sure what is causing your symptoms, but I
> don't believe this represents a serious illness. You seem to be suf-

fering a great deal with this pain, and this means we need to focus on the cause of the pain itself and also on the effect that the pain is having on your life. To provide the best possible care for you, I suggest we work on the latter problem as well. As part of this plan, I routinely obtain a consultation with a colleague who has a special interest in your symptom picture. After this consultation, I would like to see you again."

■ Family Modalities

Illness and somatization are best understood if the therapist can convene the family at least for the assessment. During these consultations, the therapist tries to determine which family subunits (i.e., smaller groups of family members that help determine the structure of a family) may be helpful as participants in later meetings.

It may be helpful to consider family members as consultants whose perspectives and information are essential for treatment success. The family often reveals that the symptomatic individual needs treatment for an underlying anxiety, mood, or personality disorder. A core somatization component is difficult to resolve, and the person continues to search for medical explanations and tests. The therapist should involve all family members who affect and are affected by the illness and pain behaviors. By focusing on the neglected interpersonal meanings of illness and illness behaviors, therapists can gain a new view of the problem and the opportunity for helpful collaboration with the primary care physician.

The family therapist working with medical illness can meet with whole families or subunits within a family, such as parent-child groups, couples, and sibling groups, to deal with their reaction to the illness and their fear of impending loss.

■ Psychoeducation

Families may benefit from learning about the illness, its prognosis, and its course. The diagnosis of a medical illness can throw a family into such crisis that they are unable to solve problems at the very time when decisions are essential. They may need help in assessing the benefits and drawbacks of procedures, hospitals, physicians, rehabilitation centers, home care, and medications, particularly if they are not used to making decisions for the index person. Anxiety about the chance of inheriting the disorder may also become prominent.

For many families, this type of education and support is the only desired intervention. Other families may want help in learning how to act around a family member who is dying of devastating diseases such as cancer or AIDS, or they may need to know how best to deal with new disabilities that arise from stroke, multiple sclerosis, or spinal cord injuries. An excellent example of a psychoeducational module for people with physical disabilities is available (Gonzalez et al. 1986). Therapists should also attempt to identify and offer therapeutic help to those families willing and able to work directly at healing relationships.

Families of somatoform patients may need help in determining what *not* to do as they attempt to participate in treatment. Many patients have unnecessary medical and surgical procedures that worsen their condition. The therapist can help family members learn how to show interest without reinforcing the pain, and to leave the scene quietly when the person starts complaining. The family can learn to reinforce an attitude of coping with rather than eliminating pain.

The therapist can also coach family members on how to avoid helping the patient obtain pain medication, especially if addictive drugs are being overused, and how to discourage further surgeries unless clear and convincing evidence of a new, correctable problem is presented. Many families find this approach too difficult to maintain successfully.

An unhelpful cycle evolves: the individual demands reassurance that nothing organic is happening, the family offers reassurances that do not work, the individual makes more demands for certainty, and the family becomes angry and frustrated. To break this cycle, families can learn to convey an attitude of interest and concern while emphasizing probabilities. This approach begins by admitting that nothing is known with absolute certainty and focuses on the risk-benefit ratio of further tests. The only reassurance offered is that waiting and watching are sometimes safer and in the person's best interest.

■ New Stories

The most crucial problem is how to use language so that links between symptoms and psychosocial dimensions can be made without making the patient feel misunderstood and angry. It is notoriously difficult to help somatizers think psychologically and pay attention to new connections. "Psychological" therapists routinely encounter the dilemma of trying to communicate via interpretation and confrontation with patients who have minimal capacity for such awareness or verbal skills.

It is important to tailor each intervention to the specifics of the family problem and allow the story of the illness to unfold in its own unique way. The therapist listens not for blame and causality but instead for ways to change the dysfunctional stories that families may have created around the illness. The therapist points out exceptions to the negative sequences—for example, times when the family has been nurturant and supportive. The therapist should scan—even in the most dysfunctional families—for specific instances in which family members' attitudes and behavior were conducive to healing and recovery (White 1979; White and Epston 1990).

The reflecting team.   Somatization is an indirect expression of emotion that is often dealt with more effectively when it is matched by indirectness and tact. This approach allows the family and index person to save face and process the comments at whatever conscious and unconscious levels they can. A Norwegian technique involving a reflecting team has been adapted to accommodate these qualities of somatizing families (Andersen 1987; Griffith and Griffith 1992). During the session, two or more therapists conduct a conversation in front of the family where the "unspeakable" about the underlying problem is discussed in a gentle, hypothesizing way. This idea can be extended to a mini-debate in which the therapists take different positions on what might be important:

> **Therapist One:** "I'm wondering if her telling her daughters so much about her pain is just a very natural expression and may also be a way to say she needs them to care for her and be close to her."
>
> **Therapist Two:** "I think she just has intense pain and is convinced that it is a physical disorder of some sort, and so she is doing her best to take care of herself and find that disease."
>
> **Therapist Three:** "I wonder if she could have closer relationships with her family if she spoke less about the pain. Then she still might not have an answer about the underlying disease, but at least she'd have better relationships with her family."
>
> **Therapist Four:** "That's a good idea. At first, I thought she was punishing and pushing her family away by the complaining, but now I am beginning to see it differently. How can she find a way to share some of her suffering in a way that allows her family to stay connected?"

Words are carefully chosen to allow the family to receive the message and use it in a positive way. The intentions of family members are positively connoted, and a deeper confrontation and interpretation may become possible when the index person and the family feel less threatened and defensive.

The solo therapist can modify this approach by musing to him- or herself about the different possible interpretations of the symptom issues.

Healing and curing.   It is best to introduce a focus on the healing of relationships rather than on the curing of disease. Because the therapist, patient, and family have no direct power over the course of the disease, a focus on the quality of relationships among all family members offers a chance to find an area where some control does exist. It is also a nonblaming stance. This venture will be of use to the family whether or not it helps cure the illness (Friedman 1985, 1986).

In undifferentiated family systems, stress in one member can produce symptoms in other members. An increase in differentiation could offer some immunity from having to somatize each other's stress and could lead to good health and higher recuperative potential. Improved differentiation acts like a broad-spectrum, multipurpose antibiotic. The therapy proceeds by helping family members focus on family-of-origin issues and any other dimensions necessary for increased differentiation and healing of current relationships. The therapist focuses on the level of anxiety of each member. Those members who are less anxious when they are in caregiving roles may need assistance in dealing with anxiety or in finding other roles.

Focusing on healing can also mean allowing one person to describe feelings about another that are usually taken for granted—especially those of gratitude, resentment, and guilt. The therapist may encourage dialogue that clarifies past family issues and legacies, which can increase the possibility of enhanced closeness and intimate moments. Children can be helped to express their debt and gratitude to a dying parent. Parents can attempt to redress injustices they feel they perpetrated over the years.

Pain as family enemy.   Externalizing techniques work well in the family treatment of medical illness and somatization. The pain, virus, or illness is discussed as a common enemy of the entire family rather than as something one person is "doing to" the others:

"It's as if the whole family has been attacked by this disease. One body has accepted the battle against the virus, but all members feel the illness."

Illness as opportunity.   Discussion can focus on whether somatoform pain is an atonement for some guilt or transgression that the person thinks is so bad it cannot be faced in any other way. The complex positive and negative aspects of this expression of illness can be emphasized to help the family look beyond the illness complaints and see the underlying issues that may now be workable.

The idea is reinforced that illness affects the present and future lives of all family members and is not just an issue involving one individual and one organ system. Illness can be seen as an opportunity for the family to work on relationship problems that otherwise would have been neglected. If they are resolved, a gift is bestowed onto the next generation.

Apparent rejection by the family may hide concern. Family members are shown to be so eager to bring relief from suffering that they feel especially inadequate when their efforts fail. The index person's pain and complaints then generate an intolerable degree of guilt in the family, which causes them to pull away from the index person.

When a person blames him- or herself for getting cancer or a chronic illness, the idea can be proposed that this attitude is a bit grandiose in assuming too much power, even if it is power to bring about bad things. While some correlation between stress and illness may exist, the relationship is far too complex to interpret so simplistically. To get at underlying helplessness, the therapist may ask, "What would you be experiencing if you did not think your actions or psyche had anything to do with your getting this illness?"

Somatic complaints as signal malfunction.   For a family that is feeling angry and rejecting, it may be useful to describe somatization as hypersensitivity to pain, part of an inborn neurological system that cannot muffle such information and indeed tends to amplify it.

The index person's disorder interferes with his or her ability to distinguish serious medical disorders from inconsequential pain. This problem is easily compounded by medical-surgical procedures that not only bring adhesions, scars, anesthesia, and side effects but may also distract attention from the attempt to relieve the signal problem. By enabling the help seeker, the family inadvertently undermines the patient's ability to identify and distinguish among various body signals, pay less attention to some of them, and deal with other issues.

Genogram.   The role of illness, health status, and injuries in the multi-generational family history is elicited. Attitudes about illness, pain, and the communication of complaints can help clarify the present context.

> Amy N., a 63-year-old woman, was being treated for somatization disorders for which she had sought innumerable medical consultations. She was angry, and one therapist had labeled her borderline. Her childhood had been spent as a nursemaid to her ill and somatizing mother. Her siblings did nothing to help, and her mother wanted care from Amy only. At the end of her mother's life, Amy realized that her efforts of overgiving had gone unacknowledged and unappreciated by all. Her own career as an angry, anxious somatizer began.
>
> Extended family interviews revealed a grown daughter who somatized even more intensely than Amy did. Also, Amy's husband had become obsessed with a fear of headaches and seizures and, like his wife, became unable to leave the house. His symptoms were related to his obsessive conviction that he would die of a brain tumor just as his father had died more than 50 years earlier. When her husband's symptoms worsened, Amy became more phobic. The multigenerational context was essential to understanding the current interrelated somatic symptoms.

Circular questioning.   Circular questioning is helpful in expanding discussion from symptoms to relational issues because it can elicit an interpersonal dimension without implying blame of any one member. Circular questioning also focuses on understanding the effects of the symptoms without implying that they are or are not physical in origin. Questions such as those that follow may be helpful:

> "Who reacts, and in what ways do they react, when Mother complains about her pain?"
> "To whom are the complaints made most often?"
> "How does each member of the family try to solve the problems created by the complaints and the illnesses?"
> "Besides the index person, who do you think is affected most by the illness?"
> "Who in the family supplies Dad's arms and legs?"
> "What has been given up for the illness?"

Circular questioning can also elicit each family member's beliefs about the cause of the problem and its possible meanings and solutions. The following questions might be used:

"What does each of you think caused this illness?"
"How much do you blame the patient or yourself for the problems?"
"What emotions seem to make the illness better or worse?"
"What do you dream life might have been like for each family member if this tragedy had not struck the family?"
"What do you think will help the illness go away?"
"How would things be different if someone else had gotten sick?"
"What do you think other people in the family believe about this illness?"

■ Additional Reading

■ Family Somatics

Berlin RM, Sluzki CE: C-L psychiatry and the family system. Psychosomatics 28:206–208, 1987

Goldberg D, Gask L, O'Dowd T: The treatment of somatization: teaching techniques of reattribution. J Psychosom Res 33:689–695, 1989

Griffith JL, Griffith ME, Slovik LS: Mind-body problems in family therapy: contrasting first- and second-order cybernetics approaches. Fam Process 29:13–28, 1990

Griffith JL, Griffith ME, Krejmas N, et al: Reflecting team consultations and their impact upon family therapy for somatic symptoms as coded by structural analysis of social behavior (SASB). Family Systems Medicine 10:53–58, 1992

Hudgens AJ: Family-oriented treatment of chronic pain. Journal of Marital and Family Therapy 5:67–78, 1979

Huygen FJ, Smits AJ: Family therapy, family somatics, and family medicine. Family Systems Medicine 1:1–23, 1983

Liebman R, Honig P, Berger H: An integrated treatment program for psychogenic pain. Fam Process 15:397–405, 1976

McDaniel SH, Campbell TL, Seaburn DB: Family Oriented Primary Care: A Manual for Medical Providers. New York, Springer-Verlag, 1990

Roy R: Family etiology of psychogenic pain: the systems perspectives. Contemporary Family Therapy 9:263–274, 1987

Turk DC, Rudy TE, Flor H: Why a family perspective for pain? International Journal of Family Therapy 7:223–234, 1985

Weakland JH: Family somatics—a neglected edge, in The Interactional View. Edited by Watzlawick P, Weakland JH. New York, WW Norton, 1987, pp 375–387

Wood BL: Beyond the "psychosomatic family": a biobehavioral family model of pediatric illness. Fam Process 32:261–278, 1993

Wood BL, Watkins JB, Boyle JT, et al: The "psychosomatic family" model: an empirical and theoretical analysis. Fam Process 28:399–417, 1989

▮ Medical Illness and the Family

Auerswald EH: The Gouverneur Health Services Program: an experiment in ecosystemic community health care delivery. Family Systems Medicine 1:5–24, 1983

Bateson G: Steps to an Ecology of Mind. New York, Ballantine Books, 1972

Bloch DA: Illness and family systems: a coevolutionary model, in Family Systems Medicine. Edited by Ramsey CN. New York, Guilford, 1989, pp 321–333

Campbell TL: Family's impact on health: a critical review. Family Systems Medicine 4:135–328, 1986

Coyne JC, Fiske V: Couples coping with chronic and catastrophic illness, in Family Health Psychology. Edited by Akamatsu TJ, Stephens MAP, Hobfoll SE, et al. Washington, DC, Hemisphere, 1992, pp 129–149

Dym B: The cybernetics of physical illness. Fam Process 26:35–48, 1987

Fisher L, Nakell LC, Terry HE, et al: The California family health project, III: emotion management and adult health. Fam Process 31:269–287, 1992

Fisher L, Ransom DC, Terry HE, et al: The California family health project, I: introduction and a description of adult health. Fam Process 31:231–250, 1992

Gonzalez S, Steinglass P, Reiss D: Family Centered Interventions for the Chronically Disabled: The Eight-Session Multiple-Family Discussion Group Program (treatment manual). Washington, DC, George Washington University Rehabilitation Research and Training Center, 1986

Keeney B, Ross J, Silverstein O: Mind in bodies: the treatment of a family that presented a migraine headache. Family Systems Medicine 1:61–77, 1983

Leahey M, Wright L: Intervening with families with chronic illness. Family Systems Medicine 3:60–69, 1985

Marcus L: Random notes—illness counseling: a proposed adjunct series for primary-care physicians. Family Systems Medicine 7:357–364, 1989

McDaniel SH, Hepworth J, Doherty WJ: Medical Family Therapy: A Biopsychosocial Approach to Families With Health Problems. New York, Basic Books, 1992

McGoldrick M, Pearce JK, Giordano J (eds): Ethnicity and Family Therapy. New York, Guilford, 1982

Ransom DC, Fisher L, Terry HE: The California family health project, II: family world view and adult health. Fam Process 31:251–267, 1992

Rolland JS: Family illness paradigms: evolution and significance. Family Systems Medicine 5:482–503, 1987

Simon R: Chronic illness as a therapeutic metaphor. Family Systems Medicine 6:262–275, 1988

Steinglass P, Horan ME: Families and chronic medical illness. Journal of Psychotherapy and the Family 3:127–142, 1987

Wynne LC, Shields CG, Sirkin MI: Illness, family theory and family therapy, I: conceptual issues. Fam Process 31:3–18, 1992

■ References

American Psychiatric Association: Family Therapy and Psychiatry: APA Task Force. Washington, DC, American Psychiatric Press, 1984

Andersen T: The reflecting team: dialogue and meta-dialogue in clinical work. Fam Process 26:415–428, 1987

Auerswald EH: Families, change, and the ecological perspective. Fam Process 10:263–280, 1971

Bass CM (ed): Somatization: Physical Symptoms and Psychological Illness. Oxford, UK, Blackwell Scientific, 1990

Coyne JC, Anderson BJ: The "psychosomatic family" reconsidered, II: recalling a defective model and looking ahead. Journal of Marital and Family Therapy 15:139–148, 1989

Friedman EH: Body and soul in family process, in Generation to Generation: Family Process in Church and Synagogue. New York, Guilford, 1985, pp 121–146

Friedman EH: Resources for healing and survival in families, in Family Resources. Edited by Karpel MA. New York, Guilford, 1986, pp 65–92

Gonzalez S, Steinglass P, Reiss D: Family Centered Interventions for the Chronically Disabled: The Eight-Session Multiple-Family Discussion Group Program (treatment manual). Washington, DC, George Washington University Rehabilitation Research and Training Center, 1986

Griffith JL, Griffith ME: Speaking the unspeakable: use of the reflecting position in therapies for somatic symptoms. Family Systems Medicine 10:41–51, 1992

Kremer EF, Sieber W, Atkinson JH: Spousal perpetuation of chronic pain behavior. International Journal of Family Therapy 7:258–270, 1985

McDaniel SH, Hepworth J, Doherty WJ: Medical Family Therapy: A Biopsychosocial Approach to Families With Health Problems. New York, Basic Books, 1992

Minuchin S, Rosman B, Baker L: Psychosomatic Families: Anorexia Nervosa in Context. Cambridge, MA, Harvard University Press, 1978

Turk DC, Rudy TE, Flor H: Why a family perspective for pain? International Journal of Family Therapy 7:223–234, 1985

Violon A: Family etiology of chronic pain. International Journal of Family Therapy 7:235–246, 1985

Violon A, Giurgea D: Familial models for chronic pain. Pain 18:199–203, 1984

White M: Structural and strategic approaches to psychosomatic families. Fam Process 18:303–314, 1979

White M, Epston D: Narrative Means to Therapeutic Ends. New York, WW Norton, 1990

Zborowski M: People in Pain. San Francisco, CA, Jossey-Bass, 1969

CHAPTER 10

Factitious Disorders

Ray P.

A 51-year-old man, Ray P., was referred for his first psychiatric consultation ever for "anxiety and obsessiveness." His history revealed itself slowly as 32 years of seeking medical attention with an ever-changing slate of symptoms. The search for medical care began in the year after his parents' divorce, when Ray was 19 years old. By the time he was seen in consultation, he had been hospitalized 250 times and had undergone innumerable surgical operations, including a Whipple procedure (removal of much of the pancreas and duodenum). Ray was now cachectic, weighed 80 pounds, and was addicted to meperidine (Demerol), which he had been taking for most of the last 30 years. His decision to give up the secrecy of his self-destructive career was related to the death of his father a few years earlier. Ray was near death himself and realized that a craving to be around people was behind much of his behavior.

Mary S.

Mary S., a 45-year-old nurse, was being worked up in the hospital for a fever of unknown origin. She was observed injecting feces into her veins at a moment when she thought she was alone. When a meeting was held to discuss this dramatic finding, her husband adamantly refused to believe the story.

Tony E.

An 18-month-old boy, Tony E., was being worked up for fever, malnutrition, diarrhea, and vomiting. No medical etiology could be found until Tony's mother was observed to be using her finger and other objects to force the child to vomit.

Jonathan R.

Jonathan R., 8 months old, was recovering from a partial pancreatectomy. The medical team had become convinced that the documented extremely low blood glucose levels and repeated hypoglycemic seizures were caused by a life-threatening insulin-secreting tumor. The behavior of the child led to an investigation of the family. The social work report disclosed strange maternal behaviors, including the mother's expectations that Jonathan should be more independent and take care of her. Later the mother was discovered injecting insulin into the child. Jonathan was removed from the home and put up for adoption.

■ Perspective on the Disorders

Psychiatry and family therapy have been extremely underutilized thus far in treating these disorders. Therapists must attempt to demonstrate expertise and tolerance and a model of intervention that can be used by the primary care providers who bear the brunt of assessment and treatment.

Factitious disorders (also known as Munchausen syndrome) are often embedded within family contexts and may be associated with seriously unhappy marriages and multigenerational patterns of cruelty and abuse. The underlying individual psychopathology of the patient with Munchausen syndrome is severe and usually contrasts with the seemingly normal presentations of many of these patients when they are first seen by medical professionals. Factitious disorder by proxy (also called Munchausen syndrome by proxy) is by definition a family disorder and is my main focus in this chapter. Factitious disorder by proxy is a form of child abuse in which medical symptoms and actual disease are induced. Almost all abusers are mothers; the father is usually distant. More than half of the abusing mothers have a factitious disorder themselves—and, incidentally, about half are nurses (Meadow 1982). Occasionally, illnesses are induced in elderly people by other adults (Smith and Ardern 1989).

The need for medical professionals to be acutely aware of these disorders is emphasized by their potentially serious collusion if the problem is not discovered. Medical helpers participate in factitious disorders when they perform excessive tests and procedures, becoming inadvertent agents of the self-mutilation aspect of the disorders (Zitelli et al. 1987).

Although factitious disorders are not as rare as was once thought, the field of family therapy of these disorders is in its infancy (Rosenberg 1987). The literature of factitious disorders and factitious disorder by proxy is sizable and almost completely descriptive. At this time, there is no consistently useful way to understand these bizarre syndromes. My introductory multidimensional look at the disorders offers a small step toward better understanding.

In this chapter, I focus on several factors associated with the development of factitious disorder or factitious disorder by proxy: an individual with an intrapsychic need to be in the sick role, usually finding support and gratification from contact with medical professionals; a family system that overemphasizes physical health and is overconcerned with physical symptoms; and a multigenerational pattern of child abuse (Griffith 1988).

Table 10–1 summarizes some aspects of the family context of these disorders, which is described in more detail in the next section.

■ Connections of the Symptoms to the System

■ Effects of the Disorder on the Family

In adult factitious disorder, the family is concerned about the severity of physical symptoms, the dramatic medical stories, and the fear that the individual will die. After many failed treatment attempts, the family becomes increasingly enraged at the individual. Many families then report intense guilt for having been so angry at a person who is so ill. Soon this guilt is again followed by anger as the person continues to be difficult and stays ill.

Families are often angry at the medical profession for not properly diagnosing and finding the physical problem. This anger can be fueled

Table 10–1.	Factitious disorders in context

Effects of the disorder on the family

- Concern over severity of physical symptoms; confrontational approach to medical professionals; rage at individual for not complying with treatment; guilt
- Family organizes around illness, symptoms, and the search for medical help

Family maintenance of the symptoms

- In factitious disorder by proxy, child's illness maintained by physical assaults on the child's body
- Existing personality disorders seen as contributing toward maintenance of factitious disorders
- Family defends actions of mother
- Can occur in two people in same family
- Existing factitious disorder or severe somatoform disorder may interact with specific family system type that predisposes to child abuse

Functions of the symptoms within the family

- Disorder forces attention to distressed child and floundering, needy family
- Demands of dealing with illness keeps family together
- Response to illness appeals to desire to give nurturance

Adverse consequences of change

- Complexity of underlying problems means extensive treatment and psychosocial support needed; lack of availability
- Addressing problems only partially seen as more dangerous than no intervention at all
- Significant increase of family stress with diagnosis or events surrounding discovered abuse of child
- Dangers of hospitalization for child; evoking of mother's pathological behavior
- Seeking of care elsewhere under aliases

by the individual's endless distorted or blatantly fabricated stories of medical disasters and mistakes. After the disclosure and confrontation of the factitious disorder, the family may show confusion ("I can't make sense out of such a thing. How could a person do that?"), anger ("What are you trying to pull?"), and impulsive denial ("Let's get out of here and get you to a hospital that helps people."). Some families move through this phase of disbelief and denial and then turn on the index person with blame, disgust, confusion, and rage over the vast deceptions and betrayals of trust.

In factitious disorder, the family may give attention to the index person only when he or she is ill; therefore, the "need" to have disease becomes a compulsive, addictive search for nurturance, parental love, and admiration. Great sacrifices can be made for such "fixes" of attention. The disorder brings the family into a pattern of organization around illness, symptoms, and the search for medical help.

■ Family Maintenance of the Symptoms

In factitious disorder by proxy, there is no subtlety in the family maintenance of the symptoms. Illness in the child is maintained by physical assaults on the child's body.

Observers of both factitious disorder and factitious disorder by proxy often note the predominance of personality disorders in these individuals. The presence of untreated personality disorders contributes toward maintaining the factitious disorders. Symbiotic ties between mother and child become visible over time and are noted repeatedly (Meadow 1982; Waller 1983). Both mother and child are uneasy about even moments of separation.

Fathers usually believe the stories of abusing mothers, no matter what evidence is presented. To helpers, this denial appears to be either an inability to grasp the effects of such bizarre behaviors on the children or a pathological need of the system to hold on to overt symptoms: "Munchausen syndrome by proxy (FDP [factitious disorder by proxy]), in at least a significant number of cases, is a disorder maintained by the family system as a whole rather than by the autonomous behavior of a perpetrating parent" (Griffith 1988, p. 433).

At least one instance of factitious disorder occurring in the same form in two family members, a mother and daughter who presented with almost identical neurological symptoms, has been reported. Their secretiveness led to further investigation, and it was later discovered that each person had elaborate histories of hundreds of workups (Janofsky 1986).

Factitious disorder by proxy develops when a mother's own factitious disorder or severe somatoform disorder interacts with the family system type that predisposes to child abuse: diffuse boundaries, sense of parental entitlement, lack of empathy with and inability to understand the child's developmental needs, authoritarianism, social isolation, poor parental nurturing ability emanating from the parent's own history of physical abuse as a child (Griffith 1988; Krener and Adelman 1988; Leeder 1990), and intolerance of the dependency of children. In general, these families tend to value autonomy and independence and may encourage premature separation of the child before he or she is biologically and psychologically ready.

Functions of the Symptoms Within the Family

Such dramatic symptoms draw attention to a distressed child and a floundering, needy family. This attention can partially correct the family's extremely negative self-image by enhancing their sense of importance. The helping system that is mobilized can also offer the possibility that the mysterious functioning of the family will be deciphered and unmasked. The family as a whole may then gain access to help, emotional support, and therapy. In this way, symptom presentation can help prevent or mitigate future child abuse.

Symptoms function to restrain family change. In one case, the child's hospitalizations occurred predictably after a parental blowup in which father would leave, and the couple would have to reunite to deal with the child's life-threatening illness together. In another case, the abusive mother reflected on how her relationship with her own parents had always focused on discussions of medical issues and had been cold and silent otherwise. This pattern continued into the next generation, and she related how her parents were part of her life only when her child was sick (Rosenberg 1987).

Responding to the symptoms may provide a way for the family to offer nurturance, which otherwise is denied to the child. A family that has suffered a loss that seems too devastating to face directly may also become absorbed in the drama of one member's illness and hence be distracted from the unresolved grief.

Adverse Consequences of Change

Identification and confrontation offer hope for change, especially if a multimodal approach that includes the family is offered. However, the underlying problems are so complex that extensive treatment and psychosocial support must be mobilized. Such services are no longer available in most areas, and addressing these problems only partially may be more dangerous than no intervention at all.

The initial diagnosis of factitious disorder or factitious disorder by proxy greatly increases family stress. In factitious disorder, the family is disrupted by the trauma of the diagnosis and is in confusion and crisis. In factitious disorder by proxy, the family loses its familiar focus on illness and hospitals and must become preoccupied with arrest, court charges, and concern about losing custody of a child.

Many children are placed in foster care, which may or may not be an improvement for the child, and partial treatment will be offered. Hospitalizing children with an uninformed treatment team may make the situation worse because the hospital setting can readily evoke the mother's pathological behavior. In one study, 70% of children's induced illness was produced in the hospital. In the same study, two children died at the hands of parents *after* parents had been confronted with the diagnosis of factitious disorder by proxy (Libow and Schreier 1986). This is not to say that treatment should not be sought, only that these possible consequences must be considered.

The unmasking of factitious behaviors in one facility can lead to increased desperation and a search for other medical facilities, where care is sought under aliases. The humiliation of the confrontation can increase the impulse for anxiety relief and attention, which may lead to an increase in self-inflicted or child-induced illness in the pursuit of more surgeries and invasive procedures.

◼ Special Systemic Dimensions

◼ Gender

In factitious disorder by proxy, mothers have been repeatedly observed and described as psychiatrically ill, yet they have the vast proportion of parenting responsibility. Women are the dominant members of these families, a reversal of stereotypical gender roles. The absent, peripheral father role is assumed or condoned, which overwhelms the mother's limited coping abilities. Perhaps physicians and other medical professionals who are mobilized in providing care assume the roles of the woman's absent husband and her own nonnurturant parents (Griffith 1988).

The syndrome of factitious disorder by proxy could be viewed as a tragic caricature, taking to the extreme the socialized expectation that women focus on their children's welfare. The disorder is a distorted, angry attempt to maintain self-esteem, validation, and power as a caretaker.

■ Intimacy

Using these disorders to regulate intimacy in conflictual marriages is repeatedly observed (Meadow 1982; Mehl et al. 1990; Nichol and Eccles 1985). The intense poverty of relational life and the presence of serious psychiatric problems can lead to desperate, disturbed attempts to fill the void.

> A desperate woman finds that the child's medical problems provide her only way to get close to her husband.

> A lonely man with limited skills and intelligence finds that his illness provides his only vehicle for human contact, as the nice doctors and nurses try so hard to find out what's wrong with him.

> Another woman finds that her own childhood abuse renders her unable to trust or get close to anyone except her 18-month-old son, who must be with her at all times. She is threatened by his developing autonomy and finds herself having strange and very strong wishes that he were ill. She could then care for him constantly and feel meaningfully employed and distracted from her isolation.

■ Loyalty

The person with a factitious disorder often comes from a closed, secretive, abusive family. Thick walls separate the family from the outside world. Asking for help from strangers is often taboo, with the notable exception of seeking medical care from doctors. The individual tries to respect these family laws by channeling all requests for help into the search for more and more medical care. This tactic may be the only sanctioned way of exposing family problems to outside awareness and possible intervention.

In factitious disorder by proxy, parent-child loyalties are discerned everywhere. The parent-child symbiosis itself is a form of loyalty. The child "agrees" to stay tied closely to the mother and in this way may help distract the mother from her own emotional pain and loneliness.

Observers often comment on how these children are trying to help the parent deal with his or her problems. In a way, these children "offer" their bodies as instruments of expression of the parental pain, inability to cope, and sense of being sick. Older children show further loyalty by denying the circumstances and protecting the person with factitious disorder by proxy; they will not disclose or speak about the abuse.

■ Map of Emotions

Pathological as they may be, factitious behaviors may translate emotionally as desperate attempts to avoid the powerlessness of the individual's life and the poverty of relationships. In factitious disorder by proxy, the mothers cannot face loneliness, ambivalence, rage, and shame. The disorder represents an extreme unconscious denial of intense affects on a scale that is difficult to comprehend.

■ Countertransference

Deliberate self-mutilation followed by elaborate lies to fool medical professionals is likely to stimulate the clinician's revulsion, confusion, and loss of objectivity. Anger and disgust will make it impossible for the therapist to achieve the perspective necessary to offer psychiatric help to the family.

Factitious disorder by proxy creates even stronger negative emotions in the therapist. The therapist can become enraged at the idea of the suffering of innocent children. It is especially difficult to accommodate the awareness that the therapist and medical practitioners are likely to have been inadvertent accomplices in the abuse.

The therapist is likely to experience more confusion and conflict, however, when faced with the knowledge that the "easy" way out (complete rejection of the offending parent) is not always in the child's best interest. Someone must try to stay involved with the parents as a means of offering help, especially because so many of the abused children are eventually returned home.

Conversely, some therapists who work individually with persons with factitious disorder by proxy become so drawn into the person's own victimizations that they lose sight of the agony of the victims. This serious drawback is inherent in a therapy that focuses on an individual and does not take the family context into account.

◼ Posterity

The best interests of the child may be served by assuming a seemingly adversarial stance with the parental abusers. Reporting of child abuse to public agencies and even breaking up a family through removal of the child may seem antithetical to family therapists, but this course may prove the best possible intervention for the child.

In other cases, the needs of children are best served by attempts to understand the family at a deeper level. The therapist searches for opportunities to intervene, to meet the needs of the desperate mother, and to preserve the child's family.

◼ Treatment

◼ Standard Individual Therapies

Persons with factitious disorder are notoriously difficult to treat individually. They reject the diagnosis when confronted, hold desperately to the sick role, and insist that the symptoms are medical. Psychiatric attention alone does not usually gratify enough, and the patient seems relentlessly dedicated to continued testing and medical or surgical procedures.

One of the most important parts of treatment may be making the diagnosis. Even if definitive help is refused or scorned, the awareness of the diagnosis by the medical team reduces the chance of harm from procedures and alerts the staff to other problems, such as child abuse. The core mystery is the strong need to be in the sick role, even if it means being harmed in the process. Some patients can be engaged in a psychotherapy that slowly works on such processes.

In treating these disorders, the team must wrestle with the ethical and legal dilemma of using surveillance and hidden cameras. They must be prepared to confront certain patients and parents with the diagnosis. In factitious disorder by proxy, the team must be ready to work with court-mandated treatment and actions aimed at protecting the child.

Court-mandated individual therapies offer one of the best options but are often characterized by the person's extreme resistance to self-disclosure and treatment in general.

■ Family Modalities

Denial by the individual and family is usually direct and absolute: "There must be some mistake. I would never do such a thing." After confrontation, responses like these have been heard: "I will never do this again. Just give me a second chance. I want my child back. I did it to protect the child from his father. If I hadn't found a way to get my baby into a hospital, her father would have kidnapped her. You must recommend to the court that the child be returned to me."

In factitious disorder by proxy, early questions involve the role of the legal system and the need to stop the abuse and save the child's life. A decision must be made regarding the return of the child to the family. The focus must be on stopping the abuse, not necessarily on separating family members. If the mother can prove she has changed and will no longer abuse her child and has learned new ways to deal with emotions, and if other family members agree to work as observers and helpers to avoid more trouble, the court can lean toward return of the child to the family.

In treating the individual with factitious disorder or factitious disorder by proxy, it is necessary to search for others who could become involved, be informed, and serve as potential resources. Family-of-origin assessment must consider possible multigenerational dimensions of the abuse. It is important to know if the mother's parents are currently abusive to her. The mother may not be able to stop abusing her child as long as she is being abused, and court placement could inadvertently be made with the abusive grandparents unless these data are obtained from an extended family assessment.

It is essential to involve the husband. The main goals are to explore hidden resources in the relationship that can help support the mother, to give the therapist another ally in halting the abuse, and to emotionally reengage the father in parenting and family life. Another goal is to reduce the oversimplified blaming of the mother while helping all family members accept their responsibility and accountability.

Confrontation, support, and protection are central to treating these disorders. In some cases of factitious disorder by proxy, it is extremely important and also extremely difficult for the hospital staff to block parental visits temporarily to see if the medical symptoms stop. The first step is to frame the blocking of visits as doctor's orders: "This family needs a short break." If this request is insufficient, some pediatricians have moved to court-ordered blocks (Meadow 1985).

■ Psychoeducation

Because individuals with factitious disorder have no interest in educational information about the disorder, the therapist focuses on education of the family. The approach to the family can include some explanation of the phenomena and the need to protect the patient or child from further mutilation. If someone in the family cannot stop the inducing of disease and the invasive procedures, an external agency will stop it.

Because others may be involved in the abuse, careful assessment must precede psychoeducation. Once evidence has been found, firm, direct confrontation has the best chance of saving the child's life (Meadow 1982). The mother should be confronted alone, because a family meeting will raise anger and defensiveness (Meadow 1985).

In some cases of factitious disorder, the education of other medical professionals in the community is as important as family education. This effort is likely to be effective in mitigating participation in the damage.

■ New Stories

The good mother. In the first phase of treating factitious disorder by proxy, the therapist has the nearly impossible job of becoming the ally of someone who considers therapy an enemy threatening to crash through denial into a world of abuses and bizarre acts. Therapeutic conversations cannot be limited to confrontation and moral lectures; they must also look for and recognize positive parental intentions. The therapist works with the assumption that most of these parents in some way want what is good for their children.

During the early phase, this assumption offers more than an alternative to the attribution of purely evil intent. Beginning with a search for the exception to the rule of abuse works on several fronts. It counterprojects the blame and disdain that the parent is expecting once the behaviors have been unmasked. This counterprojection leaves the parent a bit confused, which is a useful opening for change. It allows the possibility of an alliance, or at least raises the probability of alliance from near zero to something a little higher. This approach may make it possible for the family intervention to build upon the healthy "exception" rather than exclusively on the depths of the pathology.

These comments can be offered:

> "Tell me about all the ways you are a good mother to your children."
> "It sounds to me as if you spent a lot of time and energy thinking about what's best for your children."
> "So you have worked hard to not abuse your children as much as you were abused."

With this approach, any healthy resources that are present in the family system can be mobilized early. Later therapy can include more about the historical roots and deeper problems in the family.

Intervention in the cycle. In treating factitious disorder by proxy, it may be possible to focus on intervening in the abuse cycle. Questions such as those that follow may be helpful:

> "Would it be possible for you to stop the cycle of abuse?"
> "Are you the only one who can stop it?"
> "What would it take?"
> "Would you be able to accomplish this even if your own mother or father can't stop abusing you?"

Hypothesizing. If the disorder is hypothesized to balance power in the marital relationship, other ways of balancing need to be discussed. If the person with factitious disorder gains status and influence through the symptoms and medical attention, other ways must be found for him or her to maintain influence without creating illness. If a child is being abused and the father is passive, strengthening the weaker parent may a helpful key to stopping the harmful behaviors of the person with factitious disorder. The father is told that he *must* intervene and that doing nothing is itself an action that causes harm.

To test ideas without direct confrontation at first, the therapist can present the findings as hypotheses rather than certainties. Comments can be introduced in hypothetical ways:

"Certain members of the team got the extreme idea that induced illness is a possibility. How should we respond to such a concern?"

A less negative delivery is sometimes feasible (Rosenberg 1987):

"Even if these ideas are true, there may be medical help for your child."
"We know mothers who have done similar things and have been helped."

Hospital addiction.   The combination of firmness and compassion of the addictions model may be useful as a frame for some families or medical professionals struggling to understand these behaviors. The idea is presented that some behaviors are out of control and can take over a person's life. Analogies to alcoholism, eating disorders, gambling, pyromania, obsessive-compulsive disorder, and so on help make the point and "detoxify" the peculiar nature of the symptoms.

The underlying sense of inadequacy, desperation, and emotional pain can be reflected as common to addictive disorders. The specific underlying addictive behavior is "chosen" based on certain variables. In the case of factitious disorder, this addiction arises out of a family of origin that tended toward somatization, the individual's inherent focus on body and illness, and the sense of reward experienced only through the attention of health care providers.

One essential caution is that the individual must face and accept full responsibility for the behaviors. If this point is not made forcefully, the person will immediately sense an escape and deny responsibility for the "out-of-control" behaviors: "I couldn't help myself, Doc—So now that I admit it, you have to tell the judge to return the child to me."

After removal of the child, parents experience a panic and despair so deep that the possibility of hitting bottom emerges. The admission of powerlessness and recognition of a life out of control can be a turning point.

Adaptations gone awry.   There is a lesson in the normative parental adaptations to the brutal assault of chronic childhood illness. The distortions in parenting style brought about by a child's chronic illness may resemble characteristics associated with families that actually abuse their children. Cooperative parents may become isolated and show extreme concern and rigorous attention to the child's every symptom and body excretion. The therapist makes an effort to look at the possible connection of this illness behavior with the behavior of other parents facing similar stresses.

In families with chronically ill children, parental noncompliance with treatment can be seen as an attempt to adapt to overwhelming stressors. Similarly, it may be that the woman with factitious disorder by proxy can also be seen as knowing she could not survive another day without a break and as orchestrating a careful, minimally dangerous plan to give her a respite from 24-hour care. Then she earns at least some support and sympathy from the treatment team as a parent who saw no choice but to salvage her sanity in an effort to survive (Krener and Adelman 1988).

Genogram.   Sometimes a resource-based approach reveals members of the extended family who are reasonably good nurturers and who are not involved in the abuse. It may be possible to enlist them to help prevent the destruction of the individual and the family. In factitious disorder by proxy, these relatives may be able to provide placement options other than foster care.

A multigenerational history offers a deeper understanding of past family patterns that can suggest possibilities for family intervention. The telling of the stories of three generations of abuse helps others in the family gain a glimpse of possible connections with such disturbed symptoms.

■ Additional Reading

Alexander R: Patient profile: Munchausen's syndrome. Nursing Management 18:59–60, 1987

Asher R: Munchausen's syndrome. Lancet 1:339–341, 1951

Bhugra D: Psychiatric Munchausen's syndrome. Acta Psychiatr Scand 77:497–503, 1988

Chan DA, Salcedo JR, Atkins DM, et al: Munchausen syndrome by proxy: a review and case study. J Pediatr Psychol 11:71–80, 1986

Coons PM, Grier F: Factitious disorder (Munchausen type) involving allegations of ritual satanic abuse: a case report. Dissociation 3:177–178, 1990

Epstein MA, Markowitz RL, Gallo DM, et al: Munchausen syndrome by proxy: considerations in diagnosis and confirmation by video surveillance. Pediatrics 80:220–224, 1987

Goodwin J: Munchausen's syndrome as a dissociative disorder. Dissociation 1:54–60, 1988

Jani S, White M, Rosenberg LA, et al: Munchausen syndrome by proxy. Int J Psychiatry Med 22:343–349, 1992

Jones JG, Butler HL, Hamilton B, et al: Munchausen syndrome by proxy. Child Abuse Negl 10:33–40, 1986

Kass FC: Identification of persons with Munchausen's syndrome: ethical problems. Gen Hosp Psychiatry 7:195–200, 1985

Kaufman KL, Coury D, Pickrel E, et al: Munchausen syndrome by proxy: a survey of professionals' knowledge. Child Abuse Negl 13:141–147, 1989

King BH, Ford CV: Pseudologia fantastica. Acta Psychiatr Scand 77:1–6, 1988

Masterson J, Dunworth R, Williams N: Extreme illness exaggeration in pediatric patients: a variant of Munchausen's by proxy? Am J Orthopsychiatry 58:188–195, 1988

McGuire TL, Feldman KW: Psychologic morbidity of children subjected to Munchausen syndrome by proxy. Pediatrics 83:289–292, 1989

Meadow R: Munchausen syndrome by proxy: the hinterland of child abuse. Lancet 2:343–345, 1977

Pickford E, Buchanan N, McLaughlan S: Case report: Munchausen syndrome by proxy: a family anthology. Med J Aust 148:646–650, 1988

Sadler JZ: Ethical and management considerations in factitious illness: one and the same. Gen Hosp Psychiatry 9:31–36, 1987

Schreier HA: The perversion of mothering: Munchausen by proxy. Bull Menninger Clin 56:421–437, 1992

Schreier HA, Libow JA: Hurting for Love: Munchausen by Proxy Syndrome. New York, Guilford, 1993

■ References

Griffith JL: The family systems of Munchausen syndrome by proxy. Fam Process 27:423–437, 1988

Janofsky JS: Munchausen syndrome in a mother and daughter: an unusual presentation of folie a deux. J Nerv Ment Dis 174:368–370, 1986

Krener P, Adelman R: Parent salvage and parent sabotage in the care of chronically ill children. American Journal of Diseases of Children 142:945–951, 1988

Leeder E: Supermom or child abuser? treatment of the Munchausen mother. Women and Therapy 9:69–88, 1990

Libow JA, Schreier HA: Three forms of factitious illness in children: when is it Munchausen syndrome by proxy? Am J Orthopsychiatry 56:602–611, 1986

Meadow R: Munchausen syndrome by proxy. Arch Dis Child 57:92–98, 1982

Meadow R: Management of Munchausen syndrome by proxy. Arch Dis Child 60:385–393, 1985

Mehl AL, Coble L, Johnson S: Munchausen syndrome by proxy: a family affair. Child Abuse Negl 14:577–585, 1990

Nichol AR, Eccles M: Psychotherapy for Munchausen syndrome by proxy. Arch Dis Child 60:344–348, 1985

Rosenberg DA: Web of deceit: a literature review of Munchausen syndrome by proxy. Child Abuse Negl 11:547–563, 1987

Smith NJ, Ardern MH: "More in sickness than in health": a case study of Munchausen by proxy in the elderly. Journal of Family Therapy 11:321–334, 1989

Waller DA: Obstacles to the treatment of Munchausen by proxy syndrome. Journal of the American Academy of Child Psychiatry 22:80–85, 1983

Zitelli BJ, Seltman MF, Shannon RM: Munchausen's syndrome by proxy and its professional participants. American Journal of Diseases of Children 141:1099–1102, 1987

CHAPTER 11

Dissociative Disorders

Theresa M.

Theresa M., a 40-year-old lawyer, presented with her husband for help with depression and marital problems. She complained that her kind, passive husband was controlling and punishing, though she was also aware that these complaints were exaggerated. She began to get images of her parents, especially her father, abusing each of her siblings but never abusing her.

Theresa asked her siblings about these abusive images. She reported that her siblings were incredulous, wondering how she could have forgotten the frequent beatings inflicted on each of them approximately 30 years earlier. They said that one night the father beat her unconscious, and it was necessary to call the police and an ambulance.

Theresa was amnestic about this event until the conversation with her siblings took place. Her new awareness, horrible as it was, was the turning point of therapy. Projections onto the spouse were withdrawn as they were perceived as trauma based, and the relationship moved toward restoration.

Thomas D.

Thomas D., the 42-year-old husband of a woman with dissociative disorder, said that he did not want to hear any stories of his wife's childhood abuse; he just wanted his wife to get better. If she were a "multiple" (had dissociative identity disorder), then so be it. The only thing he cared about was that he did not want to go to bed with Henry or Sam or any of the male alters.

Bill and Sarah H.

In another couple, the husband, Bill, said that it was valuable for him to see and meet several alters that expressed spontaneously during a marital session. Hearing some of the stories of what Sarah had been subjected to in childhood helped Bill immeasurably in feeling both compassion for what she had gone through and admiration for what she had achieved. He even found it useful, though somewhat painful, to find that alters who were often "out" did not consider themselves married to him and referred to him as "that man." Bill was glad to be relieved of the anger and frustration he had experienced while he and Sarah were both oblivious to the role of childhood trauma in their current dilemmas.

Perspective on the Disorders

Family therapy of dissociative disorders is relatively unexplored territory. The study of these disorders is young, and few therapists are trained in both treating dissociative disorders and practicing family therapy. In addition, the range of issues involved in dissociative disorders is complex, controversial, and frightening. The difficulties include horror over what people can do to each other and confusion associated with memories of childhood abuse recalled by adults.

Individuals may have created abusive situations in their new families, and difficult issues of advocacy and adversarial relationship emerge when the person with dissociative disorder is or may be abusing his or her own children. In spite of these substantial obstacles, issues related to treating dissociative disorders must be addressed. Therapists must grapple with the issues and move toward an integrated systemic approach.

Dissociation that develops in response to trauma can be viewed as a mechanism of survival and psychological hiding. Although these responses are referred to as disorders, it is useful to acknowledge that they have a creatively adaptive dimension. Such responses may be a defense available only to those who have innate neural pathways for dissociation. The ability to dissociate may be seen as a merciful talent or gift for enduring the unendurable, to "leave" when one cannot literally escape.

In discussing dissociative identity disorder, the commonly accepted term of "alter," short for alternate personality, is used to refer to split-off parts of the mind that are experienced as separate states. This concept is useful for many in helping make sense of their mental world, but the idea should not be reified or concretized as more than a description of part of a person's mental functioning. The importance of responsibility for actions is emphasized and cannot be bypassed by saying "an alter made me do it."

Although dissociative disorders are incompletely understood, prevalent clinical and research beliefs associate the disorders with abuse. In this chapter, I emphasize family constellations in which abuse or allegations of abuse are an issue, which is consistent with DSM-IV's (American Psychiatric Association 1994) emphasis on stressful or traumatic events. Posttraumatic stress is discussed further in connection with anxiety disorders (see Chapter 7). Fragmentation or disintegration of self is discussed with personality disorders (see Chapter 17).

Table 11–1 summarizes key aspects of the family context of these disorders, which is discussed in more detail in the next section.

■ Connections of the Symptoms to the System

■ Effects of the Disorder on the Family

Family of origin with alleged abuse.   In many abusive families in which children are developing dissociative processes, life is so chaotic that the child's symptoms are not even noticed. Sometimes the abused person learns to use dissociation in a preemptive adaptive way. The child with dissociative disorder may learn to sense when abuse is coming and allow the part to express that best knows how to cope with or minimize the abuse. The child may retreat to an alter who is quiet, immature, seemingly indifferent, or resisting. This presentation may enrage the abusive person more as he or she interprets the retreat as the child's bad, defiant behavior and feels justified about the cruel treatment.

Table 11–1.   Dissociative disorders in context

Effects of the disorder on the family

- *Family of origin with alleged abuse*
    - Defensive retreat of child angers family further and "justifies" further abuse
    - Concern or confusion over seeing dissociative symptoms in child with no memory of having abused child
    - Need for therapist to look for hidden agendas when child brought for treatment
- *Nonabusive family of origin*
    - Anger, rage, guilt, confusion, disbelief, and sense of betrayal
    - Blame by friends and agencies
    - Denial of abuse
    - Possible eventual ability to face problem
- *Family of procreation: abusive and nonabusive*
    - Need to differentiate between patients with and without abusive spouse
    - Subtle symmetry in relationships of dissociative identity disorder patients and their spouses
    - If both spouses have dissociative identity disorder, need for assessment of violence toward each other or children
    - Perplexity and fear for kind, nonabusive spouse

Family maintenance of the symptoms

- Emotionally fragile, unpredictable family life associated with maintenance of repetitious abuse
- Marriage to abusive spouse ensures continued need for dissociative symptoms
- Children may participate in symptom maintenance by deliberately eliciting certain alters
- Tendency for abused adult to "choose" abusive spouse
- If spouse nonabusive, tendency for projected misidentifications by survivor (e.g., spouse as evil, enraged, dangerous)

Functions of the symptoms within the family

- Adaptation to abusive, almost unbearable events
- Dissociation noticed more by family than by the abused persons

Adverse consequences of change

- Threat of therapy if abuse is continuing
- Family as reluctant to give up alters, who form a kind of family of their own with many pleasurable components

---

Parents may become concerned about the development of dissociation in their children or notice other symptoms such as aggression, depression, bed-wetting, and truancy. These families may present the children for treatment, but there will be hidden agendas; for example, the parent will want the therapist to recognize that abuse may be occurring, that the abusive parent may be dissociative, or that the abusive parent also needs treatment before the children can benefit—or some combination thereof. The parents may ask for help in a way that keeps the secret. They may be vague or reluctant to disclose information and will convey to the children that they must keep the family secret of abuse, even in psychotherapy.

Nonabusive family of origin. Regardless of whether a child is abused by a day-care center worker or by a trusted friend, priest, or neighbor, the family reactions include anger, rage, guilt, confusion, disbelief, and a sense of betrayal. The tendency of friends and agencies to blame the family adds to the rage and difficulty adjusting to the worst of all possible family crises. Denial of the abuse is an understandable defense as the parents gradually accommodate the horror of the news (Finkelhor 1988). Later, the family may pull together to face the problem and will feel empowered again.

Family of procreation: abusive and nonabusive. Patients who have abusive spouses must be distinguished from those who do not. Attempts must be made to stop the abuse if the survivor is again being abused by his or her spouse, but clear resolution of this problem will not be immediate. The reabuse phenomenon is complex, and the patient can be helped to access and use inner resources, including protective alters and adult coping.

Often there is a kind of subtle symmetry in the relationships of individuals with dissociative identity disorder and their spouses. This symmetry is easy to miss because the two people appear to be different on the surface.

> The husband of one woman with dissociative identity disorder had himself suffered from severe family losses and had survived by learning to partially tune out the pain and stimuli. His distance was itself a form of dissociation, and he often did not notice the behaviors and switches of his wife.

> In another couple, the benign, gentle husband of a woman with dissociative identity disorder realized through the couples work that he had taken on an excessively passive role in the family. His passive role left his spouse to struggle with internal states and memories of abuse while she was also expected to be in complete charge of the household. He began to learn to assume clear, active, executive functions within the family.

If two adults with dissociative identity disorder have married, assessment must involve screening for violence. Once the issue of current abuse is considered, the effects on the children of the parents' changeability and strange behaviors can be discussed gradually but openly. Family sequences can be carefully assessed to determine how the children react to different dissociative symptoms. The children of dissociative parents may be experiencing extreme pain and confusion even if they are not being abused. They are exposed to behavioral extremes and have difficulty explaining them.

Many individuals with dissociative disorder marry kind, nonabusing spouses who present with perplexity, fear, and concern; these spouses wish to understand and to receive help in addressing a series of bizarre, unexplainable symptoms. The trials of the nonabusing spouse are characterized by mystery, confusion, chaos, and constant attempts to adjust to changes in mood, personality, reactions, and behavioral age. The rewards of living with a survivor of abuse and of witnessing the human drama of recovery are also real, though not often stated. The opportunity to nurture and to participate actively in the healing process can be rewarding for the patient's spouse (Cohen et al. 1991).

■ Family Maintenance of the Symptoms

Some families of children presenting with dissociative identity disorder have managed to provide a basic ego structure to the child, but this structure has not integrated. These families have been characterized based on clinical findings (Hornstein and Tyson 1991). The parents are emotionally fragile, family life is completely unpredictable, and abuse is repetitive. Boundaries between the members of the family are absent; conflicts often cannot be contained and automatically escalate. The child is often put in a double bind in which he or she is given the illusion of choice: "If you don't stop crying when I threaten you, I'm going to beat you."

There is intense overinvolvement of the parent with the children, which sometimes alternates with inadequate attention to the children's basic needs. Finally, there is intolerance of the child's affective states.

Symptom maintenance into the next generation is directly related to the adult with dissociative identity disorder's formation of new family. For those who go on to marry an abusive spouse, the need to continue the dissociative defense is ensured. The dissociative capacity remains almost as valuable as it was during childhood, and this becomes a major treatment consideration.

Ironically, children may participate in maintaining the symptom.

> One adolescent had a tendency to threaten and provoke his mother, who had dissociative identity disorder. This provocation triggered dissociation, and he could then manipulate her to get what he wanted. He knew that the violent protector alter could be summoned if he made certain threatening gestures, and he would arrange to have this alter attacking him as his father was coming in the door. The adolescent then watched as his father wrestled his mother to the floor.

> Another adolescent learned to elicit the permissive alter when he wanted his mother's car and the nurturant alter when he wanted her to listen to him and take care of him.

In a marriage, the adult survivor of abuse may alternate controlling domination with a childlike, fearful cowering. If the adult survivor is still driven to be abused, the spouse is unconsciously "chosen" for potential abusiveness.

The dynamic does not always involve a dominant, chronically abusive spouse attacking a previously abused spouse. In some couples, the spouse is chosen for gentleness and the ability to control impulses and rage, but the spouse then receives projections of being evil, abusive, enraged, and dangerous. These attributions can lead to projective identification scenes in which the adult with dissociative identity disorder badgers and insults the spouse until he or she begins to exhibit some of the behaviors most feared in the first place.

■ Functions of the Symptoms Within the Family

Dissociative symptoms develop as an adaptation to abusive, almost unbearable events. As long as the abuse continues, the dissociation manifests frequently to help the person with dissociative identity disorder survive the trauma. The symptom of dissociation persists even after its protective function fades (e.g., when the abuse stops).

For some adults, dissociation is noticed more by their family than by the index person. Later in life, with increased awareness and contact with other people, these index persons perceive differences between them and other people. The index person realizes that others have a sense of time that is continuous rather than discontinuous. They also note different, more positive, less fearful attitudes and behavior involving men, sex, violence, and children.

Adverse Consequences of Change

Removal of dissociative symptoms by a well-meaning therapist is contraindicated in children and adults who are currently being abused. The person's emotional system is using dissociative defenses as an essential mode of adaptation and survival. These defenses cannot be tampered with until relative safety can be ensured.

The chaos of dissociative switching in a family brings an understandably desperate need for relief, but the family may also be reluctant to give up the alters, who form a kind of family of their own with many pleasurable components. Children may get used to permissive, playful child alters and fear that the loss of these alters will leave an exclusively rigid, disciplinarian parent. Spouses may be reluctant to give up the "sexy alters." One husband sheepishly shared that he would really miss "the kids" and had learned to enjoy "playing" with them.

Special Systemic Dimensions

Family History and Genetics

The capacity of the mind to use dissociation to survive intolerable situations is influenced by neural connections that are themselves partially inherited and present at birth.

Abuse itself has a genetic dimension that expresses through constitutional factors. These factors include a deficit in the capacity to control impulses, a tendency toward aggression, and high sensitivity to rejection. These characteristics tend to be passed on from generation to generation, adding a biological tendency toward abuse. This biological inheritance adds to the effect of environmental factors, sharply increasing the likelihood that abused children will grow up to be abusive adults.

■ Gender

The main gender dimension relates to societal sanction of abuse of women, beginning in the commonness of physical and sexual exploitation of young girls. A related gender issue is the frequency with which males are taught aggression as an acceptable mode of behavior and coping.

Moreover, the abuse of boys by both male and female caretakers is common and may have hidden effects. The results of abuse in the mature man are often disguised by the person's alcoholism, sociopathic behaviors, or societally sanctioned aggression.

■ Intimacy

The core components of intimacy include give-and-take, trust, vulnerability, self-disclosure, wholeness, and being present and genuinely concerned for the other. The person who dissociates faces difficulties in finding a balance of power and influence that allows for the give-and-take of an intimate relationship.

Bob and Beth R.

In one couple, the wife, Beth, had clearly documented dissociative identity disorder. Her husband, Bob, was generally calm and accepting, qualities that Beth interpreted during dissociative periods as quiet rage that would soon explode—as her father's rage had in the past. She was so anxious about this expected outcome that she would insult Bob relentlessly until he lost his temper and stormed out of the house. Beth then felt that her fears had been confirmed, but she also felt abandoned.

Fred and Ruth T.

In another couple, Fred, the husband, had been abused as a child and had dissociative identity disorder. Ruth, his wife, was extremely anxious and probably agoraphobic. The T.'s were involved in a behavioral cycle in which Ruth's nervous style led her to overcontrol all the details of their lives. This behavior made Fred feel small and inadequate, and he sometimes became quietly withdrawn or depressed. At other times, he experienced her as his abusive mother and exploded in rage, though not with physical abuse. In either scenario, Ruth feared that Fred was incompetent and disturbed, and she became even more controlling.

Sam and Gina M.

Sam M., a 34-year-old accountant, was the survivor of brutal childhood abuse and was flooded with posttraumatic memories. He was unable to function at his work and was on psychiatric disability for a year after a hospitalization. During that year, his wife, Gina, became the couple's sole financial support. Resentment over this responsibility and over his tendency to "go away" or "space out" destroyed her sense of the intimate relationship that they each said had characterized their early years together.

The couple entered into sequences of mutual provocation, each believing themselves to be with a partner who was "using and abusing" them. This behavior continued until one person exploded with anger and left the house. During these times of separation, Sam and Gina "courted." They saw each other in positive ways and reexperienced intimate moments. Therapy helped bring these complicated sequences into awareness so they could be controlled.

In most individuals with dissociative disorder, trust has been so fundamentally betrayed in childhood that adult capacity to trust others is understandably damaged. The ability to be vulnerable and the willingness to self-disclose are naturally curtailed in an emotional system oriented to hiding and blocking out to ensure survival. The ability to be present is at odds with the dissociative tendency to "go away." The willingness to be genuinely concerned for another is at odds with self-protective vigilance.

With these formidable obstacles, the mystery is not why conflicts occur but why some survivors can have close (though complicated) interpersonal relations. One factor is the intense yearning to be trusting and caring, to heal the wounds. These patients are often highly motivated to sort out how much of their hostility toward the spouse is a projective or a trauma process. The person with dissociative disorder is also grateful for the spouse who does not abuse.

■ Loyalty

Fascinating and illuminating family loyalty dimensions can occur with these disorders. Seemingly mystifying phenomena include intense resistance to therapy by the child or adult with dissociative disorder, the denial of the history or severity of abuse, and an unwillingness even to describe dissociative symptoms out of fear that they will be related to past abuse.

This behavior begins to make sense when the loyalty dimension is considered. Abuse may change the nature of loyalty expression, but it does not diminish and may greatly intensify the child's loyalty to the parent. Children who have been abused will go to tremendous lengths to protect their abusing parents. The prominent symptom of amnesia functions at least in part to protect parents from painful realities or consequences of their behavior.

Abusive persons with dissociative disorder are likely to have been abused as children. Continuing this behavior in their own families is in part a way to express loyalty to their parents by imitating them. In effect, the person joins the parents in a way that absolves them and prevents negative judgments. The continuing abuse and forgetting thus form a kind of multigenerational bond.

■ Map of Emotions

Therapy can increase fear, shame, guilt, rage, denial, and sadness. Shame, guilt, and continued fear may provide the energy needed to keep memories hidden away. Shame derives from the nature of the abuse, which convinces the abused person on some level that he or she deserved abusive treatment because of dirtiness, seductive powers, inadequacy, and "badness." Guilt acquires power from the sense of having done bad things that no one must ever discover.

Fear is associated with the thought of retribution for telling a forbidden story and with the expected loss of control if all affects are experienced. The rage that appears during contact with dissociated aspects of self is part of a painful and unpleasant experience. Sadness may appear later, as the individual and family grieve for the illusion of normalcy in their past family life. Sadness can also give way to a new sense of freedom as the family gives up the illusion of their images of the past.

■ Countertransference

The main countertransference issue is vicarious or secondary posttraumatic stress disorder (PTSD). The therapist who must listen to stories of outrageous abuse is prone to become dazed and to experience intrusive pictures, images, impulses, and fear. Some therapists are particularly prone to becoming perturbed and dysfunctional if their own unhealed traumas are triggered and reexperienced.

Family therapists are taught to see the family as the organizing societal unit and as the main source of nurturance and resources for children and to see themselves as advocates of families and family life. Those therapists who find themselves working with the most severely abused adults are at risk to become disillusioned with these ideas and commit the logical error of *pars pro toto*.

Family therapy supervisors and teachers can help trainees who are floundering accommodate these experiences and readjust their world view in a way that does not destroy their ability to be agents of relational change. The limits of positive reframing and connotation must be faced. Only then might it be possible to integrate the dark side of human nature with the existence of positive resources in families.

■ Treatment

■ Standard Individual Therapies

The standard therapies for dissociative disorders include long-term individual psychotherapy, case management, crisis management, hospitalization, and psychopharmacology.

There is little role yet for psychopharmacological treatment of the core dissociative process (for which the treatment is psychotherapy), but some benefit can be gained by treating ancillary symptoms (Loewenstein 1991). Few double-blind studies are available to guide the clinician here. Clinical results suggest that posttraumatic stress symptoms may be helped by clonazepam, hyperarousal and disorganized thinking by propranolol or clonidine, and impulsivity (as in addictive self-mutilation) by naltrexone.

■ Family Modalities

In the treatment of dissociative disorders, family therapy is generally an adjunctive modality used with the primary mode of intensive individual therapy. This adjunctive use recognizes that healthy family support can reduce the length and difficulty of therapy, but also acknowledges that dissociative disorders do not remit even if the family becomes stable and nurturing and stops the abuse.

The patient, spouse, and therapist can work in conjoint session on strategies for behavioral limit setting regarding violence, suicidal threats, age regressions, flashbacks, or other problematic situations that threaten both therapy and the family. Hospitalization decisions are usually conjoint, as consensus among family members allows the hospital to be viewed more as a place of help rather than of control. Sessions can be used to plan for contingencies, such as when to hospitalize or call the individual therapist and how to pay for treatment or provide emotional support.

The individual therapist will be much more effective if he or she considers systemic forces such as lifelong loyalty dilemmas of survivors and issues of ongoing relationships with the abusers, accomplices, and witnesses.

Child with dissociative disorder.   If the child is currently being traumatized, the first intervention of any family therapy is to end the trauma. If this effort is unsuccessful, the therapist may have to end the treatment or take on a strong advocacy role that might involve child protective agencies and social services.

Parent with dissociative disorder.   If the index person is a parent, the first step is to assess how the children have been affected. Information can then be provided about dissociation and ways to relate better with the dissociative parent. The family may strongly resist efforts to discuss family events. Even if abuse has occurred, children are reluctant to incriminate their only caregiver. They may have been threatened with consequences if they tell strangers about personality changes and lapses in the parent. Younger children also may not be aware that their family life is not normal or acceptable.

An unhelpful cycle of accusation and denial of abuse of their children keeps many families from progressing in therapy. Some families express a wish for help in changing their abusive behavior, and then further structural work and healing conversations can begin. The therapist must be clear about the goals of treatment as well as persistent and gentle to move families along these dimensions. He or she must also have the courage to hold conjoint meetings of the parent with the children and spouse when needed—and, alternatively, the ability to sense when such meetings will only bring more pain.

The dissociative parent may be seen as fragile and delicate by members of the family and outside helpers, and the therapist is prone to being labeled as another abuser. The therapist must be respectful but yet firm in the belief that the children deserve information appropriate to their age and the opportunity to understand the diagnosis and the bizarre behavior they have witnessed.

In most cases, even the diagnosis of dissociative identity disorder will not be as difficult as the scenes to which the children have already been exposed. In addition, family sessions allow for the possibility of dialogue between parent and child and for the possible perception of the parent as having an illness, rather than as simply being hateful. The parent may be seen as not wishing to abuse but unable to control the impulse. The child may see that the abuse received was less than what the parent received in the last generation. Most importantly, the abusing parent has a chance to begin to make amends for injustices already committed.

Initial presentation of "marital problem."   Therapists who work with couples often report complexly disguised childhood abuse (Nadelson and Polonsky 1991). A couple may complain about a lack of closeness, intimacy, and sexuality, or one person may complain that the other spouse is distant, explosive, or hard to reason with. The couple may already be facing the end of their marriage, with both members already talking to divorce lawyers.

For some couples, change can take place only after an underlying dissociative disorder in one partner is treated. The story often begins when one person reluctantly shares that he or she has been having intrusive images of childhood abuse. A useful therapeutic stance is to remain neutral about the disclosures, be open to considering abuse and dissociation as one of several possibilities, raise the issue of corroboration, and allow treatment to continue with minimal therapist suggestion.

The difficulty assessing the reliability of these memories brings painful dilemmas with no definitive answers. Should the couple allow babysitting by the family members who appear in the intrusive images? A difficult judgment must be made that attempts to ensure the children's safety but also avoids false assumptions or accusations that may result in the unnecessary destruction of family relationships.

In those cases where abuse is admitted or confirmed, the couple realizes they have been struggling with a hidden enemy. This experience can allow the spouses to question their mutual attributions, and many couples can reconstruct the reality of their relationship. A husband may begin to understand his wife's response to sexuality in a completely different way. If she has resisted sexuality or gone into a trancelike state at bedtime, he may have taken this behavior personally and become increasingly hostile over the sexual and personal rejection.

The new reality may allow the spouse to move rapidly from retaliatory anger to compassion and sadness. Practical suggestions for day-to-day relating may be useful. The survivor should be the one to take the lead in regulating distance or disclosing intimate feelings. Sexual expression with the bedroom light on may decrease identity confusion.

The hopefulness of the new awareness sometimes fades as the spouse begins to realize that a better understanding of the issues does not change the reality of the seemingly endless psychotherapy that is often recommended or the interpersonal distance that prevails in the meantime. The therapist has a long struggle to keep the couple working and realistically hopeful while also helping them face those areas over which they are powerless. Disclosure, therefore, is just the beginning of a couple's long process of healing.

How much should the dissociative person's spouse be involved in the treatment? If the spouse is underinvolved in the treatment and hears little of the partner's abuse history, there is no opportunity for the spouse to understand what has been going on with his or her partner all these years. If the spouse is included too much and hears too many of the stories, a secondary posttraumatic stress syndrome may develop. The spouse then becomes numb and begins to detach and distance.

The therapist performs a delicate balancing act between the two extremes of spousal involvement. The couple can be asked how they feel about either sharing or hearing the stories. It may be useful to ask abused spouses how comfortable they feel in sharing these stories with their partners. It may likewise be helpful to ask nonabused spouses how much they think they can absorb before getting too upset by their partners' memories.

Psychoeducation

If it is possible to stop the abuse of a child with dissociative identity disorder, the next phase focuses on helping the family to become more consistent and nurturant and to communicate without using abusive behavior. Boundaries are strengthened. Stating clear rules and decreasing triangulation of the child (e.g., refraining from pulling the child into marital battles) become essential. The goal is to establish a parental authority that is as fair and nonabusive as is humanly possible.

If a parent is dissociative, the spouse and children may need educational information. Children are helped to see that they are not to blame for the strange and frightening behaviors of the parent. This knowledge alone can reduce a child's sense of badness.

Further information on living with the affected parent involves identifying family stressors that might encourage dissociation. Children can learn that certain noises, gestures, and comments are triggers for the parent and that stopping them is one way to offer help to the family. If the therapy involves work with alters, then the contract with the affected parent can specify that only the good parental alters or behaviors are permissible when the children are present.

A psychoeducational approach with the nonabused spouse informs about dissociation and childhood trauma. In some cases, an explanation of the phenomenology of the spouse's personality alters may help. The spouse may need support in dealing with the perturbations and emotions evoked in the treatment, especially after particularly cathartic sessions.

Spouses of those with dissociative identity disorders benefit from participation in self-help or therapist-led groups. The spouses can learn from and support each other as they negotiate the difficult problems and choices associated with the disorder. Certain readings (Cohen et al. 1991) offer perspective and knowledge to the spouse who cannot imagine that anyone else could have experienced a life like his or hers. The essential need for therapists to include the spouses in therapy in some way is emphasized most strongly by the survivors themselves.

◼ New Stories

Reauthoring relationships. The adult survivor may retain an image of him- or herself as a helpless child prone to being abused at the whim of an out-of-control, threatening parent. Therapeutic conversations, whether involving just the individual, a couple, or the whole family, can be used to reflect the person's power, influence, control, and choices. Direct questions are asked about any positive successes, relationships, and feelings. These positive changes can be discussed as part of a continuing protest and victory over the forces of oppression, injustice, and unfairness.

Credit for not abusing. The dissociative parent is usually presented as the *patient*, the bad and weird unpredictable person who is blamed for all family misery. Sometimes the children and spouse are unable to think of a single positive attribute of the affected person. Once therapy has revealed to family members the degree of abuse to which the parent was subjected, another way of thinking is possible. For parents who have dissociative symptoms but have not abused their own children, the "bad" parent can be reframed as having done an admirable job in containing the symptom by "just" showing amnesia and never abusing his or her own children. The parent who has been perceived as weak and sick is then given due credit for attempts to stop the multigenerational legacy of abuse.

Amends and healing. The realities, memories, and histories of abuse survivors are by definition obscured by amnesias and confusing, conflicting stories of what life has been like. Family and individual psychotherapies allow for the creation of a consistent reality in which the child was not bad and the past does not completely determine the future. Healing is a possibility, and the legacy of multigenerational abuse can be broken.

   In the midst of the chaos, negativity, and adversity of work with abusive families, the therapist must be alert for opportunities to help the family move toward making amends and healing.

> After years of abusing his child and denying the abuse, one father
> finally asked to be forgiven and promised to do whatever he could
> to repair the damage and earn his child's trust.

> In another case, a daughter withdrew accusations of abuse against her father and asked for his forgiveness.

Both denial and false accusations add to injury and injustice. The sooner the truth emerges, the sooner the family can begin moving toward repair and restoration of relationships. For many, however, the "truth" is never found, partly because a proven methodology for determining the veracity of memories has yet to be developed. In these cases, the cycle of uncertainty, denial, and accusations goes on.

Focus on solutions.   All too often, couples present without resources for more than a very brief therapy, To help these couples, some techniques for brief therapy using future-oriented questions are being developed. Some of these techniques consist of therapeutic questions for spouses of survivors of sexual abuse. These questions focus away from the trauma and toward healing. The therapist may ask a partner to describe signs of healing that he may be observing in his wife and then may ask how he will know that she has healed even a little more. The couple may be asked to consider what they imagine their future relationship will be like after healing begins (Y. Dolan, "Reclaiming the Self" workshop, Baltimore, MD, June 1991; Dolan 1991).

Working with uncertainty.   Work with adult patients who report childhood memories of abuse has become a quagmire for therapists. One difficulty is the legitimate fear of the allegedly abusive family of origin. Initial denial and rage at the index person are soon focused on the therapist, who is seen as the enemy and destroyer of the family for having stirred up dark secrets or for suggesting unfounded memories of abuse.

Therapists may inadvertently over- and underdiagnose abuse because no foolproof guide is available. Some decide to ignore evidence of abuse and dissociation and explain it as hysteria, suggestion, overreaction, or oedipal fantasy wishes for the father. Other therapists see trauma, past abuse, and dissociation everywhere and will find proof in any intense or unusual symptom.

Therapists who are uncomfortable with uncertainty may adopt strong dogmatic views: "If you have these memories, then incest must have occurred," or the equally dogmatic "Major memories are remembered continuously; if you are having new memories now, then you are a victim of the therapist who suggested them to you." Therapists who can accommodate uncertainty will feel the anguish of not being sure of the validity of a patient's memories. One new approach (Barrett and Scott 1994) includes the suggestion of a third reality:

> "Why do you think your child believes these things happened? Is there anything you can take responsibility for that everyone would agree did happen and that might help all of us understand these painful, strange experiences?"

In this new and controversial field, many unanswered questions are prominent. It is difficult to know whether, when, and how to confront abusive families of origin. When is it imprudent to attempt to bring out repressed traumatic memories? When the accusation of abuse is denied, how much confirmation and evidence should the patient be encouraged to uncover (Wylie 1993)? If a mother (or father) realizes in individual therapy that she has abused her children, how does a therapist conduct a session with the mother and her now-adolescent children in which she can explain her behavior and history in a way that is more healing than traumatizing for both her and her children?

Therapists must accommodate these and other unresolved issues as "givens" of consultation and therapy for these difficult disorders.

■ Additional Reading

Busby DM, Glenn E, Steggel GL, et al: Treatment issues for survivors of physical and sexual abuse. Journal of Marital and Family Therapy 19:377–392, 1993

Calof D: Facing the truth about false memory. Family Therapy Networker 17:38–45, 1993

Dell PF, Eisenhower JW: Adolescent multiple personality disorder: a preliminary study of 11 cases. J Am Acad Child Adolesc Psychiatry 29:359–366, 1990

Figley CR: Treating Stress in Families. New York, Brunner/Mazel, 1989

Kluft RP: The parental fitness of mothers with multiple personality disorder: a preliminary study. Child Abuse Negl 11:273–280, 1987

Kluft RP, Braun BG, Sachs R: Multiple personality, intrafamilial abuse, and family psychiatry. Int J Family Psychiatry 5:283–301, 1984

Sachs RG, Frischholz EJ, Wood JI: Marital and family therapy in the
treatment of multiple personality disorder. Journal of Marital and
Family Therapy 14:249–259, 1988

Williams MB: Clinical work with families of MPD patients: assessment
and issues for practice. Dissociation 4:92–98, 1991

Yapko M: The seductions of memory. Family Therapy Networker 17:30–
37, 1993

■ References

American Psychiatric Association: Diagnostic and Statistical Manual of
Mental Disorders, 4th Edition. Washington, DC, American Psychiatric Association, 1994

Barrett MJ, Scott W: Commentary on "avoiding the truth trap": responding to allegations (and denials) of sexual abuse. Family Therapy Networker 18:73–76, 1994

Cohen BM, Giller E, "WL": Multiple Personality From the Inside Out.
Baltimore, MD, Sidran Press, 1991

Dolan Y: Resolving Sexual Abuse: Solution Focused Therapy and Erick-
sonian Hypnosis for Survivors. New York, WW Norton, 1991

Finkelhor D: The sexual abuse of children: current research reviewed.
Psychiatric Annals 17:233–237, 1988

Hornstein NL, Tyson S: Inpatient treatment of children with multiple
personality/dissociative disorders and their families. Psychiatr Clin
North Am 14:631–648, 1991

Loewenstein RJ (ed): Rational psychopharmacology in the treatment
of multiple personality disorders. Psychiatr Clin North Am 14:721–
740, 1991

Nadelson C, Polonsky D: Childhood sexual abuse: the invisible ghost
in couple therapy. Psychiatric Annals 21:479–484, 1991

Wylie MS: The shadow of a doubt. Family Therapy Networker 17:18–
29, 1993

CHAPTER 12

Sleep Disorders

Steve and Christine S.

Steve and Christine S., a separated couple, entered marital therapy as a prerequisite for reuniting. During an early session, they began to talk spontaneously about the meaning of dream sharing:

> Christine: "I enjoy relating dreams. My husband doesn't want to hear about them."

> Steve: "Boring! I can't stand it. I don't remember dreams. I don't know why they fascinate you."

> Christine: "They do because the feelings that I have in real life, whether positive or negative, are intensified in dreams."

> Steve: "Crock!"

> Christine: "Well, that's what they are for me. It's a gift when you get a dream."

The sequence illustrates the underlying schisms in the relationship. Steve's repudiation of Christine's offerings precisely mirrored his need to maintain rigid defensive distance. Her earlier shared dreams had revealed her side of the avoidance of intimacy. During one session several weeks later, a surprising shift occurred: Steve began to cry and expressed sadness over his powerful dependency needs and underlying fears of abandonment. He even began to share his own anxiety dreams.

Calvin and Anne K.

The husband's insomnia was the chief complaint of another couple, Calvin and Anne K. The story unfolded to reveal that Calvin had a major drug addiction and had returned recently from a rehabilitation center. Anne's focus on the sleep problems was the only way she could express her concerns about bigger problems such as how his life was going after rehabilitation and whether their relationship could survive without drugs.

Roberta D.

Roberta, a 36-year-old woman suffering from anxiety and insomnia, was also found to be severely upset over being cut off from her brother. She was coached on how to renew contact with him and on how to define herself in that relationship. As Roberta progressed in this work, her insomnia disappeared.

■ Perspective on the Disorders

Sleep disturbance as a symptom may finally be getting some respect in psychiatric circles. Sleep disorders are important not only because one-third of life may be spent in sleep, but also because sleep is disrupted in almost all psychiatric disorders. Discerning specific patterns of sleep disruption may soon help to reliably distinguish one disorder from another or may lead to a sleep laboratory test to help diagnose certain psychiatric disorders.

Although the abnormalities of sleep patterns in affective disorders have received the most attention (shortened rapid eye movement [REM] latency, decreased slow-wave sleep, less sleep continuity), most other psychiatric disorders also include reduced sleep efficiency, reduced sleep time, and less non-REM sleep (Benca et al. 1992). The relationship of sleep and families is not as well researched. One major text on sleep disorders mentions families only once, in connection with the rare syndrome of fatal familial insomnia (Williams et al. 1988).

In sleep disorders, the family is the observer and reporter and often the complainant. In some ways, sleep disorder is an "observers' disease," especially when the distress of sleep terror and sleepwalking is reported by those who witness the behaviors rather than by those who have the disorder. In some sleep disorders, the bearer of the problem also endures and complains bitterly about the torture of sleepless nights or the inability to stay awake and function during the day.

One field of study that is bound to grow is that of "cosleeping," when family members other than the parents spend the night together. Long-standing controversies about the benefits or negative effects of cosleeping were "resolved" by relatively clear dogmatic psychoanalytical views that such arrangements are overstimulating and conflict producing. This view has merit, but it is being mitigated by many studies showing the widespread prevalence of cosleeping in many cultures with no obvious ill effects (Lozoff et al. 1984; Rosenfeld et al. 1982).

Although cosleeping usually refers to parent-child behaviors, it can be expanded to any sleeping arrangement that includes more than one person. A couple sleeping together certainly does not fit a disorder concept, but can illustrate a connection between the field of sleep and family therapy. How one person's sleep influences that of another is a new field of study (Mendelson 1987). The use of the phrase "sleeping together" to connote sexual intercourse points out implicit connections between sex and sleep that reside in our language and thoughts.

Sleep patterns offer a look into family dynamics and structure, including the family's sense of boundaries, privacy, and closeness. In cases of incest or other abusive violations, sleep patterns offer a glimpse into expressions of violence and hostility. The relationship between attachment and sleep is another area of interest and a topic for future research. For example, sleep disruption is intense at times of bereavement, separation, and divorce. Disruption of a primary relationship may be the single most potent contributor to severe sleep disturbance (Ellis 1991; Kellerman 1981). Interestingly, such interpersonal disruptions are also commonly noted among those with sleep apnea (T. Hobbins, M.D., personal communication, March 1994).

The DSM-IV (American Psychiatric Association 1994) classification formally divides the sleep disorders into dyssomnias (problems of amount, quality, and timing of sleep) and parasomnias (abnormal sleep events without particular problems with daytime arousal).

In DSM-IV, two important new categories are added. The first is *sleep disorders related to another mental condition*. With this diagnosis, the sleep symptoms of common psychiatric syndromes, such as major depression, can be viewed as bona fide diagnoses and problems of focus. The other new category is *secondary sleep disorder due to a nonpsychiatric medical condition,* which highlights the remarkable correlation of sleep problems with medical illnesses.

Table 12–1 summarizes key aspects of the family context of these disorders, which is described in more detail in the next section.

■ Connections of the Symptoms to the System

■ Effects of the Disorder on the Family

Sleep problems might seem to be personal symptoms, but actually the symptoms can be public and interpersonal. The sleeplessness of a newborn infant quickly becomes a family affair for exhausted, irritable

---

Table 12–1.   Sleep disorders in context

Effects of the disorder on the family

- Exhaustion from sleeplessness of others
- New struggles from adolescent biorhythm change
- Anxiety; canceled plans; focus of family on sleep problems
- Hypervigilance; concern over nightmares
- Increased accidents from narcolepsy and hypersomnia
- Deterioration of relationships
- Parasomnia-specific dramatic worries of families

Family maintenance of the symptoms

- Circumstances of the sleep environment, such as shift work and crowding, that disturb normal sleep patterns
- Family misattributions about sleep problems
- Strained family relationships
- Separation from person with whom one is or has been close

Functions of the symptoms within the family

- Attempts of the mind to deal with conflicts and trauma
- Public distress signal
- Distraction from family traumas
- Protection from real or perceived threat
- Dream sharing as offer of unconscious help and deep communication

Adverse consequences of change

- Loss of "productive" time with increased sleep
- Possible loss of intimate relating
- Need to deal directly with trauma

---

parents and siblings. The natural biorhythm of an adolescent shifts to later bedtimes and later rising in the morning. A schedule that includes going to sleep at 2 A.M. and rising at noon may be a sign not so much of rebellion or sloth as of physical changes. Such a schedule leads to the common problem of struggles over curfews and bedtimes and later to sleep deprivation, because school, parents, and various others "conspire" to keep teenagers from getting the sleep they need.

The story continues into adulthood.

> One woman related the interaction of her insomnia with her husband's snoring, which bothered her only when her sleep was also disturbed by her own anxieties. When she couldn't sleep, her husband's anxiety increased as he worried about her. He then woke up hourly, and neither person slept.

In both the parasomnias and the dyssomnias, the entire household feels the effects. If one member's sleep is disturbed by hypersomnia, the family quickly cancels plans and makes excuses. With insomnia, the family is aware of one person's night motions or the light that is on all night. The family becomes increasingly anxious as they become aware of a disturbance in one family member.

Hypervigilance may be one aspect of insomnia in potentially abusive situations. A parent may feel a need to protect throughout the night, or a child may be unable to trust the world enough to let go of watchful waiting.

Psychosocial effects are now part of the standard description of narcolepsy and hypersomnia (Kales et al. 1987; Manfredi and Cadieux 1987). Anxiety may increase with an increase in driving accidents and household accidents. Relationships deteriorate as the family believes that a family member is deliberately feigning sleepiness or is emotionally disturbed, and everyone feels misunderstood.

In apnea syndrome, the spouse usually presents with and identifies the problem and should be considered the expert. He or she spends 6 to 8 hours a night listening to snoring and labored breathing. Both spouses may present with the sequelae of sleep deprivation. The patient suffers from fragmented sleep and headache, and the spouse presents because of difficulties in sleeping through the snoring, gasping and snorting, and body movements and because of the terror of watching as the patient often stops breathing for 10 to 20 seconds at a time.

Parasomnias occur in both children and adults. A child brought in by parents who are upset by his or her sleepwalking behavior will often be wondering what all the fuss is about. Adult parasomnias are usually presented by a concerned spouse. The adult patient may be concerned with misplaced possessions and with items found rearranged on awakening. Sleep terror disorder and nightmares can create a family anxiety syndrome as a child's dramatic awakenings and screams repeatedly wake the rest of the household. Sometimes parents present with an inability to fall asleep because they are anticipating the child's screams. Understandably, parents may become overprotective about overnight activities such as camping and class trips. Because the person with night terrors and sleepwalking is amnestic the next morning, the clinician is completely dependent on the family for the history.

■ Family Maintenance of the Symptoms

Like mealtimes and decision making, sleep can become behaviorally disordered in families. Sleep patterns can provide a window into family life. The family usually forms what could be called the sleep environment, which can include who sleeps with whom, what sleep secrets are held by which family members, and whether and why "transitional objects" are used to accompany sleep.

In sleep disorders, the family can easily misattribute sleep disturbances to hostility or psychiatric problems. As the person realizes the family's misattributions, he or she begins to withdraw or become preoccupied, hurt, fearful, and emotionally restricted. This response confirms for the family that he or she does not like them, and their increased criticism then generates a negative cycle.

In some studies of narcolepsy, family stressors have been identified as contributing to increased symptoms. In a study of identical twins with narcolepsy, one pair was notable in that the condition of one twin improved with time, whereas the condition of the other worsened in association with a bad marital situation. She improved only after a successful remarriage (Mamelak et al. 1979).

Families are economic survival units. In families where one or both parents must work night shifts or rotating shifts, a disorder of the sleep-wake cycle will likely be added to the family's stressors. Poverty may dictate sleeping arrangements that contribute to sleep problems, such as too many siblings in one bed or the necessity of sleeping in the same room with a family member who tosses, kicks, and snores.

Parents can inadvertently condition an infant to demand middle-of-the-night feedings. A father who has spent a long day at work and sees his child only at bedtime may stimulate the baby to have time to relate, thereby unintentionally disrupting sleep onset. The effects of family and interpersonal events on sleep are just beginning to be explored. The interrupted sleep of a child separated from his or her mother and the agitated insomnia of adults after a separation are common and universal clinical observations. Sleep disruption after a disruption of one of a person's primary bonds is particularly evident and is now occasionally the subject of research (Ellis 1991; Kellerman 1981). One study addresses the relationship between REM latency and recovery from divorce-related depression. The findings imply that the psychosocial stressor of divorce may trigger affective disorders in vulnerable individuals with short REM latencies. Short REM latency was also associated with recovery from depression (Cartwright et al. 1991).

> One high-functioning patient with no depressive history or prior sleep problems reported that she was unable to sleep after her separation. She could cope with all aspects of the situation except for the chronic sleep deprivation.

> Another woman presented a similar story of finally extricating herself from a destructive marriage. She had been able to sleep only 3 or 4 hours per night since the separation more than a year earlier. Even with the treatment and remission of depressive symptoms, her nights were spent in endless rumination about being alone.

■ Functions of the Symptoms Within the Family

Sleep terrors are likely to represent organic dysfunction, whereas nightmares are complex and associated with psychological distress. Psychologically, nightmares tend to function like dreams, and both occur during REM sleep. Those who believe that dreams function as ways to work through conflicts also view nightmares as attempts of the mind to deal with conflicts and trauma. The nightmare of one member of a family may signal overwhelming family troubles that the dreamer fears discussing openly. The nightmare becomes a public distress signal that the dreamer is struggling with some sort of personal troubles. The nighttime screams can result in some sharing and problem solving.

Posttraumatic nightmares have a level of meaning that can be tied quite convincingly to current and past family life. In one research series, postcombat posttraumatic nightmares were unmasked as also associated with childhood trauma memories that were even more difficult to face than the recent adult combat trauma (Lansky and Karger 1989). Interpersonally, the nightmare is a sanctioned expression of a high level of distress that is less loaded with shame than the original traumatic memory. The sharing of the nightmare in therapy indicates movement closer to underlying conflicts and memories.

Some insomnia and chronic sleep problems represent hypervigilance in connection with an expected feared event. Current and past abuse victims must stay awake to protect themselves from injury. Patients with dissociative disorders commonly report disordered sleep.

The relationship of the family to dreaming and dream sharing has been reviewed elsewhere (Perlmutter and Babineau 1983). Possible functions of the sharing of dreams between family members include offering unconscious help, sharing information, and communicating on deeper levels. Children may offer dreams as a way to communicate thoughts and feelings that would be treated as unacceptable or disloyal if said directly. Dreams can become a vehicle for opening up blocked family communication (Markowitz et al. 1968).

■ Adverse Consequences of Change

A person who has accommodated insomnia may be ambivalent about successful treatment. Hard-driving types feel as if their wakefulness gets them ahead and worry that a return to normal sleeping may represent a loss of productive time. Some insomniac individuals have the time to read extensively only because of their sleeplessness and may be reluctant to lose the pleasures of the nighttime activities. One person said, "I hate not sleeping. It gets me agitated and I worry about how tired I'll be tomorrow, but you know I like it in a way too. It's my only quiet time and my only chance to be alone."

If communication has been through dream sharing and discussion of nightmares, the resolution of sleep problems can bring a loss of intimate relating. The therapist can convey that amelioration of a sleep disorder does not imply that all focus on family sleep life has to disappear. Dream sharing, for example, is healthy and can be nurtured.

For individuals with nightmares, especially posttraumatic nightmares, some repair work seems to take place during the nightmares through reexperiencing and desensitizing. Sometimes the dreams serve as screens, with the dreamer focusing on the content instead of facing what the dreams represent.

■ Special Systemic Dimensions

■ Family History and Genetics

Much data now support a genetic influence on sleep patterns, including twin studies that demonstrate greater monozygotic than dizygotic concordance (Hori 1986; Webb and Campbell 1983).

Narcolepsy may run in families. It shows both genetic and environmental influences, and the genetic component is thought to contribute to a "threshold of liability" for the disorder (Kessler 1976; Kessler et al. 1974; Leckman and Gershon 1976; Mamelak et al. 1979) This theory has replaced earlier assumptions of clear autosomal dominance (Zarcone 1973).

Sleep aspects such as shortened REM latency in depression are clearly familial (Cartwright et al. 1991; Giles et al. 1987, 1989), and it is possible that this sleep finding may become a laboratory sign of a person's genetic tendency toward depression (Giles et al. 1989).

Other sleep disorders thought to be familial are sleepwalking, night terrors, sleep apnea, and enuresis (American Psychiatric Association 1994; Buchholz 1987).

■ Intimacy

Intimacy issues are exemplified by dream sharing, for example, in the unconscious resonance that occurs when one member of a couple experiences deep affects when hearing the dream of the other. This effect can be seen in those uncanny moments of psychotherapy in which the hidden communications of the dream make it seem that the dreamer actually had the dream for the other.

People may sleep and dream together in complex ways. Two people sleeping together at night are thought by some to represent a kind of "pair bonding." These theories regard cosleeping as a survival instinct of primitive man. Sleeping alone was a state of extreme vulnerability that could be reduced only by bonding and sleeping in groups.

■ Treatment

■ Standard Individual Therapies

Treatment of sleep disorders emphasizes the treatment of any medical or psychiatric disorder diagnosed during the workup. Treatment of the primary sleep problems (the dyssomnias) includes psychotherapy, counseling and education regarding general "sleep hygiene," behavioral therapy, and psychopharmacology. For the insomnias, a benzodiazepine or trazodone is used most commonly (Kales et al. 1982; "The Use of Benzodiazepine Hypnotics" [special issue] 1992). Stimulants are prescribed for narcolepsy, with pemoline and methylphenidate being the most effective.

For breathing-related sleep disorder (apnea), weight loss is important, as are continuous positive airway pressure, oxygen, and surgery. In certain patients, protriptyline is used (Buchholz 1987; Manfredi and Cadieux 1987).

Treatment of the parasomnias includes educating the family about the expected course of the disorder and how to prevent injury. Psychotherapy aims to reduce stress and to develop new ways of coping with conflicts and aggression. Sleepwalking and sleep terrors are sometimes adjunctively treated with benzodiazepines, such as triazolam or flurazepam, to raise the arousal threshold. The tricyclics are also used, although their effectiveness has not been proven.

A formal sleep workup includes a careful clinical history, a physical, and sleep laboratory study. The DSM-IV categories are designed partly to ensure that psychiatrists can understand and use them, and also to mitigate against a complete dependence on sleep laboratory results for diagnosis and treatment. Screaming out, bolting up from sleep, or walking in a trancelike state during the night (when slow-wave sleep is expected) is diagnostic of the parasomnias on descriptive grounds.

In office practice, it is not feasible or practical to obtain sleep studies on most patients who complain of sleep problems. Nevertheless, polysomnography is essential to precisely identify certain disorders and is available in most areas.[1] Tests to define wake and sleep stages include electroencephalography monitoring as well as eye movement (electro-

---

[1] A list of facilities that provide polysomnography is available from the American Sleep Disorders Association.

oculographic) and muscle (electromyographic) tracings. Most labs also monitor cardiovascular, pulmonary, and penile functioning as parameters for diagnosing primary sleep disorders.

■ Family Modalities

Although the prototypical workup of sleep disorder remains the individual clinical exam and sleep study, a knowledge base now exists that allows the field to move ahead in both theory and practice. Studying a married individual alone in a sleep laboratory might be sufficient to diagnose certain primary sleep disorders, but this arrangement cannot reveal subtle or primarily interpersonal aspects of sleep. The natural state for married individuals is "couples sleep," and some early investigations have focused on variations in patterns of couples sleep.

Treatment of sleep disorders need not include the family in every case, but family assessment can be useful. In treatment of the parasomnias, responses of the family may be amenable to modification. In dyssomnias such as breathing-related sleep disorder, including family members in treatment decisions enhances the power of the treatment team. The observers already consider themselves experts in the symptoms and can be coinvestigators in the effectiveness of treatment.

Openness to the interpersonal dimensions of insomnia can add to the list of possible interventions. Including others may contribute to the discovery of underlying psychiatric disorders, many of which can be closely related to sleep problems. The relationship of some sleep problems to issues of bonding and sexuality also supports the use of a family approach to sleep disorder treatment.

Parents are involved automatically in treatment of childhood parasomnias, and partners can be incorporated routinely into the assessment and treatment of the dyssomnias. Siblings often have insightful observations into the patterns of symptoms and are also significantly affected by the behaviors.

Family members can offer information about the lives and relationships of those with sleep problems. They can provide insight about possible connections between sleep problems and interpersonal issues.

> One family brought in their 10-year-old child because of night terrors and sleep refusal. Once they recognized that the problem had begun after the mother's car accident, they could discuss the associated stresses and fears openly.

■ Psychoeducation

In psychoeducation for dyssomnias, a preliminary step may be to first rule out other psychiatric or medical disorders and then to ask if the person has tried basic sleep hygiene suggestions, which many already know from the popular media. Basic hypnotic induction methods and relaxation techniques can be useful (Buchholz 1987).

Psychoeducation can specifically address the organic etiologies and sequelae of narcolepsy and breathing-related sleep disorders. This approach can help the patient and the family understand and choose from among the treatment options (Manfredi and Cadieux 1987).

For the parasomnias, the family is eager for information about these mysterious phenomena and about what they can do to help. In sleep terror disorder of childhood, parents receive instruction that describes the disorder and helps dispel any misconceptions the family may have. Detailed instructions are given on how to improve the safety of the environment, how to reassure other children, how to handle the actual episode (e.g., don't interrupt sleep terrors, which can increase fear and confusion and make violence more likely), and how to physically restrain only when absolutely necessary (Gates and Morwessel 1989; Vela-Bueno et al. 1987). The family can be informed that a child usually outgrows this disorder within 4 months. In sleepwalking disorder, parents or spouses must learn about safety measures such as securing windows and doors with special bolts, blocking access to staircases, and having the child or adult sleep on the floor.

Education can elucidate factors that increase the incidence of the terrors, such as overtiredness, insecurities, and major life changes—new siblings, illness, new day-care arrangements, and parental battles. The therapist should remind parents to include *all* of their children in the educational sessions.

■ New Stories

Attributions. The dyssomnias, such as narcolepsy, are reframed as organic diseases over which the patient has little control. Family members may assume that the index person is lazy or is expressing anger or passive aggression. The therapist can introduce the idea that the person is more likely to be experiencing humiliation and fear.

In children, the parasomnias are explained to the family as most likely developmental. This frame alone may decrease shame, because parents often imagine that the problem reflects a parenting failure. The developmental idea also addresses the hidden question or fear that the disorder will be lifelong.

The unusual behaviors of the parasomnias can be discussed as not necessarily reflecting other psychiatric disturbances but possibly reflecting a primary organic problem that may resolve and be treatable.

Dreams as communications. The sharing of a dream during a family therapy session offers an opportunity to elicit special interpersonal meanings and communications. The therapist can ask each member first what they *felt* as the dream was being shared and then what they *thought* it was about.

> In one case, the wife shared a dream during a couples session and the following conversation took place.
>
> > Wife: "I'm in the middle of a war with two men in the middle of a large field, perhaps a battlefield . . . "
> >
> > Therapist to husband, who appeared moved: "How are you reacting and feeling inside when you hear the dream?"
> >
> > Husband (sobbing): "I know it's a dream about my own war with myself."
>
> The husband talked about how touched he was by the trust she showed in sharing a dream in front of him and also by the content of the dream. He thought she had dreamed in part for him, because the themes resonated so well with his core conflicts. Although the therapist and couple explored the personal associations with the dream, including the transference meanings, the therapist emphasized that the dream represented a shared communication "designed" in part to elicit previously inaccessible affects from the partner so relational healing could begin.

Circular questions. These circular questions can be used in the dyssomnias:

> "Who is most affected when Dad sleeps so much?"
> "Who has pitched in to help with the jobs Dad is not able to do right now?"

"Who worries most about the idea that your mother might fall asleep at bad times, such as when she is driving a car?"

"To whom does Mom talk most about the snoring or about her own fatigue?"

In the parasomnias, these questions may be used:

"Who wakes up when your brother screams or sleepwalks during the night?"

"Who is in charge of him during the episode?"

"Does the screaming seem to occur more when Dad is home or when he is away?"

"Does anyone notice any other patterns, such as the circumstances that make the episodes less of a bother?"

■ Additional Reading

Bynum EB: Families and the Interpretation of Dreams: Awakening the Intimate Web. New York, Haworth, 1993

Dolnick E: What dreams are (really) made of. Atlantic 266:41–61, 1990

Goldberg M: The use of dreams in conjoint marital therapy. Journal of Sex and Marital Therapy 1:75–81, 1974

Harris ME, Ray WJ: Dream content and its relation to self-reported interpersonal behavior. Psychiatry 40:363–368, 1977

Jimmerson KR: Maternal, environmental, and temperamental characteristics of toddlers with and without sleep problems. Journal of Pediatric Health Care 5:71–77, 1991

Keener MA, Zeanah CH, Anders TF: Infant temperament, sleep organization, and nighttime parental interventions. Pediatrics 81:762–771, 1988

Salzman C: Interpersonal problems in narcolepsy. Psychosomatics 17:49–51, 1976

■ References

American Psychiatric Association: Diagnostic and Statistical Manual of Mental Disorders, 4th Edition. Washington, DC, American Psychiatric Association, 1994

Benca RM, Obermeyer WH, Thisted RA, et al: Sleep and psychiatric disorders: a meta-analysis. Arch Gen Psychiatry 49:651–668, 1992

Buchholz D: Sleep disorders, in Current Therapy in Internal Medicine, 2nd Edition. Edited by Bayless TM, Brain MC, Cherniack RM. Toronto, Ontario, Canada, BC Decker, 1987, pp 1235–1239

Cartwright RD, Kravitz HM, Eastman CI, et al: REM latency and the recovery from depression: getting over divorce. Am J Psychiatry 148: 1530–1535, 1991

Ellis EM: Watchers in the night: an anthropological look at sleep disorders. Am J Psychother 45:211–220, 1991

Gates D, Morwessel N: Night terrors: strategies for family coping. J Pediatr Nurs 4:48–53, 1989

Giles DE, Kupfer DJ, Roffwarg HP, et al: REM latency concordance in depressed family members. Biol Psychiatry 22:907–910, 1987

Giles DE, Kupfer DJ, Roffwarg HP, et al: Polysomnographic parameters in first-degree relatives of unipolar probands. Psychiatry Res 27:127–136, 1989

Hori A: Sleep characteristics in twins. Jpn J Psychiatry Neurol 40:35–46, 1986

Kales A, Kales JD, Soldatos CR: Insomnia and other sleep disorders. Med Clin North Am 66:971–991, 1982

Kales A, Vela-Bueno A, Kales JD: Sleep disorders: sleep apnea and narcolepsy. Ann Intern Med 106:434–443, 1987

Kellerman H: Sleep Disorders: Insomnia and Narcolepsy. New York, Brunner/Mazel, 1981

Kessler S: Genetic factors in narcolepsy. Advances in Sleep Research 3:285–302, 1976

Kessler S, Guilleminault C, Dement W: A family study of 50 REM narcoleptics. Acta Neurol Scand 50:503–512, 1974

Lansky MR, Karger JE: Post-traumatic nightmares and the family. Hillside Journal of Clinical Psychiatry 11:169–183, 1989

Leckman JF, Gershon ES: A genetic model of narcolepsy. Br J Psychiatry 128:276–279, 1976

Lozoff B, Wolf AW, Davis NS: Cosleeping in urban families with young children in the United States. Pediatrics 74:171–182, 1984

Mamelak M, Caruso VJ, Stewart K: Narcolepsy: a family study. Biol Psychiatry 14:821–834, 1979

Manfredi RL, Cadieux RJ: Sleep disorders of organic origin: narcolepsy and sleep apnea. Psychiatric Annals 17:470–478, 1987

Markowitz I, Taylor G, Bokert E: Dream discussion as a means of reopening blocked familial communication. Psychother Psychosom 16:348–356, 1968

Mendelson WB: Human Sleep: Research and Clinical Care. New York, Plenum, 1987

Perlmutter RA, Babineau R: The use of dreams in couples therapy. Psychiatry 46:66–72, 1983

Rosenfeld AA, Wenegrat AO, Haavik DK, et al: Sleeping patterns in upper-middle class families when the child awakens ill or frightened. Arch Gen Psychiatry 40:277–280, 1982

The use of benzodiazepine hypnotics: a scientific examination of a clinical controversy (special issue). J Clin Psychiatry 53 (suppl 12), 1992

Vela-Bueno A, Soldatos CR, Julius DA: Parasomnias: sleepwalking, night terrors, and nightmares. Psychiatric Annals 17:465–469, 1987

Webb WB, Campbell SC: Relationships in sleep characteristics of identical and fraternal twins. Arch Gen Psychiatry 40:1093–1095, 1983

Williams RL, Karacan I, Moore CA: Sleep Disorders: Diagnosis and Treatment, 2nd Edition. Edited by Williams RL. New York, Wiley, 1988

Zarcone V: Narcolepsy. N Engl J Med 288:1156–1166, 1973

CHAPTER 13

Sexual and Gender Identity Disorders

Jeff B.

Jeff B., a 55-year-old man, and his 53-year-old wife, Nancy, presented with the chief complaint that she was anorgasmic. He attributed this problem to her desire to mock him and emphasize his inadequacy as a man. In the sessions, this attribution was deciphered as a projection of his sense of inadequacy. Nancy's underlying feelings actually related more to fear of the hurt, angry, and retaliatory state that Jeff could so easily enter when the problem occurred.

Mr. and Mrs. P.

A devout Roman Catholic Portuguese couple, Mr. and Mrs. P., presented with bitter fights after their child was born with ambiguous genitalia. In the third session, the underlying issue finally emerged: "Is it my family or your family that did this to us?" This question did not refer to a literal genetic search for similar defects in the extended family, but to the idea that the sins of the parents are transmitted to the children.

The therapist focused on the idea that blaming for such a defect was futile and presumptuous because there was no way to know for certain what the determinant was. Allowing this blame to destroy family life would go against their values and their faith. Mr. and

Mrs. P. shifted to a search for the purpose of such a defect and what meaning or message it might contain.

◼ Perspective on the Disorders

The field of sexuality has been a mental health pariah, perhaps as a result of shame associated with a Victorian moral code. Sexuality had been almost completely avoided by most fields of science, including medicine and family therapy, until the emergence of sexual treatments in the 1970s. Since then, sexuality has been treated somewhat less phobically.

While a few clinicians and scholars have achieved their own brand of systemic integrated approach to sexual disorders, very little is described in the literature that fully utilizes the knowledge of both fields. One notable exception is the marital couple, which was given full emphasis in the pioneering work of Masters and Johnson and later by others including Helen Singer Kaplan, who noted:

> The recognition that sexual difficulties are not invariably expressions of one person's intrapsychic conflict, but are often rooted in the vicissitudes of the marital relationship, is one of the truly significant advances in the behavioral sciences. . . . *it has become standard practice in the field to work with couples together rather than with the symptomatic patient alone in most clinical situations.* (Kaplan 1974, pp. 155–156 [emphasis in original])

The addiction model is one of the most promising for the integration of family systems thinking with the treatment of sexual disorders, especially the paraphilias and several of the dysfunctions. Some compulsive sexual behaviors can be approached as automatic, habitual, and beyond the sufferer's conscious control, which can help make compassion possible as an alternative to judging, automatic hate, or intense fear.

One essential caveat is that the sexual offender must accept responsibility for his or her actions. The family members must also accept responsibility for taking care of themselves, including protecting self and others from the negative effects of the person's out-of-control behaviors. A strong, clear stance can be formulated through this model.

Using the addictions model, a spouse may come to believe that the paraphiliac husband cannot control his fantasies at all and has only partial control over acting on impulses. She may insist on his getting treatment, since that is something he can control. She can then formulate an ultimatum, linking his staying in treatment with her staying in the relationship.

The sexual disorders are divided into three main categories: sexual dysfunctions such as pain and problems in sexual desire, arousal, and orgasm; paraphilias such as exhibitionism, fetishism, frotteurism, pedophilia, masochism, sadism, voyeurism, and transvestism; and gender identity disorders, in which there is a strong identification with the complementary gender and confusion about one's own.

Table 13–1 summarizes some aspects of the family context of these disorders, which is described in more detail in the next section.

■ Connections of the Symptoms to the System

■ Effects of the Disorder on the Family

Dysfunctions. The manifestation of a sexual dysfunction in one member of a couple is usually associated with affective reactions such as hurt, rejection, alarm, anger, or a sense of the other's resentment and may contribute to the erosion of otherwise healthy relationships. Fights and even violence may extend beyond the bedroom into all other aspects of the relationship. The shame and difficulty of dealing with the dysfunctions can result in divorce before any attempt is made to face and work through the problems.

In virtually every culture, the male erection is connected to a man's sense of self-esteem. It is not surprising that erectile dysfunctions would be related to poor view of self, panic, and depression in men. Women may feel fear, worry, rejection, poor self-esteem ("I must not be attractive"), and anger ("You must not care about me").

Misunderstandings and misinterpretations are also associated with premature ejaculation. In an attempt to avoid overstimulation, the man tries to withhold himself erotically. His partner is likely to sense this restraint and to take it personally as a sign of disinterest. These sexual matters are so difficult to discuss openly that clarification of the situation is blocked.

The effects of a woman's low desire or inhibition of orgasm are more variable (Kaplan 1974). The woman's enjoyment of sex has tra-

Table 13–1. Sexual and gender identity disorders in context

Effects of the disorder on the family

- *Dysfunctions*
  - Hurt, rejection, alarm, and anger in response to person's problems
  - Low desire/erectile problems and premature ejaculation taken as rejection by partner; lack of self-esteem in men
  - More variable effects with awareness of own problems in inhibition of desire or orgasm in women taken as rejection by partner
- *Paraphilias*
  - Direct effects include devastation by affected person's and spouse's disappointment, anger with each offense
  - Spouse's guilt for not satisfying affected person; guilt for staying in relationship
  - Subtle and pervasive shame, fear, secrecy, and confusion for family, especially children
- *Gender identity disorders*
  - Powerlessness, confusion, and emotional devastation with recognizing difficulties of ambiguous genitalia in child
  - Stress on family of child with sexual identity confusion

Family maintenance of the symptoms

- *Dysfunctions*
  - Closely associated with relational problems; merging of sex therapy and marital therapy
  - Connection to trust, loyalty conflict
- *Paraphilias*
  - Enabling and further isolation of index person as possible result of attempt to help
- *Gender identity disorders*
  - Possible connections to limited paternal influence and strong maternal influence, with associated relational imbalance and dissatisfaction

Functions of the symptoms within the family

- *Dysfunctions*
  - Regulation of intimacy, power, and affective expression
  - Request for help
- *Paraphilias*
  - Tendency to create secrecy and distance in relationship; possible renewed marital closeness when connected to understanding of compulsion and to limit setting

(continued)

Table 13–1.   Sexual and gender identity disorders in context *(continued)*

- *Gender identity disorders*
    - Stabilizes family characterized by paternal distance and maternal distress
    - May wake up family to their need for change

Adverse consequences of change

- *Dysfunctions*
    - Facing underlying relational problems
- *Paraphilias*
    - Weight gain and other antiandrogen side effects
    - Increased conflict because fixing sexual problem does not fix relationship
- *Gender identity disorders*
    - Difficulty in accepting sexual identity that was formerly unacknowledged or kept secret

---

ditionally been viewed with ambivalence as if unimportant. While more women today are able to see their lack of pleasure in sexuality as worthy of attention, many are still not as distressed as men are by their own obstacles to sexual pleasure. Misunderstandings can occur if a woman is relatively matter-of-fact about her lack of desire or enjoyment. Even though her focus may simply be on relational aspects other than sexuality, the man takes this as a reflection of rejection, a statement of his inadequacy, or a sign that she doesn't really care.

Paraphilias.   In paraphilias, the effects on the family are both indirect and direct. The direct effects of victimization by the offender can be catastrophic. Others are also affected; for example, the paraphiliac person's spouse expresses disappointment, anger, and rage each time an offense is revealed. Some partners, usually wives, experience guilt based on their belief that they somehow caused the disorder by not being "good enough" sexually. Guilt is also expressed by a spouse who wonders, "Why do I stay with a person who does such acts?"

Most paraphiliac acts are not incestuous (Abel and Osbourn 1992). Indirect effects on family members as observers or keepers of the secret are more common and profound. The discovery of daddy dressing in mommy's clothing will certainly have an effect on the children. The general effects can be heard from children who express shame ("My family is so bizarre I can't stand it"), secrecy ("I'd rather be dead than have anyone know that my father dresses in women's clothes" or "How could I tell anyone that my mother does weird things with animals"), fear ("If he's that strange I'm worried that he's going to do something awful to me or that I'll become strange like that"), and confusion ("My family seems so nice, how can they do things like that?").

Secrecy also has both direct and indirect effects. It is common for paraphilias to be kept secret even from the immediate family, and its influence on relationships is hidden and indirect. At some point the effects become direct. The paraphiliac individual is arrested, and the family is shocked, shamed, and publicly humiliated.

Gender identity disorders.   A painful example of a gender identity disorder is the birth of a child with ambiguous genitalia. The birth of a baby invariably brings the question: "Is it a boy or a girl?" The powerlessness of parents begins at birth, when they do not know the answer to this question. Nature has played a cruel trick, and it seems as if the doctors are "deciding" the gender of the child.

Gender identity problems in infants and children require the involvement and participation of the family. The revelation of the secret of sexual identity confusion in older children, adolescents, and adults is more complex, because the reactions of the family can become part of the problem. The common parental reactions of shame, disappointment, impulse toward cutoff, and homophobia become part of the child's burden. Familial confusion becomes an additional problem to the person already disturbed by identity confusion. Family stress is compounded when the identity problem triggers hidden uncertainties of the parents about their own sexual identities and anxieties.

◼ Family Maintenance of the Symptoms

Dysfunctions.   Relational problems are closely associated with sexual dysfunctions. The fields of sex and marital therapy are merging in response to the fact that couples presenting with sexual dysfunctions usually have underlying relational issues (Sager 1976). These issues may connect to the family of origin of one or both partners, as in trauma, incest, divorce, blame, and scenes of parental hatred. They may connect to intrapsychic issues of conflict around trust, loyalty, or oedipal issues—such as experiencing the spouse as being too much like or too much different from the same-sex parent.

The treatment of sexual dysfunctions recognizes that attempts of both spouses to try harder to resolve sexual dysfunctions almost always make things worse. Temporarily banning intercourse and assigning graduated sensate-focus exercises are strategies designed to help break negative cycles and allow new options for dealing with the problem.

Paraphilias. Often the person with a paraphilia is a loner looking for connectedness, even through the behaviors of the disorder. With paraphiliac individuals who are married, the therapist looks for well-meaning behaviors of a spouse that might make an already difficult situation much harder to change, such as the spouse's actions to isolate the person further. The spouse may cover for the paraphiliac partner instead of allowing that person to take responsibility for his or her own actions. This approach is understandable because of the spouse's shame over the behaviors, but the attempt to help may inadvertently encourage the behaviors in subtle ways.

Gender identity disorders. The findings of Stoller, the major psychoanalytic observer of gender presentations, can be extrapolated to fit the context of family forces that contribute to gender identity disorders. In greatly simplified form, his studies of effeminate boys lead to this "equation": Less father + More mother = Feminine boy.

Other factors that may need to be present include a biological predisposition away from maleness and a father that rejects the little boy in preference for daughters. The mother in these cases is not disappointed to have a son, as some would predict. Quite the contrary, she is thrilled and falls in love passionately, perhaps too much so, and this intensity does not modify with time (Stoller 1985).

Incest. Incest is typically maintained by complex family systems characterized by denial. The family may inadvertently encourage the symptom by reframing the acts as expressions of love, as a way fathers teach children, or as a form of acceptable attention from fathers: "The children should be grateful because so many people have absent fathers." The symptom may also be maintained by the forces that keep the couple from considering why their sexual needs are extending outside the couple's relationship in this way.

■ Functions of the Symptoms Within the Family

Dysfunctions.   Sexual dysfunctions can regulate intimacy. In those couples where one or both have intrapsychic conflict and terror of too intense closeness in a positive relationship, then moments of emotional intimacy may need to be balanced by some difficulty in meeting sexually. Conversely, a relationship that is drifting apart can be held together temporarily by resumption of mutually gratifying sexuality.

Hidden affects may be expressed through sexuality, which may bring out into the open such affects as guilt, hostility, hurt, and shame, feelings that usually lie below the surface of marital battles. Sexual dysfunction may serve to balance power in a relationship. For example, impotence or premature ejaculation can be seen as an unconscious way for the male to control sexual intercourse and keep the woman from dominating.

Sexual problems may signal a cry for help in resolving underlying relational problems. Therapy or dialogue may then help clarify the resources or the irreversible unworkable conflicts in the relationship. The problems can also signal a need for individual help.

> One couple presented with the overt issue of the wife's sexual unresponsiveness. By the third session, the husband's major depression and rage outbursts were the focus of discussion. These incidents terrorized the family and were incompatible with the wife's ability to be trusting or fully sexual. Once the husband's major depression was treated, both partners described the restoration of a mutually satisfying sexual relationship.

Paraphilias.   As a way of expressing sexuality, the paraphilias can contribute to secrecy and distance from other family members. Discovery and disclosure of the full story may seriously disrupt a relationship, but disclosure can also create the possibility for deeper mutual understanding.

> Jenny W. presented for individual therapy for her depression. She also related a concern about a nonexistent sex life with her husband, which she at first attributed to her lack of desire. Later she revealed something that she had been too ashamed to talk about in early sessions. She had discovered her husband dressed in her underwear and learned that he cross-dressed as his main means

of sexual expression. After this discovery, her sexual desire disappeared.

Individual therapy was indeed indicated, but for a different reason than the one for which Jenny initially presented. She needed to work out the conflict between her automatic revulsion and panic and her wish for the secret to be part of an intimate, trusting disclosure in an otherwise satisfactory relationship. She was able to feel some compassion after recognizing the compulsive nature of her husband's paraphiliac behaviors, but she also learned when to express and feel justified in her feelings that the behaviors were a turnoff. She learned to feel comfortable with her need to set clear limits on the behavior.

Gender identity disorders. A gender identity disorder such as effeminacy in a child may serve to stabilize the family. If the father is extremely distant and the mother dissatisfied, the child with the gender identity disorder fulfills the mother's need for a companion. This companionship may diminish her tendency to scold the father and may allow the father to be part of the family.

In other families, the embarrassment of public symptoms may force the whole family's attention to the needs of the children and the family as a whole. The overdistant father may comprehend the possible effects of his absence and rejoin the family to help prevent further adverse effects.

■ Adverse Consequences of Change

Dysfunctions. Successful treatment of a specific sexual dysfunction can escalate pain and fighting, which often reveal other aspects of the relationship that require attention. One spouse may secretly think he or she wants to leave the relationship and justifies leaving by focusing on the sexual problem instead of facing other issues. There may be a puzzling disappointment if the sexual problem can be fixed and the easy way out of the relationship is taken away. The other spouse must now face the underlying issues.

Paraphilias. Successful treatment may mean weight gain and other side effects of treatment with antiandrogens such as Depo-Provera (medroxyprogesterone acetate), which add to the problems more than some people would like. The spouse may be grateful that the problem is controlled but may still be too repelled or distrustful to be able to rebuild the relationship with the paraphiliac partner. The spouse may feel increased conflict over the desire to leave at a time when he or she also feels compassion for the sufferer.

Gender identity disorders.   The solution to one problem may create another problem when a spouse or offspring resolves sexual identity issues and the family does not like the outcome. If the person becomes clear about having a male or female identity, the "disorder" resolves. The family may have to deal with dramatic change in their child, and the child must determine how to present this new identity to the world.

■ Special Systemic Dimensions

■ Family History and Genetics

The field of sexuality articulates models of development that account for the relationship of nature-nurture. Dichotomous concepts are replaced with the complex interactions and influence of biology and environment, embryology, and family gender roles as described in the work of John Money. All human beings receive a genetic program that specifies a range of possibilities within which the organism is to develop sexually. This genetic program interacts first with the environment of the embryo and fetus and later with the family and the whole social world (Money and Ehrhardt 1972).

Psychoanalytic studies elaborate a complex schemata of the variations of gender identity. This work complements the field's emphasis on genetic determinants of sexual behaviors by elaborating on the vicissitudes of early life for the infant, especially by detailing the influence of social and family forces on hormonal and sexual expression. Stoller approaches treatment from a psychoanalytical rather than a family systems model, but does endorse the need to study at least three generations in order to understand the process of femininization in boys (Stoller 1985). Family systems theory also supports the need to study three generations to find connections in the current generation (Bowen 1994).

The interrelation of biology-genetics and family environment is fascinating and begs for synthesis. Scientific literature is challenging and expanding our assumptions about what may be genetically transmitted. The new field of biological correlates of homosexuality is one example. In the next few years, science promises to connect the pieces in ways that will strongly affect our views of patients' sexual histories and their choices regarding sexual orientation, degree of drive, and deviant behaviors.

■ Gender

The treatment of the dysfunctions has been impacted by changes in gender expectations. Men are now more likely to ask for affection and touching in addition to intercourse as part of a more complex sexuality. Women may express desires without thinking this reflects poorly on them and may broaden their perspective beyond exclusive concern for the feelings of the other.

There is a growing awareness that family therapy has not always served the best interests of women. Basic systems theory sometimes neglects the issue of power imbalances. In practice, the therapist must watch the tendency to blame women for the sexual dysfunctions of men or to mistake women's wish for relationships and connectedness for nagging or undue demandingness. Men who suffer from an inability to grasp or express feelings cannot accommodate the vulnerability of sexual moments that are not based strictly on performance. These feelings can be discussed in a very different way than was possible 30 years ago. Men may be open to going beyond the emotional limits of their socialization (Mason 1991).

Gender stereotypes define much of the content of gender identity disorders. According to these stereotypes, boys should play with boys and be interested in the sexual conquest of girls. They should play with boys' toys, and they should play roughly. Girls should be feminine and should identify with mothers and dolls. The degree of attachment to the stereotypes is illustrated by the panic seen in parents who present feminine sons or gender-rejecting daughters. The distress cannot be explained completely by antiquated destructive gender biases.

The importance of sex assignment at birth is taken for granted, but studies of cases of hermaphroditism and ambiguous genitalia have demonstrated the power of the family and social aspects of gender assignment (Money and Ehrhardt 1972; Stoller 1985; Touzimsky and Rybakowa 1985).

■ Intimacy

The relationship of intimacy and sexuality is complex, and the two can enhance or detract from each other. Intense moments of mutual sexual pleasuring can help create moments of closeness and bonding. In English, the word *intimacy* connotes the experience of intercourse. On the other hand, sexuality can serve to oppose intimacy, as when sexual partners are used compulsively and exclusively for one's own pleasure without the mutuality and care for the other that must be present for the intimate moment.

In paraphilias, the quest for intimacy is the driving force. The paraphiliac person experiences the self as so inadequate, so uncomfortable socially, and so dependent on others that interaction with the object of the paraphilia seems the only interpersonal comfort possible. A pedophiliac individual may be comfortable only around children, and transvestites may be most peaceful when gazing at themselves in the mirror while cross-dressed (M. F. Schwartz and Masters 1983).

Although the paraphiliac individual creates a closeness on one level, the deficits of self prevent deeper intimacy because the other is being used. The nature of the disorder can draw the paraphiliac person into him- or herself. The inability to focus on, understand, or empathize with the feelings of another becomes the obstacle to genuine interrelation.

■ Loyalty

As the old saying goes, there are at least six people in the marital bed. A rebalancing of loyalties occurs when adults form sexual partnerships and allegiances expand from family of origin to include the new family. Closeness to the spouse or "stranger" comes at a price because it disturbs the exclusive allegiance to the original family. If this rebalancing is conflictual, the conflict will have a strong effect on the sexual intimacy of the couple. The ability to give oneself physically to this stranger requires a certain amount of "permission" from the original family.

The image of the parent may be transferred onto the spouse as a kind of loyalty payment to the family of origin, thereby maintaining the parents' presence and the adult child's connection to the original family. The cost may express as a sexual dysfunction if the spouse becomes angry at the other for being so much like an abusive parent and sex becomes impossible. Alternatively, the similarity of the spouse to the parent may make sexual intimacy feel incestuous (Boszormenyi-Nagy and Krasner 1986).

■ Map of Emotions

Affects in a relationship are expressed through sexuality, and sexuality generates affects in a relationship. A relational model of sexuality that accommodates the full reality is needed.

A consideration of emotional aspects of sexual disorders must begin with shame. Shame has so permeated sexuality in Western cultures that it is sometimes hard to sort out attitudes about sex from shame itself. If normal sexuality creates such emotional reactions, then it is understandable that shame would be a significant part of dysfunctions such as impotence, ejaculatory incompetence, and syndromes of low desire. If the problem makes the partner feel hurt and angry, the symptom bearer feels increased shame, guilt, or defensive anger. This situation allows a cycle of anticipatory fear before sexual behaviors, which necessarily exacerbates the dysfunction.

Old theories that sexual problems result from unconscious anger still have merit in some couples, but the story is much more complex. Sex may be more an attempt to discharge anxiety than an attempt to express angry affects or to find and give sexual pleasure.

Compulsive sexuality can translate emotionally as avoidance of aloneness; it may also be a way of discharging high levels of anxiety. The paraphiliac impulse and act emerge under stress or high anxiety. When the person with the paraphilia is not feeling anxious or powerless, the impulses are more likely to be resisted and controlled.

Powerlessness that becomes intolerable can lead to sadistic acts in which the person assumes control and mastery over the one being dominated.

■ Countertransference

Therapist discomfort and judgmentalism regarding sexual matters are an expected product of most upbringings. The training of the sexual therapist therefore usually includes desensitization, raising of consciousness about attitudes, and emotional reeducation. In general family therapy practice, it is important to convey verbally and nonverbally that sexual matters can be discussed. The therapist must have enough self-awareness, knowledge of his or her own conflicts, and objectivity to allow sex into the therapy room without undue anxiety, fear, and rejection. The effort to achieve this openness is much of the battle.

■ Treatment

■ Standard Individual Therapies

Initially, all the dysfunctions (and what used to be called perversions) were thought to be treatable only by long-term psychoanalysis. In 1970, the publication of Masters and Johnson's *Human Sexual Inadequacy* introduced specific behavioral and relational techniques for each of the sexual dysfunctions (Masters and Johnson 1970). A few years later, this approach was applied to some of the paraphilias (Adson 1992; Langevin 1992; B. K. Schwartz 1992; M. F. Schwartz and Masters 1983).

The paraphilias have received much less attention than the sexual dysfunctions, but recently treatment has progressed significantly. There are now sophisticated integrative approaches that use treatment techniques for sexual dysfunctions to address the special deficits of ego and relatedness that characterize the paraphilias (M. F. Schwartz and Masters 1983). Antiandrogen therapy (e.g., with Depo-Provera) is controversial, but it is accepted in specialized treatment settings as a pragmatic way to reduce the need to act on the impulses.

■ Family Modalities

The ideal treatment for a couple with sexual dysfunction involves a combination of specific behavioral sexual therapy and conjoint marital therapy aimed at underlying relational problems. A systemic view adds much to the treatment possibilities but is insufficient by itself. Conversely, some sexual dysfunctions do not resolve even with the best sexual therapy because underlying relational problems predominate. Other couples who engage in long-term marital therapy may resolve many relational problems and yet emerge from therapy with their sexual difficulties unchanged. During the evaluation phase, the therapist must judge the proper mix of these two modalities in treatment.

During the past decade, the field of sexual therapies has moved further toward considering the relationship as the unit of treatment. Both individual and conjoint sessions are helpful in approaching this goal. Some writers advocate that one therapist should focus on the sex therapy while another therapist meets with the couple on relationship issues (Mason 1991). This approach may be useful in some cases but may contribute to an artificial separation of issues. Ideally, one therapist will have the skills and aptitude to work on both issues.

Dysfunctions.   Multigenerational sessions have not been widely considered in helping couples with sexual dysfunction and are almost nonexistent in practice, which blocks the potential contribution of parents and grandparents as resources during the treatment period. Although the reason for avoiding these sessions can be a desire to maintain appropriate boundaries, more likely the main reasons are secrecy and shame.

The historical perspective can still be conveyed effectively through individual and couples sessions. The central focus of these sessions is a consideration of the ways that love, touching, affection, and attitudes about sexuality have been passed down through the generations.

Paraphilias.   Treatment models for paraphilias emphasize individual and group therapy and include an interpersonal perspective. Because not much is known about specific family treatment, there are new possibilities for including family members at least in the assessment phase, with some family members being included throughout therapy. The family can offer an essential perspective on what might be the most effective motivations for change.

As in treatment of impulse or substance use disorders, the family must be involved to stop enabling, to protect children and others from the consequences of the behavior, and to exert pressure on the individual to maintain treatment. Children may be included later in treatment, especially if the paraphilia is a secret. The spouse who has discovered this secret may demand to be included in the treatment.

Gender identity disorders.   More descriptions of family process exist for those families in which the disorder manifests in childhood. In work with families with effeminate boys, one suggested model is individual therapy of the child with a male therapist and simultaneous family work with a different therapist to work on strengthening the marriage and the father-son relationship and weakening the mother-son context. Alternative gratifications for the mother are explored, and the parents are engaged in a behavioral program.

The superiority of a more systemic approach was described in the case of Tom N., an effeminate boy who had been treated for several years in a clinic and in traditional individual and parental sessions. The decision was made to move to a stricter family system model. The boy's attachment to his mother was understood as maintaining homeostasis by providing someone to respond to the mother's distress after the father refused. When therapy tasks were assigned in which father was to get closer to his son and roughhouse with him, the mother complained of migraines.

A three-generational perspective in this case was dramatic in elucidating patterns similar to those in the index family, including coalition patterns and a wish for female offspring. The resistance of the parents to changing the maladaptive behaviors emerged on many levels, but the treatment ended successfully (Wrate and Gulens 1986).

■ Psychoeducation

Dysfunctions.   Sexual ignorance is common. From the beginning, the treatment of dysfunctions included a strong emphasis on basic teaching and attitudinal adjustment. The teaching is both general and specific, emphasizing normal sexual response and anatomy and the normalcy of a wide range of feelings and desires.

Some teaching points apply to particular dysfunctions, as when anorgasmia is treated by educating the patient and her spouse through progressive methods of stimulation and communication. Like the treatment of many dysfunctions, male erectile disorder begins with an understanding of the role of anxiety. Teaching about this sexual disorder also considers the insidious, paradoxical cycle that occurs when the erection becomes a goal in itself. For example, trying to "will" or work at arousal usually increases anxiety and decreases erectile function.

Sexual therapists often use what is referred to as the P-LI-SS-IT model, in which the first three levels of intervention are psychoeducational and the last phase is intensive therapy (IT). The three psychoeducational levels involve permission (P) to talk about sex to an understanding, nonjudgmental audience, the acquiring of limited information (LI) through basic sex education and readings, and a focus on specific suggestions (SS) for exercises and tasks such as sensate focus exercises or the squeeze technique for premature ejaculation.

Paraphilias.   Spouse education is essential to relieve any guilt that the spouse caused the paraphilia, although there is an openness to seeing ways in which the family might be inadvertently maintaining the symptoms. A disease model similar to that described for schizophrenia and other disorders is used to reflect the sexual disorder as hormonal or as a compulsive organic problem that is complex and imperfectly understood. The therapist conveys the attitude that the family should hold the offender strictly responsible for the actions while at the same time viewing the problem with compassion. The person is viewed as suffering from an illness that makes it impossible to express affection in more adaptive modes (M. F. Schwartz and Masters 1983).

Because paraphilias often express themselves first in childhood and adolescence, early sex education that includes these topics could do much to reduce shame and encourage earlier intervention.

Gender identity disorders.   Psychoeducation includes information about genital birth defects. Parents are educated on how to live with the ambiguity for the first 10 to 12 weeks of life, when tests are performed. Specialized clinics provide support, readings, and other sufferers with whom to share the experience (Renshaw 1993).

Some experts in the treatment of effeminate boys advocate behavioral programs for parents that teach how to bring out more masculine behaviors. These programs advocate that the son spend more time with males and forbid mother/son cosleeping. The parents are helped to mitigate overprotectiveness and to encourage the child to play with other boys (Bates et al. 1975; Green 1975; Heiman et al. 1981; Stein and Chittenden 1985).

All judgments concerning effeminacy must be scanned for a cultural or countertransference bias on the part of the therapist. The intervention is designed to help reduce the overall suffering of the child and family, rather than to extinguish behaviors because of outmoded cultural views about what maleness and femaleness are supposed to be.

■ New Stories

Attributions.   Attributions in sexual disorders warrant much attention. Poor communication and tendencies toward projective defenses can lead to misattributions about the meanings of behavioral symptoms.

> One scenario involves "the husband who always says the wrong thing." Just as lovemaking is beginning, he may say, "I notice you're getting a little fat," "Do you think the kids can hear us?" or "Did you remember to put the garbage out?" Naturally enough, the wife presents to a therapist with the idea that her husband is expressing hostility and ambivalence about her by these comments.

Although certainly there may be some validity to the wife's attributions, the therapist must be alert for additional explanations. The husband may be sabotaging sexual experience out of his fear of impotence, which he then never has to face consciously. His comments affect his spouse in such a way that the sexual experience ends, and he can then view the trouble as her problem. Therapy may also unveil that he unconsciously believes that he doesn't really deserve such pleasuring with such a good woman. These completely different attributions open up new therapeutic possibilities.

In treating couples' sexual dysfunctions, an attempt is made to find positive attributions for specific behaviors. The therapist may focus on the wife's attributions of her husband's well-intended attempts to solve the problem of premature ejaculation:

> "Are you saying that perhaps his holding back is, on one level, his attempt to provide you a better experience?"

Similarly, the therapist's comment to a husband complaining about his wife's lack of concern about her anorgasmia might go like this:

> "Her matter-of-fact attitude could reflect that her assessment of the overall relationship is positive and shows the faith she has in you to maintain the relationship and forgive her problem rather than see it as disinterest."

Dilemma of change.   The systemic therapist views noncompliance with specific sexual tasks as an expression of the inevitable conflict between the wish for sameness and the wish for change (Keeney and Silverstein 1986; Papp 1983). Some noncompliance is expected and becomes the subject of investigation in an effort to clarify its significance and meaning. This investigation assumes respect for the family's attachment to the symptom, familiarity with it, and fear of losing it along with their simultaneous desperate wish to be relieved of it. Dialogue might be focused as in this example:

> "Both of you know and have stated that all kinds of therapy have not succeeded in helping with this sexual problem. We know that if you follow through on these exercises, as difficult as they are, the chance of improvement is excellent. Now that you are finding yourselves unable to do the exercises, despite all your wishes to improve, you feel disappointed and stuck. I know this is sad for you because you had such high hopes for this therapy to bring change. Would you be willing to prepare further for the change by using your imagination to create a list with me of negative consequences you would have to deal with in your relationship or within each of you if the tasks succeed and you do achieve a mutually satisfying sexual life?"

This dialogue variation can also be effective:

> "You both wish for this therapy and the tasks to succeed, and yet sometimes I get concerned from what you've told me that success would create a deeper fear in you that she really does not love you and in fact that you are not lovable. I find myself wondering if keeping the sexual problem around avoids this awful notion."

Another focus might also be tried:

> "If you resolve the sexual difficulty, are you hinting you might feel you sold out? As I hear it, satisfying a man is what you were taught you had to do, and now when you feel that's what you're being asked to do again, you feel threatened and rebellious."

Genogram. The three-generational history or genogram can elucidate inherited belief systems about sex. All sexual disorders are better understood in this family context. In gender identity disorders, the therapist elicits family attitudes about what makes up a boy and what makes up a girl, what is male and what is female. With sexual dysfunctions, the genogram is taken for both partners to gain a preliminary understanding of intrapsychic, familial, and sexual issues (Hof and Berman 1986; Offit 1977).

Usually it is best to take this history in a matter-of-fact way as something done routinely in all first evaluations rather than draw attention to some of the family patterns that may be contributing to the symptoms. Disorders are better understood in connection with the couple's perceptions regarding sex as pleasure or sin, their norms of touching and expression of affection, and the degree of shame they associate with sexual matters.

Parable technique.   To overcome the family's discomfort in discussing sexual matters, the therapist may tell a "parable" or story involving a person of the same age as the index person (Money 1994). Even if the story does not exactly match a given situation, this method can serve to open up public discussion of issues or events that a couple or family believes must be kept private.

■ Additional Reading

Calderone MS, Johnson EW: The Family Book About Sexuality. New York, Harper & Row, 1981

Faber A, Mazlish E: How to Talk So Kids Will Listen & Listen So Kids Will Talk. New York, Rawson, Wade, 1980

Gitchel S, Foster L: Let's Talk About S-E-X: A Read-and-Discuss Guide for People 9 to 12 and Their Parents. Fresno, CA, Planned Parenthood of Central California, 1986

Glick ID: Treating the new American couple. J Sex Marital Ther 12:297–306, 1986

Gordon S, Gordon J: Raising a Child Conservatively in a Sexually Permissive World. New York, Simon & Schuster, 1983

Higham E: Case management of the gender incongruity syndrome in childhood and adolescence. J Homosex 2:49–57, 1976

Lim MH, Bottomley V: A combined approach to the treatment of effeminate behavior in a boy: a case study. J Child Psychol Psychiatry 24:469–479, 1983

Masters W, Johnson V: The Pleasure Bond. Boston, MA, Little, Brown, 1970

Newman LE: Treatment for the parents of feminine boys. Am J Psychiatry 133:683–687, 1976

Quattrin T, Aronica S, Mazur T: Management of male pseudohermaphroditism: a case report spanning 21 years. J Pediatr Psychol 15:699–709, 1990

Sipe AWR: A Secret World: Sexuality and the Search for Celibacy. New York, Brunner/Mazel, 1990

Woody JD: The reality of an integrative sex therapy. J Sex Marital Ther 15:62–73, 1989

References

Abel GG, Osbourn C: Stopping sexual violence. Psychiatric Annals 22:301–306, 1992

Adson PR: Treatment of paraphilias and related disorders. Psychiatric Annals 22:299–300, 1992

Bates JE, Skilbeck WM, Smith KVR, et al: Intervention with families of gender-disturbed boys. Am J Orthopsychiatry 45:150–157, 1975

Boszormenyi-Nagy I, Krasner BR: Between Give and Take: A Clinical Guide to Contextual Therapy. New York, Brunner/Mazel, 1986

Bowen M: Family Therapy in Clinical Practice, 9th Edition. Northvale, NJ, Jason Aronson, 1994

Green R: The significance of feminine behaviour in boys. J Child Psychol Psychiatry 16:341–344, 1975

Heiman JR, Lopiccolo L, Lopiccolo J: The treatment of sexual dysfunction, in Handbook of Family Therapy. Edited by Gurman AS, Kniskern DP. New York, Brunner/Mazel, 1981, pp 592–627

Hof L, Berman E: The sexual genogram. Journal of Marital and Family Therapy 12:39–47, 1986

Kaplan HS: The New Sex Therapy: Active Treatment of Sexual Dysfunctions. New York, Brunner/Mazel, 1974

Keeney B, Silverstein O: The Therapeutic Voice of Olga Silverstein. New York, Guilford, 1986

Langevin R: Biological factors contributing to paraphiliac behavior. Psychiatric Annals 22:307–314, 1992

Mason MJ: Family therapy as the emerging context for sex therapy, in Handbook of Family Therapy, Vol 2. Edited by Gurman AS, Kniskern DP. New York, Brunner/Mazel, 1991, pp 479–507

Masters W, Johnson M: Human Sexual Inadequacy. Boston, MA, Little, Brown, 1970

Money J: Sex Errors of the Body and Related Syndromes: A Guide for Counseling Children, Adolescents, and Their Families. Baltimore, MD, Paul H. Brookes, 1994

Money J, Ehrhardt H: Man and Woman, Boy and Girl. Baltimore, MD, Johns Hopkins University Press, 1972

Offit A: The Sexual Self. Philadelphia, PA, JB Lippincott, 1977

Papp P: The Process of Change. New York, Guilford, 1983

Renshaw DC: Sexual birth defects: telling the parents. Resident and Staff Physician 39:87–90, 1993

Sager CJ: Marriage Contracts and Couple Therapy. New York, Brunner/Mazel, 1976

Schwartz BK: Effective treatment techniques for sex offenders. Psychiatric Annals 22:315–319, 1992

Schwartz MF, Masters WH: Conceptual factors in the treatment of paraphilias: a preliminary report. J Sex Marital Ther 9:3–18, 1983

Stein GS, Chittenden CL: Collaboration between therapists in the simultaneous treatments of a father and son with disorders of masculine identity formation. International Journal of Psychoanalytic Psychotherapy 11:339–368, 1985

Stoller RJ: Presentations of Gender. New Haven, CT, Yale University Press, 1985

Touzimsky Z, Rybakowa M: Ethical problems in family psychotherapy of patients with hermaphroditism. Mater Med Pol 17:257–260, 1985

Wrate RM, Gulens V: A systems approach to child effeminacy and the prevention of adolescent transsexualism. Journal of Adolescence 9:215–229, 1986

CHAPTER 14

Delirium, Dementia, and Amnestic and Other Cognitive Disorders

Jane D.

Jane D., a 70-year-old woman, was dealing with intense conflict with her siblings. The present eruption occurred over the family's expectation that she would automatically become the caregiver for family members, especially a widowed brother with advanced Alzheimer's disease. This expectation led to rage and resentment that Jane traced back 40 years, when the caregiving for both parents had fallen to her in what she perceived as a highly unjust arrangement. Her siblings claimed that she enjoyed this role and were shocked by her protests. However, they were very reluctant to review the family history in an effort to find a new balance of responsibility that would include their carrying a share of the present caregiving load.

Carl G.

Carl G., a youthful 67-year-old executive who had just retired, enjoyed excellent health until he suffered a stroke one Saturday. His cognitive capacity was severely compromised. Even after the initial delirium cleared, Carl was unable to orient to place or time, could not recognize family and friends, and became so irritable, hostile, and demanding that it was clear his care could not be managed at home. His wife gradually became aware that she had in essence lost her husband and must grieve, but without the clarity and finality of death. She suddenly found herself having to make health care decisions and placement options that she felt unprepared to handle.

■ Perspective on the Disorders

The category of organic mental disorders was dropped in DSM-IV (American Psychiatric Association 1994) because of the artificial and unhelpful connotation of mind-body dualism. If a psychiatric disorder is judged to be caused by a medical disease such as hypothyroidism, a diagnosis of "secondary disorder due to hypothyroidism" is made on Axis I.

The slow insidious deterioration of thinking and functioning associated with the dementias brings a family crisis that is characterized by chronic depletion of hope, energy, and resources. The deliriums are the acute rapid-onset changes of mental status with altered level of consciousness. The appearance of delirium in a family member represents an emergency for a confused and shocked family. The patient provides much information, but may be unreliable in terms of logic, sequencing, and facts. The family report provides the basis for the evaluation and offers clues to any underlying medical etiologies.

The complaints that lead to diagnoses of both delirium and dementia are usually brought by the family rather than by the patient. In the early phases of the dementias, the individual may complain of memory lapses, confused periods, difficulty maintaining level of function, and a vague sense of loss. This awareness changes notably in later stages of the disorder, when chronic dementia becomes "the observers' disease." The affected person may be distressed but is just as likely to be obliviously content, while those around feel grief and hopelessness.

Demographic trends suggest that 5% to 10% of the population over age 65 will suffer from dementing disorders at some point (Gwyther et al. 1984). The percentage of the population over age 65 is expanding rapidly, and therapists will inevitably be confronting issues relating to dementia. It is estimated that by the year 2050, there will be about 6 million people in the United States with severe dementia (Malmgren 1994).

Table 14–1 summarizes some aspects of the family context of these disorders, which is described in more detail in the next section.

Table 14–1.   Cognitive impairment disorders in context

Effects of the disorder on the family

- Sense of "ambiguous loss"
- Need for problem solving related to aging and loss of function
- Pressure on family to pursue medical differential diagnosis for index person
- Caregiving leads to burden
- Reversal of family roles
- Frustration of hopes for resolution of old conflicts involving index person
- Current conflicts related to caregiving
- Pain associated with index person's inability to recognize family

Family maintenance of the symptoms

- Disturbed family dynamics and behaviors affect still-sensitive individual
- Lack of family cooperation with therapeutic suggestions
- Well-meaning "memory tests" by family introduce conflict
- Worsening state could be related to psychosocial events
- Need to consider issue of elder abuse and the needs of overwhelmed caregiver
- Certain deficits of dementia tolerated by family if individual has competence in valued area of functioning

Functions of the symptoms within the family

- Family's interpretation of behavior as "pathological" can be accurate or misattribution; may continue established isolating of individual within family; effect on interventions
- Symptoms of caregiver also considered; need to assess for guilt motivation
- Symptoms may elicit positive resources in family

Adverse consequences of change

- Concerns regarding the "unemployed caregiver" (loss, uncertainty about identity)
- Need to restore more balanced relationships and responsibilities (e.g., for caregiving)

■ Connections of the Symptoms to the System

■ Effects of the Disorder on the Family

The effects on the family fall into several general categories. When an individual has a cognitive impairment disorder, the family suffers what has been described as "ambiguous loss" (Boss 1990). Some families of individuals with Alzheimer's disease pass through a series of reactions to the diagnosis. One schema for this family response resembles a description of the phases of reaction to a diagnosis of terminal illness—denial, overinvolvement, anger, guilt, and acceptance (Teusink and Mahler 1984).

The family must now face issues related to the individual's loss of memory and function. Family problem solving focuses on issues such as guardianship, financial arrangements for care, placement and/or providing for 24-hour care, and dilemmas related to behavioral changes such as wandering, violence, sexual advances, emotional lability, outbursts, safety lapses (e.g., with hot stoves), and incontinence.

The family is responsible for actively pushing the patient's work-ups to conclusion. This responsibility can pose a major challenge if the person is uncooperative and confused and cannot understand why all the doctor's visits and tests are needed.

The effects on the primary caregiver for patients with a cognitive impairment disorder have been well studied (Poulshock and Deimling 1984; Pruchno and Potasknik 1989) and suggest that caregivers have an increased frequency of medical disorders and emotional effects such as depression. The higher the degree of cognitive impairment, the heavier the burden (Poulshock and Deimling 1984). Studies comparing stress levels for those caring for physically ill or demented elderly patients suggest that caregivers of demented patients suffer greater stress (Houlihan 1987), possibly because of the patient's progressive deterioration and the absence of the psychological rewards that might derive from episodes of clear improvement.

The family must determine how to deal with reversed family roles (i.e., when the child becomes the caregiver of the parent). The dominant member of a couple might become dependent after developing a disorder, and then the formerly dependent spouse must become the caregiver.

Resolution of old conflicts and restoration of good relations between family members and the index person are extremely important possibilities in this last phase of life. With irreversible dementia, the possibility for such resolutions is lost and must be mourned. With delirium, family members may get another chance. Experiencing the person's temporary loss of memory and personality function can dramatize the need to heal relationships when the delirium clears and the mind and essence "return."

Caregiving for individuals with dementia is associated with an unusually high incidence of family conflict, most commonly between the caregiver and one or two siblings. The unavoidable conflicts that might occur in any family accommodating a major stress are compounded by differences in the siblings' expectations of each other, often with each person able to justify his or her position. This conflict is usually reported to be painful and is sometimes described as a burden equal to the caregiving itself.

Those around the person with Alzheimer's disease are often distraught and overwhelmed with anger, sadness, powerlessness, and fear. The anger relates to the powerlessness and helplessness associated with watching a loved one lose the essence of his or her intellect and character.

Families living with a member with a cognitive impairment disorder suffer the pain of being with a loved one who cannot recognize even close family members. This eerie, upsetting experience can lead to a sense of helplessness and loss of hope.

■ Family Maintenance of the Symptoms

The most obvious family contribution to symptom maintenance or exacerbation may relate to disturbed family dynamics and behaviors. Individuals with cognitive impairment disorders may lose many cognitive functions, but they may remain sensitive to their environment. An Alzheimer's patient living in a chaotic or violent situation is likely to present with severe behavior problems and family demands for placement (Silliman et al. 1988).

The course of both acute and chronic cognitive impairment disorders is greatly influenced by the family environment. Sometimes well-meaning family members try to "help" by repeatedly testing the patient's memory just as the doctor does, assuming that it must somehow have an effect on the dementia: "What is today's date? Who visited us last night? What did we do yesterday?" These questions lead to conflict and to angry outbursts by the person who is being asked to focus on what he or she cannot recall. Medications may not be administered at all or may be given irregularly, and the family may ignore suggestions regarding memory aids and orientation signs. The family may not heed medical evaluations and recommendations. The course of the disorder can be influenced as much by these factors as by the underlying pathology.

A sudden increase in difficulty managing a chronically demented patient may be a result of medical complications of other conditions or new infarcts. Psychosocial events must also be considered in the differential diagnosis—especially a disruption of the relationship with the primary caregiver. The demented patient can sense danger or fear and is sensitive to changes in the caregiver, such as illness or burnout, but has lost much of the cognitive ability needed to process these perceptions. The elderly person then presents with agitation that often requires hospitalization.

Therapists must be alert for the possible connection between worsening cognitive condition of a patient and elder abuse or exploitation. The abuse or exploitation may be a manifestation of the caregiver's own impulse or substance-related disorder, and these behaviors must be met with sanctions and consequences. More often, the behaviors are the family's only way of signaling that the caregiver is overwhelmed, needs care him- or herself, and can no longer function without assistance.

The spouse or children commonly blame the person for the cognitive or personality deterioration, and this environment does not help the functioning of the impaired person. The family may also interpret demented behaviors as hostility. Such attitudes may originate in old grudges, injustices, and negative projections. They may also reflect the psychological need to avoid the fear of one's own aging, infirmity, dependency, and death.

Family members may respond differently to different deficits, almost as if each member has a special relationship with different parts of the person's brain.

> One woman with multi-infarct dementia had deteriorated markedly. She lived at home with her family and was showing marked impairment in dominant parietal lobe functions, which the family tolerated without any problem. The family presented for help only after a small nondominant parietal stroke left her unable to care for her granddaughter.

■ Functions of the Symptoms Within the Family

The family defines, categorizes, and "bundles" new behaviors as dementia, delirium, or amnesia rather than as "normal forgetting," "just getting old," or "pretty good recall for someone his age." The family's interpretation of behavior as pathological may have varied functions. In cases of serious cognitive changes, the family can function as objective factual observers who bypass denial and minimization and ensure that memory and mental status changes are addressed and urgent medical issues are investigated.

In other families, the practice of labeling behaviors and memory lapses as dementia may be applied a bit too readily to a family member who has tended to be isolated in the past and who has a history of problems in the family. If this is the case, the assessment says more about family discord than it does about the measurement of cognitive deterioration and therefore cannot be accepted as objective (Hanson 1989). This awareness of family context in the presentation of a parent with dementia is useful in understanding and generating hypotheses about those cases in which the demand for placement or elaborate medical workup seems excessive, based on objective clinical findings. The interventions will be different if the family's complaint seems more related to anger, blaming, and isolation of a parent rather than to the individual's cortical atrophy or delirium.

The function of symptoms in family members must also be considered. Caregivers often present with depression, anger, isolation, and confusion. A person with depression may offer to be the caregiver partly out of a mature wish to contribute and partly out of a guilty, depressed martyrdom that will eventually take a toll elsewhere.

Cognitive deterioration may function to help balance power in a relationship. The most common example is the tyrannical spouse who becomes the concerned caregiver in response to the diagnosis of dementia or delirium. The disorders may elicit nurturance from family members who express caring behaviors only in response to illness.

The disorders may also elicit hidden resources in families. Conflict and discord may be overcome and families may be reunited in an attempt to deal with the extreme stress of 24-hour caregiving for a parent or spouse. Occasionally a child will express gratitude at the opportunity to give back to the parent through providing such care.

■ Adverse Consequences of Change

Beware the compulsive caregiver who suddenly has no one to care for. "Unemployed caregivers" are likely to become medically ill. For those whose identities are completely intertwined with their role as caregivers, the death of a parent or spouse with chronic dementia or the recovery of a more acutely ill patient leaves the caregiver searching for meaning and uncertain of identity. These caregivers have lost other interests, friends, and skills during the years spent fulfilling 24-hour responsibilities. When the extreme demands are suddenly removed, relief mixes with emptiness and panic.

When a delirium is successfully treated, old relationship problems are likely to return. If a depressed overfunctioning caregiver becomes less depressed, she may demand that other family members share the caregiver role. This demand can ignite family conflicts that were merely smoldering when the caregiver was bearing the burden for the larger group.

■ Special Systemic Dimensions

■ Family History and Genetics

The complexities of medical and dementing illness in an aging parent usually occur as the children are themselves entering middle age, feeling a bit more forgetful, and becoming obsessed with aging. To then see parents "lose their minds" is terrifying and creates intense concern with inheritability of the disorder.

Although there is evidence of overall increased risk for first-degree relatives of Alzheimer's patients, this evidence is complicated by the existence of both a familial and nonfamilial form, the suggestion of an increased risk if the onset of dementia is before age 70, and continuing questions about the significance of abnormality in chromosome 21. Estimates of risk to relatives vary from about 8% by age 65 (Mace and Rabins 1991) to 50% by age 90 (Mohs et al. 1987). The complex patterns of risk are still being elucidated (Silverman et al. 1994).

■ Gender

The caregiving role is often filled by oldest daughters or daughters-in-law. Because women outlive men, women commonly find themselves taking care of first their husbands and then their own mothers. The overrepresentation of women as caregivers is likely to increase.

Male caregivers report less stress than their female counterparts. Men seem to take a more detached stance in caring for patients with dementia. Interestingly, however, reports show that women's approach to caregiving becomes more similar to that of men as the patient's dementia progresses (Goldstein 1990).

■ Intimacy

Delirium and dementia obstruct the capacity for intimacy by limiting the level of awareness of self and other. Family members may comment that their relationship with the index person is dead because the person's mind or soul is gone. It is impossible to have intimate moments when a delirious person confuses one family member with other real or imagined people.

Moments of intimacy are still possible for some, though the expression may be subtle and brief. A caregiver of a parent with dementia may describe quiet moments of caregiving in which the person has a certain look or moment of lucidity. Warmth and gratitude are expressed, and the moment is experienced as brief though deep intimacy.

Cognitive impairment disorders have an effect on other family members' experience of intimacy. Caregivers may note a negative impact on their own marriages when their energies are absorbed in nursing a parent with chronic dementia. Sometimes the caregiver avoids spousal intimacy by overfocusing on the parent with dementia. Even if this loss of intimacy is not the caregiver's intention, the spouse may not be able to deal with the competitive or rejected feelings associated with having effectively lost a spouse to an in-law. At the same time, the caregiver feels trapped between loyalty to the spouse and loyalty to the parent with dementia.

■ Loyalty

Loyalty is a crucial part of the kinship bond that accrues throughout a person's life, and the issue of what the child owes the parent becomes prominent during the last years of the parent's life.

The rules of loyalty vary from one family to another and must be investigated rather than assumed. In some families, children are seen as owing complete self-sacrifice to the aging parent and must fulfill this obligation to express their love. Other families believe that sacrifice should never be asked of one's children, and aging parents do not feel entitled to caregiving by their children. These parents feel they violate their loyalty to their children if they impose any burden on the children.

Children also vary in their need or desire to give back to parents. Occasionally, an adult child expresses pleasurable anticipation of being the child who will care for an elderly parent, seeing this care as a chance to give back to the parent for all that the child has received throughout a lifetime. Adults without a system of accountability or a "ledger" of what is owed to a parent may experience extreme conflict as the parent's disorder worsens and decisions must be made.

Family loyalty is a major issue in the "choice" of which child will be the caregiver, a decision that involves a complex and often unconscious selection process. The child who feels the most obligation, guilt, or need to return past favors is the most likely to step forward. This person may have made a promise to a parent or sibling who died. This selection process may also offer the last chance for one sibling to attain the role of "favorite child." Expectations of oldest and unmarried daughters as well as hopes for inheritance all play a role in choosing the primary caregiver.

Countertransference

Therapists working with families of the aging must deal with prejudice against the old. Therapists will feel a pull to devalue the elderly, especially if the person is demented and ill. Work with cognitive impairment disorders means facing one's own fear of death and infirmity. Clinicians rely on their memory and have a strong fear of cognitive impairment. The therapist must be aware of the tendency to overidentify with, distance from, ridicule, or patronize those who trigger this fear.

Families are often enraged with the patient but feel too guilty to recognize this anger. Their rage may instead be directed at the professional who tries to help but can do nothing to stop the progression of the disorder. Therapists may be shamed by their inability to have any significant effect on the course of the disorder. This shame may push the therapist to avoid the family members or to become angry with them.

■ Posterity

Grandchildren may feel left out or competitive with the cognitively impaired grandparent because the parent may give more to the elder than to the younger generation. At other times, small children especially will ally with a grandparent because of their similar vulnerability and need for protection. The family dealing with a member with delirium or dementia sends a message to children about the rules and obligations to the parent's generation. The children perceive a model of caregiving that may someday involve the parent.

■ Treatment

■ Standard Individual Therapies

The main treatments of delirium and the amnestic disorders are the treatments of the underlying disorders. These include psychiatric disorders, such as depression, and medical factors, such as infection or toxicity, which may make the patient appear much more deteriorated than he or she really is. If these factors are not addressed, the family may consider placement and guardianship questions prematurely.

For the primary dementias, the present treatments are at a rudimentary level and include psychopharmacology and environmental changes. No known pharmacological agents have been proven consistently useful in double-blind studies for treating memory loss. Most research and clinical strategies have been with cholinergic agents.

■ Family Modalities

Family therapy for individuals with delirium or dementia takes place largely without the active participation of the person him- or herself. Although it is respectful to have the person present for many sessions (e.g., when the diagnosis is presented), it can be disrespectful to always include someone who will be confused by discussion in a therapy session.

Multigenerational family sessions can be extremely valuable. During these sessions, members of each generation can see what they might owe to aging, frail parents in return for a lifetime of care.

Sibling sessions are crucial when the individual with cognitive impairment disorder is the sole surviving parent. Dividing up the caregiving can either draw a family together as they share a meaningful task or ignite new or existing grievances that can last for generations, especially if one branch of the family perceives themselves as carrying a disproportionate load.

Marital sessions are indicated when the caregiving role of one spouse for a parent is creating jealousy and discord. Parent-child sessions can be enlightening when the parent is making caregiver decisions about his or her own parent and can share dilemmas and family expectations.

■ Psychoeducation

For patients with delirium, the distraught family is usually seen in the hospital, often in an intensive care unit. Family members do not know what to do or say when the individual suddenly does not know who they are. The clinician can explain delirium and the medical workup to the family; he or she can ask the family to help by orienting the patient frequently. The clinician explains that their familiar faces have a greater chance of getting through to the individual and thanks the family for their efforts.

Most treatment approaches for dementia include family and multifamily group educational sessions during which the disorders are explained. These sessions emphasize the practical problems and expected developments in the course of the illness, in terms of both the individual's illness progression and the family's likely range of responses. Specific blocks to solutions are identified and resolved as fully as possible. For example, if a family's assumption that only women can take care of others is causing hardship and resentment for the women, the discussion focuses on finding ways to include male family members in the caregiving.

Family members can be taught to recognize two types of changes: *adaptations,* which are readily controlled, and *deficits* (memory failings, personality changes, and decreased impulse control), which have a physiological basis and are beyond control. The family can learn how to discourage maladaptations, such as temper tantrums, and how to reinforce positive adaptations, such as having the individual make lists and use memory aids. The family can insist on rigid adherence to specific storage places for tools and utensils.

Families appreciate instruction about both the cognitive and personality changes of these syndromes. An understanding of the classic personality changes (labile affects, superficial affects, impulsivity and unpredictability, self-centeredness) helps the family gain a better sense of control over their world of loss and chaos. They can begin to grasp the effects of the disorder on the *person*, not only on the thoughts and reasoning capacity.

Treatment for cognitive impairment disorders can include referral of interested family members to self-help groups such as the Alzheimer's Association, which has an extensive network of chapters. The group offers education and a chance to share information, emotions, and support with others confronting the same struggles. The caregiver support group is one of the main therapeutic modalities for families of patients with degenerative dementia. The same research literature that documents increased medical and emotional disorders in caregivers also advocates the participation of primary caregivers in self-help and psychoeducational support groups (Goldstein 1990; Perkins and Poynton 1990; Shields 1992). Families report some relief from the feelings of isolation, a greater understanding of the disorders and of their conflicted feelings, and an enhanced ability to set limits and tend to their own needs with less guilt.

Other studies suggest that individual and family counseling is more effective than support groups in providing relief and enhanced functioning for the family involved in caregiving (Whitlatch et al. 1991).

■ New Stories

Martyrdom as overfunctioning. Caregiving can destroy a sense of identity and interest in life; it can also be associated with a sense of martyrdom. The therapist can offer alternate realities that may free the martyr for other roles. Alternatives for the caregiver may include insisting on help and respite, taking care of him- or herself in crucial ways, or even investigating placement.

Burden as privilege. The caregiver who feels martyred may become open to a new way of thinking about his or her lot in having to care for an aging spouse or parent with dementia. The caregiver may be asked to consider whether any positive aspects at all can be gleaned from what certainly is an unbelievably heavy burden. If none can be found, the therapist can share the story of the adult child who sincerely said, "How fortunate and privileged I am to be able to give back in this way." This example does not minimize the contributions of the caregiver or the trauma and intensity of the demands, but it can be seen as demonstrating one possible positive aspect of the responsibility of caring for an impaired spouse or parent (Boss 1990).

One result of a long life.   Most researchers conclude that all people would become demented if they lived long enough. Improved health care can be seen as the reason we now live long enough to become demented, instead of having the shorter lives that were typical before medical advances took place. This view may offer the family a somewhat more accepting attitude toward the individual and toward dementia itself.

Ambiguous loss.   The concept of a vague, almost indescribable sense of loss has been extremely helpful for many families after a cognitive impairment disorder is diagnosed. In some ways, the clarity of death is envied. The idea of ambiguous loss helps many families tolerate the particular form of grief they must endure for an extended and uncertain length of time (Boss 1990).

Opportunities for family repair.   The crisis of adapting to a cognitive impairment disorder forces families together, for better or worse. Previously cut-off and distant families, both nuclear and extended, find themselves bound by a common history and an urgent need to solve the problem together. In some families, the crisis can reactivate old conflicts; in others, it brings new possibilities for healing their relationships. The parent with dementia can thus be seen as offering a kind of gift to the next generations by bringing the family together at this time.

Family as refugees.   The sudden onset of delirium or amnestic disorders pushes families— against their will —into a new way of life in a new place, much like political refugees (Sachs 1991). In cognitive impairment disorders, this new place is full of strange facilities such as hospitals, nursing homes, and rehabilitation centers. The "dislocated" family can focus on the same things refugees focus on: adapting to constantly changing circumstances and maintaining their sense of purpose.

Deconstructing dementia. Some families show a pattern of magnifying cognitive deficit and minimizing cognitive competence. The family member labeled as having a cognitive deficit is the person who has been isolated or discredited for years (Hanson 1989). In such cases, the therapist can experiment with efforts to decrease the emotional isolation of the individual, perhaps by identifying an ally.

An objective assessment for cognitive impairment can be made. If these signs are either absent or equivocal, the therapist and family can discuss the idea that the deficits are either normal and no worse than those experienced by other family members or not serious enough to decrease function.

Questions and comments can focus on examples of "remembering" episodes, or times when the individual has shown competence. Examples of situations in which the allegedly demented person remembered better than others can be playfully introduced.

Genogram. During this exercise, families reveal the patterns and expectations of caregiving based on past examples of dementing and chronic illnesses in grandparents and great-grandparents. This story will help explain the current generation's both resourceful and conflictual handling of cognitive impairment disorders. The degree to which each member fears inheriting the disorder will emerge during this assessment. Past sibling conflicts will be revealed and will help both the therapist and the family to grasp some of the predeterminants of the present conflicts (e.g., perceptions about who was the favorite or who owes the most).

■ Additional Reading

Aronson MK (ed): Understanding Alzheimer's Disease. New York, Charles Scribner's Sons, 1988

Eisdorfer D, Cohen D: Management of the patient and family coping with dementing illness. J Fam Pract 12:831–837, 1981

Goldberg JR: The new frontier: marriage and family therapy with aging families. Family Therapy News 23:1, 1992

Haley WE: A family–behavioral approach to the treatment of the cognitively impaired elderly. Gerontologist 23:18–20, 1983

Herr JJ, Weakland JH: Counseling Elders and Their Families: Practical Techniques for Applied Gerontology. New York, Springer-Verlag, 1979

Rabins PV, Mace NL, Lucas MJ: The impact of dementia on the family. JAMA 248:333–335, 1982

Raia PA: Helping patients and families to take control. Psychiatric Annals 24:192–196, 1994

Scott JP, Roberto KA, Hutton JT: Families of Alzheimer's victims: family support to the caregivers. J Am Geriatr Soc 34:348–354, 1986

Spitzer RL, First MB, Williams JBW, et al: Now is the time to retire the term "organic mental disorders." Am J Psychiatry 149:240–244, 1992

Williams JM, Kay T (eds): Head Injury: A Family Matter. Baltimore, MD, Paul H. Brookes, 1991

Zarit SH, Anthony CR, Boutselis M: Interventions with caregivers of dementia patients: comparison of two approaches. Psychol Aging 2:225–232, 1987

■ References

American Psychiatric Association: Diagnostic and Statistical Manual of Mental Disorders, 4th Edition. Washington, DC, American Psychiatric Association, 1994

Boss P: Ambiguous loss, in Living Beyond Loss: Death in the Family. Edited by Walsh F, McGoldrick M. New York, WW Norton, 1990, pp 164–175

Goldstein MZ: The role of mutual support groups and family therapy for caregivers of demented elderly. Journal of Geriatric Psychiatry 23:117–128, 1990

Gwyther LP, Blazer DF: Family therapy and the dementia patient. Am Fam Physician 29:149–156, 1984

Hanson BG: Definitional deficit: a model of senile dementia in context. Fam Process 28:281–289, 1989

Houlihan JP: Families caring for frail and demented elderly: a review of selected findings. Family Systems Medicine 5:344–356, 1987

Mace NL, Rabins PV: The Thirty-Six Hour Day: A Family Guide to Caring for Persons With Alzheimer's Disease, Related Dementing Illnesses, and Memory Loss in Later Life, 2nd Edition. Baltimore, MD, Johns Hopkins University Press, 1991

Malmgren R: Epidemiology of aging, in Textbook of Geriatric Neuropsychiatry. Edited by Coffey CE, Cummings JL. Washington, DC, American Psychiatric Press, 1994, pp 17–33

Mohs RC, Breitner JCS, Silverman JM, et al: Alzheimer's disease: morbid risk among first-degree relatives approximates 50% by 90 years of age. Arch Gen Psychiatry 44:405–408, 1987

Perkins RE, Poynton CF: Group counseling for relatives of hospitalized presenile dementia patients: a controlled study. British Journal of Clinical Psychology 29:287–295, 1990

Poulshock W, Deimling G: Families caring for elders in residence: issues in the measurement of burden. J Gerontol 39:230–239, 1984

Pruchno RA, Potasknik SL: Caregiving spouses: physical and mental health in perspective. J Am Geriatr Soc 37:697–705, 1989

Sachs PR: Treating Families of Brain Injury Survivors. New York, Springer-Verlag, 1991

Shields CG: Family interaction and caregivers of Alzheimer's disease patients: correlates of depression. Fam Process 31:19–33, 1992

Silliman RA, Sternberg J, Fretwell M: Disruptive behavior in demented patients living within disturbed families. J Am Geriatr Soc 36:617–618, 1988

Silverman JM, Li G, Zaccario ML, et al: Patterns of risk in first-degree relatives of patients with Alzheimer's disease. Arch Gen Psychiatry 51:577–586, 1994

Teusink JP, Mahler S: Helping families cope with Alzheimer's disease. Hosp Community Psychiatry 35:152–156, 1984

Whitlatch CJ, Zarit SH, von Eye A: Efficacy of interventions with caregivers: a reanalysis. Gerontologist 31:9–14, 1991

CHAPTER 15

Impulse-Control Disorders Not Elsewhere Classified

Ann M.

Ann M., a 35-year-old schoolteacher, described her husband Paul's gambling problem and said that her father was also a gambler. Later, Ann said that her father often berated Paul for his gambling sprees but would then invite him to go on all-expense-paid trips to a nearby casino resort, where her father provided cash to get Paul started.

Debbie L.

Debbie L., a 17-year-old who was seen in individual therapy, had experienced her parents' unhappy marriage and divorce and had engaged in considerable shoplifting as well as stealing from her mother's friends. Her mother was described as alcoholic and had unstable relationships with men. The mother's own mother was also alcoholic and was still deeply involved in their family life. When Debbie stayed with her father, she felt a greater sense of stability and social acceptability.

As Debbie began to improve with treatment, she began to focus on her father's lifestyle. Although he engaged in substantial drug use and had accumulated many large debts that went unpaid, she emphasized his external signs of success—a young wife, a large house, and new cars. Debbie began to see that her father was not as consistent and reliable as she had thought, and she saw that she could not learn to understand herself better by continuing her relationship with him as it was then defined. When Debbie began to question her father about his actions or ideas, he reneged on his promise to pay her treatment expenses. The therapist then realized it would be impossible to ignore family forces and switched to an approach that involved several family members.

Terri E.

Terri E., an 18-year-old, presented to the emergency room following an overdose. After she was medically treated, she was evaluated psychiatrically and interviewed with her parents, who had been present the entire time. The parents said that their daughter stole things, even though the family was well-off financially. Their theory about the overdose was that she was upset and ashamed after having been caught stealing once again—this time a sweater from a store near her college. The school expelled her, as they had promised they would if she shoplifted again.

During the family interview, the mother acted cold and at times hostile. Terri said they had never related well to each other, but father and daughter had always been close. The father and mother had been getting along poorly since Terri left for school 5 months ago. Her father agreed that life was more fun around the house when Terri was home, and Terri said she felt guilty leaving Dad alone with Mom. Now she would be able to keep her father company and help restore balance to the floundering family.

■ Perspective on the Disorders

The impulse disorders are grouped together somewhat loosely based on the presence of tension that builds, pushes for release, and cannot be resisted. The person then acts on the impulse and feels relief. Many of the impulse disorders just miss meeting the criteria that define other disorders. For example, pathological gambling is strongly related to obsessive-compulsive disorder and addiction. Pathological gambling and obsessive-compulsive disorder are both characterized by out-of-control, irresistible impulses that are expressed compulsively. DSM-IV

(American Psychiatric Association 1994) recognizes addictions only if the attachment is to a substance. If that definition broadens, pathological gambling will likely be considered an addiction. Trichotillomania is likely to be reclassified as a type of obsessive-compulsive disorder.

New neurobiological findings involving impulsivity and aggression may suggest a recategorizing of obsessive-compulsive disorders from anxiety to impulse disorders (Lopez-Ibor 1990; Stein and Hollander 1993) as a relationship between compulsivity and impulsivity is elucidated. Both compulsive and impulsive behavior may be associated with dysregulation of serotonergic transmission and with behavioral disorders. One appealing theory puts them at opposite ends of a "risk" continuum. In compulsivity, the behavior is typically inhibited, fearful, and risk avoiding. In impulsivity, the behavior is typically disinhibited and risk seeking (Hollander 1993; Stein and Hollander 1993).

A crucial area of study for family therapy will be the assessment of the family's role in triggering and reacting to problematic behaviors and the examination of differential responses to impulsive and compulsive actions. For example, fearful compulsive behaviors are so well suited to an anxious, inhibited family that the symptoms will not be brought to a therapist's attention until they are extreme and impairing. A tougher, more machismo family can tolerate aggressive behaviors but may panic at the risk-aversive nature of anxious obsessive-compulsive symptoms.

Family violence, especially specific patterns of couples violence, is considered here in connection with intermittent explosive disorder. Although family violence encompasses much more than its impulsivity component, the pervasive problem of battering fits intermittent explosive disorder in that much violence is episodic and the behaviors are grossly out of proportion to the precipitants. The distinctive patterns of spousal abuse may require a separate definition, and the category of "Abuse Disorder" (Zeitlin 1989) has been proposed.

Further study of the role of intermittent explosive disorder may help provide much-needed insight into the family context of violence and may suggest possible therapeutic interventions for this pervasive problem. Many have attempted to define the nature of this violent disorder in terms of the individual. Initially, the disorders referred to as intermittent explosive disorders were thought to be neurological or related to seizures, but these criteria have been dropped. Some might categorize intermittent explosive disorder as a conduct disorder or severe personality disorder.

Such diagnostic considerations of violence are helpful, but they might best be applied in describing the state of the abuser *between* episodes of violence. To understand the violent act itself, therapists need a more complete understanding of the family contexts in which so much of this violence occurs.

Acts of explosive aggression are most usefully considered as part of relational cycles that involve at least the relationship between the people involved, the neurobiology of the impulsively aggressive offender, and the larger societal and cultural context, which may subtly or explicitly condone violence.

Table 15–1 summarizes some aspects of the family context of impulse disorders, which is described in more detail in the next section.

Table 15–1. Adjustment disorders in context

Effects of the disorder on the family
- Marital problems
- Constant state of vigilance for next episode
- "Walking on eggs"
- Financial worries; related anxiety

Family maintenance of the symptoms
- External stresses
- Difficulty in marriages
- Any interpersonal turmoil
- Inability of parents to meet child's needs
- Enabling behaviors by spouse or others
- Societal ambivalence about violence

Functions of the symptoms within the family
- Control of underlying psychiatric disorders
- Maintenance of family stability
- Diverting of attention from other problem

Adverse consequences of change
- Potential for facilitating violence in couples
- In pyromania, legal problems and rejection by helping agencies
- Depression and low self-esteem emerge when person not engaged in impulsive behavior

---

■ Connections of the Symptoms to the System

■ Effects of the Disorder on the Family

Each impulse disorder episode leaves families in a state of vigilance for the next episode and brings its own kind of worry. An episode of pyromania is a sporadic but devastating event, and the stress of waiting for the next episode can be extreme. Sleep is destroyed as parents listen for sounds that could mean a threat to the rest of the family or to someone outside the family.

The marriage of the pathological gambler is usually in trouble. The spouse suffers from the stress of constant financial problems, phone calls from creditors, and distrust of the gambler. Rage, shame, hurt, and uncertainty build. The gambler's words cannot be trusted because the need to gamble takes over all other motivations. The spouse may not even have the advantage of knowing when the gambling behavior is taking place because it can be conducted in secret with no immediate telltale signs, such as alcohol on the breath (Rosenthal 1992). In pathological gambling, financial worries lead to a pervasive anxiety for all members. Long absences of the gambler and bitter marital battles on his or her return do not bode well for the home atmosphere.

In intermittent explosive disorder, the "walking on eggs" phenomenon occurs as the spouse or children carefully watch the face of the abusive parent to see if something has set off that terrifying state. The family believes that if they are attentive enough they can control impulse-driven behavior, a belief that persists. Hypervigilance and fear of the next episode predominate.

■ Family Maintenance of the Symptoms

Any interpersonal turmoil can increase gambling behavior in someone who is already hooked. The gambler's anger at his spouse, for instance, creates intolerable negative feelings. Gambling is relied on to soothe the feelings and distract the person from them. If the gambler is angry at the spouse, the trip to the racetrack is a way of getting back at her without confronting her directly. Eventually, any action by the spouse becomes an excuse for the behavior. A familiar cycle is launched wherein the spouse nags or expresses anger about the gambling. The unreflective gambler quickly escapes the turmoil by going to the casino, which enrages the spouse further and inspires an increase in the attack.

In fire setting in children, families are observed to show poor parental supervision, much external stress, more symptoms overall (such as depression), less affective expression, poor marriages (Kazdin and Kolko 1986), and higher rates of divorce and adoption (Kunhley et al. 1982). One theory about childhood origins of pyromania implicates a period where the child demonstrates an increased demand for support. The family is revealed as unable to respond well to this demand, largely because of chronic crises. Tension and rage build in the child and push for expression (Soltys 1992).

Male violence in couples is a study of cycles. In one common form of the cycle, a man is predisposed to violence by a subtle nervous system defect. He has been raised to believe that his identity as a man requires never submitting to the influence of a woman, and he has been taught that manhood means not having needs and not depending on anyone. Then he meets a woman who has X-ray eyes that see the caring, hurt little boy beneath the wrathful bravado and who wants to nurture him. His hidden need to be cared for makes her irresistible and central to his survival, and he must guard her from other men or interests. If she tries to assert her own identity, his own survival is threatened and he cannot control the affective storm within.

The larger social context is ambivalent about containing or stopping violence against women and presents no consistent threat of censure. The impulse to dominate is unchecked, and the abuser rages. He demonstrates his loyalty to the family of origin as he shows himself to be *their* kind of man. The next day he feels guilty and contrite, and his wife sees the hurt little boy and forgives the abuse.

This forgiveness and willingness to stay in the relationship have long puzzled therapists. It is more understandable when the observer realizes that, for her own reasons, the woman partly believes the accusations the violent person screams at her and is struggling with the guilty sense that she somehow caused the whole episode. In this way, the cycle begins again (Goldner et al. 1990; Serra 1993).

◼ Functions of the Symptoms Within the Family

The gambler may be warding off depression or panic. The family is accustomed to the impulse problem and is spared having to deal with the underlying disorder. The public nature of an impulse problem, such as stealing, may gain the family's attention and provide the incentive for seeking help. At this point, underlying impulse problems with substances, sexuality, or other similarly driven behaviors may be discovered.

The impulse disorders serve to decrease the tension of one member of the family and may play a role in maintaining family stability.

> One husband related a severe problem with rejection sensitivity that led him to become enraged and to direct his anger at his wife and children. His wife had filed divorce papers, and while they awaited a court date, the husband's anxiety drove him back to an old gambling habit. This habit took him out of the house much of the week, which had a calming effect on the family. The family discovered that the rage attacks were gone when he was at home between gambling episodes. His wife withdrew her divorce request because she felt she could live with the absences and gambling as long as she and the children were not targets of the rages.

Trichotillomania and pyromania offer dramatic possibilities for diverting attention away from almost any other problem in the family. Even an estranged or distant family may pull together to deal with the larger threat.

■ Adverse Consequences of Change

Attempts to deal with violence through couples therapy can introduce the troubling possibility that family therapists may inadvertently facilitate violence. The wife may be open and frank in the couples session, perhaps to please the therapist or just to be honest. The husband, who has not yet learned how to control his behavior, may become angry because his wife told these secrets to a stranger or insulted him and "made him feel small." He will label her action as disloyal and demeaning. The wife's safety is now a concern because abuse may occur after the session.

To reduce the risk of contributing to violent behavior, individual sessions may be preferable. Any family therapy sessions that are held for impulse disorders must emphasize accountability of the person for his or her actions and for getting treatment for the disorder. Other family members must understand that therapy may make the situation more tense and that no one but the index person can control the violent assaults. The violent person is responsible for his behavior regardless of the perceived provocation, and the spouse's first concern is for her own and the children's safety.

Recognition and diagnosis of pyromania brings legal troubles and difficulty finding help. The doors of helping agencies are often closed to the pyromaniac. Every school and residential or hospital facility will refuse to offer assistance. Fire setters may be the most outcast of all groups because of the potential threat they represent to all other occupants of a building.

Diagnosis may also bring depression.

> A 10-year-old boy was caught after having set three fires, one of which had burned down an apartment building. Once an inpatient psychiatric facility was found that was willing to assess and treat the child, he became suicidally depressed and attempted to jump from the third floor of the hospital parking garage.
>
> Family sessions later revealed a series of multigenerational secrets about impulse problems, including the suicide of an uncle. The conversations helped the parents recognize how these past secrets had paralyzed their ability to react to their son's out-of-control behavior and his cries for strong intervention. The family reported their first glimmer of hope that they would get some control over this overwhelming problem.

Stopping the impulsive action often leads to the expression of other disorders and affects. Most gamblers are overt about wondering if they can tolerate the low feelings about self that overwhelm them when they are not gambling (McElroy et al. 1992).

■ Special Systemic Dimensions

■ Family History and Genetics

The families of those with impulse disorders are generally a depressed, substance-abusing group. Family studies of pathological gamblers report that 18% to 50% of the gamblers have at least one alcoholic parent. From 21% to 28% have parents who were pathological gamblers, and approximately 33% have parents with mood disorders. In violent offenders, one study showed that 81% had alcoholic first- and second-degree relatives (McElroy et al. 1992).

Gender

New insights into couples violence shed light on the familiar phenomenon of futile therapeutic attempts to convince abused persons to leave the abusive situation. These women are viewed as "resisting" therapist advice, admonitions, and interpretations, but it is far more likely that women stay in these relationships in response to relational and cultural forces—not as a result of intrapsychic masochism (Goldner et al. 1990; Serra 1993; Symonds 1979).

The woman is asking for help not in leaving the husband but in stopping the abuse. Ironically, the woman feels betrayed by therapists who urge her to leave the abusive husband instead of stopping the abuse so she can stay. Again ironically, the woman who does leave ends up being the punished one, as she is usually left with full responsibility for the children, much of the guilt for the breakup of the family, and little or no money or support.

Intimacy

In intermittent explosive disorder and pathological gambling, as with substance-related disorders, the "morning after" phenomenon provides moments of unparalleled closeness.

The capacity of the abusive couple for this temporary but strong, loving closeness is a mystery to observers ("Why does he treat her so badly when he seems so attached to her? Why does she keep forgiving him?"). These times of intimate relatedness can be strengthened even further by an underlying bond created by the secret of abuse that the couple keeps from the world.

Loyalty

The abuser's family of origin often defines manhood as equal to absolute strength and invulnerability and demands that offspring maintain a primary allegiance to kin. When this man is drawn toward his wife and feels her influence over him, he becomes confused and panicked, feels he is losing his manhood, and senses that he is being disloyal to his family of origin. At these moments, he is easily incited to violence.

To assert his authority, the abuser may demand the same fierce loyalty from his spouse that his family demands of him. He experiences as betrayal and threat any connections she has with her own family of origin. If she simply mentions her father, for example, he hears only that she must prefer her father to him. Again he feels a boiling, primitive rage.

For the woman, loyalty to her husband and to her family of origin can be simultaneously demonstrated by remaining in the relationship. Her family has trained her to put others first, and she will preserve a sense of compassion for her contrite spouse.

Map of Emotions

Impulses are acted upon because the person is unable to imagine experiencing the related affects. Relief is obtained only from the impulsive actions, and the behaviors become an addictive and repetitive way to avoid emotional pain.

Violence can be viewed partly as the result of powerlessness that becomes intolerable. The grandiosity of the angry, out-of-control moment allows the person to feel temporarily powerful and dominating. This response is especially tempting for men who have been taught that fear and vulnerability represent weakness, feminization, and the end of the hoped-for closeness with the father. Closeness to a woman is seen as shameful because it represents subjugation, weakness, and dependence.

Many of the other impulse disorders are associated with shame and inadequacy over the inability to control oneself, a highly valued ability that is recognized as the essence of mature functioning.

Countertransference

The more the clinician struggles with his or her own impulse-control issues or exerts excessive self-control to compensate for such impulse-control problems, the more he or she is likely to reject or become enraged with impulse-disordered patients. Certain actions such as fire setting, spouse abuse, and child beating are likely to elicit primitive responses in almost any therapist.

The therapist who becomes aware of hating the abusive person because of a frustrated need to help can make an effort to wait until a more productive understanding of the person comes. Taking a genogram, or multigenerational history, may help elucidate the index person's story. Therapy must continue at least until the victimizer can be understood as also having been victimized.

Therapists can also attempt to see themselves as researchers and to realize that no one else has yet determined how to offer definitive help to violent abusers or those with other impulse disorders. This stance can help reduce the pressure to fix problems completely. The therapist is free to experiment with therapies that might work, and an interested yet detached stance may be achieved. Sometimes treatable aspects of the disorder can then be uncovered.

Posterity

Much parenting focuses on helping children mature, delay gratification, and find alternatives to acting on impulses. A parent with an impulse disorder has severe deficiencies as a role model. The other parent must work especially hard to teach delay of gratification and to model being a more restrained, patient, mature adult. The parent with impulse disorder may be able to contribute by providing a model in areas in which he or she does have restraint. For example, the gambler may have no problem controlling his or her temper or food intake.

Children living in a family dominated by poor impulse control find that uncertainty is the only certainty. "Will this be a good or bad day? Will they fight again tonight? Should I take responsibility for protecting Mom or for keeping the cash hidden from Dad?"

Treatment

Standard Individual Therapies

Impulse disorders have been treated with almost every known pharmacological agent, but studies have been largely uncontrolled (American Psychiatric Association 1988; Lion 1992). The work of neurobiology in suggesting new relationships between aggressive impulsivity and dysregulation of the serotonergic systems will have major implications for pharmacotherapeutic interventions.

Psychotherapy approaches have emphasized increasing the index person's affective awareness, with the assumption that increased toleration of affect will lead to enhanced control over the need to act. Psychoanalytical approaches try to repair underlying ego weaknesses that have resulted from earlier traumas.

Social-behavioral approaches emphasize that the index person should leave the scene when impulses or rage is building. After an inappropriate expression of rage, the index person is also expected not only to take responsibility for the damage he or she has caused but also to make amends with those who were affected. Personal responsibility has the additional effect of reducing the likelihood of denial, blaming, and shame.

In kleptomania, no therapy has been found to be consistently useful. Some suggestion of benefit has been attributed to behavioral therapy, to antidepressants, and to the banning of all shopping (Rosenthal 1992).

Family Modalities

The treatment of impulse disorders is so difficult that the therapist will often need help, and so must consider bringing in the spouse, parents, children, and siblings. These meetings can give family members a chance to tell their stories. They can also further motivate the family to convince the index person that he or she must face the devastation associated with the impulsive behaviors. The threatened loss of family can help push the index person toward "hitting bottom" and encourage a serious engagement in treatment.

Therapy sessions might increase the same painful affects and thoughts that push toward impulsive discharge. This risk can be mentioned to the family to enhance their understanding of what feeds impulsiveness and to provide the experience of helping the index person find alternatives.

In pathological gambling, the threat of loss of the spouse connects to the "crunch" and the "bailout." As is true of alcoholic patients, the impulse disorder patient cannot get help until he or she has no choice but to face the problem (Boyd and Bolen 1970; Victor and Krug 1967).

Psychoeducation

Each disorder can be objectified and demystified by a discussion of prevalence, theories of etiology, treatments, natural course, and the experience of other families. Treatment of some disorders, such as gambling, can include referral to a 12-step program that provides a necessary spiritual component and emphasizes responsibility, humility, and an understanding of the disorder as addiction.

For disorders that affect children, such as pyromania, parent training is essential to define a nurturant parent-child relationship that includes clear, consistent limit setting, rewards for evidence of self-control, and consequences for transgressions.

Individuals and their families can learn about the emotions that are related to episodes of the disorder. They can learn to identify the feelings and events that are present before the impulse pushes for discharge and try to develop a strategy for change. With temper outbursts, the index person can learn to recognize the tension buildup; once the index person can sense the temper outburst coming, he or she can progress to learning how to let go of the tension—or, if unable to let go, then at least to be self-aware enough to leave the scene before the outburst occurs.

■ New Stories

A special bond.   In the treatment of intermittent explosive disorder or pathological gambling, a focus on positive aspects of the marital relationship may reveal the heavily guarded secret of the couples bond (Goldner et al. 1990). This positive focus can help expose what often shames both partners—their love for each other and their participation in a relationship that looks sick to observers. Outsiders blame them for maintaining the relationship (but rarely do anything to put a stop to the abuse). The therapist may be able to convey understanding of the hidden positive aspects of the relationship, which can lead to a productive consideration of the complex interpersonal reasons that the man abuses and the woman stays.

From "either/or" to "both/and."   An all-or-nothing perspective characterizes the intermittently violent couple. The couple may get along well until there is an empathic failure in either person, the wife's contact with her family of origin threatens the husband's tenuous sense of security, or a comment made during a therapy session leaves one person competing for the role of "most loved" ("Do you love me or your father the most?"). If the love is not perfect, all-consuming, and directed at the index person, what was formerly "all good" is transformed to "all bad" through the person's paranoia, cognitive all-or-nothing style, and perception of threat.

Therapy attempts to suggest that there are different kinds of love and that it is possible to love several people at once. Actions and people are discussed in a balanced way—as a combination of good and bad, rather than all good or all bad. Conversations emphasize exoneration (understanding) and accountability rather than oversimplified blaming.

He (she) still needs you.   Maladaptive impulsive behavior can be discussed in terms of how the behavior indicates immaturity. The family's view of the index person as evil or crazy may be recast if they see that he or she has not fully learned a central lesson of childhood: to delay gratification and to refrain from acting on every impulse (Imber Coppersmith 1981). Seeing the index person as functionally young and immature expands the family obligation from control and punishing to include continued parenting. This parenting will attempt to teach the difficult lessons of tolerating painful affects rather than taking the more immature and easier path of giving in to impulses.

A related idea for therapy is to engage the family as helpers in monitoring the progress or lack of progress in the index person's efforts to control impulsivity. This approach engages the family as more detached observers, thereby easing overengagement. The family can then deal with their powerlessness by focusing on something they *can* contribute.

He (She) can't help it; you can't help him (her).   Sometimes the family's simplistic blaming and enabling of the index person adds to their already excessive involvement in the person's concerns. Therapy can emphasize that the impulses are stronger and more powerful than the person who has them, and they may arise from forces that are out of the person's control, such as past learning or biology or both. The family's efforts to force the person to stop will be futile. Dialogue based on the following ideas might be useful:

> "The impulses seem to have proved too powerful to be influenced by any member of the family, even after tremendous effort, will, and collaborative energy. This has me wondering if it would be possible to give up trying, perhaps to take a short break just as an experiment. Then you can return to your usual approach until we meet next time. What do you think of this? What would happen?"

"If all of this energy could be freed from focusing on the problem,
what else might it be used for? Could the family's energy be used
to care for neglected members of the family for awhile? Or might
the energy bring all of you together to really put pressure on the
person to stay in treatment or to face the consequences of his or
her behavior?"

Amends.   The middle and end phases of therapy must include conversations about resolving some of the injustices that resulted from the
impulsivity. The early phase of therapy prepares the family for later
phases by discussing the injustices without minimizing their impact.
Anger and hurt are expressed throughout therapy. By the middle and
end phases, the abusive person is seen as having also been abused in
his or her own way but at the same time is expected to take responsibility for past actions and for present and future control of impulsive
behavior.

From this mature stance, the person with impulse disorder can
gradually work to rebuild trust in those who have been hurt. Creative
ways to make amends can be sought. The sessions can be used to encourage the beginnings of these difficult conversations.

Control.   Because impulse disorders involve a lack of control, many
comments that address aspects of power, willpower, self-control, or
self-determination are fitting. It can be helpful for families to consider
that control applies to behavior and not to feelings. Feelings are described as having a life of their own, whereas behavioral choices can be
made by the individual. This emphasis limits the excusing of inappropriate behavior that is based on feeling and can facilitate the understanding that in most cases feelings change only after the behavior
changes.

Solution-oriented questions can attempt to find aspects of maturity
that may have gone unnoticed by the family. Examples of the index
person's ability to delay gratification, to be self-sufficient in some small
way, or to be responsible about fulfilling a task can be discussed as
evidence of mature functioning. Questions such as those that follow
can be asked:

"How can you show that you are in charge of your own life?"
"How will your parents (children, spouse) begin to recognize that
you have taken charge of yourself (or your business, finances, gambling, temper)?"

> "What do you think it would take to get to a situation where others could leave you alone and know that you no longer needed to be watched, distrusted, and controlled?"
>
> "How could you demonstrate that you are no longer a slave to your impulses and addictions but instead are their master?"

Genogram.   The extended family history is likely to reveal impulse-control problems in past generations. The present disorder is then seen as a continuation of past family problems that may include substance abuse, temper, violence, gambling, eating disorders, sexual disorders, and compulsive rituals.

In some cases, family members may experience compassion for the first time in therapy as they recognize that the index person had very poor models. They may be surprised that the person is not even more out of control as a result of this difficult past.

The multigenerational investigation can also scan for rigid, destructive views of identity and gender roles.

Circular questions.   Each person has his or her own map of impulsivity and impulse-control mechanisms. The family can focus on impulses that cannot be resisted by discussing their own vulnerabilities. The therapist can inquire about each member's irresistible stimulus:

> "I know each of you has something you give in to, even though you would rather not. Can you each think of an example? It may be chocolate chip cookies, beer, the *New York Times*, books, gossiping, pretzels, or movies."

Impulse-control issues can also be discussed in a circular way:

> "Who in the family keeps control of emotions, impulses, and actions the most? How does that person accomplish this? If your husband (or other index person) could become open to such instruction, would you be willing to teach him? Who has difficulty controlling themselves? What are the costs of being impulsive, and what would be the cost of being in perfect control?"

New weapons.   The therapist can offer this perspective:

> "We seem to be losing the battle against the enemy: anger and impulsivity. Would you be willing to think about a radical step such

as medication, let's say one of the new serotonin agents? Many people say these agents help them deal with impulses, bad feelings, and the automatic emotional reaction to shaming events. They also say they then have more choice and control over their own actions. If this works, it would give you a chance to weaken or destroy the enemy and save the family from defeat and destruction."

■ Additional Reading

Favazza AR: Repetitive self-mutilation. Psychiatric Annals 22:60–63, 1992

Goldman MJ: Kleptomania: an overview. Psychiatric Annals 22:68–71, 1992

Goldner V: Generation and gender: normative and covert hierarchies. Fam Process 27:17–31, 1988

Kavoussi RJ, Liu J, Coccaro EF: An open trial of sertraline in personality disordered patients with impulsive aggression. J Clin Psychiatry 55:137–141, 1994

Swedo SE: Trichotillomania. Psychiatric Annals 23:402–407, 1993

Winchel RM: Trichotillomania: presentation and treatment. Psychiatric Annals 22:84–89, 1992

■ References

American Psychiatric Association: Treatment of Psychiatric Disorders. Washington, DC, American Psychiatric Press, 1988

American Psychiatric Association: Diagnostic and Statistical Manual of Mental Disorders, 4th Edition. Washington, DC, American Psychiatric Association, 1994

Boyd WH, Bolen DW: The compulsive gambler and spouse in group psychotherapy. Int J Group Psychother 10:77–90, 1970

Goldner V, Penn P, Sheinberg M, et al: Love and violence: gender paradoxes in volatile attachments. Fam Process 29:343–364, 1990

Hollander E: Obsessive-compulsive spectrum disorders: an overview. Psychiatric Annals 23:355–358, 1993

Imber Coppersmith E: "Developmental" reframing: he's not bad, he's not mad, he's just young. Journal of Strategic and Systemic Therapies 1:1–8, 1981

Kazdin AE, Kolko DJ: Parent psychopathology and family functioning among childhood firesetters. J Abnorm Child Psychol 14:315–329, 1986

Kunhley EF, Hendred R, Quinlan DM: Fire-setting by children. Journal of the American Academy of Child Psychiatry 21:560–563, 1982

Lion JR: The intermittent explosive disorder. Psychiatric Annals 22:64–71, 1992

Lopez-Ibor JJ: Impulse control in obsessive-compulsive disorders: a biopsychopathological approach. Prog Neuropsychopharmacol Biol Psychiatry 14:709–718, 1990

McElroy SL, Hudson JI, Pope HG, et al: The DSM-III-R impulse control disorders not elsewhere classified: clinical characteristics and relationship to other psychiatric disorders. Am J Psychiatry 149:318–327, 1992

Rosenthal RJ: Pathological gambling. Psychiatric Annals 22:72–78, 1992

Serra P: Physical violence in the couple relationship: a contribution toward the analysis of the context. Fam Process 32:21–33, 1993

Soltys SM: Pyromania and firesetting behaviors. Psychiatric Annals 22:79–83, 1992

Stein DJ, Hollander E: Impulsive aggression and obsessive-compulsive disorder. Psychiatric Annals 23:389–395, 1993

Symonds A: Violence against women—the myth of masochism. Am J Psychother 33:161–173, 1979

Victor RG, Krug CM: "Paradoxical intention" in the treatment of compulsive gamblers. Am J Psychiatry 21:808–814, 1967

Zeitlin PA: A proposal for a new diagnostic category: abuse disorder. Journal of Feminist Family Therapy 1:67–84, 1989

CHAPTER 16

Disorders Usually First Diagnosed During Infancy, Childhood, or Adolescence

Mark N.

Mark N., the 9-year-old youngest son in one family, was referred with the diagnoses of overanxious disorder and attention-deficit/hyperactivity disorder (ADHD). His parents believed he was passive, sad, immature, and overly competitive, and Mark blamed his peers and teachers for his problems. During the family session, the issues of medication and peer problems were discussed, and the child's passivity was reframed as "passive power." The boy began to talk with his parents about how to solve peer problems.

Over the course of these sessions, Mark attempted new challenges at school and felt more anxious. He began sleeping on a mattress next to his mother's side of the bed. In a meeting alone

This chapter was written in collaboration with Peter A. Kahn, M.D., Senior Child Psychiatrist, Sheppard and Enoch Pratt Hospital, Towson, Maryland.

with the therapist, his parents decided to ask their son to sleep in his own room. They did not take this step, however. In the next session, the mother said that perhaps she was more worried about the move than the child was, and she felt she should have more faith in her son. The father finally took the initiative in asking for the move, and the child complied.

During the next session, the mother made an appropriate demand for the child's participation immediately upon seeing her son slump passively in his seat. The boy smiled and joined in confidently, and the family was also pleased as the therapist commented on the family's newfound faith in their son.

■ Perspective on the Disorders

The treatment of children requires a knowledge of both the disorders and family therapy. Child-onset disorders can be divided into categories that reflect similarities in family themes and interventions. In this chapter, we group the disorders loosely into three categories of prototype: 1) internalizing disorders, which include anxiety and depressive disorders; 2) attention-deficit and disruptive behavior disorders, which include conduct disorders, oppositional defiant disorder, and ADHD; and 3) developmental disorders.

The child's developmental level strongly influences the assessment of certain behaviors as pathological (Dulcan and Popper 1991). Angry, negative, oppositional behavior is more commonly demonstrated by preschool children than by 10-year-olds. Further, a child's behavior may vary from situation to situation. A child with separation anxiety may demonstrate far fewer symptoms within the family therapy setting than he or she does within the home on Monday mornings. In work with children, data from the family and others are necessary for proper diagnosis. Individual observations of children are normally influenced by individual bias (Dulcan and Popper 1991; M. Lewis 1991).

The relationship between the child's temperament and the parents' temperaments, expectations, and parenting skills influences both personality and psychopathology development (Chess and Thomas 1986; Dulcan and Popper 1991).

An irritable, hypomanic mother relates differently to a child with severe ADHD than she does to an easygoing, docile child. The first child's early life experience will be very different from that of the second child, in part due to great differences in the interpersonal field.

Comorbidity is very common (Angold and Costello 1993; Biederman et al. 1991; Brown and Gammon 1993; Caron 1991; Dulcan and Popper 1991; Fergusson et al. 1993). Some childhood disorders continue into adulthood (Biederman et al. 1991; Hechtman 1992), although the symptoms may present differently. Similar disorders in other family members may have a significant impact on the outcome of family treatment. For example, a parent who does not comply with treatment suggestions may have had difficulty in processing the information because of his or her own learning disorder.

A systemic approach to child- and adolescent-onset disorders requires an integrated consideration of the individual's physical condition and behavior, the family system, and the school.

It should be noted that there is almost no literature on the family therapy of childhood schizophrenia, mood, or other major psychiatric disorders. The efficacy of family-based approaches has been well documented, however, for conditions such as autism and conduct disorder (Estrada and Pinsof 1995; Pinsof and Wynne 1995).

Table 16–1 summarizes some aspects of the family context of these disorders, which is described in more detail in the next section.

▮ Connections of the Symptoms to the System

▮ Effects of the Disorder on the Family

Internalizing disorders.   Children with anxiety disorders may cry, scream, and complain of abdominal pain or headaches, enuresis, and many other physical and emotional symptoms. They may worry about potential harm to attachment figures, their own competence, events in the past or future, loss of control, or death. They may develop sleep problems and may reexperience traumatic events from the past. If unable to avoid traumatic thoughts or situations, an anxious child may exhibit shaky speech, trembling hands, and other signs of distress (Barrios and Hartmann 1988; Kendall et al. 1992).

A loving parent's initial reaction to an anxious child is to provide reassurance and comfort, but this response can turn to anger if it repeatedly fails to calm the child. Eventually, the child's anxiety becomes

---

Table 16–1.   Childhood-onset disorders in context

Effects of the disorder on the family

- *Internalizing disorders*
    - Terror of anxious child leads to clinging or avoidant behaviors, sleep disturbances, and physical symptoms such as pain and enuresis
    - Parent overcompensation or increased strictness in response to child's problems
    - Sibling resentment of attention to anxious or depressed child
    - Family sense of helplessness when unable to entertain depressed child
    - Contagion of depression
- *Attention-deficit and disruptive behavior disorders*
    - Family denial and anger or guilt and dysphoria upon diagnosis of ADHD
    - Lack of information about disorder may worsen effects
- *Developmental disorders*
    - Diagnosis creates or becomes family crisis
    - With previous denial of problem, family members' response to diagnosis may be shock, anger, sadness, sense of unfairness, chronic sorrow
    - Marital strain as a result of chronic stress of child's prolonged dependent stages
    - Siblings affected by ridicule and shaming
    - Sense of family pride in accomplishments

Family maintenance of the symptoms

- *Internalizing disorders*
    - Tension and arguments intensify child's anxiety
    - Sibling teasing adds to child's stress
    - Family blame part of child's view of self as "bad" or "ruining the family"
- *Attention-deficit and disruptive behavior disorders*
    - Incorrect attribution of child's negative intentions; associated with unrealistic expectations of children
    - Parental anxiety supports child's sense of helplessness and dependency
    - Possible confusion through overexplanation
    - Overcontrolling or loss of control in dealing with child; associated with escalation of oppositional behavior
    - Peer group rejection contributes to overall sense of difference

(continued)

Table 16–1. Childhood-onset disorders in context *(continued)*

- *Developmental disorders*
    - Complex etiologies and effects considered; misinformation or family dysfunction possibly associated with worsening of disorder
    - Underorganization and chaos in family have strong effect
    - Importance of family attributions, expectations, and values in labeling of child as "bad," lazy, or stupid

Functions of the symptoms within the family

- *Internalizing disorders*
    - Parents feel needed, even if helpless
    - Crisis may unite family
- *Attention-deficit and disruptive behavior disorders*
    - Distraction from marital or other relational troubles in family
- *Developmental disorders*
    - Tendency to preserve status quo and avoid change and threats to identity
    Focuses family energy and attention on child, leading to neglect of other challenges

Adverse consequences of change

- *Internalizing disorders*
    - Family members must face discontent in other areas of their lives
- *Attention-deficit and disruptive behavior disorders*
    - Remission of externalizing disorder can lead to expression of internalizing disorder
    - Initial buildup of anxiety as family members are able or are forced to face other problems in family
    - Adaptation to relative peace and boredom
- *Developmental disorders*
    - Family confronts own insecurities about academic achievement and qualities of self
    - Emptiness rather than joy as child's potential revealed and strengths developed
    - Acceptance of severe limitations for child's future
    - Expression of underlying family dysfunctions

---

anxiety producing or frustrating for other family members because they are unable to help the child. In the two-parent family, one parent might identify with the anxious child and provide even more reassurance while the other parent insists on firmer limits. The single parent might swing from one extreme to the other.

Siblings quickly learn to resent the large share of emotional re-sources that the child seems to require. Siblings may also be discontented with the restrictions imposed by the need to alter the family's lifestyle to help alleviate the child's anxiety.

Children with major depressive disorders often appear sad and hopeless and describe themselves as "stupid" or "dumb." They complain of headaches and stomachaches and lose interest in activities, and their academic performance deteriorates. Their parents describe them as irritable, whiny, agitated, and moody. Sometimes suicidality and deep despair are directly expressed.

The profound changes associated with a depressive episode have a dramatic effect on other family members. Unsuccessful efforts to please, cajole, and entertain the child leave them feeling helpless and inadequate. Others often feel irritable and angry; this may be especially true for parents who suffer from affective disorders themselves. The child's depression may increase the difficulty for a parent struggling with his or her own problems.

Depression is also contagious. The family of a depressed child may become bogged down and glum as they try to live with the irritable, agitated child. Siblings are frightened by the behavior of the depressed child. They perceive their parents' helplessness and wonder who will take care of them. An older sibling may initially feel protective of the sad, withdrawn child—a position often reinforced by the parents. Other family members may feel guilty about being happy themselves and may avoid talking about positive aspects of their lives.

Attention-deficit and disruptive behavior disorders.   When presented with the diagnosis of ADHD, many parents react with denial and anger. They feel overwhelmed and helpless and may direct their anger outward. If the anger is turned inward, parents feel guilt and dysphoria and may withdraw from the child or each other. They may also express guilt by overprotecting the child. The family may search endlessly for a doctor who will give a different diagnosis, or they may be uncooperative and blaming toward doctors.

Other children in the family may feel jealous and angry when the child with ADHD receives extra time with parents to attend tutoring or therapy or when there is not enough money for other activities because of the extra bills. When they are told that the index person is unable to control his or her behavior, siblings who have taken out their anger on the patient may either stay angry or feel guilty.

Developmental disorders. Families with a child with developmental disorder usually enter the mental health world in the crisis of diagnosis. For some parents, the world changes when the child is born and is diagnosed with brain damage or Down's syndrome. For other parents, anxiety grows slowly with the ominous sense that something is wrong with the young child.

In some cases, parents are bothered by the child's poor school performance but deny any serious problem for years before a learning disorder is diagnosed. At this point, recognition of the problem usually brings shock, anger, sadness, and a sense of unfairness. The anger may be directed at self, spouse, child, obstetricians, and other experts. In pervasive developmental disorder and mental retardation, parents express a chronic sorrow.

It is difficult enough for a family to raise children who are developing normally; it is far more difficult to raise a child with developmental disorder. In autism and mental retardation, the family must provide special care around the clock. In autism, there is a constant need to protect the child from self-injury. The constant stress of the child's prolonged dependent stage puts a great strain on marriages because the focus of the adults must remain on the child rather than on each other. Marital discord may also connect to shame or to blame and mutual negative projections.

The effects on siblings cannot be underestimated. The experience of ridicule and shaming by peers and neighbors becomes an organizing principle of the childhoods of many siblings of children with developmental disorder.

In some memorable families, sorrow and grieving transform into a kind of joy as meaning is found in the demanding experience of raising special children. The achievements of a child with a developmental disorder become a source of special pride.

▉ Family Maintenance of the Symptoms

Internalizing disorders. The anxiety of the family with an anxious child may lead to tension and arguments, which can intensify the child's anxiety. Some parents tend to acquiesce to the child's demands in an effort to calm both the child and the rest of the family, which may mean allowing the child into the parents' bed, letting the child stay home with the parent, and allowing the child to avoid other activities and challenges appropriate to the child's age.

Siblings may overprotect the child or add to the stress by teasing, "poor little mama's baby can't even sleep alone." The parents' sense of incompetence is reinforced by members of the extended family and even by the idea that a professional eventually should take charge of the situation (Combrinck-Graham 1989), and a lack of parental confidence can increase the child's anxiety.

In the family with a depressed child, comments that blame the child for the lack of fun contribute to the child's view of self as "bad" or "ruining the family." The parents' failure or inability to help remediate poor social skills can also support the child's view of him- or herself as incompetent. Social skills deficits are a risk factor for further depressive episodes.

Attention-deficit and disruptive behavior disorders.   The child's disruptive behaviors may be inadvertently maintained by the parents' beliefs and misattributions about the problem. The parents may believe that the child's behavior is intentionally disruptive and is a reflection of a stable negative character trait, or they may believe that the behavior reflects their own deficiencies as parents. All-or-none thinking may occur ("my child never behaves" or "I never know what to do").

Parents may have unrealistic expectations related to the child's development of self-control, for example, when a toddler is expected to sit quietly throughout a meal while the adults talk. Parents may also perceive natural behavior as disruptive or inappropriate (Braswell and Bloomquist 1991).

If they continually seek new medical opinions, parents decrease the child's ability to trust doctors and may increase the child's fears that he or she is sick or bad. Dedicated parents who drain themselves caring for the child may not have enough energy for other family members. These protective parents may also help maintain the child's sense of helplessness and dependency (Silver 1990).

Many parents spontaneously use the expression "catch-22" or "vicious cycle" to describe their interactions with their children.

Certain parental behaviors appear to maintain oppositional defiant behavior in children with and without AD disorders. Parents often respond to oppositional defiant behaviors with increased efforts to control the child, sometimes by giving too many directions ("Now remember, when we get to grandmother's house, we are not to . . . "). When problems occur, some parents are aware of their natural inclination to further overexplain or give even more confusing commands.

Overburdened parents may reinforce oppositional behavior if they themselves lose control during interactions with the child, which may increase the risk that the child will become involved with a deviant peer group, antisocial behaviors, and substance abuse (Patterson et al. 1992).

Patterson elaborated a number of parent constellations from his research on antisocial children. These constellations included the unattached distant parents who could not be interested in the child's stealing, the overwhelmed parents who knew how to manage the behaviors but were just too preoccupied to act, and the perfect parents who warmly and rationally lecture the child but do not confront (Patterson 1982).

The peer group at school reacts to the child's negative behavior with systematic rejection, which is likely to continue even if the child's behavior changes.

Developmental disorders.   Past views that autism is related to inadequate mothering or that learning disabilities are products of a chaotic family life have been replaced by an awareness of complex etiologies and effects. Perhaps the most promising opening stance is that a child with a biological deficit and complex problems has been born to well-meaning parents who need help, information, and problem-solving support. The therapist must also help the parents remain open to the possibility that relational problems may be contributing to the child's problems.

Many disorders present at times when the family is in crisis and the parents' marriage is in trouble. This connection may be clearest with problems such as conduct disorder, enuresis, or overanxious disorder, but it is also part of the context of learning disorders, pervasive developmental disorder, Tourette syndrome, and mental retardation.

The relationship of family function to learning disorders is particularly well studied. On the one hand, the underorganized, chaotic family is reported to be conducive to learning disorders. On the other hand, an enmeshed, overprotective, conflict-avoiding family of the type that is also associated with somatization and eating disorders is seen as exacerbating a learning disorder that is primarily a neurological dysfunction (Perosa 1980). Thus, learning disorders have been related to families that are both *underinvolved* with the child (i.e., an underorganized, chaotic family life seems to correlate with attentional deficits and conduct disorders [Green 1989]) and *overinvolved* with the child (i.e., an overorganized, intrusive family life seems to correlate with having children with learning disorders who become anxious and perfectionistic and later oppositional and provocative).

The family's attributions and value systems also play a role. If the parents are hard-driving professionals who value education and achievement above all, a child with learning disorder or mental retardation is likely to suffer a sense of failure. The same child might fare better in a family that emphasizes physical labor, sports, and religion. It is possible, however, that the professionally or academically oriented family of a child with a learning or other disorder provides access to tutoring and other resources to help overcome the impact of the disability. For all developmental disorders, the issue of unrealistic expectations is central and may become an organizing therapeutic theme.

Certain attributions maintain and maximize the suffering of the child with learning disorder, pervasive developmental disorder, or mental retardation. The child may be incorrectly labeled as lazy, stupid, and unchangeable at the same time that the family maintains impossible perfectionist expectations that deny the existence of a biological deficit and guarantee a mutual sense of disappointment and failure between parent and child.

■ Functions of the Symptoms Within the Family

Internalizing disorders.   Even if they feel helpless, the parents of an anxious child at least feel needed. The symptoms may move the family closer together as they create a barrier between themselves and the outside world. Anxious phobic parents now have company and a potential confidant. Anxiety gives a kind of reprieve to a family facing what feels like a painful loss with the child's increasing independence.

Depressive symptoms in a child may unite separated parents or keep the parents from separating. The child's problem may also force the parents to deal with each other as they avoid expressing anger at their "sensitive" child. Some children have also been able to gain a desired change of residency as part of their "recovery."

> One 13-year-old girl was hospitalized for suicidality and continued to threaten suicide until a change was made in an untenable living arrangement with her obsessively strict stepmother.

Attention-deficit and disruptive behavior disorders.   Tending to the child with ADHD, oppositional defiant disorder, or conduct disorder may distract from marital problems or other personal struggles. Sometimes the dramatic presentation of the child upstages the acting-out behaviors of other siblings or allows the family to ignore anxiety or depressive disorders in other family members.

Developmental disorders.   The developmental disorders are determined more by biology than by psychology, but the family's particular response to symptoms can hamper adjustment and coping. If parents apply intense pressure for academic achievement to a child who is constitutionally unable to meet high expectations, the pressure may encourage depression, rebellion, rage, conduct disorders, or anxiety disorders. The child's inevitable failure then functions to make the disorder the focus of the family's emotional life.

The family's anger may be associated with a sense of injustice or inadequacy that the family cannot face directly; instead, the family focuses on the child. If the parents unconsciously see the child as representing their own deficits, their focus on the child is even more intense.

The excessively prolonged dependent state of the child may serve to allow the parents to avoid the dread of facing the next phase of their lives.

■ Adverse Consequences of Change

Many parents put aside their own needs and feelings to help the child. As the child recovers, the family must now face the discontent in other areas of their life. Parents who have postponed their own treatment because of the "need" to focus on the child now have time to deal with their own problems. Many families would have been dysfunctional even without a child with developmental disorder. Focus on the child "saves" family members from other problems. The child may even be the force behind positive cooperation and problem solving as otherwise angry people pull together in a meaningful cause. If the child becomes less of a burden, the underlying dysfunctions may express more fully.

Remission of an attention-deficit or disruptive behavior disorder can easily lead to expression of an internalizing disorder. As acting-out conduct disorder behaviors fade, underlying depressive or anxious moods and fears emerge to which the family may have to adapt.

The family may also have to adapt to relative peace and boredom as the loss of possibly dramatic symptoms also brings the loss of exciting battles and adventures.

In developmental disorders, the family organization may evolve away from a focus on the child with developmental disorder. Family members must then confront their own insecurities about academic achievement and qualities of self. This awareness can lead to panic, despair, and new behaviors or distractions.

If the prolonged caretaking of the child has offered parents a meaningful role in life, the possibility of the child's maturing or developing independent skills may be thrilling in one way and threatening in another. Parents may feel a vague emptiness as the child's need for them decreases.

If the change for the family involves their moving beyond denial, this improvement brings an extremely difficult awareness of the extent of the nervous system deficit and its implications for the child's future.

■ Special Systemic Dimensions

■ Family History and Genetics

Genetic predisposition plays a role in the disorders. Often, parents themselves have struggled with the same or similar childhood-onset disorders. First-degree relatives of children with learning disorder have a higher rate of learning disorders. In specific disorders such as reading disorder, as many as 60% of children have a positive family history (Arnold 1990). There is some suggestion of genetic transmission of autism. Siblings are at greater risk for both autism and other developmental disorders (Volkmar and Cohen 1994). Genetic abnormalities are considered to be the major cause of mental retardation in those cases with known organic etiology (Tanguay and Russell 1991).

Parents often express shame, guilt, and sadness over transmitting genetically linked disorders. Mothers of children with developmental disorders may focus on having taken a particular medication or having had a virus during the first trimester of their pregnancy.

A child with generalized anxiety disorder or separation anxiety disorder is likely to have a parent, more often the mother, with an anxiety disorder during her lifetime (Bell-Dolan and Brazreal 1993). One study concluded that although relatives of children with anxiety disorders have a higher rate of anxiety disorder, there is no specific correlation between the child's disorder and that of relatives (Last et al. 1991). These findings do not preclude the significance of other etiologies such as anxious attachment, losses, modeling, and behavioral reinforcement.

Adult relatives of depressed children have higher rates of depression than the general population (Weller and Weller 1990). Earlier-onset depressive disorder correlates with greater family loading for depression (McCracken 1992). Relatives of depressed children have higher rates of suicide attempts (Todd et al. 1993), and the extended families of children with bipolar disorders have higher rates of affective-spectrum disorders (Fristad et al. 1992).

Compared with the relatives of well children, the relatives of children with ADHD have higher rates of bipolar, attention-deficit, mood, and anxiety disorders. Fathers of children with ADHD are more antisocial than the norm, and fathers of children with comorbid attention-deficit and conduct disorder are much more antisocial and aggressive than the norm. Childhood conduct disorder has been associated with parental antisocial behavior as well as alcoholism (Biederman et al. 1991).

Inheritance can be complex in that each disorder may have several etiologies—a reality that can prevent the concise prediction of inheritance likelihood. Learning disorder shows a hint of sex-linked dominant transmission with variable penetrance. In Tourette syndrome, the data lean toward autosomal dominance with variable penetrance. Mental retardation is associated with a long list of different genetic syndromes.

Inheritability may also vary widely among the disorders. ADHD (Barkley 1990) and pervasive developmental disorder are among the most inheritable. Pervasive developmental disorder occurs in siblings 50 times more often than it does in the general population (Pomeroy 1990).

Enuresis also shows high inheritability, with 75% of affected children having a first-degree relative with a history of bed-wetting (American Psychiatric Association 1994). Enuresis also exemplifies the etiological complexities in these disorders. Other factors, such as the number of urinary tract infections and low socioeconomic status, are also associated with bed-wetting disorder.

■ Intimacy

Most childhood disorders do not preclude the capacity for close, warm relationships between the child and family or friends. Nevertheless, many aspects interfere with positive relationships. Some children seem different and are likely to be ostracized and isolated, especially if the child reminds others of their own deficiencies. The child may also have deficiencies in processing interpersonal information and may misperceive the comments of others.

In internalizing disorders, relationships are made more difficult by the inward, isolating withdrawal of a child with depression or the clinging fearfulness of a child with overanxious disorder.

In attention-deficit and disruptive behavior disorders, relationships are by definition strained because the behaviors are interpersonal, difficult, and aimed at pushing others away. Sometimes the behaviors contain attempts to sacrifice closeness to parents and authority figures for closeness to peers. In ADHD, the child may want to relate more closely, but perception of the needs of others may be compromised by the restless, impulsive, inattentive stance.

■ Loyalty

The symptoms of anxious children serve to keep children home, which sometimes can be associated partly with loyalty to a parent who also remains in the home. The child's behavior may resemble that of an anxious or depressed parent and may represent the child's desire to share the parent's problems.

In developmental disorder, even the child with severe disabilities has a need to express loyalty and caregiving to the parents. If the child perceives that the parents want to be rid of him or her, the child may become suicidal or run away. A child with a learning disorder may "understand" how seriously the family regards academic underachievement; increasing marital arguments may be accompanied by school failure as an attempt to shock the parents out of their movement toward a separation (Perlmutter 1985).

The loyalty of parent to children with problems is found in all disorders. It is exemplified by the devotion of overworked, dedicated parents to children with developmental disorders who often cannot express appreciation.

◼ Countertransference

The therapist may feel the urge to change the child's behavior too quickly—before understanding the problem sufficiently—as parents label behaviors intolerable and beg for or demand action. The therapist may respond to such pressure to intervene immediately out of anxiety, guilt, or a sense of incompetence.

A therapist who is older and also a parent may see the parents' point of view and may wonder if he or she could deal with such a difficult child. The therapist may feel guilty for the sense of relief that his or her own children are not as challenging. The young therapist may unconsciously align with the symptomatic child against the parents, who are seen as the root of the problem because of their suppressiveness and lack of understanding of the child's point of view.

The therapist must know about remediation and school programming when treating learning disorders. With mental retardation, knowledge of community resources is essential; in pervasive developmental disorder, the therapist must understand the depth of despair of the early years.

The therapist may blame the family for biological illness in the child. This age-old issue is not as inevitable as it once was, but it can sneak into the unsuspecting therapist's thinking and language. This stance manifests as anger and impatience with the family.

◼ Treatment

◼ Standard Individual Therapies

Most children are treated with a combination of psychotherapy, medications, family education, parent counseling, skill remediation, and school collaboration.

Individual psychodynamic therapy has been the traditional approach to treating anxious or depressed children (Bemporad et al. 1993). While adolescents usually participate on a verbal level, school-age and younger children are frequently engaged in some kind of expressive play activity on a nonverbal symbolic level.

Cognitive-behavior therapy and behavioral therapy for anxiety are well researched and clearly described. Effective behavioral techniques include modeling, systematic desensitization, relaxation, and operant procedures (Bell-Dolan and Brazreal 1993). Cognitive-behavior therapy is one of the most useful forms of psychotherapy for developmental disorders.

Psychopharmacological research is limited, and medication is rarely the only treatment provided for children and adolescents (Allen et al. 1993; Rapoport 1993). The more commonly prescribed medications for anxiety disorders include tricyclic antidepressants (often nortriptyline [Pamelor, Aventyl]), selective serotonin reuptake inhibitors (e.g., fluoxetine [Prozac]), and benzodiazepines such as clonazepam (Klonopin). Buspirone (BuSpar) and propranolol (Inderal) are also prescribed (Allen et al. 1995).

The effectiveness of antidepressants in the treatment of depression is not as well documented in children and adolescents as it is in adults. Nevertheless, agents such as tricyclic antidepressants are commonly prescribed and have been effective in many individual cases (Joshi 1995). A few recent studies suggest efficacy for selective serotonin reuptake inhibitors (Colle et al. 1994; DeVane and Sallee 1996). While lithium carbonate is effective in treating bipolar disorders, there are fewer data for the use of valproate and carbamazepine in children and adolescents (Campbell and Cueva 1995). Nevertheless, both are prescribed, and a few studies do support their efficacy for treating mixed bipolar disorders (Potter and Ketter 1993; West et al. 1995).

Psychostimulants such as methylphenidate (Ritalin), dextroamphetamine (Dexedrine), and pemoline (Cylert) are the most effective medications for attention-deficit disorders, and bupropion (Wellbutrin) is promising. Other medications include clonidine (Catpres), guanfacine (Temex), tricyclic antidepressants, and selective serotonin reuptake inhibitors (Spencer et al. 1996). There is no pharmacological treatment for pure oppositional defiant disorder. Children with conduct disorders may have any one of many comorbid disorders, and medication is used to treat the comorbid disorder (D. O. Lewis 1991).

In autism and related disorders, recent studies have shown the usefulness of medications that increase serotonin transmission in reducing interfering repetitive behaviors and aggression. Traditionally, antipsychotics such as haloperidol (Haldol) or pimozide (Orap) are prescribed. Beta-blockers such as propranolol have been prescribed to reduce aggression, and clonidine may decrease symptoms of inattention, impulsivity, or hyperactivity (McDougle et al. 1994).

Antipsychotics have been overused in individuals with mental re-

tardation to treat aggressive outbursts, which can be treated with propranolol, buspirone, or selective serotonin reuptake inhibitors. Comorbid conditions are treated appropriately, but individuals with mental
retardation may have increased sensitivity to medication effects (Volkmar 1991). Children with IQs of greater than 45 respond better to
stimulants than those with lower IQs (Greenhill 1992).

There are no specific medications to treat learning disabilities, but
treatment is indicated for comorbid conditions that interfere with the
child's best functioning (e.g., stimulants for ADHD and antidepressants
for depression). Some studies suggest that stimulants may enhance the
learning process (McDougle et al. 1994).

■ Family Modalities

Family work with child-focused symptoms involves skills in several modalities. Conjoint meetings with parents and children support the welcoming of children into therapy. The neglect of small children in family therapy has reawakened a need for therapists to develop skills and
techniques for including them (Chasin 1989; Combrinck-Graham 1986;
Zilbach 1986). Dealing with adolescents is a special skill, and adolescents with disorders may present a particularly difficult dilemma. Because of their problems, they feel anger and shame in struggling to
adjust to the world of adult responsibilities. The need for therapeutic
intervention is high, but the ability to communicate with some adolescents is often blocked.

With children who present with academic or conduct problems, the
therapist should automatically consider psychological and educational
testing for learning, speech, hearing, and language disorders. The therapist must be open to an understanding of schools and to the idea of
intervening in the child's school. The family therapy field has begun
to integrate therapy with school intervention (Fisher 1986; Lusterman
1985).

Sibling meetings may tap a neglected resource with its own power
and curative potential. The needs of siblings of children with developmental disorder are enormous, and the effort to address these needs
is an important form of preventive psychiatry.

Therapists should have some knowledge of marital relationships
and therapies to respond to the needs of couples. Although this approach is not generally followed, child therapists can also do the mari-

tal work. The parents then do not feel excluded from the child's therapy and can focus on active preparation for positive changes in the child. If the child's symptoms are unmasked in the individual therapy as partly a concern for the parents, the therapist says, in effect: "You can turn over responsibility for your parents' troubles to me, so you are more free to continue your positive changes." Therapists who are uncomfortable with integrated therapy for the child and the parents or who believe that the child needs his or her own special place can make a well-timed and carefully worded referral for marital therapy.

Individual meetings with family members may be useful. The father's need to appear strong and perfect may inhibit his participation in family therapy. An initial meeting with the "head" of the family allows the father to tell his story without having to face his family. Such a meeting may also facilitate his later participation in family sessions.

If a child with ADHD cannot sit through conjoint sessions comfortably, the use of conjoint sessions beyond the diagnostic phase must be reviewed critically for goals. The therapist must determine whether it is worth putting the child, the family, and the therapist through what is likely to be an ordeal.

■ Psychoeducation

When a child looks physically healthy, it can be difficult for the family to accept that his or her behavior is the result of an invisible and poorly understood disease of the brain. Diagnostic labels may be confusing. Parents usually remember only a single phrase, such as "chemical imbalance" or "developmental problem," to sum up information provided to them.

Concise printed material available from sources such as the American Academy of Child and Adolescent Psychiatry and the National Alliance for the Mentally Ill reinforces the therapist's explanation of the disorder.

Parent counseling can be adapted to a systemic approach. Empathic reflection of the child's affects has a place even in severe disorders. Basic parenting skills should not be assumed and can be taught through the parent training model, supplemented by communicational skills training, anger and conflict management, and problem solving (Barkley 1990; Griest and Wells 1983; Patterson et al. 1992; Wells and Forehand 1985).

The application of social learning behavioral principles—especially the teaching of consistent family management skills—has been shown to deter the development of aggressive, antisocial disorders (Patterson 1988).

■ New Stories

Realistic expectations.   In pervasive developmental disorder, parents may view the child's accomplishments as meager and disappointing. The therapy can help adjust expectations to realistic levels. The parents are helped to see the child's accomplishments as signs of great effort in the face of extreme adversity. Parents can be credited with effort, support, and caring perseverance in helping the child move toward what progress has been achieved.

If a learning disorder has just been discovered in a workup for school problems, a complaint about poor grades may be changed to a sense of admiration that the child is able to achieve so much.

Sadness is normal.   Sadness over the child's fate may be reframed as an expected emotional reaction. This reaction can be accepted and even encouraged rather than considered as guilty thoughts that a good parent would suppress. Parents who worry that they don't love the troublesome child can be helped to see that ambivalent love is part of life and coping; it is not necessarily part of a problem.

Externalization.   With a symptom such as enuresis, a child is often seen as wetting the bed to punish the parents. This problem can be discussed instead as a developmental delay or as a sign of physical immaturity over which neither the child nor parents have control. Encopresis may be hypothesized as a developmental bowel problem that is often amenable to laxatives and intervention by a pediatrician rather than as a sign that the child is mean or spoiled.

Family-oriented therapeutic reconstructions must consider the findings of Michael White, whose work focused largely on discrete symptoms of children (White and Epston 1990).

> One well-known story involved "sneaky poo," an externalized force that was creating havoc through severe soiling and smearing of feces. In therapy, "sneaky poo" became the common enemy of a 6-year-old boy and his despairing parents.

> The therapy included a detailed account of the influence of the problem on the family's relationships and their outside lives. Conversations were structured to elicit and focus on exceptions to the devastating power of "sneaky poo." The family was able to reconsider their relationship to the problem through a kind of family celebration of the areas in which they did have power, such as their success in keeping this problem from destroying all their love and good times. Symptom relief was obtained rapidly.

This story is recounted here as an example of the creative use of focus, meaning, and language—not as a formula for rapid cure of complex problems.

Such ideas can be applied in addressing a wide range of child-focused complaints, especially where the family has an angry, blaming way of viewing the child and the problems. Developmental disorders can be framed as problems faced by a family united in a battle to minimize the destructive power of even the most severe disorder. This is a significant shift in meaning from parents who are either enraged with the child for the deficit or are blaming themselves in an internalized, guilty way.

Family as classroom and tutors.   Therapy should identify and build upon the strengths and resources of the family. For learning disorders and other school-related dysfunctions, the home can be viewed as a classroom and the family can be helped to become better tutors. The goal is to help keep the disability from becoming a total family handicap. The therapist looks for opportunities to encourage the family to suggest areas of family functioning that are preserved, even under the stress and reorganization associated with developmental disorders.

Power of labels.   Labels are powerful and should be used with great care in support of useful change. The therapist should not underestimate the influence that labels such as autism, learning disability, and mental retardation can have on the family's self-esteem and relationships.

The diagnosis of learning disorder can be a blessing in a family that previously labeled the child lazy or stupid, and the child may be tremendously relieved as teachers and parents behave more reasonably with their new concept of the source of educational and behavioral problems. The label of disability, however, may have a strong negative effect. Phrases such as "learning difference" and "academic under-achievement" are sometimes more helpful in normalizing and detoxifying the attribution.

You don't understand.   Attempts can be made to accommodate and reframe the anger of the adolescent with oppositional defiant disorder, who states that others "don't understand" and then remains stuck in angry defiance. The therapist can try asking, "What would your parents have to do so that you would know that they understood?" If the adolescent protests about decisions or attitudes being unfair, this question may be asked: "What did your parents seem to be trying to do?" The parents are then able to hear how their behavior was interpreted, and they may contribute what their underlying intentions had been.

Antagonistic behavior can be discussed as normal developmental attempts toward independence:

> "Could it be that these actions are his way of trying to be more independent, which of course is his job as an adolescent, and that these actions went awry or overshot the mark? How else could you have made this point? How else could you have let your child know of your concerns?"

Typical adolescent.   In families in which parents and adolescents both have unipolar or bipolar disorders, the onset of illness can occur much earlier in life for the children. Parents tend to forget the stresses inherent in the passage through adolescence, especially if they did not have the disorder until after adolescence and if they have had a good medication response. They tend to view every expression by the child as part of their "disease."

A daughter who dislikes her mother's overdependence on the mother's live-in boyfriend is reported to have "breakthrough depression." In these situations, depression can be discussed in terms of both a communication about relational issues and a biological phenomenon.

Circular questioning.   Each family member is asked to describe his or her theories, ideas, fantasies, and assumptions about how the child became retarded, developed learning disorder, became persistently oppositional, or became unable to stop wetting or soiling the bed.

This go-around can focus on family attributions about the disorders themselves:

> "What do you think the problem means? What message is there in
> it? What do you think might be the child's intent in acting this way
> or in doing such things?"

Executive functioning.   A family presenting in crisis may not notice
that the control of the family has been taken over by a child or an
illness. Single-parent families or two-parent families with one parent
essentially absent are particularly vulnerable to this skewing of power.

Identifying the importance of clear structure and discipline can
help set the stage for the parental exertion of authority as a sign of
love rather than of suppression. Children who have behavioral difficulties benefit from the establishment of the parent as "benevolent
dictator."

In families who tend to overdominate the younger generation, parents must consider the importance of listening to what children say,
validating their perceptions, and distinguishing between clear structure and tyranny or abuse of power.

Medication doubts considered.   Many parents are confused, anxious, and guilty about the idea of medicating children. Noncompliance
with medication regimens is a common problem. It is essential to allow
parents to express their concerns and doubts and to treat these opinions as important. The therapist and family consider the disadvan-
tages of medications as worth weighing to see if the possible benefits
prevail.

If the child has a clear psychiatric disorder and the parental issue
appears related to attitudes about psychiatric medications in particular,
the therapist can ask whether treatment for diabetes or heart disease
would be considered in the same way.

> One mother felt guilty about the use of methylphenidate to treat
> her son's severe attentional deficits and school failure. Her guilt
> dissipated when she realized she would not hesitate to buy him
> glasses if he had difficulty seeing clearly.

Fragility and sensitivity.   The therapist may suggest that the child
brought for treatment of a learning disability happens to have fragile
academic abilities and heightened sensitivity to a less-than-ideal environment. The child's performance and emotional state may be optimal only when all the right pieces are in place:

1. The family is generally supportive.
2. The mother or father is available emotionally and for homework help.
3. Parents and teachers are collaborating well.
4. Parents have sufficient energy and optimism, and the child is reasonably happy and secure, not distracted by fights or other problems at home.

Other meanings for silence. A family typically presents with a silent adolescent and the request to "make him or her talk." Often the usual go-around questioning yields more silence, and the therapist must be ready to respond with other techniques. The therapist can state the ground rule that no one has to speak during the session. Silence can be reframed as strength, fear, or shame; it can be commented on as reflecting normal adolescent needs for autonomy, boundaries, and choice. The idea is to offer the family other explanations for silence so that they have alternatives to power struggles and rage.

The adolescent may even be asked to avoid speaking as one way to keep from getting upset, and the adolescent is then praised for taking care of him- or herself by keeping emotions in check. The interviewer then continues the session with other members of the family.

■ Additional Reading

Alexander JF, Waldron HB, Barton C, et al: The minimizing of blaming attributions and behaviors in delinquent families. J Consult Clin Psychol 57:19–24, 1989

Beavers J: Physical and cognitive handicaps, in Children in Family Contexts. Edited by Combrinck-Graham L. New York, Guilford, 1989, pp 193–212

Beidel D, Morris T: Avoidant disorder of childhood and social phobia. Child and Adolescent Psychiatric Clinics of North America 2:623–638, 1993

Berenson C: Evaluation and treatment of anxiety in the general pediatric population. Child and Adolescent Psychiatric Clinics of North America 2:727–747, 1993

Biederman J, Newcorn J, Sprich S: Comorbidity of attention-deficit/hyperactivity disorder with conduct, depressive, anxiety, and other disorders. Am J Psychiatry 148:564–577, 1991

Biederman J, Faraone SV, Spencer T, et al: Patterns of psychiatric comorbidity, cognition, and psychosocial functioning in adults with attention-deficit/hyperactivity disorder. Am J Psychiatry 150:1792–1798, 1993

Bullrich S: The process of immigration, in Children in Family Contexts. Edited by Combrinck-Graham L. New York, Guilford, 1989, pp 482–500

Chasin R, White T: The child in family therapy: guidelines for active engagement across the age span, in Children in Family Contexts. Edited by Combrinck-Graham L. New York, Guilford, 1989, pp 5–25

Combrinck-Graham L: Family models of childhood psychopathology, in Children in Family Contexts. Edited by Combrinck-Graham L. New York, Guilford, 1989, pp 67–89

Combrinck-Graham L: Developments in family systems theory and research. J Am Acad Child Adolesc Psychiatry 29:501–512, 1990

Drobes D, Strauss C: Behavioral treatment of childhood anxiety disorders. Child and Adolescent Psychiatric Clinics of North America 2:779–793, 1993

Forehand RL, McMahon RJ: Helping the Noncompliant Child: A Clinician's Guide to Parent Training. New York, Guilford, 1981

Garfinkel BD, Carlson GA, Weller EB (eds): Psychiatric Disorders in Children and Adolescents. Philadelphia, PA, WB Saunders, 1990

Gartner D, Schultz NM: Establishing the first stages of early reciprocal interactions between mothers and their autistic children. Women and Therapy 10:159–167, 1990

Halperin J, Newcorn J, Matier K, et al: Discriminant validity of attention-deficit hyperactivity disorder. J Am Acad Child Adolesc Psychiatry 32:1038–1043, 1993

Jones BH: Diagnosing the dyslexic child. Family Therapy Networker 15:67–69, 1991

Kendall P, Chansky T, Friedman KR, et al: Treating anxiety disorders in children and adolescents, in Child and Adolescent Therapy: Cognitive-Behavioral Procedures. Edited by Kendall P. New York, Guilford, 1991, pp 131–164

Levy J: Family response and adaptation to a handicap, in The Psychiatry of Children and Adolescents: Managing Emotional and Behavioral Problems. Edited by Gerring JP, McCarthy PM. Boston, MA, Little, Brown, 1988, pp 215–245

Lindblad-Goldberg M: Successful minority single-parent families, in Children in Family Contexts. Edited by Combrinck-Graham L. New York, Guilford, 1989, pp 116–134

Margalit M: Learning disabled children and their families: strategies of extension and adaptation of family therapy. Journal of Learning Disabilities 15:594–595, 1982

Mufson L, Moreau D, Weissman M, et al: Interpersonal Psychotherapy for Depressed Adolescents. New York, Guilford, 1993

Ostrander R, Silver L: Psychological interventions and therapies for children and adolescents with learning disabilities. Child and Adolescent Psychiatric Clinics of North America 2:323–337, 1993

Patterson GR, DeBaryshe BD, Ramsey E: A developmental perspective on antisocial behavior. Am Psychol 44:329–335, 1989

Puig-Antich J, Lukens E, Davies M, et al: Psychosocial functioning in prepubertal depressive disorders, I: interpersonal relationships during the depressive episode. Arch Gen Psychiatry 42:500–507, 1985

Puig-Antich J, Lukens E, Davies M, et al: Psychosocial functioning in prepubertal depressive disorders, II: interpersonal relationships after sustained recovery from affective episode. Arch Gen Psychiatry 42:511–517, 1985

Rey JM: Oppositional defiant disorder. Am J Psychiatry 150:1769–1778, 1993

Schopler E: A statewide program for the treatment and education of autistic and related communication handicapped children (TEACCH). Child and Adolescent Psychiatric Clinics of North America 3:91–103, 1994

Sloman L, Konstantareas MM: Why families of children with biological deficits require a systems approach. Fam Process 29:417–429, 1990

Spacone C, Hansen JC: Therapy with a family with a learning-disabled child, in Family Therapy With School-Related Problems. Edited by Okun B. Rockville, MD, Aspen, 1984, pp 46–58

Webb-Watson L: Ethnicity: an epistemology of child rearing, in Children in Family Contexts. Edited by Combrinck-Graham L. New York, Guilford, 1989, pp 463–481

Weller EB, Weller RA: Mood disorders, in Child and Adolescent Psychiatry. Edited by Lewis M. Baltimore, MD, Williams & Wilkins, 1991, pp 646–663

Wells KC, Egan J: Social learning and systems family therapy for childhood oppositional disorder: comparative treatment outcome. Compr Psychiatry 29:138–146, 1988

Wendorf DJ, Frey J: Family therapy with the intellectually gifted. American Journal of Family Therapy 13:31–38, 1985

Zapella M: Young autistic children treated with ethologically oriented family therapy. Family Systems Medicine 8:14–27, 1990

Zilbach JJ: Young Children in Family Therapy. New York, Brunner/Mazel, 1986

■ References

Allen A, Rapoport J, Swedo S: Psychopharmacologic treatment of childhood anxiety disorders. Child and Adolescent Psychiatric Clinics of North America 2:795–817, 1993

Allen A, Leonard H, Swedo S: Current knowledge of medications for the treatment of childhood anxiety disorders. J Am Acad Child Adolesc Psychiatry 34:976–986, 1995

American Psychiatric Association: Diagnostic and Statistical Manual of Mental Disorders, 4th Edition. Washington, DC, American Psychiatric Association, 1994

Angold A, Costello EJ: Depressive comorbidity in children and adolescents: empirical, theoretical, and methodological issues. Am J Psychiatry 150:1779–1791, 1993

Arnold LE: Learning disorders, in Psychiatric Disorders in Children and Adolescents. Edited by Garfinkel BD, Carlson GA, Weller EB. Philadelphia, PA, WB Saunders, 1990, pp 237–256

Barkley RA: Attention-Deficit Hyperactivity Disorder: A Handbook for Diagnosis and Treatment. New York, Guilford, 1990

Barrios BA, Hartmann DB: Fears and anxieties, in Behavioral Assessment of Childhood Disorders. Edited by Mash EJ, Terdol LG. New York, Guilford, 1988, pp 196–264

Bell-Dolan D, Brazreal T: Separation anxiety disorder, overanxious disorder, and school refusal. Child and Adolescent Psychiatric Clinics of North America 2:563–580, 1993

Bemporad J, Beresin E, Rauch P: Psychodynamic theories and treatment of childhood anxiety disorders. Child and Adolescent Psychiatric Clinics of North America 2:763–777, 1993

Biederman J, Newcorn J, Sprich S: Comorbidity of attention-deficit/hyperactivity disorder with conduct, depressive, anxiety, and other disorders. Am J Psychiatry 148:564–577, 1991

Braswell L, Bloomquist M: Cognitive-Behavioral Therapy With ADHD Children. New York, Guilford, 1991

Brown T, Gammon G (co-chairs): Attention deficit disorders: subtypes and comorbidity. Institute VI, Annual Meeting, American Academy of Child and Adolescent Psychiatry, San Antonio, TX, October 1993

Campbell M, Cueva JE: Psychopharmacology in child and adolescent psychiatry: a review of the past seven years, II. J Am Acad Child Adolesc Psychiatry 34:1262–1272, 1995

Caron C: Comorbidity in child psychopathology: concepts, issues and research strategies. J Child Psychol Psychiatry 32:1063–1080, 1991

Chasin R: Interviewing families with children: guidelines and suggestions. Journal of Psychotherapy and the Family 5:15–30, 1989

Chess S, Thomas A: Temperament in Clinical Practice. New York, Guilford, 1986

Colle L, Belair J, DeFeo M, et al: Extended open-label fluoxetine treatment of adolescents with major depression. J Am Acad Child Adolesc Psychiatry 33:225–232, 1994

Combrinck-Graham L: Treating Young Children in Family Therapy. Rockville, MD, Aspen, 1986

Combrinck-Graham L: Family models of childhood psychopathology, in Children in Family Contexts. Edited by Combrinck-Graham L. New York, Guilford, 1989, pp 67–89

DeVane C, Sallee F: Serotonin selective reuptake inhibitors in child and adolescent psychopharmacology: a review of published experience. J Clin Psychiatry 57:55–66, 1996

Dulcan M, Popper C: Concise Guide to Child and Adolescent Psychiatry. Washington, DC, American Psychiatric Press, 1991

Estrada AU, Pinsof WM: The effectiveness of family therapies for selected behavioral disorders of childhood. Journal of Marital and Family Therapy 21:403–440, 1995

Fergusson DM, Horwood LJ, Michael T: Prevalence and comorbidity of DSM-III-R diagnoses in a birth cohort of 15-year-olds. J Am Acad Child Adolesc Psychiatry 32:1127–1134, 1993

Fisher L: System based consultation with schools, in Systems Consultation: A New Perspective for Family Therapy. Edited by Wynne LC, McDaniel SH, Webber TL. New York, Guilford, 1986, pp 342–356

Fristad MA, Weller EB, Weller RA: Bipolar disorder in children and adolescents. Child and Adolescent Psychiatric Clinics of North America 1:13–29, 1992

Green RJ: "Learning to learn" and the family system: new perspectives on underachievement and learning disorders. Journal of Marital and Family Therapy 15:187–203, 1989

Greenhill L: Pharmacotherapy-stimulants. Child and Adolescent Psychiatric Clinics of North America 1:411–447, 1992

Griest DL, Wells KC: Behavioral family therapy with conduct disorders in children. Behavior Therapy 14:37–53, 1983

Hechtman L: Long-term outcome in attention-deficit hyperactivity disorder. Child and Adolescent Psychiatric Clinics of North America 1:553–565, 1992

Joshi P: Major depressive and manic-depressive disorders. Paper presented at the American Academy of Child and Adolescent Psychiatry Institute Annual Meeting ("Child and Adolescent Psychopharmacology: Clinical Management"), New Orleans, LA, October 1995

Kendall P, Chansky T, Kane MT, et al: Anxiety Disorders in Youth: Cognitive-Behavioral Interventions. Boston, MA, Allyn & Bacon, 1992

Last CG, Hersen M, Kazdin A: Anxiety disorders in children and their families. Arch Gen Psychiatry 48:928–934, 1991

Lewis DO: Conduct disorder, in Child and Adolescent Psychiatry. Edited by Lewis M. Baltimore, MD, Williams & Wilkins, 1991, pp 561–572

Lewis M: Psychiatric assessment of infants, children, and adolescents, in Child and Adolescent Psychiatry. Edited by Lewis M. Baltimore, MD, Williams & Wilkins, 1991, pp 561–572

Lusterman DD: An ecosystemic approach to family–school problems. American Journal of Family Therapy 13:22–30, 1985

McCracken JT: The epidemiology of child and adolescent mood disorders. Child and Adolescent Psychiatric Clinics of North America 1:53–72, 1992

McDougle CJ, Price L, Volkmar F: Recent advances in the pharmacotherapy of autism and related conditions. Child and Adolescent Psychiatric Clinics of North America 3:71–89, 1994

Patterson GR: Coercive Family Process. Eugene, OR, Castalia, 1982

Patterson GR: Family process: loops, levels and linkages, in Persons in Context: Developmental Processes. Edited by Bolger N, Caspi A, Downey G, et al. Cambridge, UK, Cambridge University Press, 1988, pp 114–151

Patterson GR, Reid J, Dishion T: Antisocial Boys. Eugene, OR, Castalia, 1992

Perlmutter RA: Academic failure as a family crisis, in Working With the Parents of College Students. Edited by Cohen RD. San Francisco, CA, Jossey-Bass, 1985, pp 77–92

Perosa ML: The development of a questionnaire to measure Minuchin's structural family concepts and the application of his psychosomatic family model to learning disabled families. Ph.D. dissertation, State University of New York at Buffalo, 1980

Pinsof WM, Wynne LC: The efficacy of marital and family therapy: an empirical overview, conclusions, and recommendations. Journal of Marital and Family Therapy 21:585–613, 1995

Pomeroy JC: Infantile autism and childhood psychosis, in Psychiatric Disorders in Children and Adolescents. Edited by Garfinkel BD, Carlson GA, Weller EB. Philadelphia, PA, WB Saunders, 1990, pp 271–290

Potter WZ, Ketter TA: Pharmacological issues in the treatment of bipolar disorders: focus on mood-stabilizing compounds. Can J Psychiatry 38:51–56, 1993

Rapoport J: Overview of drugs used in child psychiatry, in Psychopharmacology in Practice: Clinical and Research Update 1993. Bethesda, MD, Foundation for Advanced Education in the Sciences, November 1993

Silver LB: The Misunderstood Child: A Guide for Parents of Children With Learning Disabilities. Blue Ridge Summit, PA, TAB Books, 1990

Spencer T, Biederman J, Wilens T, et al: Pharmacotherapy of attention-deficit hyperactivity disorder across the life cycle. J Am Acad Child Adolesc Psychiatry 35:409–432, 1996

Tanguay P, Russell A: Mental retardation, in Child and Adolescent Psychiatry. Edited by Lewis M. Baltimore, MD, Williams & Wilkins, 1991, pp 508–516

Todd RD, Neuman R, Geller B, et al: Genetic studies of affective disorders: should we be starting with childhood onset probands? J Am Acad Child Adolesc Psychiatry 32:1164–1171, 1993

Volkmar F: Autism and pervasive developmental disorders, in Child and Adolescent Psychiatry. Edited by Lewis M. Baltimore, MD, Williams & Wilkins, 1991, pp 499–508

Volkmar F, Cohen D: Autism: current concepts. Child Adolesc Psychiatr Clin North Am 3:43–52, 1994

Weller EB, Weller RA: Depressive disorders in children and adolescents, in Psychiatric Disorders in Children and Adolescents. Edited by Garfinkel BD, Carlson GA, Weller EB. Philadelphia, PA, WB Saunders, 1990, pp 3–20

Wells KC, Forehand RL: Conduct and oppositional disorders, in Handbook of Clinical Behavior Therapy With Children. Edited by Bornstein PH, Kazdin AE. Homewood, IL, Dorsey Press, 1985, pp 218–266

West SA, Keck PE, McElroy SL: Oral loading doses in the valproate treatment of adolescents with mixed bipolar disorders. Journal of Child and Adolescent Psychopharmacology 5:225–231, 1995

White M, Epston D: Narrative Means to Therapeutic Ends. New York, WW Norton, 1990

Zilbach JJ: Young Children in Family Therapy. New York, Brunner/ Mazel, 1986

CHAPTER 17

Personality Disorders

A second-year psychiatric resident was treating Marie C., a 28-year-old woman with a known borderline personality disorder, in a tumultuous unsuccessful individual therapy. One day, Marie presented to the emergency room with the most recent of many overdoses and was seen with her family as part of a research project about families in psychiatric emergencies that a colleague and I were conducting. The resident was amazed at the family drama when he viewed the tape of the family interview—especially at the clarity and intensity of the family's projections. Until then, he had had no idea that Marie's perceptions of the family were not all her own projections. Although it was uncertain whether the family was able to benefit directly from the intervention, the individual therapy was transformed. With a deeper and more respectful understanding of the family's struggles and hidden forces, the resident therapist was able to help Marie toward a healthy differentiation.

Dorothy G.

A psychiatric consultation was requested for Dorothy G., a 71-year-old woman who was admitted to a medical hospital for an overdose. All of her previous hospital admissions had been for congestive heart disease, which was now end stage. After the overdose at 3 A.M., she alerted her sister, her physician, and (using an emergency telephone number) the police. Dorothy said that she had no self-destructive intent and that the act was strictly to express her rage at her nursing aide for not taking care of all her needs adequately. Her physician revealed he had been tolerating years of her outrageous, demanding behaviors and repeated phone calls. During the interview, Dorothy related all her symptoms and behaviors to her intolerance of being ill, her impatience, and her expectation of an immediate cure. When she asked for help, she insisted on a rapid response and became enraged if this response did not come.

When the patient's sister was interviewed, it emerged that Dorothy had been ill as a child and was overindulged and "spoiled rotten" by frightened and overwhelmed parents. She had been impulsive and easy to enrage all her life, leaving those around her terrified of crossing or disappointing her. With this awareness of a long-standing narcissistic personality disorder, the consultation intervention could then include suggestions for her helpers on how to understand her hypersensitivity to being out of control, dependent, and hurt.

The staff tried a number of ways to treat Dorothy as "special," including tolerating her behaviors as much as possible. Limits on her critical, rageful behaviors were discussed and established for use when absolutely necessary. One way limits were set was to frame certain behaviors as being especially powerful and thus able to devastate others with souls as sensitive as her own.

Interviews with Dorothy's family helped the consulting psychiatrist highlight the history and family dynamics. Although the work ahead was still difficult, having these guideposts gave the therapist a chance to avoid many traps and to use the knowledge to inform the intervention. This knowledge of the family also helped identify what had worked to solve the problem in the past. The therapist then had a sense of the strengths and resources in the family, which may not have been discovered in an interview with Dorothy alone. This intervention was brief, consisting of two 45-minute clinical interviews and one meeting with staff.

■ Perspective on the Disorders

There is no sharp distinction between normal and disordered when it comes to personality. Everyone has some repetitive, habitual ways of behaving, and almost anyone could be at risk of being labeled "personality disordered," especially during times of crisis or imbalance. Awareness of the family context of the disorders also introduces a degree of "relativism" to the criteria for personality disorder. It is common to find that the whole family has the same traits or idiosyncrasies found in the individual patient. The whole family may be avoidant, hysterical, or schizotypal. In a way, the family itself could be conceptualized as meeting the descriptive criteria for a particular personality disorder.

Personality formation is related to a complex of developmental factors, including the unfolding of genetics, the family social environment, the person's experiences, and fate. The family is the context in which the individual first learns and experiments with ways of interacting with others. Some of this behavior may eventually become habitual and influence all areas of the person's life. The original use of "defenses" takes place within the family; the family constitutes the original "offense" against which the child learns to defend him- or herself.

"Personality disordered" is a phrase often used synonymously with impossible, hopeless cases. There is great potential to offer a new perspective for intransigent cases by considering the family context. Long-term psychoanalytic therapy alone is appropriate in some cases of borderline disorder. In most cases, however, this view is limiting and inadequate, especially if it neglects the attachment dimension and the interpersonal meaning of behaviors such as suicidal gestures. It is almost always helpful to try to discover how the behaviors might connect to an impending divorce, correlate with a parent's depressions, or provide one way for the individual to keep the family united.

The therapist must respect the adaptive nature of symptoms and personality style as it is expressed as persistent adulthood patterns. A Sufi legend illustrates this point. An Indian man is traveling on a small ship with 10 other men when a raging storm destroys the ship. As the ship goes down, the man grabs hold of a raft that is floating free. He soon realizes he is the only survivor and floats alone at sea day after day. He is washed onto a beach almost unconscious and is found there by some passersby, who give him drink and food and nurse him back to health. When he is strong enough, he stands up, picks up his raft, and lifts it onto his head, where he carries it for the rest of his life.

Table 17–1 summarizes some aspects of the family context of these disorders, which is described in more detail in the next section.

Table 17–1.   Personality disorders in context

Effects of the disorder on the family
- Organization of family around personality problems
- Confusion
- Apprehension
- Avoidance of negative responses from symptomatic person

Family maintenance of the symptoms
- Marriage problems (but with hidden admiration for the other)
- Marriage of people with different personality disorders
- Problematic, difficult family of origin; habitual, repetitive, intransigent behaviors
- Overinvolvement of family
- Parental inconsistency
- Forces against autonomy of family member
- Nurturance offered only in crisis
- Infantilizing of individual into adulthood

Functions of the symptoms within the family
- Distraction from more serious family problems
- Regulation of emotional distance
- Protection of family from outside threats
- Entertainment
- Allegiance to family, especially in showing distrust of outsiders

Adverse consequences of change
- Difficult adjustment because symptoms are integrated into individual's and family's identity
- Worry over how individual will cope in dangerous world if defenses are reduced and trust is encouraged
- Anger with perception that recovering individual no longer needs the family as much

---

■ Connections of the Symptoms to the System

■ Effects of the Symptoms on the Family

Like the family of an individual with substance addiction organizes around the addiction, so, too, the family of an individual with personality disorder organizes around the personality problems. In the narcissistic-borderline-histrionic spectrum of personality disorders, therapists often observe families who are "walking on eggs," living in an atmosphere of fear, tension, and apprehension that something will hurt or offend the index person and trigger a dramatic and angry response.

A parent with personality disorder may fly into rages or withdraw when children disagree or act differently from what he or she expects. It is easy to understand the family's tendency to automatically adjust to avoid these habitual negative responses. Many families are confused by the rapidly shifting moods of the individual and by the predominance of anger (Schulz et al. 1985).

■ Family Maintenance of the Symptoms

New family.   The literature is sparse regarding the marriages of individuals with character disorders. Contributions focus on descriptions of the hysteric-obsessive marriage, the borderline-borderline marriage, the borderline-narcissist marriage, and the borderline-schizoid marriage (Bergner 1977; Koch and Ingram 1985; Lansky 1981; McCormack 1989; Solomon 1985).

On the surface, these relationships seem to be filled with disappointment and unremitting misery. The person with histrionic personality disorder complains bitterly about the obsessive spouse's lack of affection, spontaneity, and emotion and about his or her passivity and unwillingness to take a stand. The obsessive person complains more quietly about the hysteric partner's dramatics, out-of-control emotionality, and lack of practicality. The person with borderline personality disorder complains and rages about the inability of the spouse and others to make him or her feel whole, fulfilled, and soothed.

In these marriages, the spouses may secretly admire and be attracted to the very aspects about which they complain. The person with hysterical behavior benefits from the stability of the obsessive person, and the obsessive person enjoys the entertainment and liveliness of the more emotional spouse. The borderline person experiences a kind of safety in the cool aloofness of the schizoid person, who certainly will not threaten with engulfment.

Two people with complementary character problems and deficits can enjoy an excellent marital relationship regardless of how disturbed they may appear as individuals. Although the negative side of the other's effect cannot be minimized, there is also a communicated empathy, or at least an awareness that each serves to keep at bay the other's terror of aloneness or annihilation.

Family of origin.   No single clinical description of the family is associated with personality disorders, but the family of origin is likely to fall within a certain behavioral range. At one end of the continuum, a family appears to be free of gross psychopathology and is appropriately upset and mobilized during times of crisis. At the other end of the continuum, a family is highly problematic, very difficult for helpers to interact with, highly provocative, easily enraged, and even violent (Perlmutter 1982). Often one observes rigid, tense family transactions that are themselves "characterological" in the sense that they show habitual, repetitive, seemingly intransigent behaviors that are maladaptive to current problem solving. These families appear unable to grow, evolve, or learn from experience.

The family of the person with borderline behavior has been the most thoroughly studied and can be considered a prototype. The usual description of the dynamic of families with a borderline child includes maternal overinvolvement with the child at early phases, followed by communicated retaliation and withdrawal in response to the child's moves toward autonomy (Green 1983). Epidemiological studies point to the common observation of both overinvolvement and the subsequent withdrawal of parental figures as predictive factors for people who will manifest borderline personality (Berzirganian et al. 1993).

This parental inconsistency and attitude toward growth interfere with the psychological tasks of both the toddler and adolescent stages, where the development of independence is prominent. The child is often locked into an intense relationship with a parent who exhibits regressive, childlike, or aggressive behaviors. This parent-child sequence becomes cyclical; for example, when an adolescent with borderline disorder adopts provocative, regressive behavior that encourages the parents to be immature, emotional, and overcontrolling. This response by the parents in turn increases the adolescent's anger and provocations, and the cycle continues.

In borderline personality disorder, the family presenting in crisis can be described as showing a "family group regression" (Shapiro 1978) connected to the child's striving for autonomy. The family inadvertently rewards the individual's regression by offering nurturance only at times of mutilation, suicide attempts, or brief psychosis, which become the times of greatest family closeness. Any indication of autonomy in the individual with personality disorder brings the certain threat of abandonment by the family. The other family members carry unresolved conflicts over autonomy and differentiation that "haunt the interview room" (Perlmutter 1982).

In borderline or narcissistic personality disorder, the family may continue to degrade and infantilize the individual even into adulthood, which perpetuates the original injury inflicted upon the child's self-esteem.

■ Functions of the Symptoms Within the Family

Borderline personality disorder.   Persistent borderline acting-out behaviors may function to distract the family from the equally serious problems of other family members. The blatant, colorful symptoms of the person with borderline behavior also help other family members "save face." In many cases, the symptoms may also be seen as attempts toward very difficult differentiation of the individual.

> Elaine N., a 26-year-old woman with borderline personality disorder, presented to the psychiatric emergency room after her fifth serious overdose. The nuclear family (father, older sister, and younger brother) were persuaded to participate in a joint interview to help problem-solve in this difficult situation. During the interview, the family agreed on the central problem: *"She has a mind of her own."* They sincerely believed that Elaine lost her value as a daughter and person when she did not think and act exactly as the father and brother prescribed.
>
> The negative sequences invariably began when Elaine mentioned getting a job in another state, a plan vehemently opposed by all family members. They became threatened and attacked her, reminding her of her history, her inadequacy, and her inability to survive away from the family. Elaine participated in this cycle by sporadically behaving in ways that reinforced or justified these assertions (i.e., by stealing drugs from medical units, abusing substances, and overdosing). This behavior alternated with periods of relative calmness and high functioning.
>
> During discussions, we found that another sister was anorectic and had suffered severe crises equal in severity to Elaine's. Elaine's mother was later revealed to have overdosed repeatedly, which created an aura of such strain and tension for the four children that it was an almost welcome diversion to focus on Elaine. The sense of powerlessness that the family felt over the mother's situation was balanced by their belief that they could control Elaine if they were dogmatic enough.
>
> In the interview, the father's hypertension and chest pains were discussed openly for the first time. He disliked talking about his health

concerns and hated having to face his own vulnerability and mortality. He had been spared having to share much about himself because the family moved so rapidly from one dramatic crisis to the next.

The outspoken brother claimed a fierce loyalty to the family and a wish to help Elaine, but he was overtly dysfunctional himself, could barely contain his emotion, and almost became violent in the emergency room. He was 22 years old and still living at home—with no prospects for any other arrangement.

Only one sister showed even a hint of having differentiated. The interviewer persistently asked that sister how she managed to leave the family to lead her own life. She admitted that Elaine's struggles were the same ones she dealt with and that her achievement of a somewhat separate existence had come at a cost. She described a troubled marriage and a strong attachment to a fanatic religious sect.

For a long time, the family held rigidly to their initial view of the problem. They did not notice that Elaine had fewer troubles and no overdoses when living away from home or that her struggle to differentiate from a wild, chaotic family life was not all craziness.

Other disorders.   Compulsive personality disorder serves to *regulate distance* in a context of individual and family anxieties, bringing some family members closer and keeping others further away.

The person with avoidant behavior suffers from high interpersonal anxiety and fears that closeness to others will lead to loss of self. The family itself may be fearful of having any stranger (i.e., anyone who is not a family member) enter their sphere. The "disorder" *protects* the whole family from having to relax boundaries and experience the accompanying anxiety.

The person with hysterical behavior may offer *entertainment* to dull or chaotic families.

A person with schizoid personality disorder demonstrates *allegiance* to family members and their beliefs, which reflect their strong distrust of the world.

■ Adverse Consequences of Change

Characterological disturbance implies a rigidity, a reluctance, and sometimes a powerlessness to change one's patterns of behavior. Personality disorder symptoms are personality traits that are integrated into the individual's identity and help define who the person is. Thus, the paranoid person clings tenaciously to suspicions; the person with narcissistic personality disorder finds it difficult to relinquish a lifelong need to be adored and spared all criticism; and the dependent person relies on a network of caregivers who have grown accustomed to their roles.

Many families have found ways to accommodate the demands of living with an individual with personality disorder. Because personality change in the individual would imply a change in interactive patterns, the family is directly affected by change. Some families are relieved to see the person suffer less, act more adaptively, and move closer to maturity. Other families are panicked, threatened, and confused by the changes.

The family may wonder how the index person will cope without the habitual, familiar behavioral patterns. The family of the person with paranoid behavior comments on how useful it is to be suspicious of all the criminals in the world. The family of the person with compulsive behavior inquires about the troubles the individual may get into with a new, looser style. If the family of the person with histrionic personality disorder is also histrionic, they may notice only the most extreme, dramatic changes or may react to change only as it reflects on or affects them.

The family of origin of the person with borderline personality disorder may become enraged at the individual for not needing them as intensely and for choosing "strangers" over them.

> One man had a mutually rewarding fused relationship with his own mother and had virtually no other human contact. As he began to date women his age, his mother found fault with each woman and never showed any pleasure in seeing her painfully isolated son take new risks.

The marital problems of the person with borderline personality disorder can be particularly resistant to therapeutic change because the emotional pain of the interactions is at least familiar and certainly preferable to aloneness and abandonment.

◼ Special Systemic Dimensions

◼ Family History and Genetics

Factors leading to antisocial personality disorder are well described (Loeber 1990). Borderline personality disorder is the most studied of

the personality disorders. First-degree relatives of individuals with borderline personality disorder have an increased incidence of affective
disorders (Soloff and Millward 1983), alcoholism, and antisocial personality disorder (Clarkin et al. 1991; Goldman et al. 1993).

Borderline personality disorder has been linked with childhood
sexual abuse. This significant research field (Goldman et al. 1992; Herman et al. 1989; Links 1990) raises the question of a possible overlap
between Axis I and II, because what appear to be personality disorders
are sometimes found to resemble posttraumatic stress disorder (PTSD).

One main research effort is to define qualities that characterize the
families of individuals with borderline personality disorder. Studies of
these families have found a very tight parental marriage that excludes
one or more of the children (Gunderson et al. 1980). The father in
these families is remembered as the neglectful parent (Frank and Paris
1981). The adolescent child's minor behavioral problems are likely to
be ignored. The child then behaves more and more outrageously until
a crisis results and the family presents in mutual blame and anger.

The more purely biological contributions to personality disorder
development have been well studied. Older twin studies showed inheritability of roughly 50% for monozygotic twins and 30% for dizygotic
twins (Loehlin and Nichols 1976). Newer models of research are designed to distinguish genetic and environmental factors. They tend to
point toward strong inheritability of most personality factors except
dependency and attachment (Bouchard et al. 1990; Livesley et al. 1993).

■ Gender

The behavior of men with personality disorder may be exaggerations
of the stereotypical masculine tendency toward isolation, competition,
lack of emotion, and a view of people as objects to be used or avoided.
Women with personality disorder are more likely to exhibit a desperate
need for relationships that provide a longed-for fusion, an ideal meeting of their deepest needs. Rage, hurt, and many other symptoms appear when these needs are not met. The behaviors associated with personality disorders for both men and women could be seen as exaggerations of sexual stereotypes in which men fear relationships and women
search for everything within them.

These observations relate moderately well to the research findings,
which show a higher prevalence of antisocial, schizoid, and narcissistic

personality disorders in men and a higher prevalence of histrionic and dependent diagnoses in women (Golomb et al. 1995), with borderline personality disorder equally prevalent in men and women.

■ Intimacy

Schizoid personality disorder is defined by the lack of enjoyment of close relationships. It implies a lack of connectedness with people that may include the family (American Psychiatric Association 1994), but it is common to find individuals with schizoid personality disorder who relate only to their parents.

In couples and family work, narcissistic issues in one or more family members are central. The individual demands that the child or spouse be a perfect extension of self, and this demand makes it impossible to achieve affectionate, loving, mutual parent-child or spousal relationships. Narcissistic rage is often behind the parents' intolerance of the anger directed toward them by their teenage child.

Control and suspicion are major obstacles to intimacy in personality disorders. Each personality disorder can be considered in terms of how the repetitive behaviors help the person gain control over others and protect the self from the actions of others. The behaviors represent attempts to control relationships and regulate the distance between self and others.

The individual is also suspicious out of fear that the past will be repeated and that the individual will be hurt again in the same way. In avoidant personality disorder, other people do not get close enough to hurt the individual. In borderline personality disorder, suspicions are projected onto a world of angry, depriving predators from whom the individual hungers for love. The individual with antisocial personality disorder escapes vulnerability by using and exploiting other people. In histrionic personality disorder, the individual is distracted by other complaints and is unaware of underlying suspicions and fears.

■ Loyalty

The behaviors associated with personality disorders are often found to be somehow consistent with the needs of the family. The individual with avoidant personality disorder may be found in a family that distrusts outsiders and is often overtly unhappy when the children develop attachments to friends or decide to marry. The person with borderline personality disorder may be carrying on characteristics found in each of the last three generations. The person with compulsive personality disorder is likely to be found in a family that is concerned with maintaining the image of perfect control and would be uncomfortable if a child became too relaxed in relating to others outside the family.

■ Map of Emotions

In each personality disorder, the individual handles emotions in certain habitual ways that lock the person into moody, dysfunctional modes. In histrionic personality disorder, deeper emotions are often not experienced or are expressed flamboyantly. In antisocial personality disorder, deep emotions would be overwhelming and therefore never threaten to enter conscious awareness.

Spouses are routinely the object of narcissistic rage. This rage can be unmasked as the injury experienced by the individual when the spouse does not live up to the ideal and does not meet every need. Because the index person is burdened by feeling entitled to having all needs met, he or she automatically attacks, criticizes, and rejects the imperfect spouse. Negative feelings are experienced as if the anger were fully justified. The individual is unaware that these expectations originated in the deprivations, injustices, and other narcissistic injuries of earlier times.

Borderline personality disorder is characterized by desperate, out-of-control attempts to fill the emptiness within. These efforts lead to a series of clinging, hostile-dependent relationships in an attempt to avoid the emotions of helplessness, hopelessness, sadness, emptiness, and aloneness.

A powerful therapeutic moment can occur around the issue of emotional avoidance. The person's fear of aloneness and the desperate search to have others fill the void are unmasked, and the person realizes that others will never be able to fill it. The person then feels intense panic, despondency, and desperation. If these emotions can be faced and grasped, they may give way to deep sadness and then lightness and relief, as the individual discovers that he or she no longer feels the need to demand that others fill the void.

As the desperate dream subsides, the individual becomes sadder and wiser, but may now have access to interpersonal relationships. Expectations of others become much more modest. The hidden demand for relief from all pain is gone, and this is in itself relieving. The individual may be amused to find that interpersonal needs can be met only after a person stops demanding that they be met.

■ Countertransference

In common clinical parlance, the label of a personality disorder in either a family or an individual connotes a warning as much as a description. The warning is that the therapist will be the object of intense projected rage and distortion and that the individual and family will cling to their symptoms if the therapy threatens to take them away. The therapist preparing to see a group of people previously labeled "borderline" or "character-disordered" may deal with countertransference fear and anger long before the referred people present in the office.

Specific personality constellations can be associated with specific traps. In hysterical personality disorder, the therapist may feel sexually aroused or just plain confused, because the patient's tendency toward distraction makes it impossible to arrive at any understanding of the information being offered. In avoidant personality disorder, the urge for the therapist to withdraw, distance, or refer away resembles the individual's way of dealing with the world.

In narcissistic personality disorder, the therapist becomes exhausted from the effort of meticulously monitoring his or her own words, tone, and frames to avoid hurting or enraging the patient. This effort can lead to anger and withdrawal on the part of the therapist, both of which are sensed immediately by the index person and result in exactly the rage and perception of insult that the therapist is trying to avoid. An opportunity for understanding may emerge from this situation, but the therapy can also end and prove unsalvageable.

This delicate situation is well known in individual psychotherapy and is even more complex in family work, where each family member may have narcissistic vulnerabilities and may react upon perceiving the therapist's slightest error or upon hearing certain comments from any member of the family. Often a person with narcissistic behavior claims that the therapist is siding with another member against them. It is easy to side against people who have a grossly exaggerated perception of their own entitlement. The therapist must consider the validity of the accusation of favoritism before interpreting it as distortion.

■ Posterity

Can the therapist focus on the effects on the next generation as a motivation for change? The person with personality disorder often denies or is unable to perceive the effects his or her behaviors have on other people. Even hatred projected onto children is denied.

> One 36-year-old woman with borderline personality disorder who was well known to staff presented with her 2-year-old daughter and asked to be seen as a walk-in patient. When the nurse entered the room, the woman showed her self-mutilated arms and continued cutting with a bloody razor until the staff subdued her. Later it became clear that the woman had cut herself in full view of her young daughter, but she was oblivious to possible negative effects on the child. Attending to the child's posttraumatic stress and arranging the mother's admission were equally important.

■ Treatment

■ Standard Individual Therapies

The traditional modal treatment for personality disorders has been long-term psychoanalytic-psychodynamic therapy aimed at altering character structure. In recent years, virtually every form of psychotherapy has been used in treating individuals with personality disorder.

A developing school of thought proposes that more and more Axis II diagnoses can be reformulated as unrecognized Axis I entities and then treated as such. Borderline conditions are conceptualized by some as affective disorders, implying a deficit of affect regulation and a need for antidepressant treatment.

In pharmacotherapy, the hope for the future is agents that address deficits of affect and impulse regulation. Promising work is emerging on the treatment of impulse problems with selective serotonin reuptake inhibitors, mood-stabilizing agents, phenothiazines, or some combination of these agents. A notable body of literature is also accumulating on the pharmacotherapy of borderline personality disorder (Cornelius et al. 1993).

■ Family Modalities

Offices of marital therapists are filled with couples in which one or both spouses could be described as having a personality disorder. A notable subgroup is characterized by persistent mutual externalization and blaming stances that lead to endless rageful battles and demands that the other partner change or be changed by the therapist. This phenomenon can occur in any disorder but is most commonly associated with Cluster B disorders (antisocial, borderline, histrionic, and narcissistic).

The crucial dilemma for the therapist is how to proceed therapeutically with family members who are exquisitely sensitive to narcissistic injury. Language is used carefully to avoid blame and to frame intentions in positive ways. History can be used to reflect how much better the parent is doing than his own parents were able to do. Emotional reactivity is discouraged as unhelpful and potentially harmful to each member's sense of self and not worth the risk. At the first hint of narcissistic vulnerability, the therapist should consider individual sessions, because the blaming and negative attributions of some conjoint meetings can trigger a suicidal despair (Lansky 1982).

If destructive rage and blaming persist despite ongoing therapy, the therapist can inquire gently about other options, such as separation, accepting powerlessness (giving up the belief in changing the other), medications (especially if the problem is rage attacks or mood swings), initiating individual therapy with new therapists, or alternating individual sessions with the current therapist. The therapist's admission of powerlessness to alter the couple's painful sequences reminds the couple that they are ultimately responsible for the outcome of the treatment. Many impasses can be broken in this way.

Treatment of a child or adolescent with borderline personality disorder illustrates the difficulty of choosing a modality or modalities for family therapy. When the predominant issues are overprotection and anxiety, conjoint meetings are often fruitful. If the family is angry and the parent-child relationship is characterized by neglect, it is often better to see the parents separately from the child at first (Gunderson et al. 1980).

Where anger and neglect predominate, conjoint parent-child sessions can too easily become rageful disasters. Some parents are terrified that the child will somehow get between them, cause them to blame each other, or otherwise force them apart. The anxiety of all family members will be so high that the sessions may consist completely of endless mutual accusations. Family meetings may be useful later to help the family adjust to therapeutic change and to discover whether further closeness is possible without loss of boundaries.

■ Psychoeducation

Psychoeducational approaches to personality disorders are not mainstream, but educational efforts may be underutilized and should be considered. In families where the index person is a child, most parents need education as much as do parents of children with schizophrenia. With some families, family therapy can be greatly enhanced by educational discussions about the types of disorders, their relationship to other disorders such as affective disorders, and the results of biological (genetic and medication) studies (Schulz et al. 1985).

If the parents have psychopathology that blocks empathic responses, the therapist identifies and works with the parent who has the more nurturant, protective responses (Feldman and Guttman 1984). A psychoeducational family approach may help family members understand personality disorders and may suggest ways to live with very difficult people.

For example, many young people and adult children of all ages present with a psychotherapy request for help in going home. Work with college students has shown that holidays become a time of panic as students prepare to visit their dysfunctional families. The students express intense loyalties to their families but feel that these ties to family are in direct conflict with the escape and the increased differentiation that seem possible in their life away from home.

Many students must return home to parents who have personality problems and to homes in which thoughts, feelings, and behaviors that are different from what the parent expects can precipitate painful struggles. Coaching techniques (Bowen 1994; Carter et al. 1976)—whereby the therapist and the young adult child review the family story together plan interventions—may be very useful. These planned interventions may include experiments of behaving differently when provoked or of providing a response that will surprise the family, such as agreeing when the other person is accustomed to receiving an argument or taking a stand on an issue on which silence was formerly maintained.

Sometimes a family meeting can form part of the intervention. Parents may be willing to fly hundreds of miles to meet about the problems of their child, and much useful work can be done quickly through these conversations. In most cases, a psychoeducational therapy with the student alone has been used successfully.

During these sessions, the behaviors of the parents were usually framed as positive even if the behaviors were unjust. Coaching ideas were combined with exoneration (Boszormenyi-Nagy 1987; Perlmutter 1985), a concept that builds on an understanding of the parents' lives. This approach does not ignore or minimize the injustices committed against the children, but it can help the adult child view the parents as people who did the best they could.

> Diane W., a 20-year-old college sophomore who presented with depressive-anxious symptoms, thought she should drop out of school and move home with her mother, who lived 200 miles away. Later in therapy it emerged that her mother had often trapped Diane in double binds and shown other borderline behaviors. At the time Diane requested therapy, her mother was calling her daily to find out why Diane was not visiting her and stayed at school so much.
>
> A discussion of her mother's health status revealed that her mother suffered from severe diabetes. The illness was difficult to control, and a strict diet had been prescribed. Diane's extreme anxiety focused on whether or not to bring her mother a gift of a large box of candy. If she did, she would feel as if she were trying to hurt her mother, and her mother would accuse her of even worse intentions. But if Diane did not bring this gift, her mother would scream accusations that Diane didn't love her. The battles with her mother would make her vacation time a living hell.
>
> The therapy consisted largely of gaining an understanding of the intense double bind Diane was presently experiencing and then discussing how the mother might have developed such defense mechanisms in her own family of origin. This approach led to a collaborative strategizing of how Diane might extricate herself from the family role of overresponsible, guilty caretaker.
>
> Diane was to go home to see her mother only after she had a sense of what she wanted to accomplish from the visit. Instead of attempting the impossible task of making her mother happy, Diane focused on defining the more manageable objective of understanding her mother better and understanding her own role within the family. Once this change was accomplished, it was safe for Diane to make the visit without the same degree of risk of a major depression or crisis.
>
> Diane was fascinated by the stunned looks on family members' faces when she didn't act in the predictable ways. When her mother talked about illness, Diane changed the topic to her problems at school and her uncertainty over whether she could stand living in a city far away from her mother. Sometimes she expressed the double binds: "I want to bring you candy, which I know you will love

but which we both know would also be a hateful thing to do to a
diabetic. I want to do the right thing, but it's so hard to decide
what's right that I think I might go crazy."

When Diane returned to therapy, she said she actually experienced pleasure as well as sadness when she was visiting her mother.
She had suddenly realized that the overall situation was not her
fault or hers alone to fix.

■ New Stories

From smothering to protecting.   Overprotectiveness by parents may
become so extreme that independence is punished. During the early
therapy sessions, the tendency toward overprotectiveness is positively
approached and reflected rather than critically confronted. The therapist says to the parents:

> "Now I think I understand the degree of worry and concern you
> feel for your child, which of course is made more intense by your
> child's irresponsible and sometimes dangerous behaviors. You feel
> the need to control and protect more, and your child then gets
> angry and defies you. Do you see any way out of this cycle? Is there
> any way for protection to be a little less work so you don't become
> exhausted?"

Discussion may focus on solutions that have worked:

> "Have you had any experiences in which you and your child solved
> a problem together and each contributed to the solution?"

Loyalty to family.   In avoidant or schizoid personality disorder, the
therapist may comment as follows:

> "Based on what you just said, I am wondering if, in your isolation,
> you are trying to spare your family the stress of meeting strangers
> or the burden of having to consider new ideas that might make
> them uncomfortable?"

In narcissistic personality disorder, the behaviors are framed as attempts to protect the self from too much assault.

> Patricia B., a 37-year-old woman, presented with anxiety and
> panic, and connections to a parent-child problem emerged in ther-

apy. Patricia's mother called her daily and made demands for attention: "If you loved me, you would call me every day." The two were locked in a severe hostile-dependent arrangement and battled constantly. Patricia was engaged in a graduate program but had been unable to finish, partly because of these conflicts. The mother ridiculed her daughter's successes, but Patricia seemed unaware of how her own success threatened her mother with the fear that she would lose her daughter.

The frame to Patricia was as follows: "I was wondering as you spoke if it could be true that, at least in part, your mother has such a low view of herself from her abusive and deprived childhood that she feels she cannot survive if she loses you. And losing you seems to be equivalent in her mind to your being successful and separating from her. So out of her fear and her survival instinct, she unconsciously tries to keep you down so you do not become powerful and independent enough to separate. Your symptoms, such as your inability to finish your degree, then, if I am understanding what you have been saying, might be related to your attempts to help your mom, to let her win, to not hurt her any more than you have to. Sure, you and I understand that this means you must sacrifice your adult life, but this represents loyalty and concern for your desperately insecure mother."

Patricia visited her mother and studied the mother-daughter sequences, asked many questions about her mother's life, and experimented with new behaviors. Gradually, she found ways to achieve small successes in her life and to couple these successes with increased contact with her mother rather than withdrawing and hiding. As she allowed more good things into her life, she also increased reassurance that there would be room for her mother in her life. Patricia was patient and calm when her mother made destructive comments because these had been anticipated in the therapy-coaching sessions.

When therapy ended, Patricia was finally preparing to get her graduate degree after 15 years of sporadic schooling, and she was closer to a mutually rewarding relationship with her family.

Narcissistic injury as bad reception. In the personality disorders, many family members struggle with projections based on past experience. Treatment usually focuses on correcting the individual's tendency to perceive the comments of others exclusively in terms that reflect poorly on him- or herself. Family members can be taught the importance of doubting their perceptions to allow them to question their automatically negative interpretations of the comments or actions of others. Their interpretation is reflected as theory or hypothesis, rather than as truth. The therapist may comment:

> "Oh, I see. When your father says he needs something from you or wishes you could do something, you take it as criticism and feel angry and hurt. Your interpretation is certainly *one* reasonable way of hearing the comments."

The therapist can stop here at first and observe for any hints of curiosity or change. During later sessions, the discussion may continue:

> "Are there any other ways of hearing your father's comments? How can you find out if your perceptions are correct? It sure would be sad if he meant something else and you suffered needlessly all these years because of your misreadings. And yet if he is attacking, it's understandable that you are always ready to defend. By the way, if he is being critical, do you know much about how your father learned that style? Do you think he criticizes you more or less than he was criticized by his own family?"

Bad behaviors as good.   Withdrawal of a narcissistic spouse is easily experienced as abandonment by the other spouse. Overinvolved control is experienced as tyranny. These patterns can be revealed as attempts at distance-closeness regulation by fragile, vulnerable individuals. The therapist wonders aloud whether such interpersonal maneuvers are helping to prevent the feeling of being overwhelmed, disorganized, fragmented, or enraged.

Personality-disordered behaviors are viewed as understandable attempts to avoid having one's defenses overwhelmed by shame. Even withdrawal and attacking behaviors are discussed in terms of their wisdom, adaptation, and usefulness for preservation of self and family function (Lansky 1982, 1991).

Solution orientation.   The therapist may focus on the future by commenting:

> "What do you think it would take for this person to begin to relate differently to other people? How will you know when he is beginning to change? What do you imagine are the thoughts or feelings that make him act in these ways? If he began to trust others more,

in what ways would that be good for him? In what ways does such change sound risky or scary?"

Defiance-based frames.   When a therapist is able to join rather than fight the family resistance, change is more likely. Joining resistance can be a way for the therapist to genuinely empathize with the family's dilemma and their reasons for fearing change.

Techniques for dealing with resistance and defiance are among the most innovative and effective contributions of the family field to psychotherapy. Many people present after having "defeated" a number of other therapists. They seem to want help but actually ignore or fight any suggestions toward change made by the series of therapists. If the therapist confronts these maneuvers directly, the family feels hurt and rejected. Techniques to confront defiance indirectly and redirect the energy of the resistance will be invaluable to the therapist.

The key is to respectfully connect the symptom with its role in the family (Jones 1987; Papp 1983). These techniques are especially applicable to work with individuals with personality disorders, in whom resistance to change is extremely common. Although a more detailed repertoire is available (Papp 1983; Perlmutter and Jones 1987; Rohrbaugh et al. 1981), the following selection is representative:

1. **Caution against too-rapid change.**   "The three of you seem to be getting along better. The last time you experienced an improvement like this, there was a huge blow-up. Are you sure you're not changing a bit too rapidly?"
2. **Speak the inferred defiant thought.**   A 37-year-old chronically paranoid man presented with his wife, and they told the story of new behaviors and increasing suspicions that were about to cost him his job and marriage. He had refused to follow the advice of family, friends, doctors, and other helpers. We thought that prescribing low-dose Stelazine (trifluoperazine) and finding the couple a family psychiatrist could avert hospitalization, but we also knew the man was resistant toward direct offers of help. We switched to a defiance-based intervention (Perlmutter and Jones 1985):

    > "I could give you a medication that would help, but from what you say you are pretty suspicious. How would you know for sure that what I'm giving you is good and that I'm not just poisoning you? I understand how these suspicions may cost you everything and that the medicine is likely to help you sort out these

thoughts, but there is no way you could trust strangers like us to help, especially at a time when your mind can send you only messages of distrust. So I'll prescribe these pills even though I'm sure you won't be able to take them."

A week later, a follow-up indicated that the man was doing better, had taken the medications, and had called to say, "Tell those guys they were wrong, and I took the pills just to show them how wrong they were."

3. **Approach the truth in terms of irony.**   Paradox is a way to express seeming contradictions in the family's behavior that may actually reveal an aspect of the truth. Discussion begins with the positive reframing or connotation of a symptom. Then the therapist suggests paradoxical reasons for the individual's behavior. The dilemma of change can be openly discussed.

In chronically self-destructive borderline, histrionic, or narcissistic personality disorders, the therapist could offer the idea that behavioral patterns may in part reflect a learning problem: the person may wish very much to be happier or to be less trouble to his or her family but has never learned to like or take good care of him- or herself. In adult life, these problems lead the person to make choices that will bring the worst possible outcome:

> "If I am correctly understanding the pattern you just described, he is certain to reject any healthy, mature option because he will feel he doesn't deserve it? If we refer him to a good therapist or if a medication is found to be helpful, he must not accept this help because he feels he deserves only bad things? This is certainly sad."

4. **Prescribe the symptom.**   With an individual with a history of treatment defiance and an avoidant personality disorder, the therapist can ask:

> "Would you be willing to isolate yourself a bit more for two weeks just so we can gather information about the effects this would have on you and those around you?"

Genogram.   Questions that focus on three generations of the family may help with exoneration and avoidance of blame:

"How did your parents and their parents learn to take care of themselves in this way? What happened to them in their lives? What kind of person was your father, grandmother, grandfather? How did others get along with him or her? What were all the relationships like?"

Circular questioning.   The therapist begins:

"I would like to ask each of you in turn to say something about the problem the individual is having. I would like to know what you believe is the meaning or message in the behaviors, how you think the problem developed, and what you think would be important elements of the solution."

The therapist may wish to assess for a "family personality disorder":

"Is the family as a whole or are any other family members suspicious of others? Does anyone else have the same sort of troubles in relationships? Who is the most shy member of the family? Who is next? Can you think of other members who are easily hurt and sensitive to rejection?"

Additional Reading

Beck MJ: Treatment of the character-disordered family member. Family Therapy 4:43–48, 1977

Beck MJ: Pathological narcissism and the psychology of the married victim. Family Therapy 6:155–159, 1979

Lachkar J: Narcissistic/borderline couples: theoretical implications for treatment. Dynamic Psychotherapy 3:109–125, 1985

Paris J: Family theory and character pathology. International Journal of Family Psychiatry 3:475–485, 1982

Shapiro ER: Family dynamics and borderline personality disorder, in Handbook of Borderline Disorders. Edited by Silver D, Rosenbluth M. Madison, CT, International Universities Press, 1992, pp 471–493

Slavik S, Carlson J, Sperry L: Adlerian marital therapy with the passive-aggressive partner. American Journal of Family Therapy 20:25–35, 1992

■ References

American Psychiatric Association: Diagnostic and Statistical Manual of Mental Disorders, 4th Edition. Washington, DC, American Psychiatric Association, 1994

Bergner RM: The marital system of the hysterical individual. Fam Process 16:85–95, 1977

Berzirganian S, Cohen P, Brook JS: The impact of mother-child interaction on the development of borderline personality disorder. Am J Psychiatry 150:1836–1842, 1993

Boszormenyi-Nagy I: Foundations of Contextual Therapy: Collected Papers of Ivan Boszormenyi-Nagy. New York, Brunner/Mazel, 1987

Bouchard TJ, Lykken DT, McGue M, et al: Sources of human psychological differences: the Minnesota study of twins reared apart. Science 250:223–228, 1990

Bowen M: Family Therapy in Clinical Practice, 9th Edition. Northvale, NJ, Jason Aronson, 1994

Carter EA, McGoldrick M, Orfandis M: Family therapy with one person and the therapist's own family, in Family Therapy: Theory and Practice. Edited by Guerin PJ. New York, Gardner, 1976, pp 193–219

Clarkin JF, Marziali E, Munroe-Blum H: Group and family treatments for borderline personality disorder. Hosp Community Psychiatry 42:1038–1043, 1991

Cornelius JR, Soloff PH, Perel JM, et al: Continuation pharmacotherapy of borderline personality disorder with haloperidol and phenelzine. Am J Psychiatry 150:1843–1848, 1993

Feldman RB, Guttman HA: Families of borderline patients: literal-minded parents, borderline parents, and parental protectiveness. Am J Psychiatry 14:1392–1396, 1984

Frank H, Paris J: Recollections of family experience in borderline patients. Arch Gen Psychiatry 38:1031–1034, 1981

Goldman SJ, D'Angelo EJ, DeMaso DR, et al: Physical and sexual abuse histories among children with borderline personality disorder. Am J Psychiatry 149:1723–1726, 1992

Goldman SJ, D'Angelo EJ, DeMaso DR: Psychopathology in the families of children and adolescents with borderline personality disorder. Am J Psychiatry 150:1832–1835, 1993

Golomb M, Fava M, Abraham M, et al: Gender differences in personality disorders. Am J Psychiatry 152:579–582, 1995

Green MR: Treatment of borderline adolescents. Adolescence 18:729–738, 1983

Gunderson JG, Kerr J, Englund DW: The families of borderlines: a comparative study. Arch Gen Psychiatry 37:27–33, 1980

Herman JL, Perry JC, van der Kolk BA: Childhood trauma in borderline personality disorder. Am J Psychiatry 146:490–495, 1989

Jones SA: Family therapy with borderline and narcissistic patients. Bull Menninger Clin 51:285–295, 1987

Koch A, Ingram T: The treatment of borderline personality disorder within a distressed relationship. Journal of Marital and Family Therapy 11:373–380, 1985

Lansky MR: Treatment of the narcissistically vulnerable marriage, in Family Therapy and Major Psychopathology. Edited by Lansky MR. New York, Grune & Stratton, 1981, pp 163–182

Lansky MR: Masks of the narcissistically vulnerable marriage. International Journal of Family Psychiatry 3:439–449, 1982

Lansky MR: Shame and fragmentation in the marital dyad. Contemporary Family Therapy 13:17–31, 1991

Links PS (ed): Family Environment and Borderline Personality Disorder. Washington, DC, American Psychiatric Press, 1990

Livesley WJ, Jang KL, Jackson DN, et al: Genetic and environmental contributions to dimensions of personality disorder. Am J Psychiatry 150:1826–1831, 1993

Loeber R: Development and risk factors of juvenile antisocial behavior and delinquency. Clinical Psychology Review 10:1–41, 1990

Loehlin JC, Nichols RC: Heredity, Environment, and Personality. Austin, TX, University of Texas Press, 1976

McCormack CC: The borderline/schizoid marriage: the holding environment as an essential treatment construct. Journal of Marital and Family Therapy 15:299–309, 1989

Papp P: The Process of Change. New York, Guilford, 1983

Perlmutter RA: The borderline patient in the emergency department: an approach to evaluation and management. Psychiatr Q 54:190–197, 1982

Perlmutter RA: Academic failure as a family crisis, in Working With the Parents of College Students. Edited by Cohen RD. San Francisco, CA, Jossey-Bass, 1985, pp 77–92

Perlmutter RA, Jones JE: Problem solving with families in psychiatric emergencies. Psychiatr Q 57:23–32, 1985

Perlmutter RA, Jones JE: On not recommending family therapy to families in psychiatric emergencies. Family Systems Medicine 5:333–343, 1987

Rohrbaugh M, Tennen H, Press S, et al: Compliance, defiance, and therapeutic paradox: guidelines for strategic use of paradoxical interventions. Am J Orthopsychiatry 51:454–466, 1981

Schulz PM, Schulz SC, Hamer R, et al: The impact of borderline and schizotypal personality disorders on patients and their families. Hosp Community Psychiatry 36:879–881, 1985

Shapiro ER: The psychodynamics and developmental psychology of the borderline patient: a review of the literature. Am J Psychiatry 135:1305–1315, 1978

Soloff PH, Millward JW: Psychiatric disorders in the families of borderline patients. Arch Gen Psychiatry 40:37–44, 1983

Solomon MF: Treatment of narcissistic and borderline disorders in marital therapy: suggestions toward an enhanced therapeutic approach. Clinical Social Work Journal 13:141–156, 1985

GLOSSARY

affects The automatic, biological, and fluctuating components of the emotional system; the innate mechanisms of response to experiences. We are *affected* by something when it stimulates our emotions. Affect theory includes nine affect states: *interest-excitement, enjoyment-joy, surprise-startle, fear-terror, distress-anguish, anger-rage, shame-humiliation, "dissmell"* (a pulling away from or rejection of something that initially seemed appealing), and *disgust* (Nathanson 1992).

attachment The emotional bond between two people; feeling that binds one to another person; the most basic of the relational processes. In attachment theory, mutual and reciprocal behavior patterns lead to the state of attachment.

autonomy The state that is relatively free or independent of family or environment. It is achieved by a process of individuation, differentiation, or emancipation; for example, a child going through adolescence gradually becomes more stable and self-sufficient. Autonomy usually implies an ability to act and think as a separate self while maintaining interaction with one's family and environment.

belief systems Our assumptions about how and why things are, what governs people and relationships, what causes disorders, how men and women should act and relate, and what being in a marriage or a family means.

boundary A concept most often associated with structural family therapy to describe emotional barriers that protect and enhance the integrity of individuals, subsystems, and families. This concept includes the rules defining who participates and how they will participate in a subsystem (Minuchin 1974). Boundaries are normal descriptive phenomena that can become troublesome in extreme forms along a continuum from disengagement to enmeshment.

circular questioning   A way of asking questions that elicits new, systemic information from the family. This method is based on interviewing techniques developed by the Milan Associates (Selvini-Palazzoli et al. 1980) in which questions are asked that highlight differences and relationships among family members. The gathering of information helps in formulating and validating hypotheses regarding the family's dynamics, structure, and approaches to problems. This way of interviewing aims at changing the individual's and the family's views of themselves.

conjoint therapy   Treatment of two or more persons in a session together.

constructivism   A point of view that emphasizes the relative, subjective construction of reality. Rather than advocating a search for the "truth," the constructivist pays attention to the cognitive maps, the beliefs, and the models of knowing from which individuals and families construct and order their views of the world. Constructivism implies that what we see in families may be based more on our preconceptions and our own maps than on a perception of some objective reality. With this philosophical position, the therapist treats the family as being as much of an expert as the therapist and is open to new meanings of symptoms.

context   In general, the frame or surrounding field in which a behavior or symptom can be understood. The context of a problem helps clarify the meaning of symptoms, disorders, and reactions of individuals as part of a larger family or environmental picture. In contextual therapy, context has a broader meaning and refers to considerations of all of a person's relationships—past, present, and future. It includes relational dimensions such as fairness, resources, justice, ledgers, and ethics.

contextual therapy   Applications of the complex multigenerational theory of Boszormenyi-Nagy based on four dimensions of relationships: facts, psychology, transactions, and relational ethics. The loyalty dimension of symptoms discussed for the disorders in this book is one central concept of contextual therapy. Other concepts are merit, entitlement, ledgers, fairness, trust, exoneration, and families as resources. Its methodology is the use of dialogue and multidirectional partiality (understanding and siding with each member) in the hope of creating the "healing moment" and a restoration of trust (Boszormenyi-Nagy and Krasner 1986).

detouring A strategy, usually outside of conscious awareness, used by family members to distract from pain. This maneuver involves diffusing conflict between family members by designating another party as the source of their problem. The focus on the third person can be intense, attacking, or solicitous.

differentiation A concept in Bowen's family systems theory describing the ability of a person to be in emotional contact with others yet still be autonomous in one's emotional functioning (Kerr and Bowen 1988). Differentiation can also refer to the psychological ability to separate intellect and emotions.

diffuse boundaries A concept in structural family therapy that describes relatively weak or thin barriers among family subsystems. Diffuse boundaries imply an increased vulnerability of the subsystem to the influence of outside forces. Diffuse boundaries may be associated with enmeshment.

double bind A situation in which an individual receives contradictory messages on different levels of abstraction and logical types, the relationship with the sender of the message is an important one, and the person cannot leave or comment. In other words, no matter what the person does, he or she cannot win.

emotion In affect theory, the complex blending of a triggered affect with memory. An event triggers a particular emotion because of past experiences with such events. Compared with *affects*, which are biological and brief, emotions can last a long time once the associated memories are activated. Joy, sorrow, sadness, shame, fear, and rage can all be triggered for a few seconds by an experience and then will pass unless memories of similar experiences carry the affect into emotion. In the map of emotions, emotions represent those ways of experiencing the world that are available when thoughts can be stopped and moods are enabled to transmute into their underlying emotions. In this book, Berenson's map of emotions is described as one important aspect of psychiatric disorders and is used as a technique to "liberate" family members from stuck positions.

enmeshment Overly close ties and permeable boundaries between any members of a group. Enmeshment implies loss of autonomy and decreased ability of the individual family members to think for themselves.

entitlement   Earning of credit for acting in positive, ethical, giving ways in relationships. Entitlement especially pertains to the accumulation of credits by parents who nurture and give to children without expectation of full return of what is given. Destructive entitlement is a term idiosyncratic to contextual therapy and refers to a sense of overentitlement accumulated by children who have been unjustly treated. They enter adult life with a sense that the world owes it to them to make up for the past, which can lead to negative, exploitative interpersonal relationships.

executive functions   The actions of the leadership subsystem of the family; control, guidance, and the effective use of authority and power. In the ideal family defined by structural family therapy, executive functions best belong with parents.

exoneration   A goal of therapy whereby blame is removed from parents or others and replaced with mature understanding of how the victimizer was also victimized. This reassessment does not minimize past injustices or offer "forgiveness," and the offending person is still accountable; but the child or adult child experiences the parent in a different, more balanced way.

externalization   Michael White's constructivist technique of moving away from "problem saturated" stories (White 1995). Families are helped to change the attribution of an oppressive problem from a characteristic of one person to an oppressive enemy menacing the person and family from outside. The attribution of blame to a single member becomes instead a story of the whole family's valiant struggle against a common enemy.

family   Natural grouping of individuals linked by biological, psychological, social, and economic concerns. The term is used expansively to include both the traditional nuclear family (two unrelated married adults plus their offspring) and the many possible variations. Variations include single-parent families, stepfamilies, homosexual couples and families, and so on.

family ecology   The interdependence of members of a family that parallel the reciprocal relationships of all organisms with their environments. Family ecology implies a "survival unit" of a person and certain members of the family.

family myths   Firmly held ideas shared by each member of a family that serve to protect them from conflict or painful awareness, such as occurs in the family that sees itself as happy and harmonious despite blatant evidence of discord.

family of origin   A person's parents and siblings; the original nuclear family of an adult.

family somatics   The study of the interrelationships of systemic family processes and all the manifestations of physical complaints and disease. Family somatics includes the development and the reactions to medical illness. It implies a holistic, nonreductionist stance open to social, biological, and psychological dimensions of illness.

family systems theory   The influential theory of Murray Bowen, subsequently added to by his students. Bowen's theory centers around two counterbalancing forces: those that bind people in family togetherness and those that push toward individuality. His theory comprises eight interlocking concepts: 1) differentiation of self, 2) triangles, 3) nuclear family emotional process, 4) family projection process, 5) multigenerational transmission process, 6) sibling position, 7) emotional cutoff, and 8) societal emotional process. Bowen's work on the use of family-of-origin connections becomes the treatment of choice for most family problems and even many disorders (Bowen 1994; Kerr and Bowen 1988).

feelings   The experience when we become consciously aware of affects.

frame   Meaning attributed to behaviors or observations. A shared frame on the definition of a problem is important in family therapy and emanates from negotiation in the early phases of the therapist-family interview. Because the therapist and family members may initially be proceeding from different assumptions about the nature of the problem, a process of mutual influence is necessary to arrive at a common ground of acceptable language and belief. Without this foundation of jointly held assumptions, agreement on a solution is unlikely to be reached.

genogram   A schematic diagram of the family system. As an interview technique, it helps the therapist structure the early sessions in a way that is easily learned and nets a great deal of information for later therapeutic use.

go-around   A technique of asking each member of the family to respond in turn to the same question; for example, "What do you believe is the main problem facing the family now?" or "What things have you tried that work best to help solve the problem?"

index person   The family member with the psychiatric diagnosis, the symptom bearer, or the official "patient" as identified by the family. This term is used instead of the more traditional "identified patient," which implies that the family as a whole is really the patient and that they have chosen to scapegoat one member rather than face this fact. Such a notion is dangerous and poorly received in dealing with families with psychiatric disorders because it leaves families feeling blamed for the problems.

intimacy   A state of being that is experienced in those moments with another where there is trust, vulnerability, and mutual self-disclosure. In the language of Martin Buber, it is the experience of treating another as a subject, as "Thou," rather than as an object or an "It" (Buber 1958).

legacies   Stories and expectations from past generations that affect later generations. The contextual therapy definition adds an obligation to use legacies in a way that helps future generations.

loyalty   A feeling of solidarity, commitment, or attachment to a group or person. Loyalty implies the mutual obligation by virtue of birth into a family. In contextual therapy, loyalty is an existential fact; constructivists might see loyalty more as the product of belief systems.

loyalty conflict   A competitive pull felt by a person when obligation to one person conflicts with obligation to another and both are "entitled" to the loyalty. Loyalty conflict refers to the competition between horizontal (spousal) and vertical (parental) claims to the child's loyalty and devotion. The usual example is the battle for a husband's loyalty between the wife and mother. A particularly damaging example of split loyalty occurs when a child is pulled by two warring parents who, during the process of divorce, demand exclusive loyalty and feel betrayed if the child gives to the other parent.

maturity of function   A family systems concept in which individuals and families exist on a continuum of capacity to function with less anxiety and more differentiation. Maturity of function usually implies the capacity of the family to solve problems and deal with crises.

metamessage   Two simultaneous communications, one relating to content and the other commenting on the communication. The metamessage includes the relationship aspect. It is related to metacommunication, which is communication about communication.

moods   In affect theory, moods result when the intensity of thoughts and feelings cannot be dissipated and instead is compounded by memories and becomes a persistent state. In both the map of emotions and affect theory, moods are the stuck places that keep us from deeper, richer, more varied ways of experiencing the world. Mood disorders emerge when these moods take on lives of their own, connect to habitual thought patterns, and strengthen because they are fed heavily by biology.

multigenerational perspective An approach to the current problems and resources of a family that takes into account the parents' families of origin and extended families. Psychiatric problems seen in this context can be viewed as the expression of problems and interactional patterns from past generations; but this perspective also points out positive, resource-based possibilities. For example, this perspective can include knowledge of coping skills acquired from past generations as well as a concern for how the disorder is affecting the extended family. The approach includes history taking via a genogram and elicitation of facts, myths, legacies, and belief systems of past generations. In psychiatric practice, this process includes eliciting family histories of past psychiatric disorders.

nurturance The provision of what another person needs (such as nourishment, support, and encouragement) during stages of growth to promote development.

parentified child A child who is chosen by parents to assume a caretaking or parental role within the family system; usually a role reversal in which the child is assigned to be responsible and nurturant toward the parent, but also a role in which the child is assigned to take care of younger siblings. In contextual theory, this arrangement is viewed as adaptive if the child learns responsibility, is able to help a family get through a crisis, is credited for the efforts to give to the parents, and if the demands are not depleting or exploitative. The arrangement can be quite destructive if it results in blurred generational boundaries, an overburdened child, and abdication of parental responsibilities.

posterity Concern for future generations and the youngest living family members.

reauthoring Changing the family's meanings and interpretations about problems and symptoms. This is done by first mapping the "influence of the problem" on their lives and then focusing on the untold stories about those times when the problem was *not* allowed to influence lives and relationships.

reconstruction A therapeutic offering of new more helpful interpretations of events, relationships, and behaviors. The old beliefs held by families form the family's stories about themselves, and new information is incorporated through these stories. Therapy offers families a chance to reexamine their constructions of the reality of the world and their place in it. At least the possibility is offered to see beliefs as constructions, rather than as an objective, unchangeable reality. This process opens the family up to the telling of new stories.

reflecting team   A form of live supervision and therapy where a team of therapists and/or students observes a family session. At chosen moments, the arrangement reverses so that the family and therapist observe the team as they discuss the dilemmas posed in the session for both the family and therapist. The conversation explores new, more helpful ways for the family to think about their strengths, symptoms, relationships, and attempts to solve problems.

reframe   Use of language to therapeutically modify the meaning attributed to a behavior, thought, feeling, or intent. The new labels are chosen to help the family or individual become more open to change. Usually, the new frame offers small shifts in the family's internal view, or map, of reality.

strategic approach   Planned orientation to change based on cybernetic principles such as the interconnectedness of parts of a system and the feedback loops that influence the system. Strategic approaches connote the study of the attempted solutions the family has already tried, with the idea that these efforts have become part of the problem. Insight and understanding are de-emphasized in favor of comments, directives, and tasks designed to change the way family members relate to each other.

structure   Generally, the linkages and recurrent patterns of relating between members of a system; more specifically, the structural family therapy study of the family's boundaries, coalitions, distribution of power, and hierarchies.

subunits   Smaller groups of family members that help determine the structure of a family. Subunits are sometimes defined by generation, sex, or function. Parents, children, males, females, or siblings serve as examples. Subunits are circumscribed and regulated by emotional boundaries.

systemic therapy   A term often used to refer to the Milan model of family therapy (Selvini-Palazzoli et al. 1980; Tomm 1985). In this book, I use this term to convey a therapy that treats problems not as residing purely in individuals but instead as issues best understood by including the study of relationships.

systemically informed individual treatment   Psychotherapy with one person that takes into account the person's context, especially past and current family relationships. This perspective implies some attention to the effects on other family members to be expected from therapeutic change. In family systems therapy, this approach implies coaching techniques to help the person change current relationships with family members.

systems theory   The study of interrelated parts that interact as a whole entity; encompasses general systems theory and cybernetics. Systems theory implies that features (such as feedback loops) are the same for all systems, regardless of whether a person or a molecule is the object of study.

triangulation   Bowen's term for a "three-person emotional configuration" (Bowen 1976). In this situation, a third person has been drawn in to help solve the conflict between two other people who cannot or will not solve a problem themselves. As a result of this process, which is usually unconscious or out of awareness, the conflict is said to be "detoured" or "defused." This solution is often at a cost, especially to the triangulated person, especially if a child is drawn in to solve or diffuse marital problems.

undifferentiated family system   Also known by Bowen's famous phrase, "undifferentiated family ego mass" (Bowen 1994); emotional "stuck-togetherness" or fusion among family members. It implies that members cannot figure out what their positions are in terms of others or cannot tell where their ideas and identities begin and end and which are really the ideas of someone else. Other authors describe similar situations as enmeshment or pseudomutuality.

■ Additional Reading

Gurman AS, Kniskern DP: Handbook of Family Therapy. New York, Brunner/Mazel, 1982

Kelly VC Jr: Affect and intimacy. Psychiatric Annals 23:556–566, 1993

Nichols MP, Schwartz RC: Family Therapy Concepts and Methods. Needham Heights, MA, Allyn & Bacon, 1991

Simon FB, Stierlin H, Wynne LC: The Language of Family Therapy: A Systemic Vocabulary and Sourcebook. New York, Family Process Press, 1985

◼ References

Boszormenyi-Nagy I, Krasner BR: Between Give and Take: A Clinical Guide to Contextual Therapy. New York, Brunner/Mazel, 1986

Bowen M: Theory in the practice of psychotherapy, in Family Therapy. Edited by Guerin PJ. New York, Gardner, 1976, pp 42–90

Bowen M: Family Therapy in Clinical Practice, 9th Edition. Northvale, NJ, Jason Aronson, 1994

Buber M: I and Thou. New York, Charles Scribner's Sons, 1958

Kerr ME, Bowen M: Family Evaluation. New York, WW Norton, 1988

Minuchin S: Families and Family Therapy. Cambridge, MA, Harvard University Press, 1974

Nathanson DL: Shame and Pride: Affect, Sex, and the Birth of the Self. New York, WW Norton, 1992

Selvini-Palazzoli M, Boscolo L, Cecchin G, et al: Hypothesizing-circularity-neutrality: three guidelines for the conductor of the session. Fam Process 19:3–12, 1980

Tomm K: Circular interviewing: a multifaceted tool, in Applications of Systemic Family Therapy: The Milan Approach. Edited by Campbell D, Draper R. Orlando, FL, Grune & Stratton, 1985, pp 33–45

White M: Re-Authoring Lives: Interviews & Essays. Adelaide, South Australia, Dulwich Centre Publications, 1995

INDEX

*Page numbers printed in **boldface** type refer to tables or figures.*